D0883981

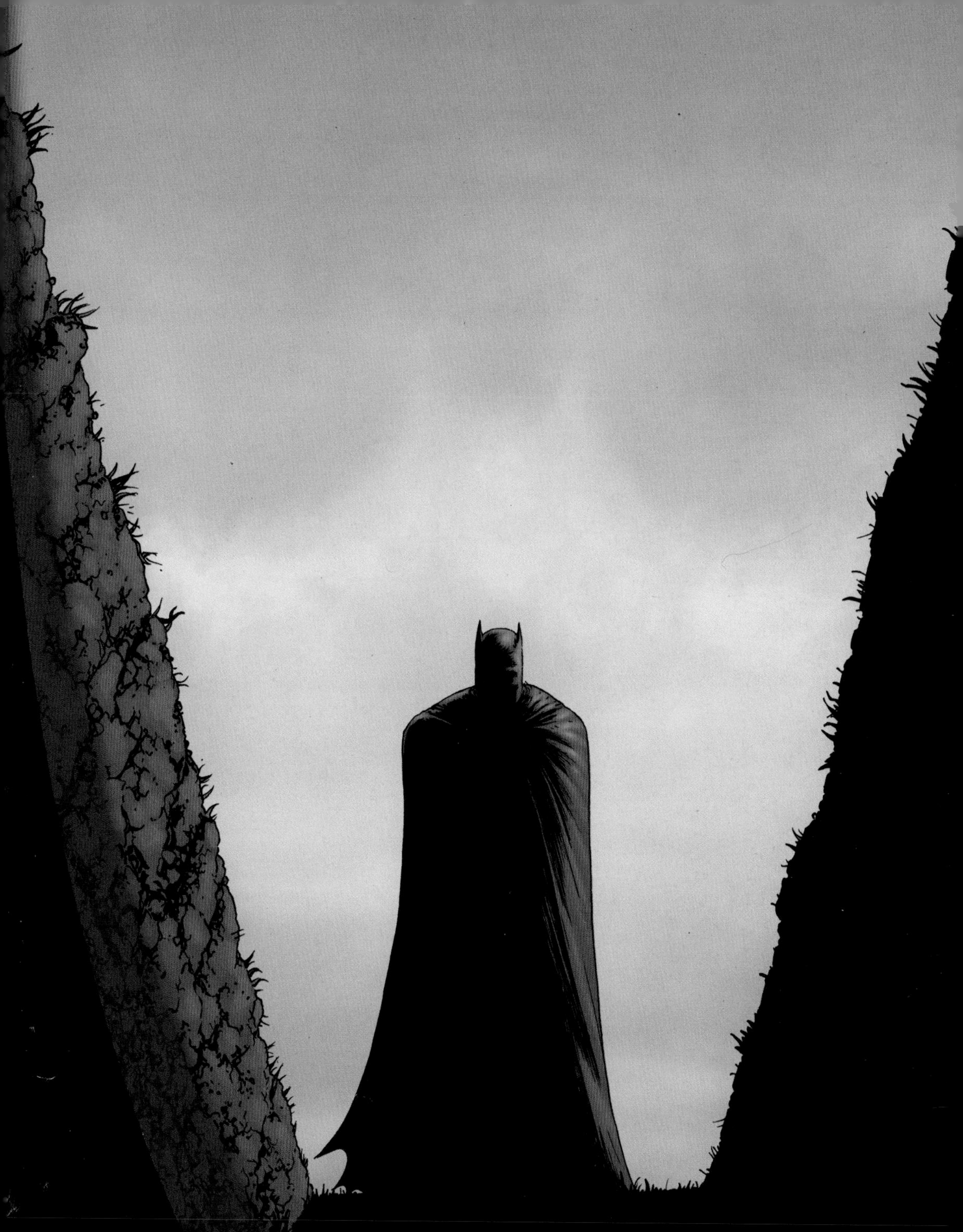

BATMAN INCORPORATED

VOLUME 2 GOTHAM'S MOST WANTED

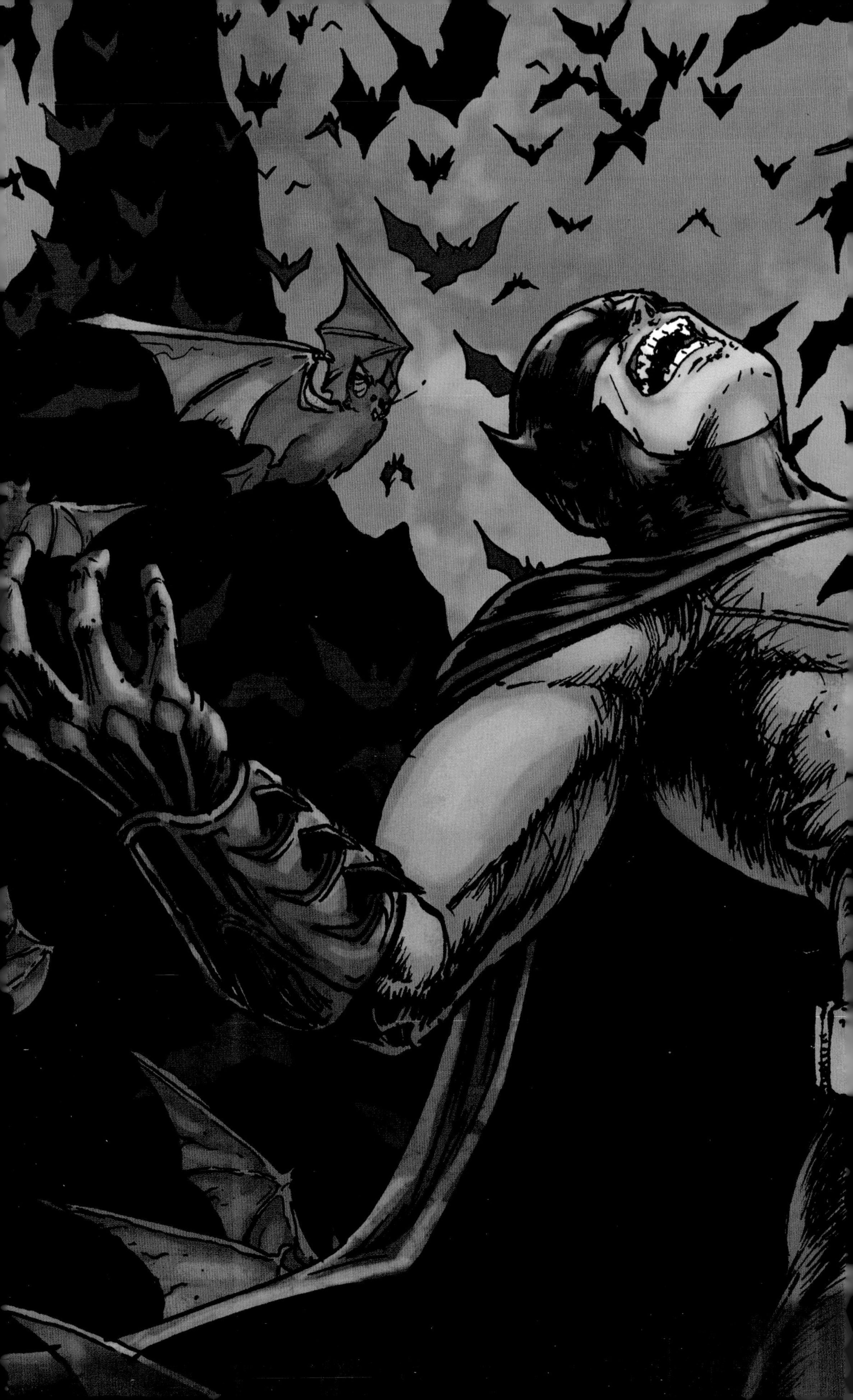

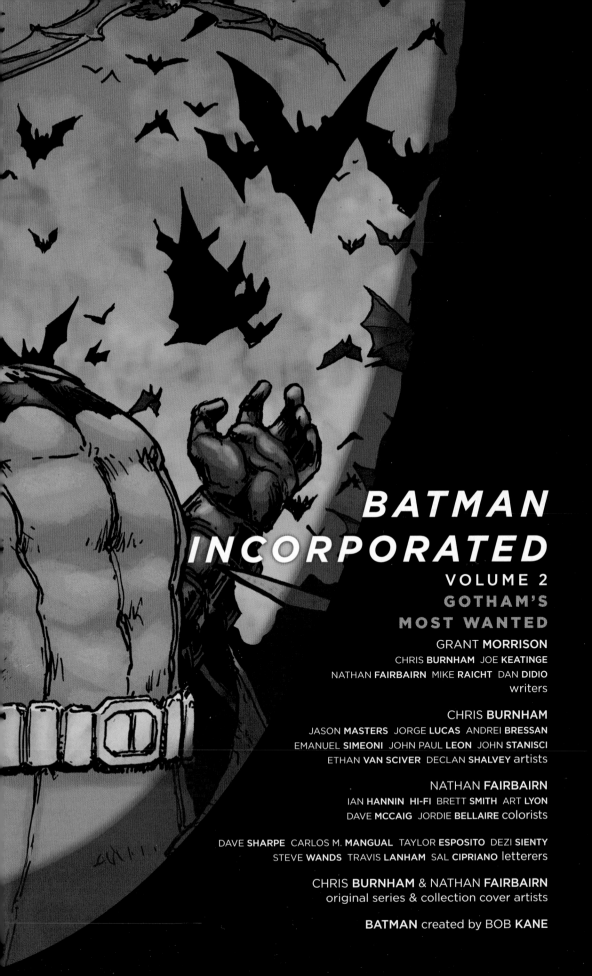

BATMAN INCORPORATED

VOLUME 2
GOTHAM'S
MOST WANTED

GRANT MORRISON

CHRIS **BURNHAM** JOE **KEATINGE**
NATHAN **FAIRBAIRN** MIKE **RAICHT** DAN **DIDIO**
writers

CHRIS BURNHAM

JASON **MASTERS** JORGE **LUCAS** ANDREI **BRESSAN**
EMANUEL **SIMEONI** JOHN PAUL **LEON** JOHN **STANISCI**
ETHAN **VAN SCIVER** DECLAN **SHALVEY** artists

NATHAN FAIRBAIRN

IAN **HANNIN** HI-FI BRETT **SMITH** ART **LYON**
DAVE **MCCAIG** JORDIE **BELLAIRE** colorists

DAVE **SHARPE** CARLOS M. **MANGUAL** TAYLOR **ESPOSITO** DEZI **SIENTY**
STEVE **WANDS** TRAVIS **LANHAM** SAL **CIPRIANO** letterers

CHRIS BURNHAM & NATHAN FAIRBAIRN
original series & collection cover artists

BATMAN created by BOB **KANE**

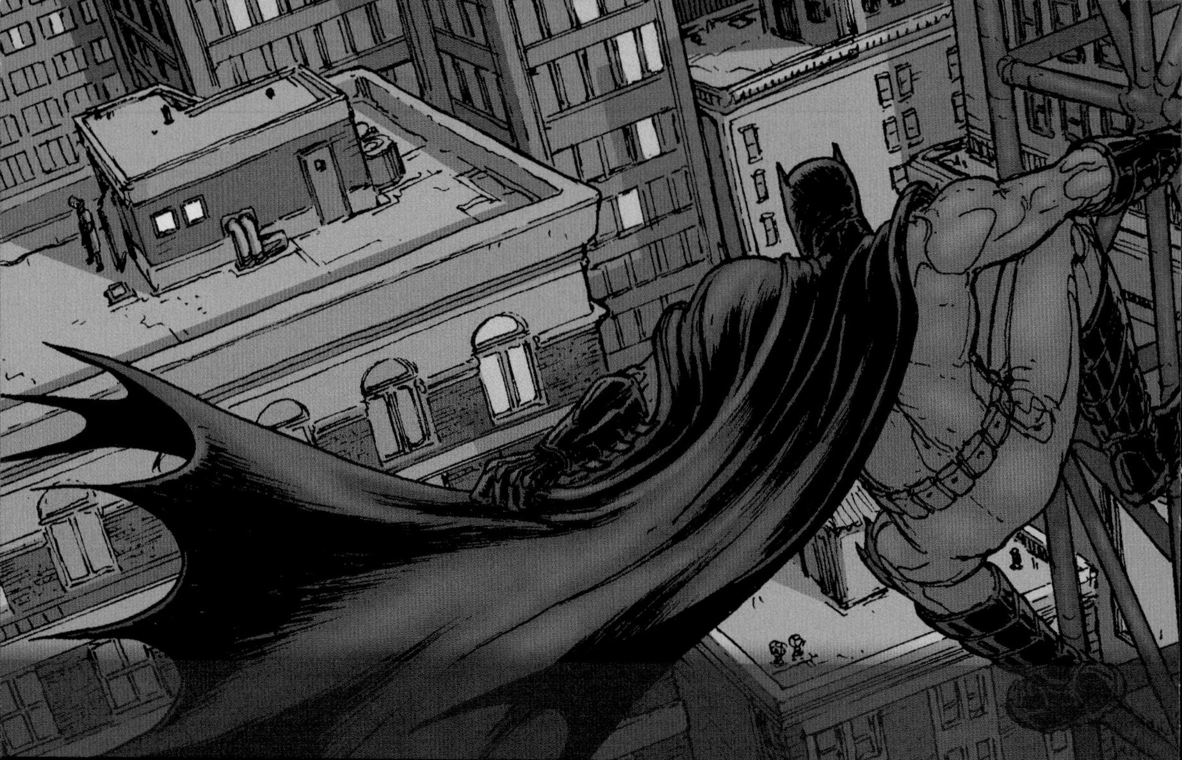

MIKE MARTS Editor - Original Series RICKEY PURDIN Associate Editor - Original Series
DARREN SHAN Assistant Editor - Original Series PETER HAMBOUSSI Editor
ROBBIN BROSTERMAN Design Director - Books ROBBIE BIEDERMAN Publication Design

BOB HARRAS Senior VP - Editor-in-Chief, DC Comics

DIANE NELSON President DAN DIDIO and JIM LEE Co-Publishers
GEOFF JOHNS Chief Creative Officer
JOHN ROOD Executive VP - Sales, Marketing and Business Development
AMY GENKINS Senior VP - Business and Legal Affairs NAIRI GARDINER Senior VP - Finance
JEFF BOISON VP - Publishing Planning MARK CHIARELLO VP - Art Direction and Design
JOHN CUNNINGHAM VP - Marketing TERRI CUNNINGHAM VP - Editorial Administration
ALISON GILL Senior VP - Manufacturing and Operations HANK KANALZ Senior VP - Vertigo and Integrated Publishing
JAY KOGAN VP - Business and Legal Affairs, Publishing JACK MAHAN VP - Business Affairs, Talent
NICK NAPOLITANO VP - Manufacturing Administration SUE POHJA VP - Book Sales
COURTNEY SIMMONS Senior VP - Publicity BOB WAYNE Senior VP - Sales

BATMAN INCORPORATED VOLUME 2: GOTHAM'S MOST WANTED

DC Comics, 1700 Broadway, New York, NY 10019
A Warner Bros. Entertainment Company.
Printed by RR Donnelley, Salem, VA, USA. 10/25/13. First Printing.

HC ISBN: 978-1-4012-4400-2
SC ISBN: 978-1-4012-4697-6

Library of Congress Cataloging-in-Publication Data

Morrison, Grant, author.
Batman Incorporated. Volume 2, Gotham's Most Wanted / Grant Morrison, Chris Burnham.
pages cm. — (The New 52!)
Summary: "Years of epic storylines converge as Batman Incorporated battles Talia and Leviathan for the very soul of Gotham City! Tragedy and triumph are the hallmarks of the second volume of Grant Morrison's epic Batman Incorporated. Batman and his allies must strengthen their resolve as Leviathan moves to take Gotham City. Everything since Batman Incorporated #1 has been leading to this!" Provided by publisher.
ISBN 978-1-4012-4400-2 (hardback)
1. Graphic novels. I. Burnham, Chris, 1977- illustrator. II. Title. III. Title: Gotham's Most Wanted.
PN6728.B36M6753 2013
741.5'973—dc23
2013031169

SUSTAINABLE FORESTRY INITIATIVE
Certified Chain of Custody
At Least 20% Certified Forest Content
www.sfiprogram.org
SFI-01042
APPLIES TO TEXT STOCK ONLY

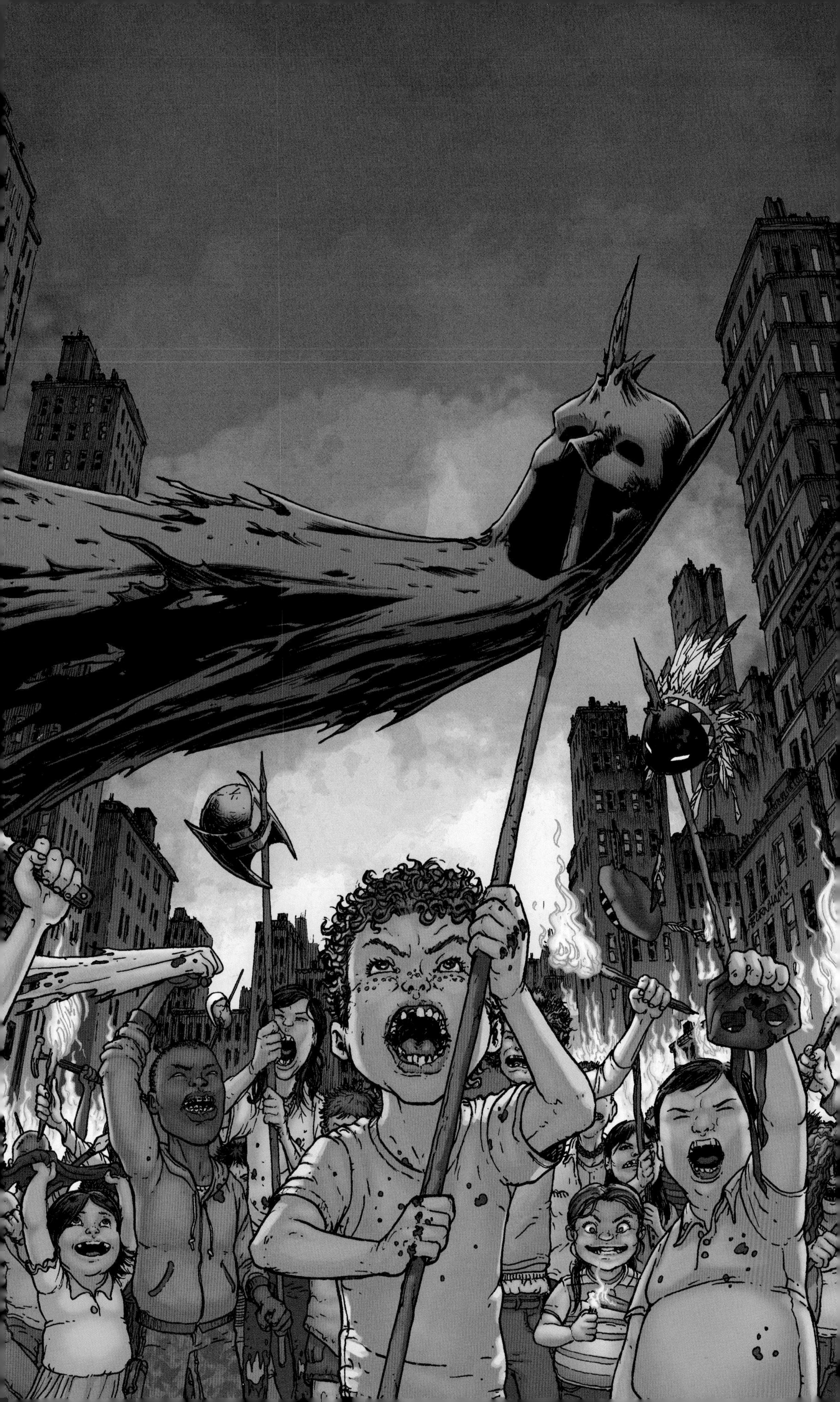

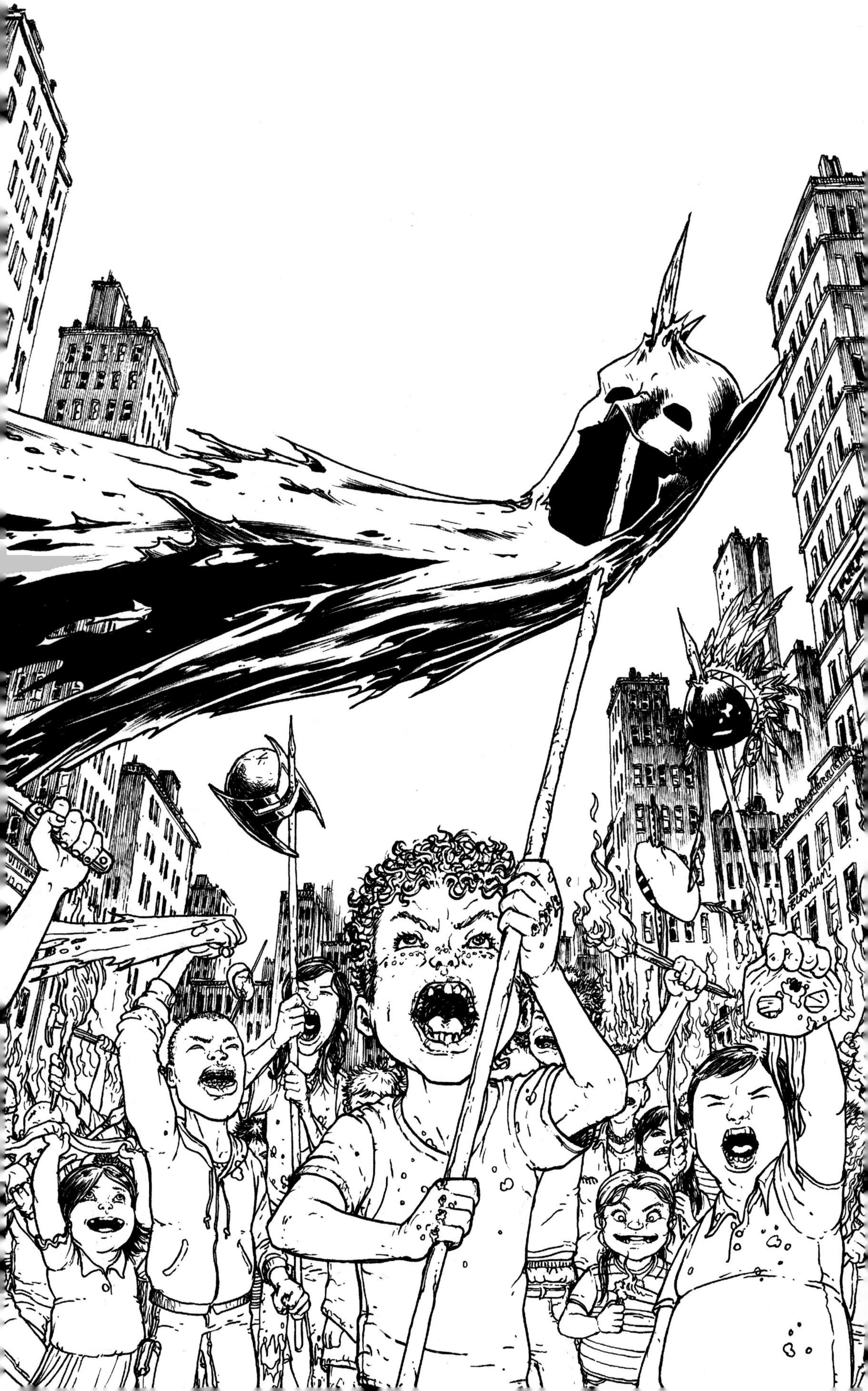

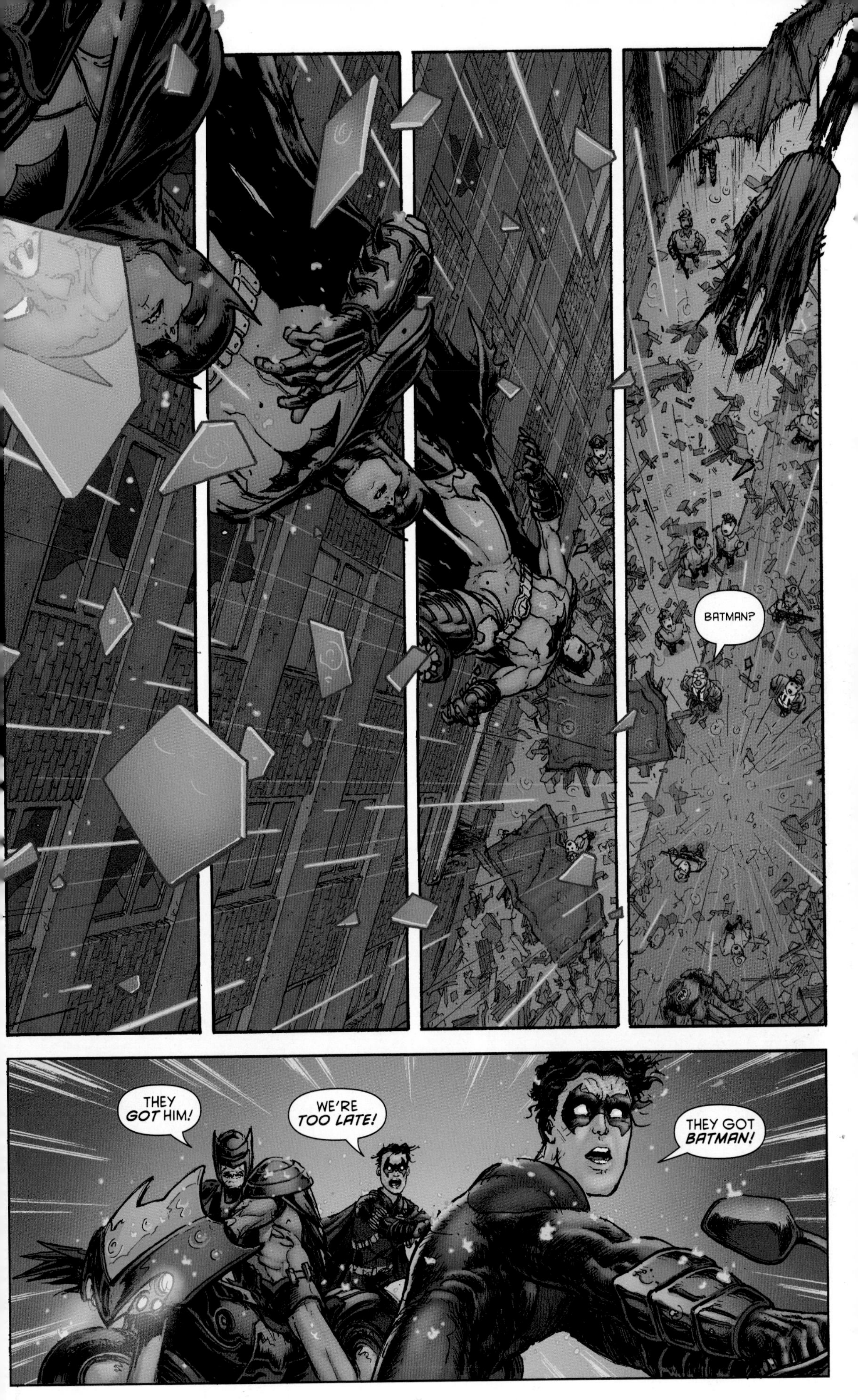
BATMAN?
THEY GOT HIM!
WE'RE TOO LATE!
THEY GOT BATMAN!

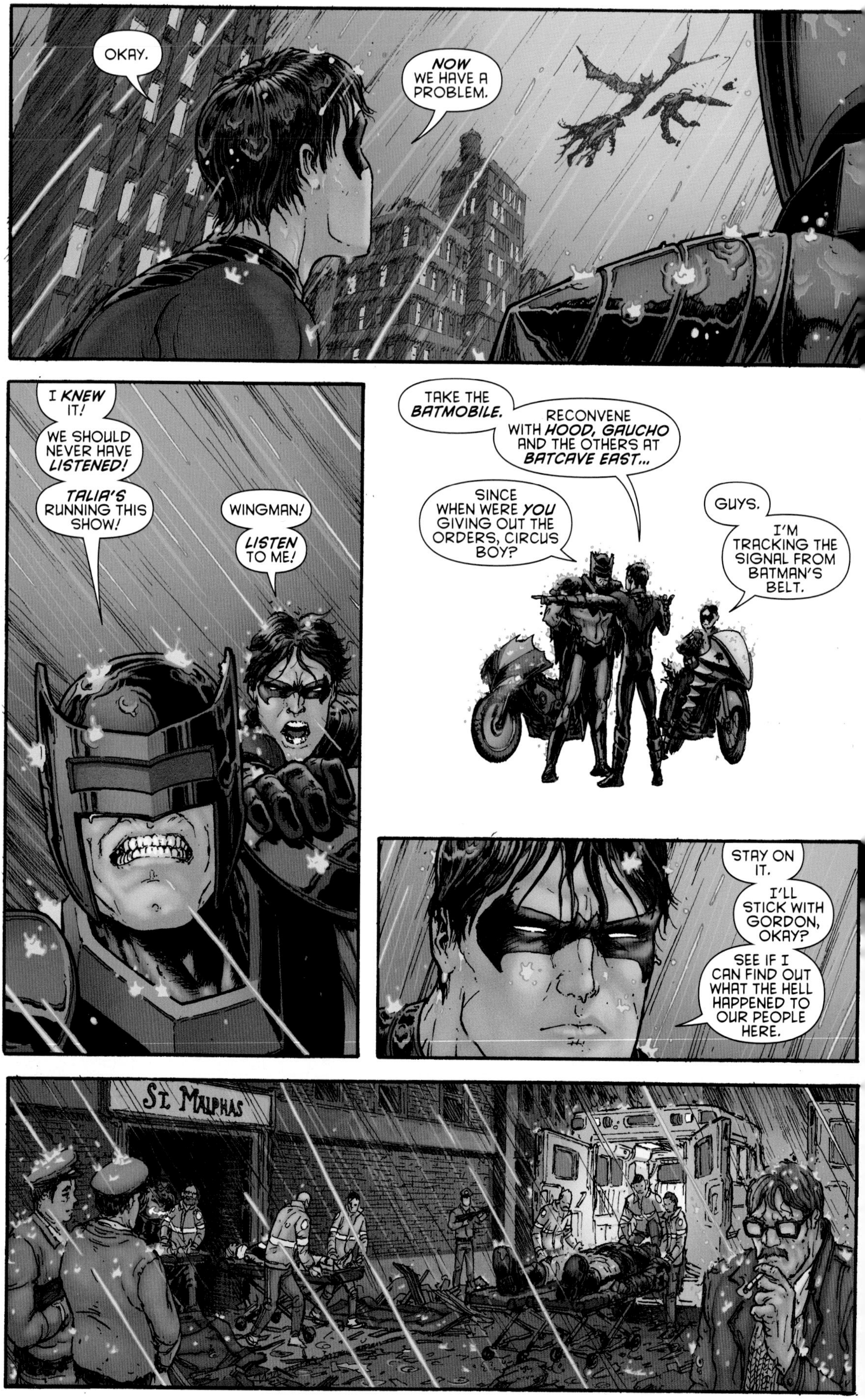
OKAY.
NOW WE HAVE A PROBLEM.
I KNEW IT!
WE SHOULD NEVER HAVE LISTENED!
TALIA'S RUNNING THIS SHOW!
WINGMAN!
LISTEN TO ME!
TAKE THE BATMOBILE.
RECONVENE WITH HOOD, GAUCHO AND THE OTHERS AT BATCAVE EAST...
SINCE WHEN WERE YOU GIVING OUT THE ORDERS, CIRCUS BOY?
GUYS.
I'M TRACKING THE SIGNAL FROM BATMAN'S BELT.
STAY ON IT.
I'LL STICK WITH GORDON, OKAY?
SEE IF I CAN FIND OUT WHAT THE HELL HAPPENED TO OUR PEOPLE HERE.
ST. MALPHAS

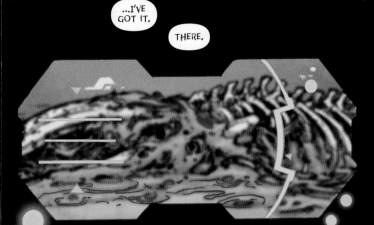

...I'VE GOT IT.

THERE.

AH.

YOU SEE THIS NOW, EH? THIS IS WHAT YOU WANT TO SEE?

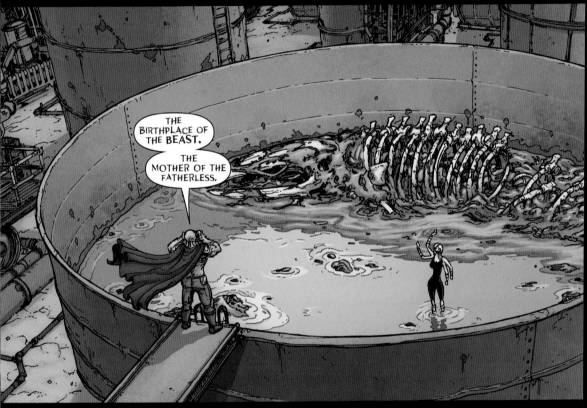

THE BIRTHPLACE OF THE BEAST.

THE MOTHER OF THE FATHERLESS.

WRITER
GRANT MORRISON
ARTIST
CHRIS BURNHAM

BELLY OF THE WHALE

ART (PGS 15, 20-21) - JASON MASTERS COLOR - NATHAN FAIRBAIRN LETTERING - CARLOS M. MANGUAL
COVER BY BURNHAM WITH FAIRBAIRN

...I SEE IT, TRAKTIR.

I'M PASSING ON THE IMAGES TO THE CENTRAL BAT-COMPUTER.

BE CAREFUL-- THE SITUATION HERE IN GOTHAM IS DETERIORATING RAPIDLY.

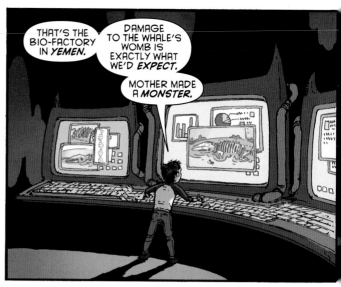

THAT'S THE BIO-FACTORY IN YEMEN.

DAMAGE TO THE WHALE'S WOMB IS EXACTLY WHAT WE'D EXPECT.

MOTHER MADE A MONSTER.

WE HAVE COMPANY. TRAKTIR SIGNING OFF.

THEY'RE ON THEIR WAY TO ERASE ALL EVIDENCE!

BOTH OF YOU!

GET OUT OF THERE!

THIS IS OUR HOME.

TRAKTIR STAYS.

SPIDRA FIGHTS.

YOU CALL YOURSELF BATWING, RIGHT?

YOU'RE BLEEDING FROM A DOZEN PLACES.

THE MAN WHO KILLED THE KNIGHT, HE HIT ME WITH THE FORCE OF A TANK.

I CAN'T BELIEVE THIS.

EVERYTHING WENT WRONG AT ONCE.

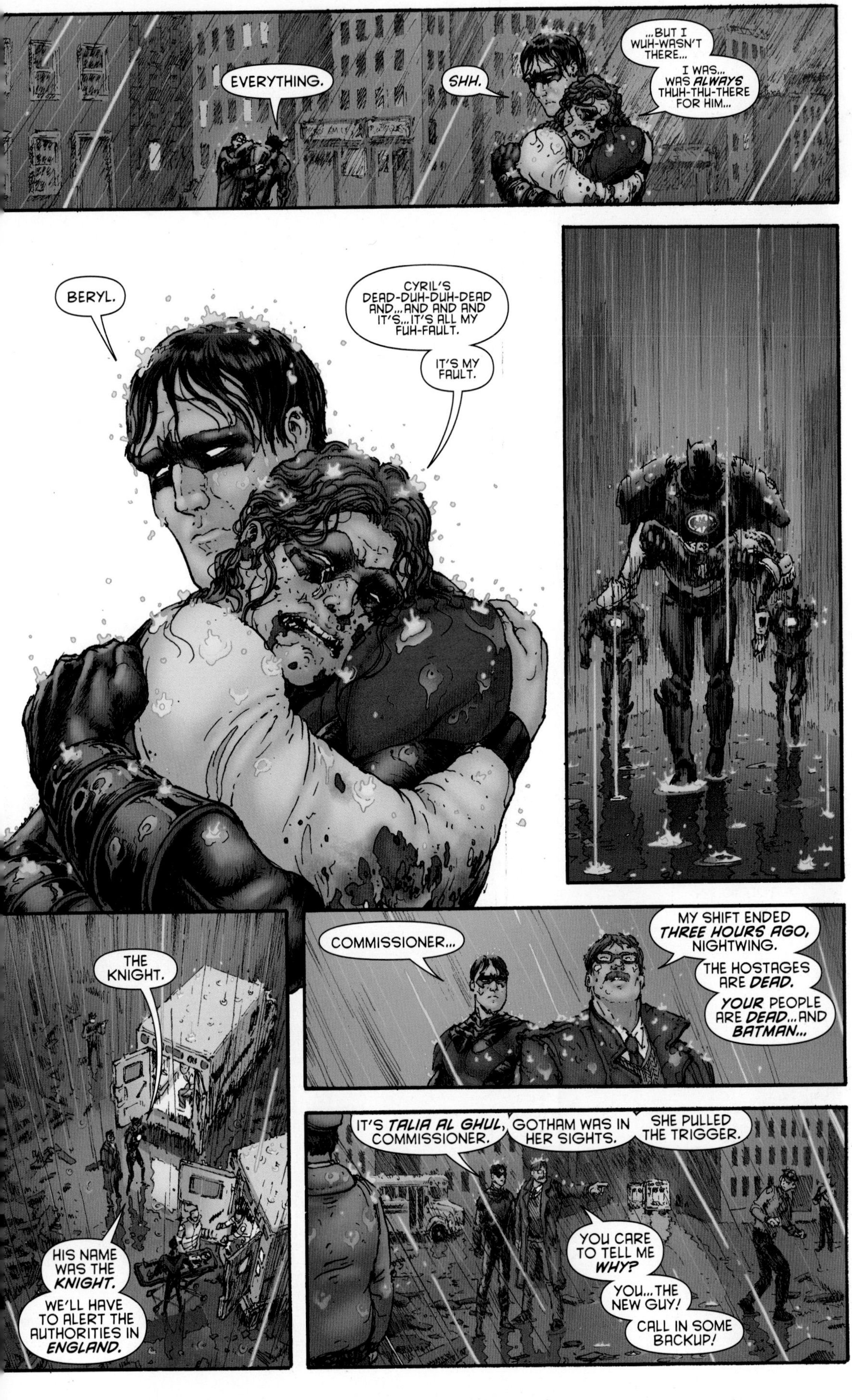
EVERYTHING.
SHH.
...BUT I WUH-WASN'T THERE...
I WAS... WAS ALWAYS THUH-THU-THERE FOR HIM...
BERYL.
CYRIL'S DEAD-DUH-DUH-DEAD AND...AND AND AND IT'S...IT'S ALL MY FUH-FAULT.
IT'S MY FAULT.
THE KNIGHT.
HIS NAME WAS THE KNIGHT.
WE'LL HAVE TO ALERT THE AUTHORITIES IN ENGLAND.
COMMISSIONER...
MY SHIFT ENDED THREE HOURS AGO, NIGHTWING.
THE HOSTAGES ARE DEAD.
YOUR PEOPLE ARE DEAD...AND BATMAN...
IT'S TALIA AL GHUL, COMMISSIONER.
GOTHAM WAS IN HER SIGHTS.
SHE PULLED THE TRIGGER.
YOU CARE TO TELL ME WHY?
YOU...THE NEW GUY!
CALL IN SOME BACKUP!

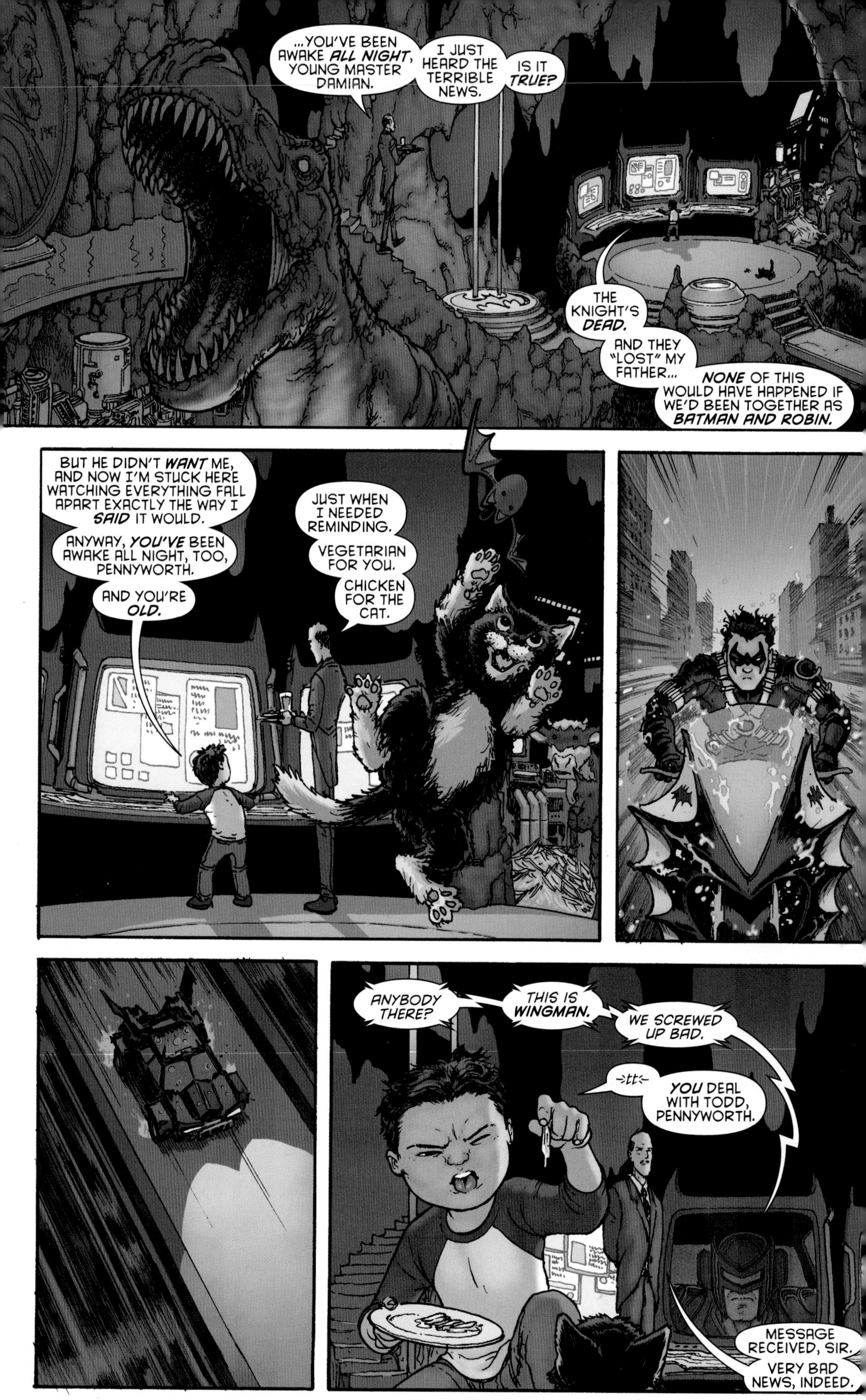

...YOU'VE BEEN AWAKE ALL NIGHT, YOUNG MASTER DAMIAN.
I JUST HEARD THE TERRIBLE NEWS.
IS IT TRUE?
THE KNIGHT'S DEAD.
AND THEY "LOST" MY FATHER...
NONE OF THIS WOULD HAVE HAPPENED IF WE'D BEEN TOGETHER AS BATMAN AND ROBIN.
BUT HE DIDN'T WANT ME, AND NOW I'M STUCK HERE WATCHING EVERYTHING FALL APART EXACTLY THE WAY I SAID IT WOULD.
ANYWAY, YOU'VE BEEN AWAKE ALL NIGHT, TOO, PENNYWORTH.
AND YOU'RE OLD.
JUST WHEN I NEEDED REMINDING.
VEGETARIAN FOR YOU.
CHICKEN FOR THE CAT.
ANYBODY THERE?
THIS IS WINGMAN.
WE SCREWED UP BAD.
-tt-
YOU DEAL WITH TODD, PENNYWORTH.
MESSAGE RECEIVED, SIR.
VERY BAD NEWS, INDEED.

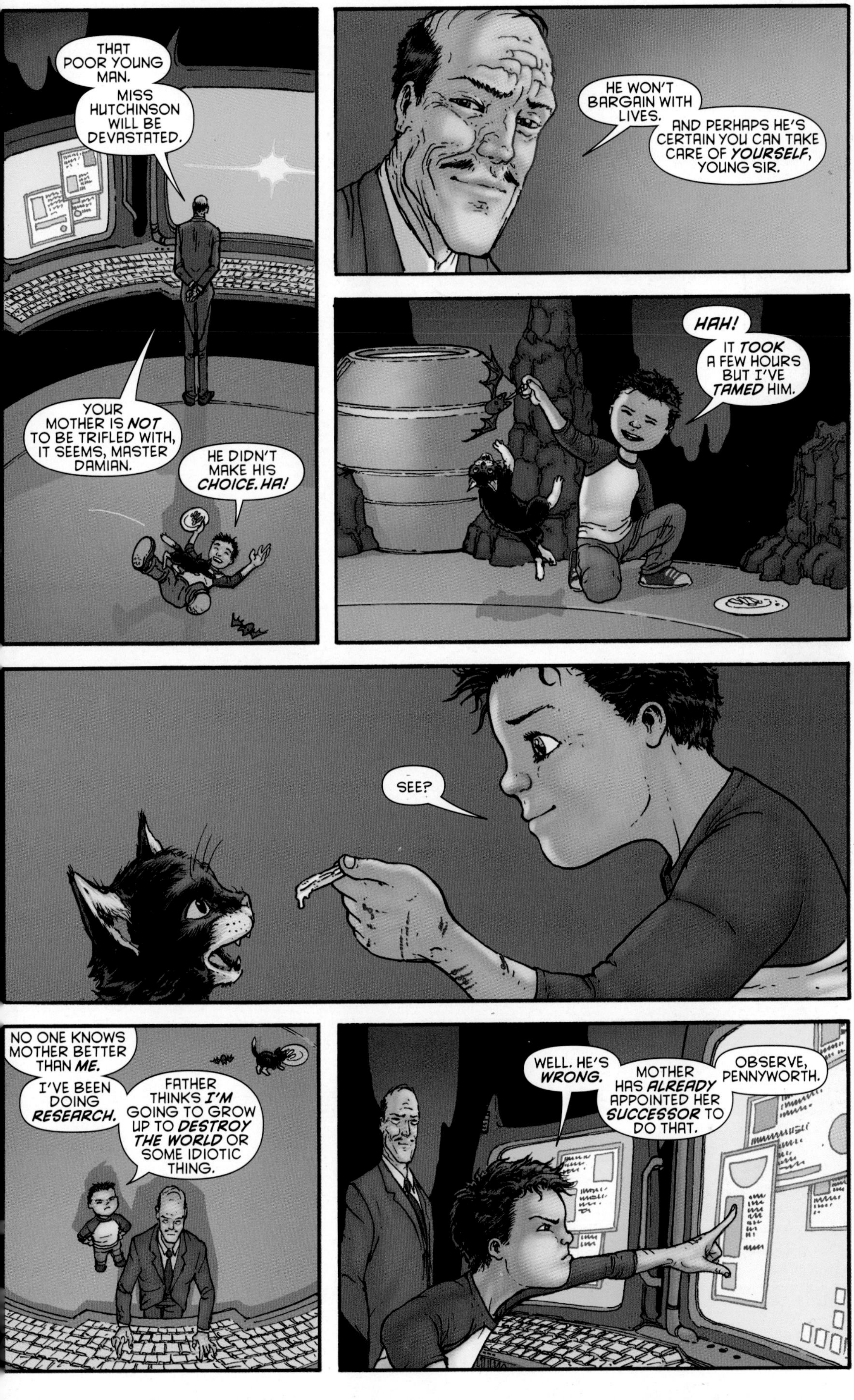
THAT POOR YOUNG MAN.
MISS HUTCHINSON WILL BE DEVASTATED.
YOUR MOTHER IS *NOT* TO BE TRIFLED WITH, IT SEEMS, MASTER DAMIAN.
HE DIDN'T MAKE HIS *CHOICE. HA!*
HE WON'T BARGAIN WITH LIVES.
AND PERHAPS HE'S CERTAIN YOU CAN TAKE CARE OF *YOURSELF*, YOUNG SIR.
HAH!
IT *TOOK* A FEW HOURS BUT I'VE *TAMED* HIM.
SEE?
NO ONE KNOWS MOTHER BETTER THAN *ME.*
I'VE BEEN DOING *RESEARCH.*
FATHER THINKS *I'M* GOING TO GROW UP TO *DESTROY THE WORLD* OR SOME IDIOTIC THING.
WELL. HE'S *WRONG.*
MOTHER HAS *ALREADY* APPOINTED HER *SUCCESSOR* TO DO THAT.
OBSERVE, PENNYWORTH.

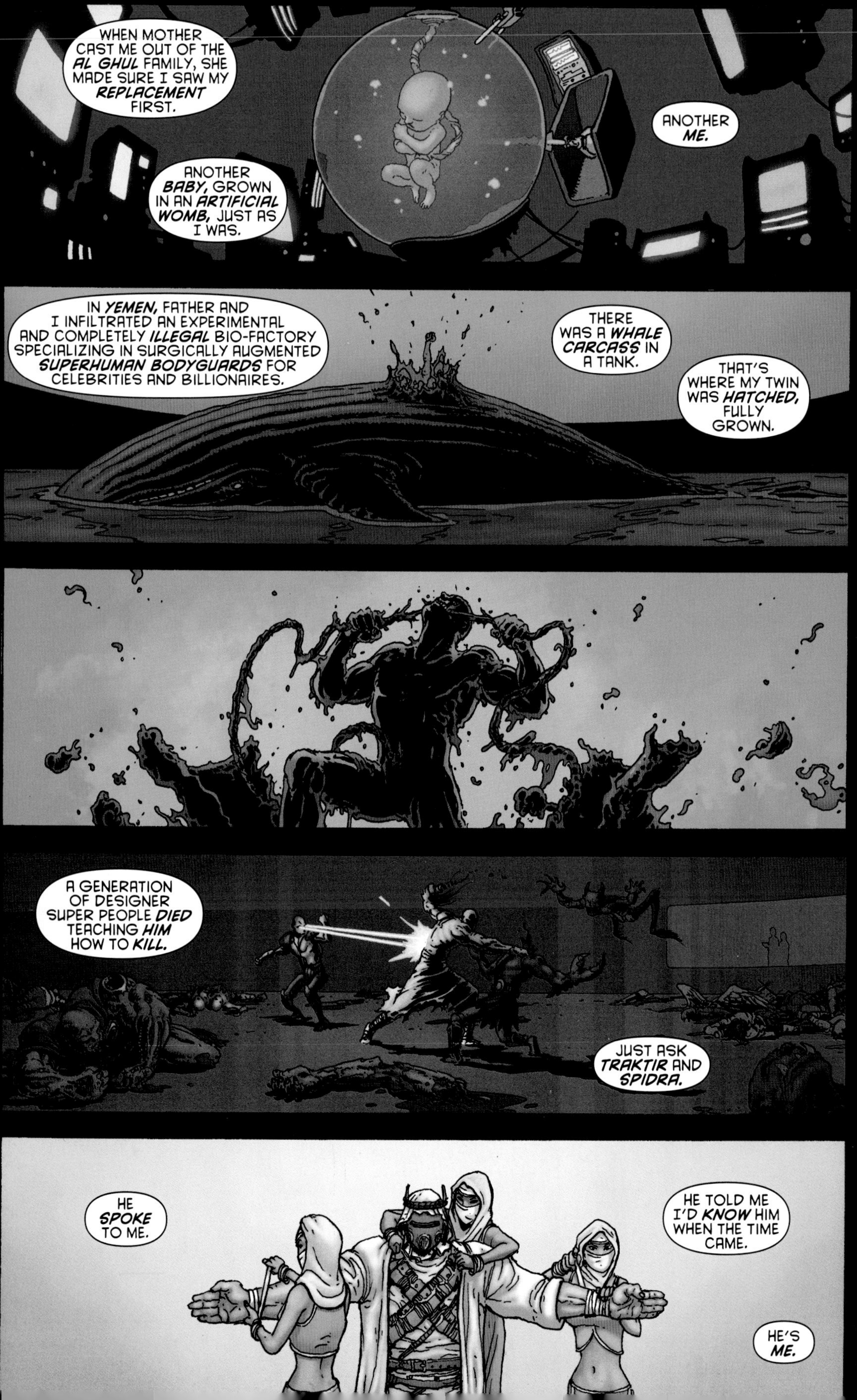
WHEN MOTHER CAST ME OUT OF THE AL GHUL FAMILY, SHE MADE SURE I SAW MY REPLACEMENT FIRST.
ANOTHER BABY, GROWN IN AN ARTIFICIAL WOMB, JUST AS I WAS.
ANOTHER ME.
IN YEMEN, FATHER AND I INFILTRATED AN EXPERIMENTAL AND COMPLETELY ILLEGAL BIO-FACTORY SPECIALIZING IN SURGICALLY AUGMENTED SUPERHUMAN BODYGUARDS FOR CELEBRITIES AND BILLIONAIRES.
THERE WAS A WHALE CARCASS IN A TANK.
THAT'S WHERE MY TWIN WAS HATCHED, FULLY GROWN.
A GENERATION OF DESIGNER SUPER PEOPLE DIED TEACHING HIM HOW TO KILL.
JUST ASK TRAKTIR AND SPIDRA.
HE SPOKE TO ME.
HE TOLD ME I'D KNOW HIM WHEN THE TIME CAME.
HE'S ME.

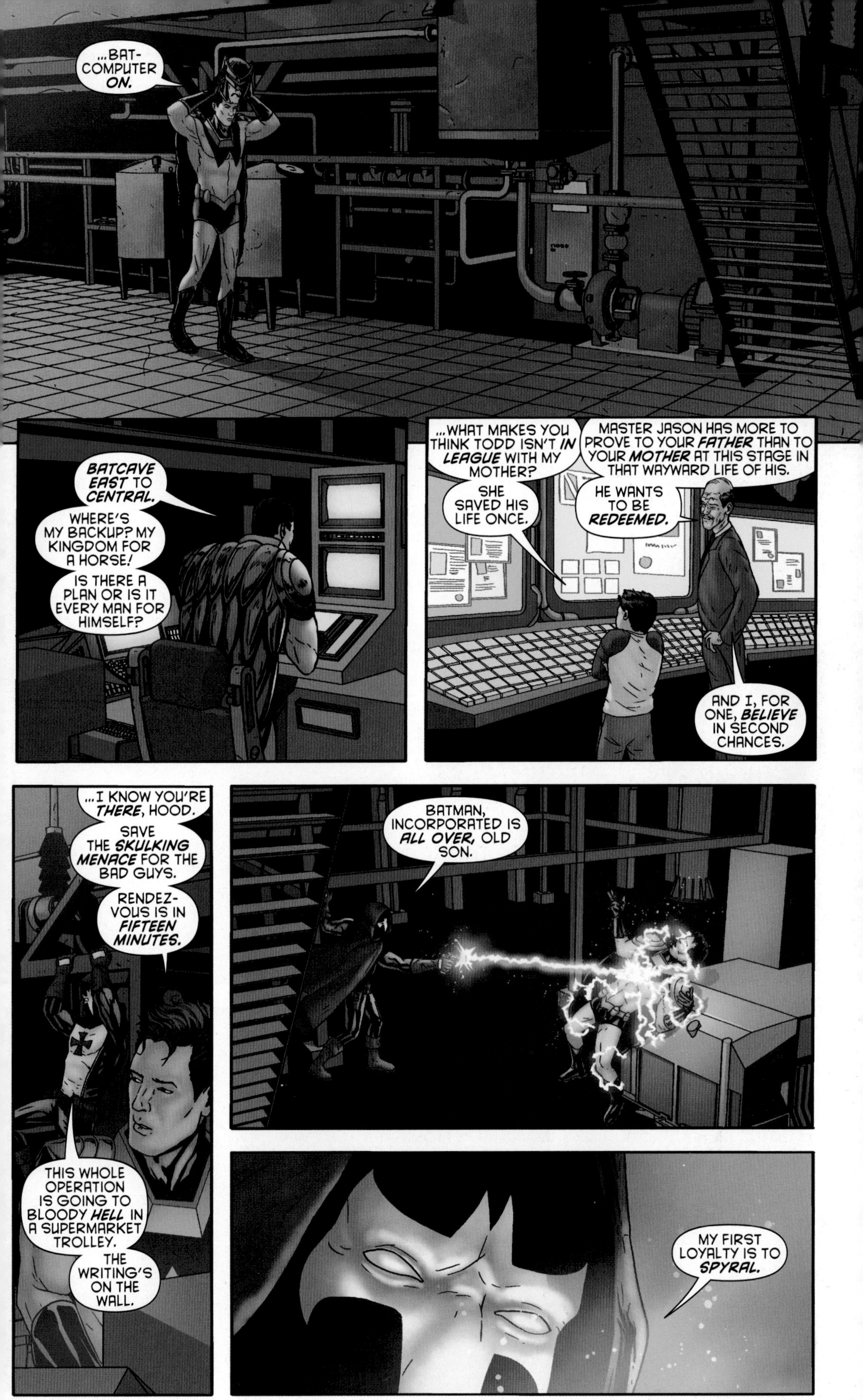
...BAT-COMPUTER ON.
BATCAVE EAST TO CENTRAL.
WHERE'S MY BACKUP? MY KINGDOM FOR A HORSE!
IS THERE A PLAN OR IS IT EVERY MAN FOR HIMSELF?
...WHAT MAKES YOU THINK TODD ISN'T IN LEAGUE WITH MY MOTHER?
SHE SAVED HIS LIFE ONCE.
MASTER JASON HAS MORE TO PROVE TO YOUR FATHER THAN TO YOUR MOTHER AT THIS STAGE IN THAT WAYWARD LIFE OF HIS.
HE WANTS TO BE REDEEMED.
AND I, FOR ONE, BELIEVE IN SECOND CHANCES.
...I KNOW YOU'RE THERE, HOOD.
SAVE THE SKULKING MENACE FOR THE BAD GUYS.
RENDEZ-VOUS IS IN FIFTEEN MINUTES.
THIS WHOLE OPERATION IS GOING TO BLOODY HELL IN A SUPERMARKET TROLLEY.
THE WRITING'S ON THE WALL.
BATMAN, INCORPORATED IS ALL OVER, OLD SON.
MY FIRST LOYALTY IS TO SPYRAL.

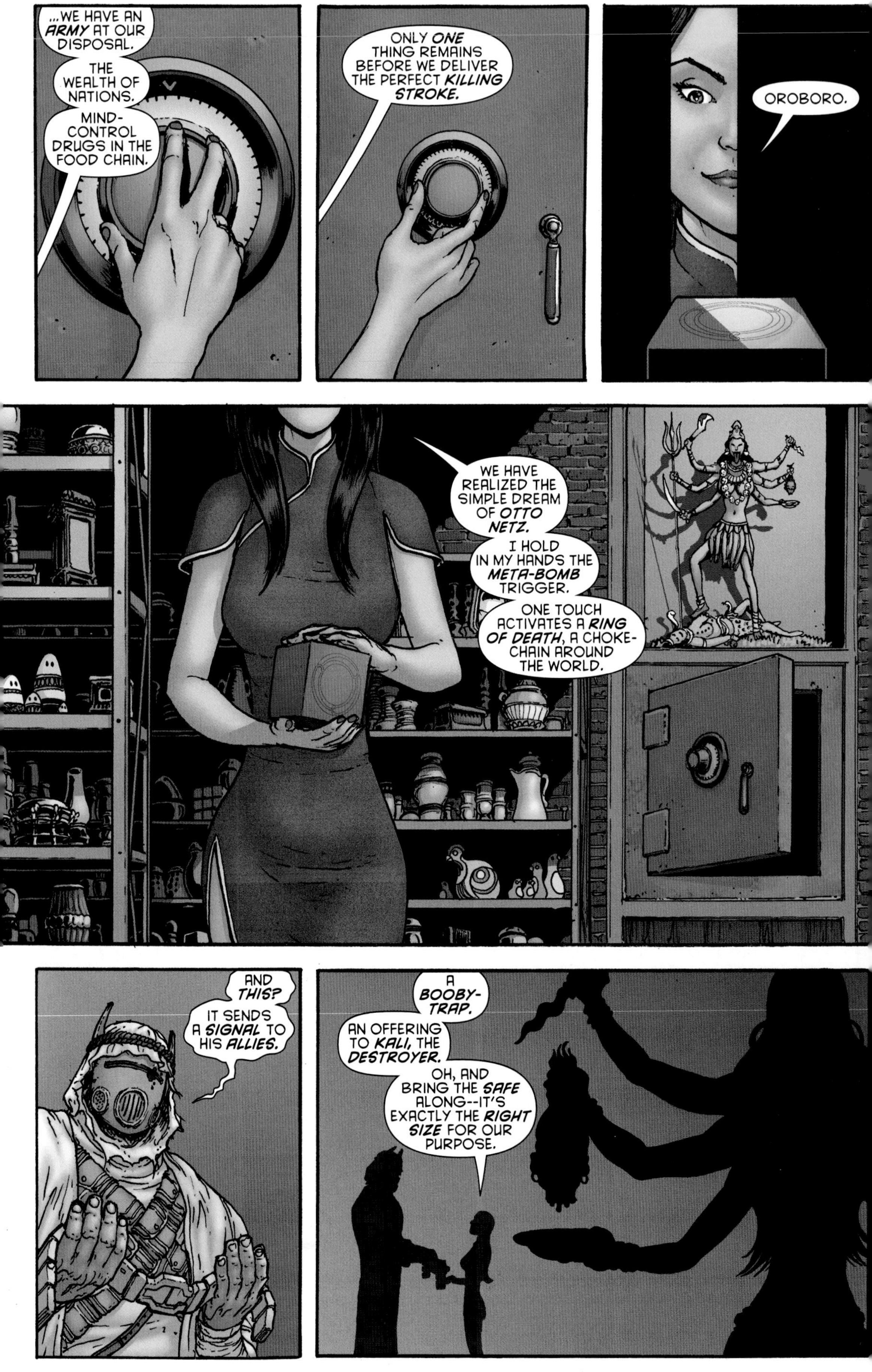

...WE HAVE AN ARMY AT OUR DISPOSAL.
THE WEALTH OF NATIONS.
MIND-CONTROL DRUGS IN THE FOOD CHAIN.
ONLY ONE THING REMAINS BEFORE WE DELIVER THE PERFECT KILLING STROKE.
OROBORO.
WE HAVE REALIZED THE SIMPLE DREAM OF OTTO NETZ.
I HOLD IN MY HANDS THE META-BOMB TRIGGER.
ONE TOUCH ACTIVATES A RING OF DEATH, A CHOKE-CHAIN AROUND THE WORLD.
AND THIS?
IT SENDS A SIGNAL TO HIS ALLIES.
A BOOBY-TRAP.
AN OFFERING TO KALI, THE DESTROYER.
OH, AND BRING THE SAFE ALONG--IT'S EXACTLY THE RIGHT SIZE FOR OUR PURPOSE.

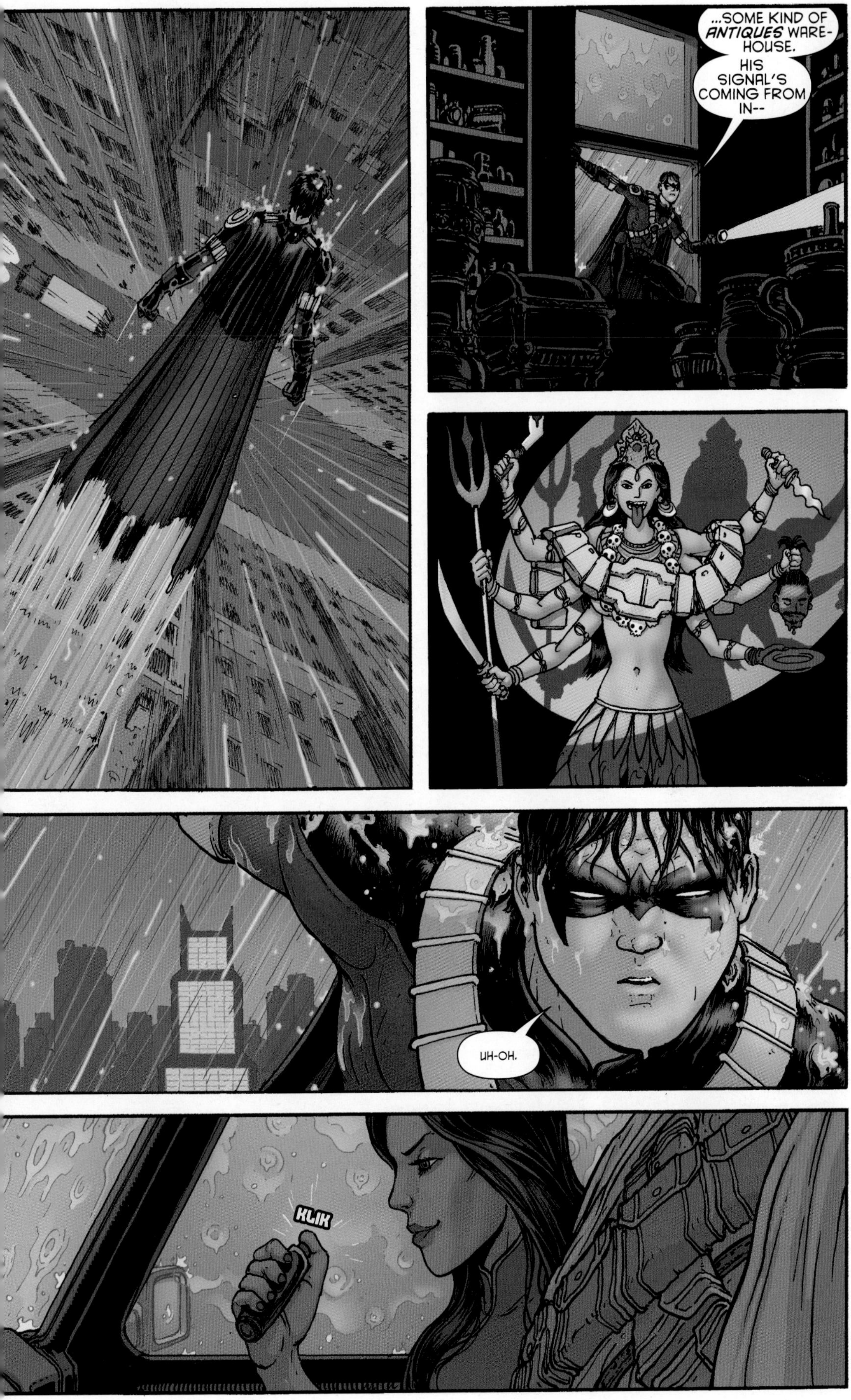

...SOME KIND OF ANTIQUES WAREHOUSE.
HIS SIGNAL'S COMING FROM IN--
UH-OH.
KLIK

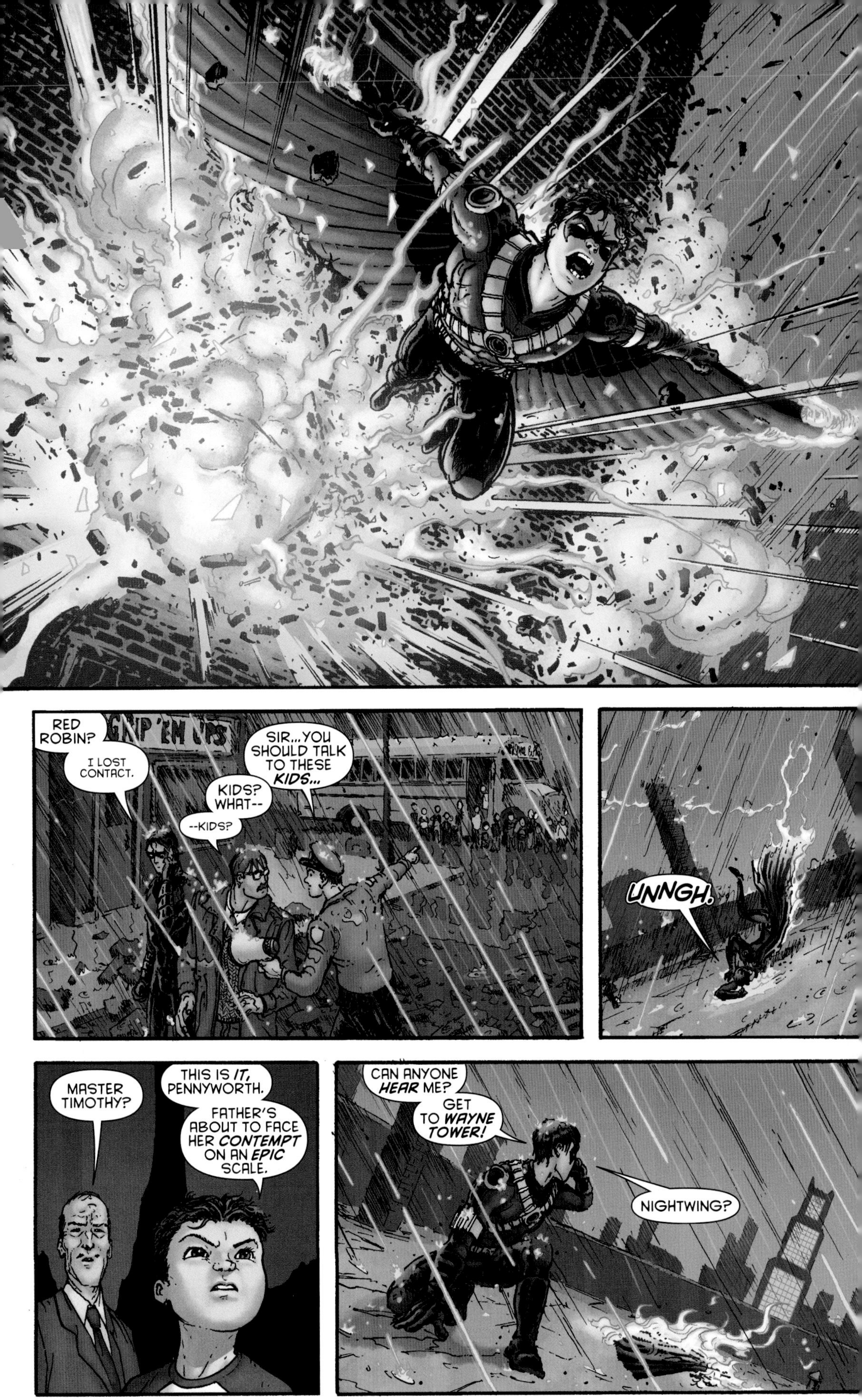
GRIP 'EM UPS
RED ROBIN?
I LOST CONTACT.
SIR...YOU SHOULD TALK TO THESE *KIDS...*
KIDS? WHAT--
--KIDS?
UNNGH.
MASTER TIMOTHY?
THIS IS *IT,* PENNYWORTH.
FATHER'S ABOUT TO FACE HER *CONTEMPT* ON AN *EPIC* SCALE.
CAN ANYONE *HEAR* ME?
GET TO *WAYNE TOWER!*
NIGHTWING?

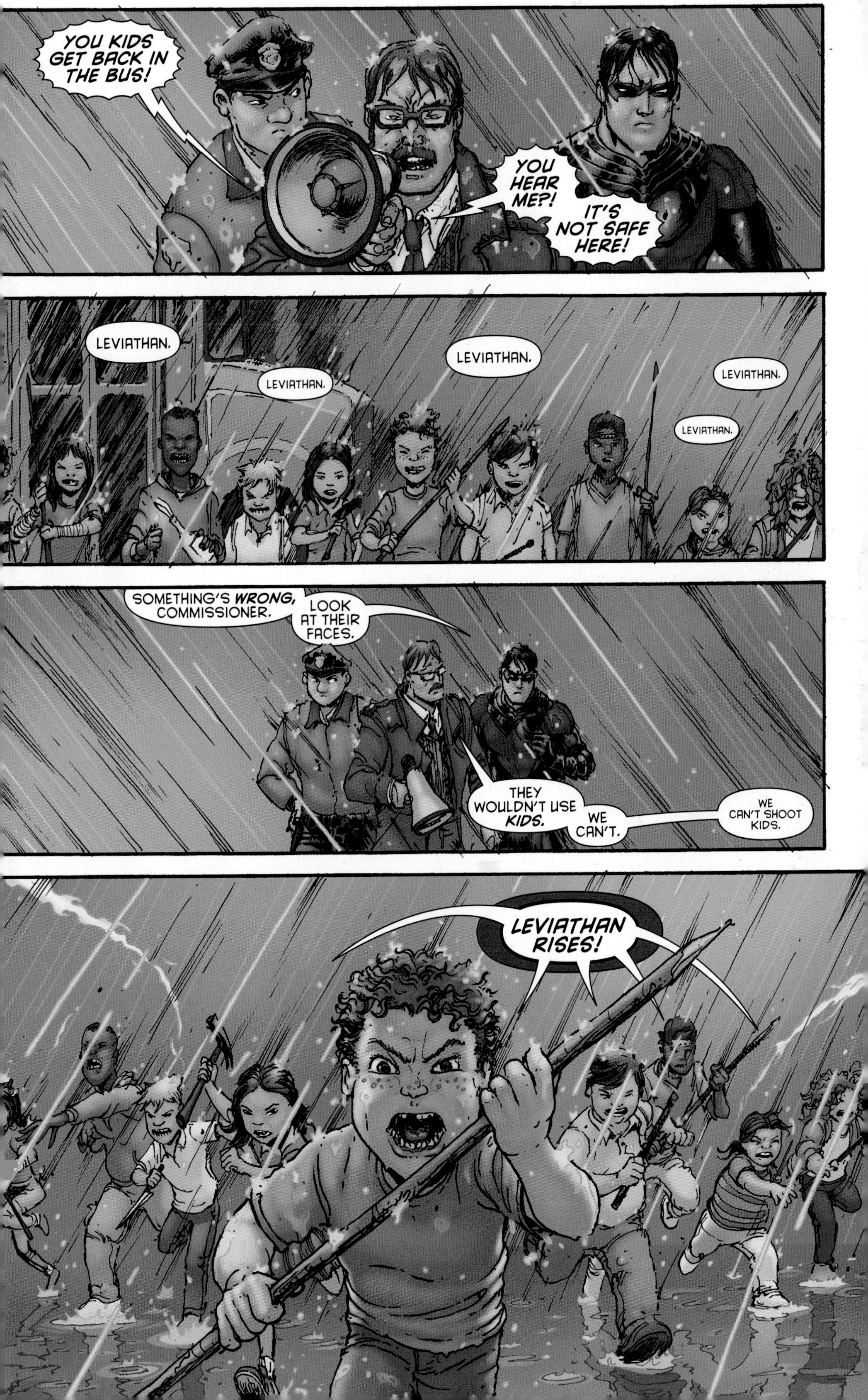

YOU KIDS GET BACK IN THE BUS!
YOU HEAR ME?!
IT'S NOT SAFE HERE!
LEVIATHAN.
LEVIATHAN.
LEVIATHAN.
LEVIATHAN.
LEVIATHAN.
SOMETHING'S WRONG, COMMISSIONER.
LOOK AT THEIR FACES.
THEY WOULDN'T USE KIDS.
WE CAN'T.
WE CAN'T SHOOT KIDS.
LEVIATHAN RISES!

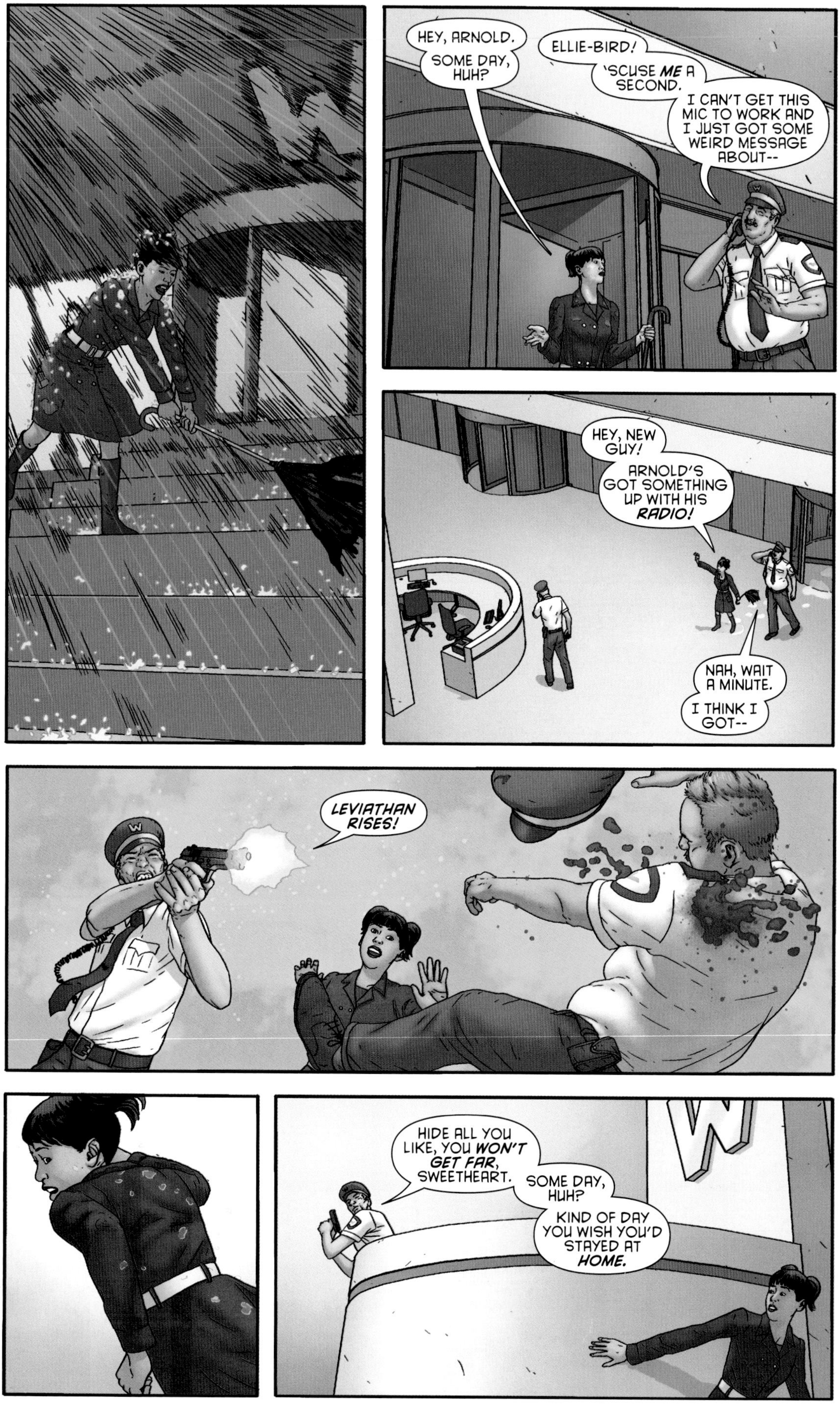
HEY, ARNOLD.
SOME DAY, HUH?
ELLIE-BIRD!
'SCUSE ME A SECOND.
I CAN'T GET THIS MIC TO WORK AND I JUST GOT SOME WEIRD MESSAGE ABOUT--
HEY, NEW GUY!
ARNOLD'S GOT SOMETHING UP WITH HIS RADIO!
NAH, WAIT A MINUTE.
I THINK I GOT--
LEVIATHAN RISES!
HIDE ALL YOU LIKE, YOU WON'T GET FAR, SWEETHEART.
SOME DAY, HUH?
KIND OF DAY YOU WISH YOU'D STAYED AT HOME.

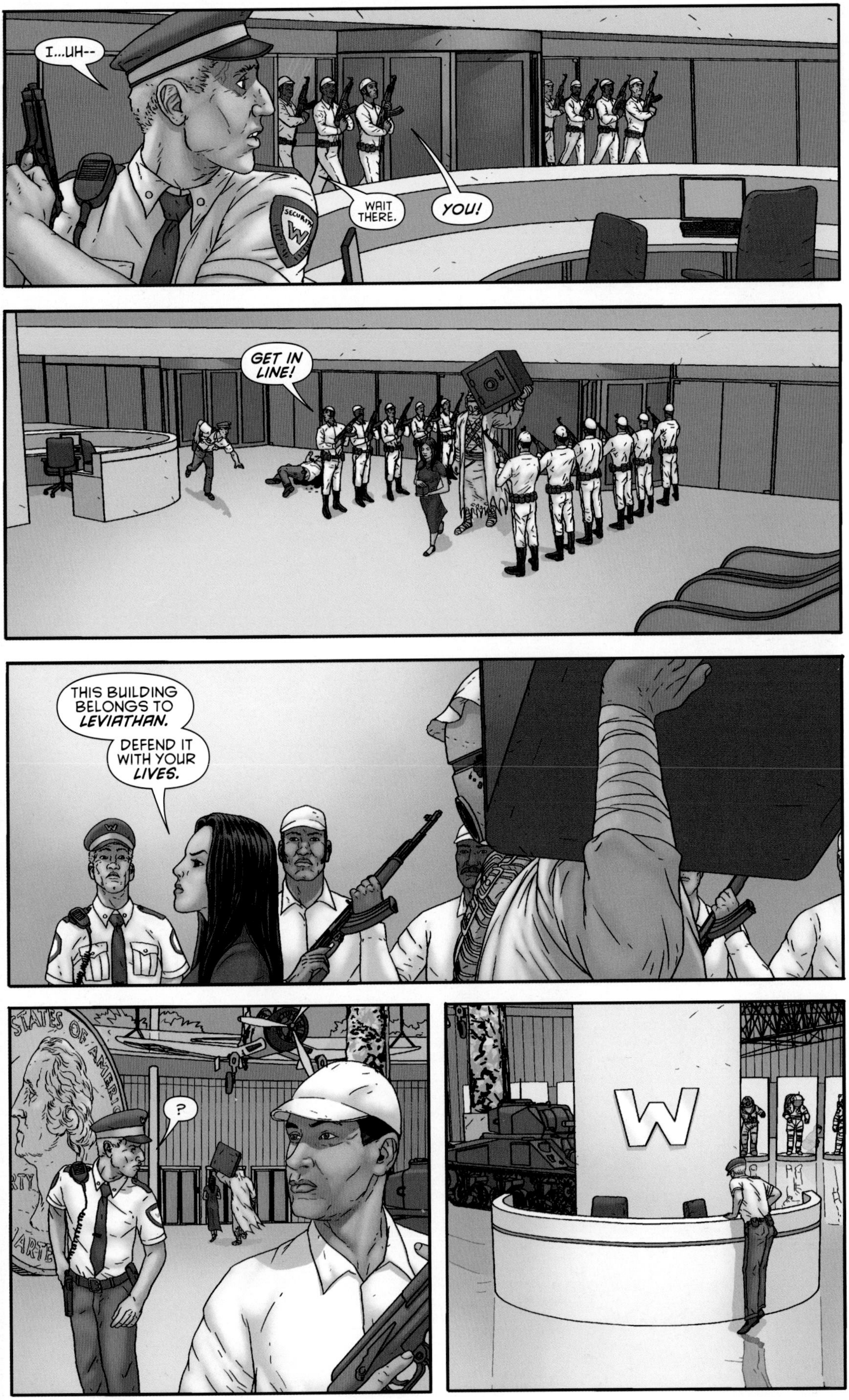
I...UH--
WAIT THERE.
YOU!
GET IN LINE!
THIS BUILDING BELONGS TO LEVIATHAN.
DEFEND IT WITH YOUR LIVES.
?

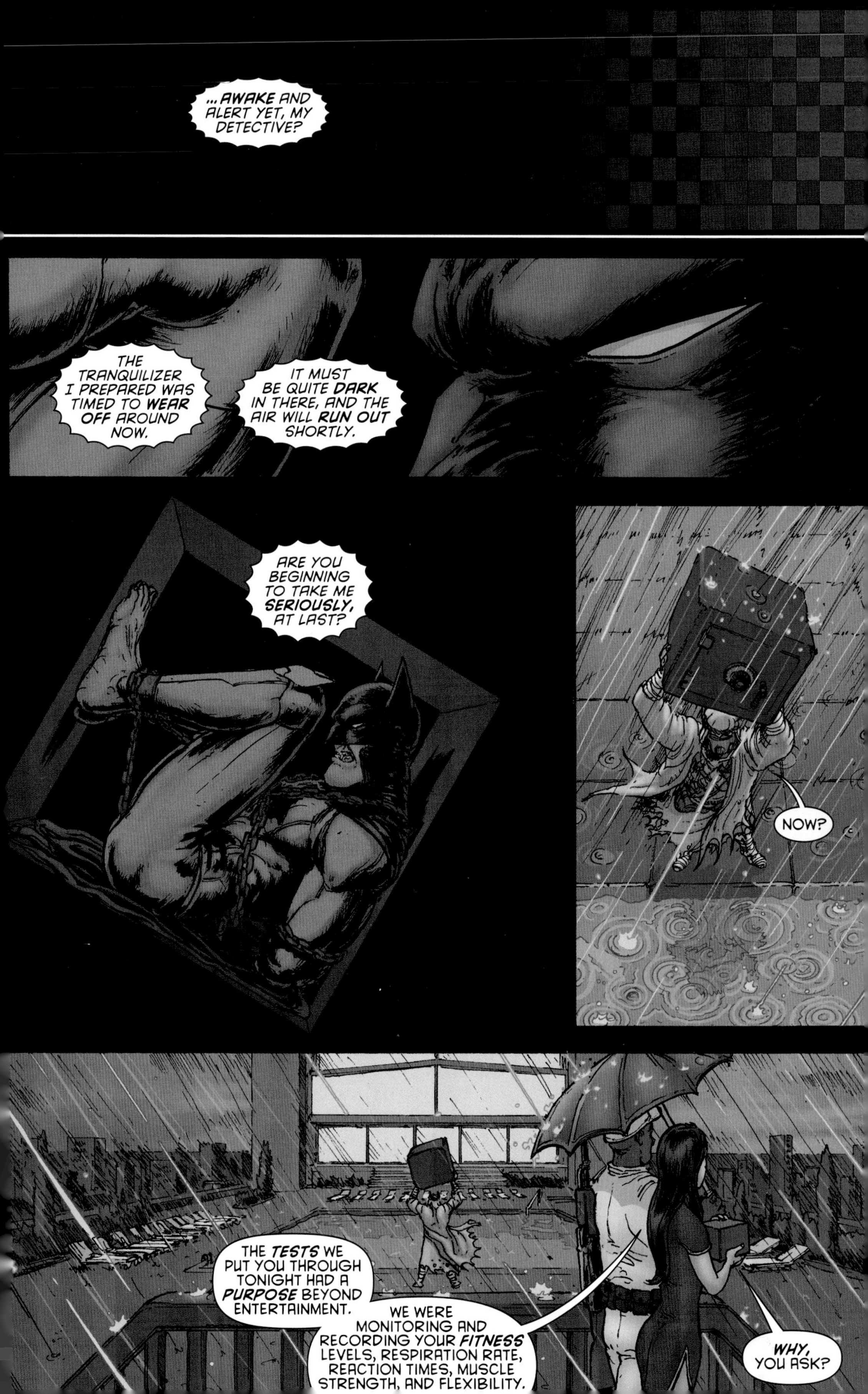
...AWAKE AND ALERT YET, MY DETECTIVE?
THE TRANQUILIZER I PREPARED WAS TIMED TO WEAR OFF AROUND NOW.
IT MUST BE QUITE DARK IN THERE, AND THE AIR WILL RUN OUT SHORTLY.
ARE YOU BEGINNING TO TAKE ME SERIOUSLY, AT LAST?
NOW?
THE TESTS WE PUT YOU THROUGH TONIGHT HAD A PURPOSE BEYOND ENTERTAINMENT.
WE WERE MONITORING AND RECORDING YOUR FITNESS LEVELS, RESPIRATION RATE, REACTION TIMES, MUSCLE STRENGTH, AND FLEXIBILITY.
WHY, YOU ASK?

EVERY DETAIL WAS NECESSARY FOR ME TO CALCULATE TO THE *MICROSECOND* EXACTLY *HOW LONG* IT WOULD TAKE YOU TO *ESCAPE* THIS RIDICULOUS TRAP.

NOW.

DURING EACH OF THOSE FUTILE SECONDS AS YOU STRUGGLE TO *FREE* YOUSELF...

...KNOW THAT I'VE *BEATEN* YOU AT YOUR OWN STUPID, CHILDISH GAME OF CLUES AND TRAPS, MASKS AND TOYS.

KNOW THAT BY THE TIME YOU GET *FREE*, ALL OF IT WILL BE *GONE*.

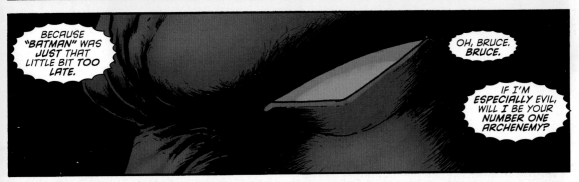

BECAUSE "BATMAN" WAS JUST THAT LITTLE BIT *TOO* LATE.

OH, BRUCE. BRUCE.

IF I'M *ESPECIALLY EVIL*, WILL I BE YOUR *NUMBER ONE ARCHENEMY?*

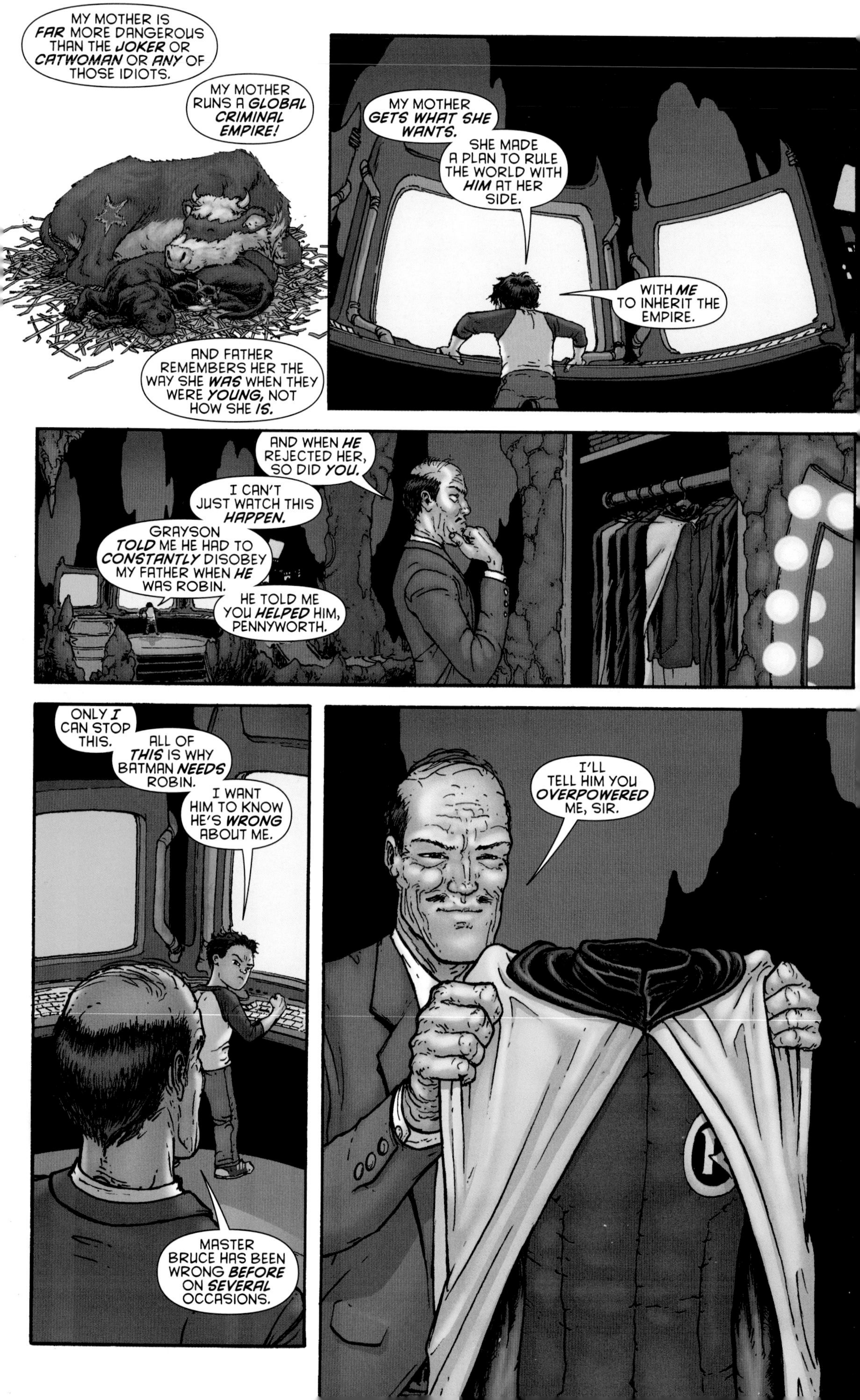
MY MOTHER IS FAR MORE DANGEROUS THAN THE JOKER OR CATWOMAN OR ANY OF THOSE IDIOTS.
MY MOTHER RUNS A GLOBAL CRIMINAL EMPIRE!
AND FATHER REMEMBERS HER THE WAY SHE WAS WHEN THEY WERE YOUNG, NOT HOW SHE IS.
MY MOTHER GETS WHAT SHE WANTS.
SHE MADE A PLAN TO RULE THE WORLD WITH HIM AT HER SIDE.
WITH ME TO INHERIT THE EMPIRE.
AND WHEN HE REJECTED HER, SO DID YOU.
I CAN'T JUST WATCH THIS HAPPEN.
GRAYSON TOLD ME HE HAD TO CONSTANTLY DISOBEY MY FATHER WHEN HE WAS ROBIN.
HE TOLD ME YOU HELPED HIM, PENNYWORTH.
ONLY I CAN STOP THIS.
ALL OF THIS IS WHY BATMAN NEEDS ROBIN.
I WANT HIM TO KNOW HE'S WRONG ABOUT ME.
MASTER BRUCE HAS BEEN WRONG BEFORE ON SEVERAL OCCASIONS.
I'LL TELL HIM YOU OVERPOWERED ME, SIR.

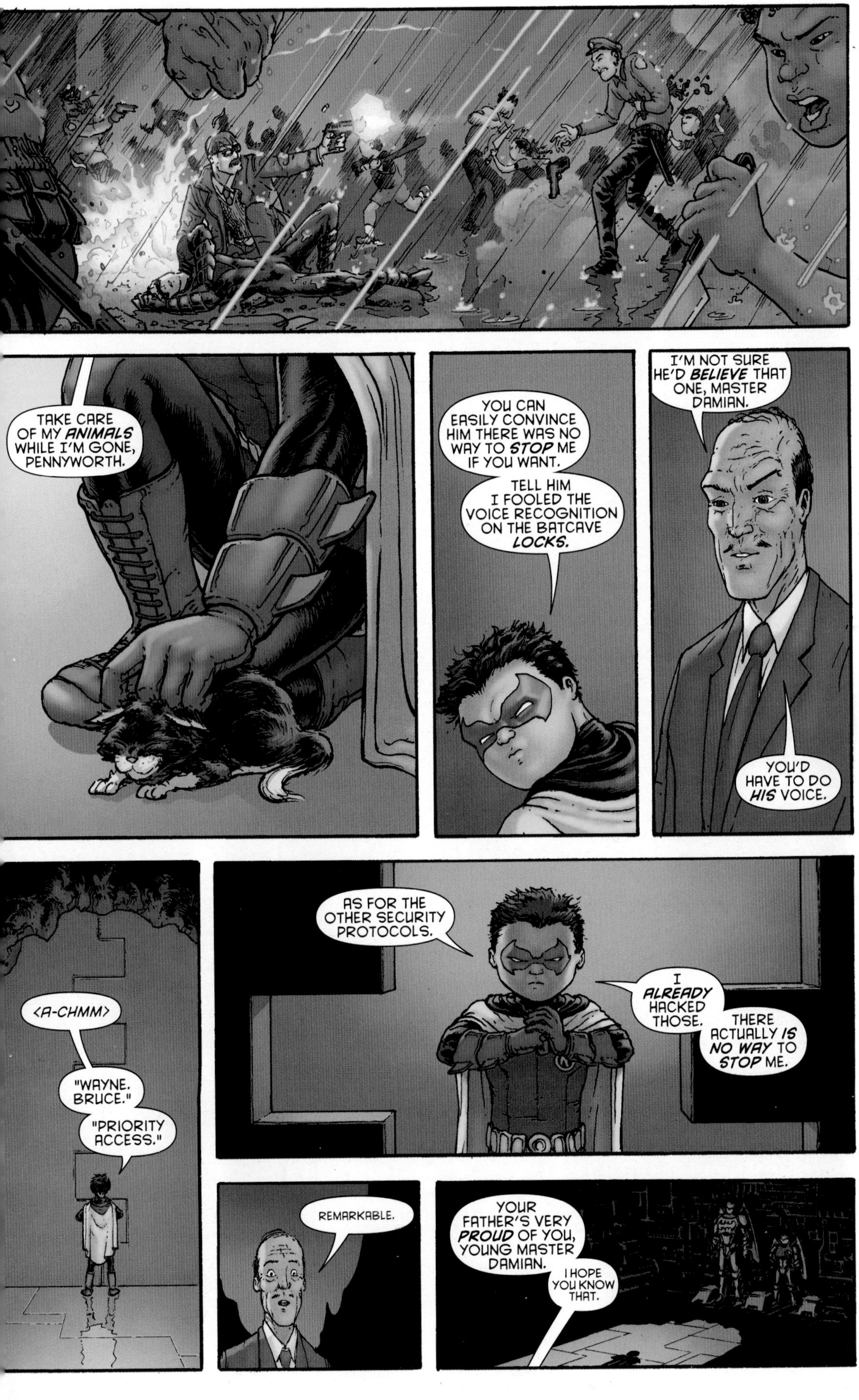

TAKE CARE OF MY ANIMALS WHILE I'M GONE, PENNYWORTH.
YOU CAN EASILY CONVINCE HIM THERE WAS NO WAY TO STOP ME IF YOU WANT.
TELL HIM I FOOLED THE VOICE RECOGNITION ON THE BATCAVE LOCKS.
I'M NOT SURE HE'D BELIEVE THAT ONE, MASTER DAMIAN.
YOU'D HAVE TO DO HIS VOICE.
<A-CHMM>
"WAYNE. BRUCE."
"PRIORITY ACCESS."
AS FOR THE OTHER SECURITY PROTOCOLS.
I ALREADY HACKED THOSE.
THERE ACTUALLY IS NO WAY TO STOP ME.
REMARKABLE.
YOUR FATHER'S VERY PROUD OF YOU, YOUNG MASTER DAMIAN.
I HOPE YOU KNOW THAT.

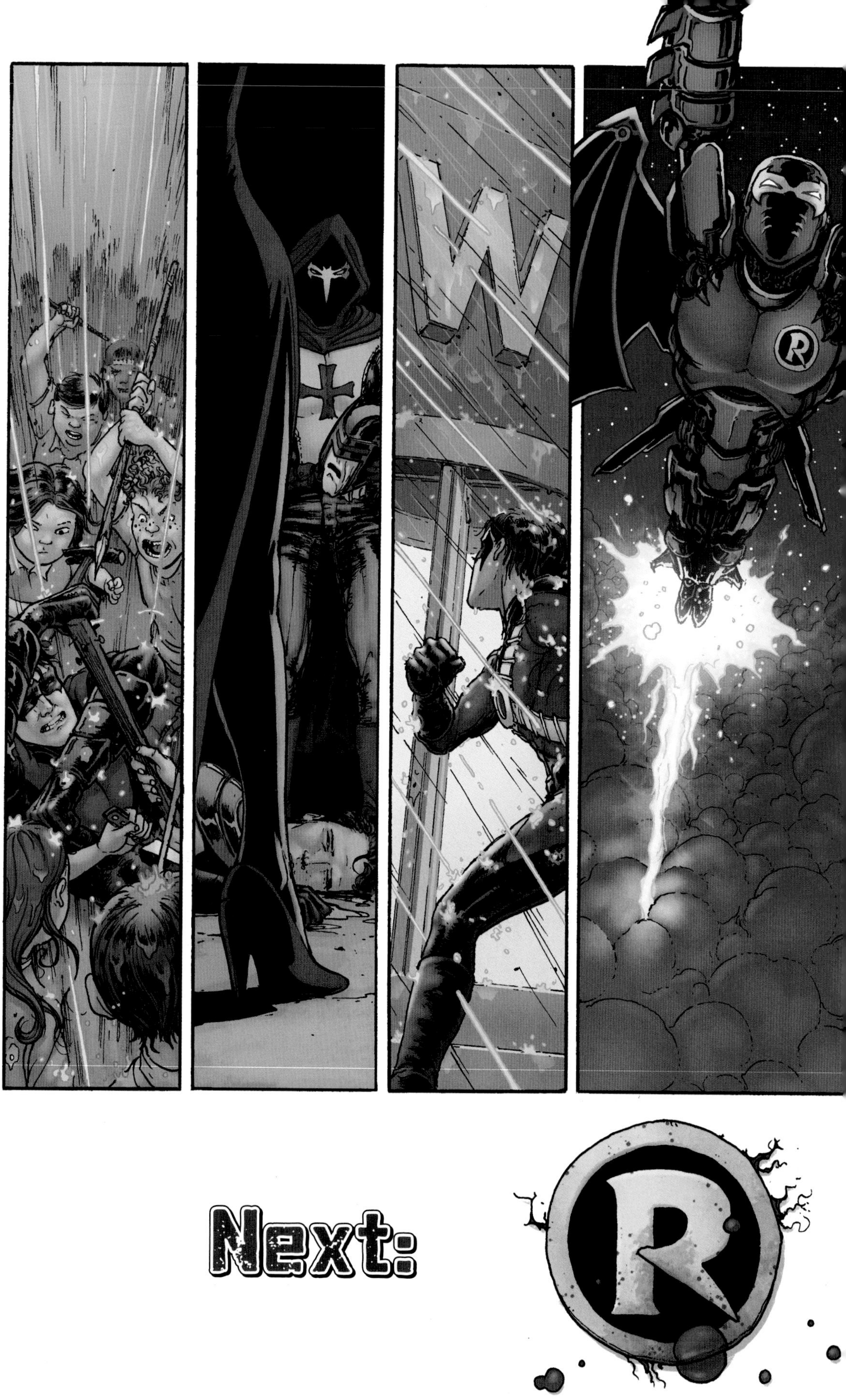

Next:

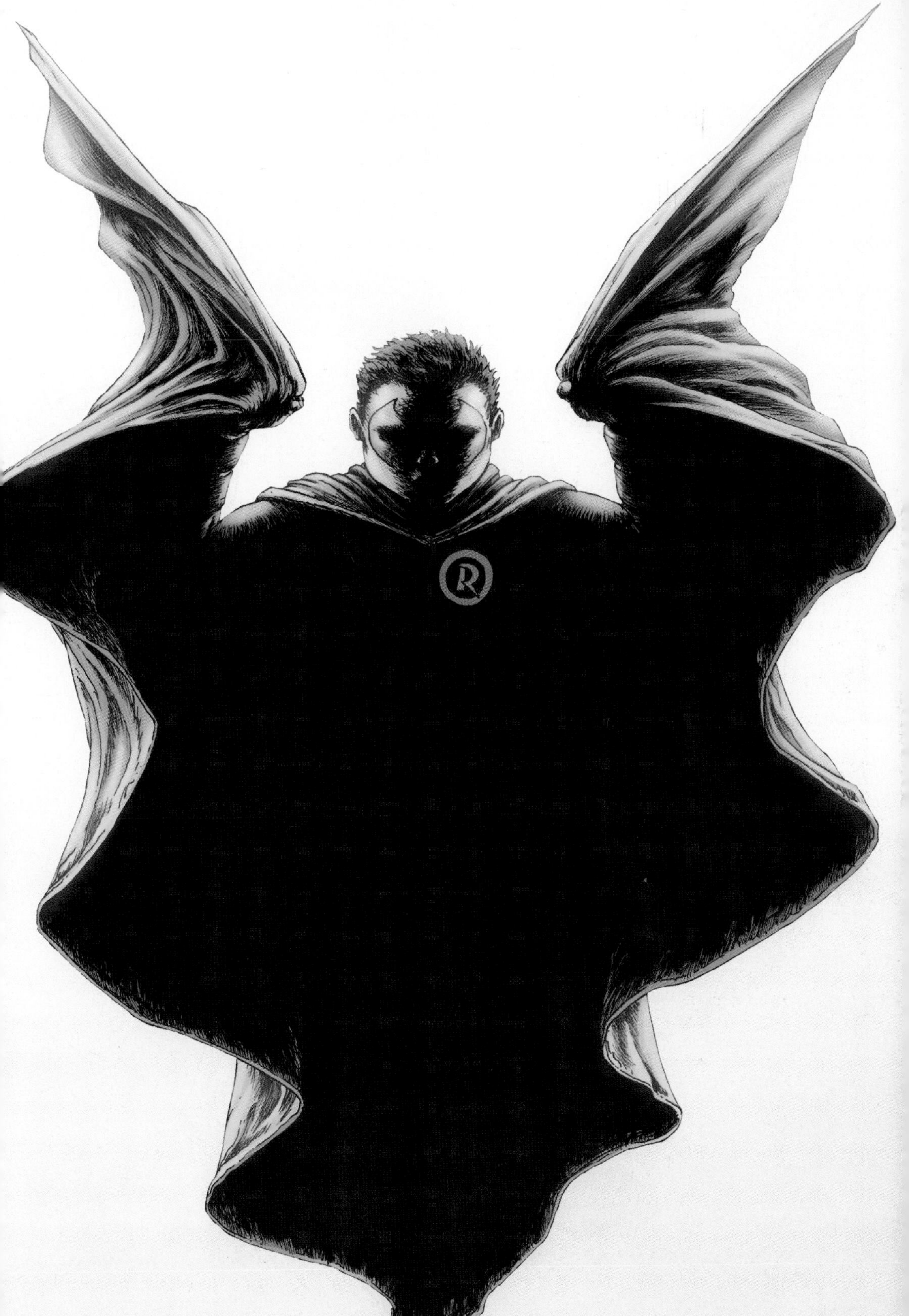

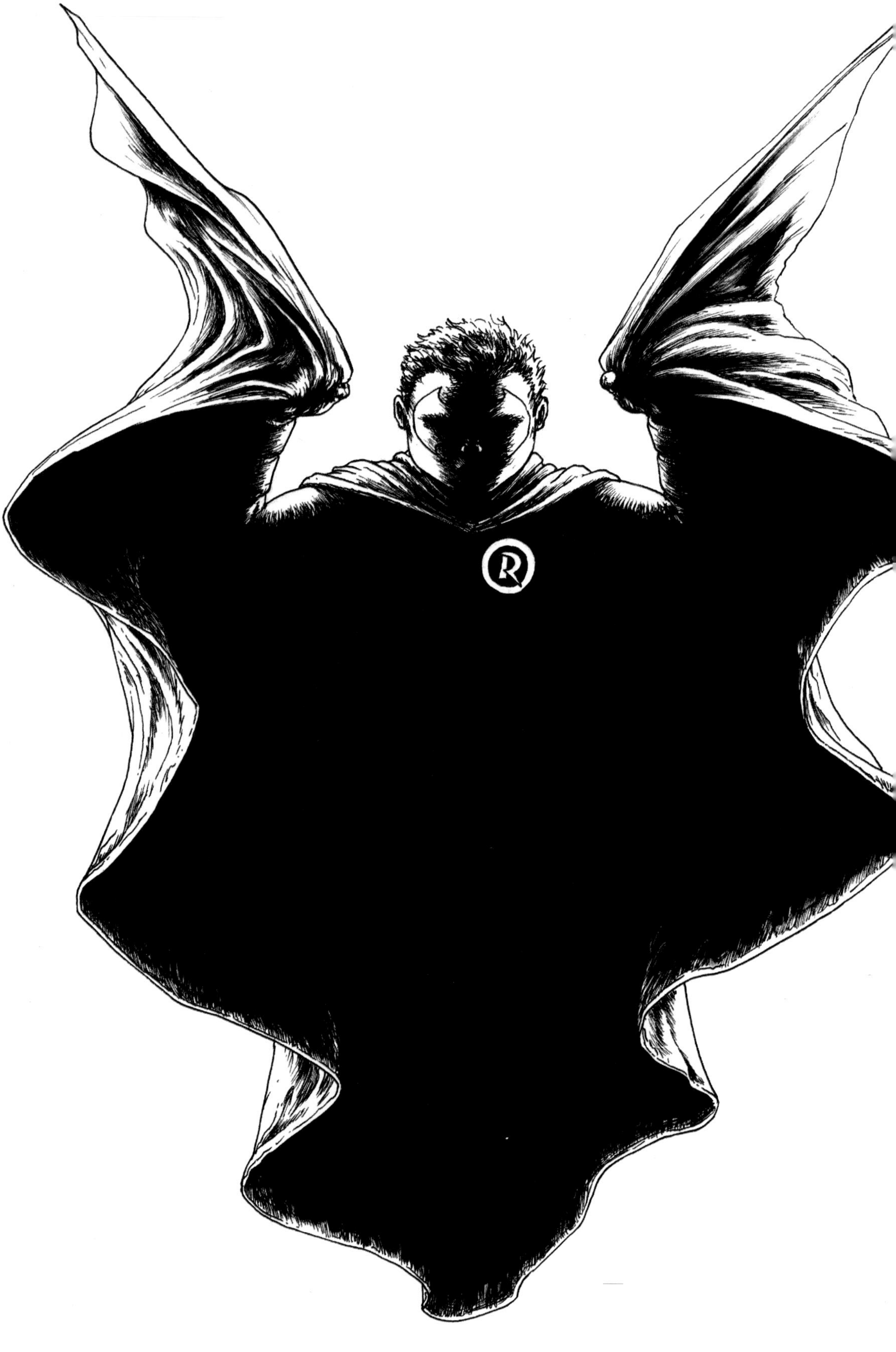

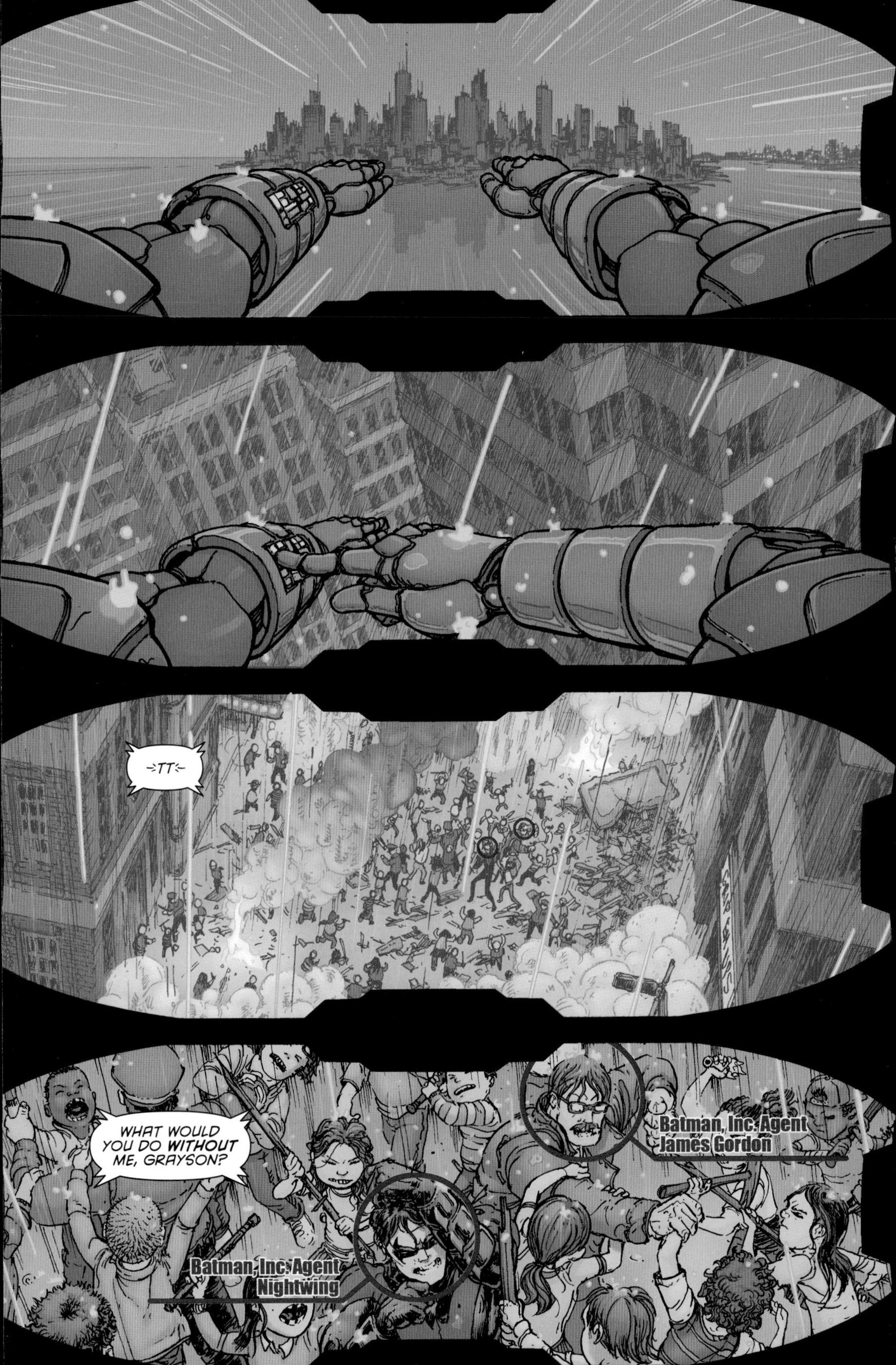
TT
WHAT WOULD YOU DO WITHOUT ME, GRAYSON?
Batman, Inc. Agent James Gordon
Batman, Inc. Agent Nightwing

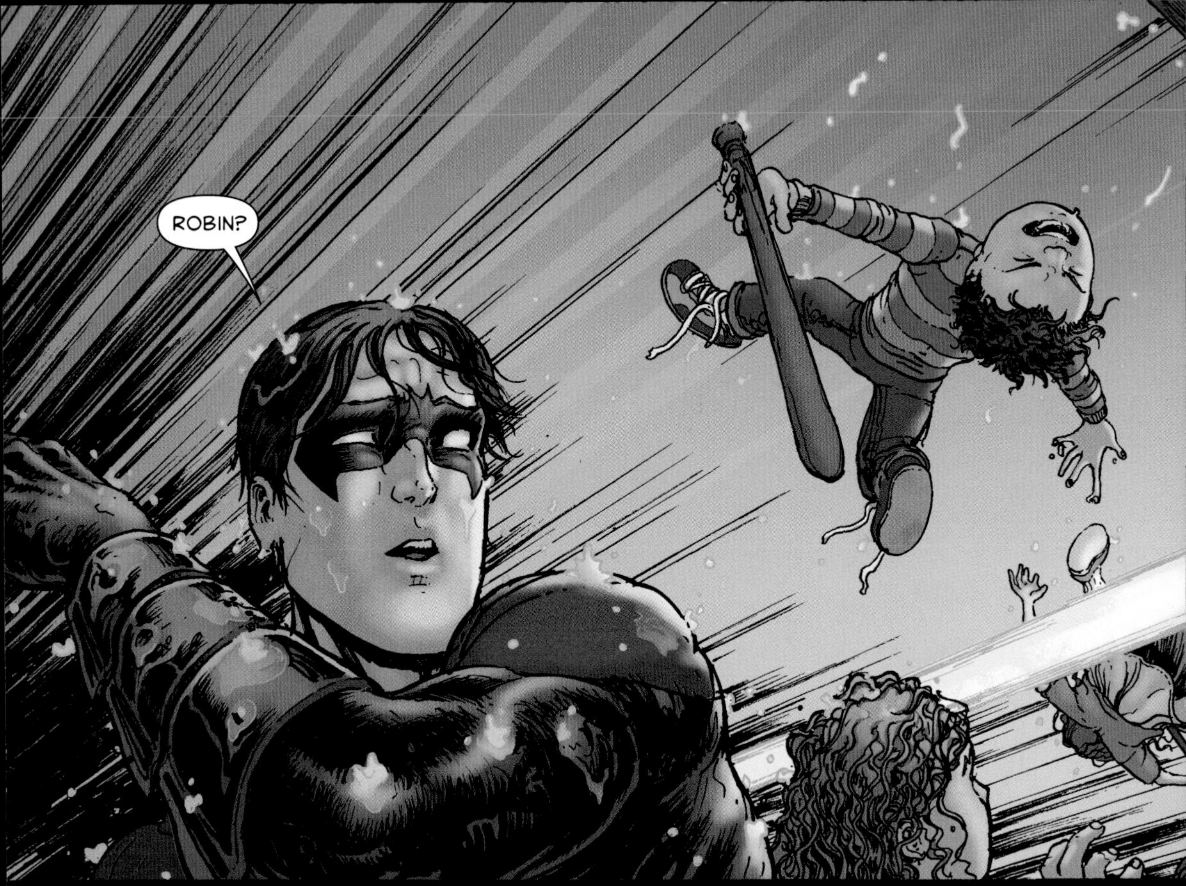
ROBIN?

THE BOY WONDER

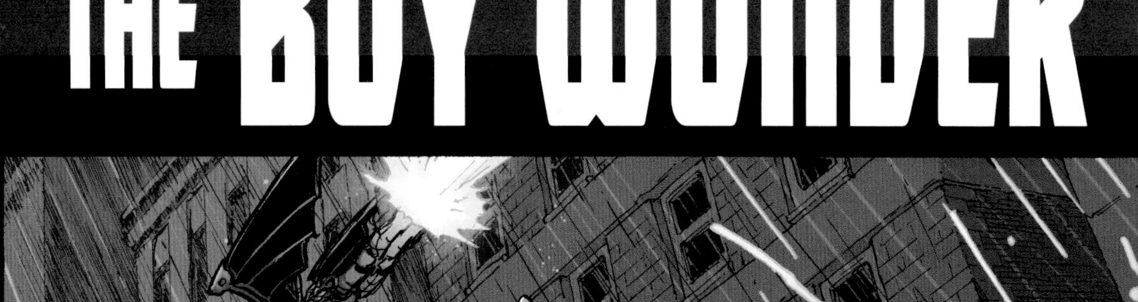

GRANT MORRISON WRITER
JASON MASTERS ART (PGS 34-37) NATHAN FAIRBAIRN COLORIST

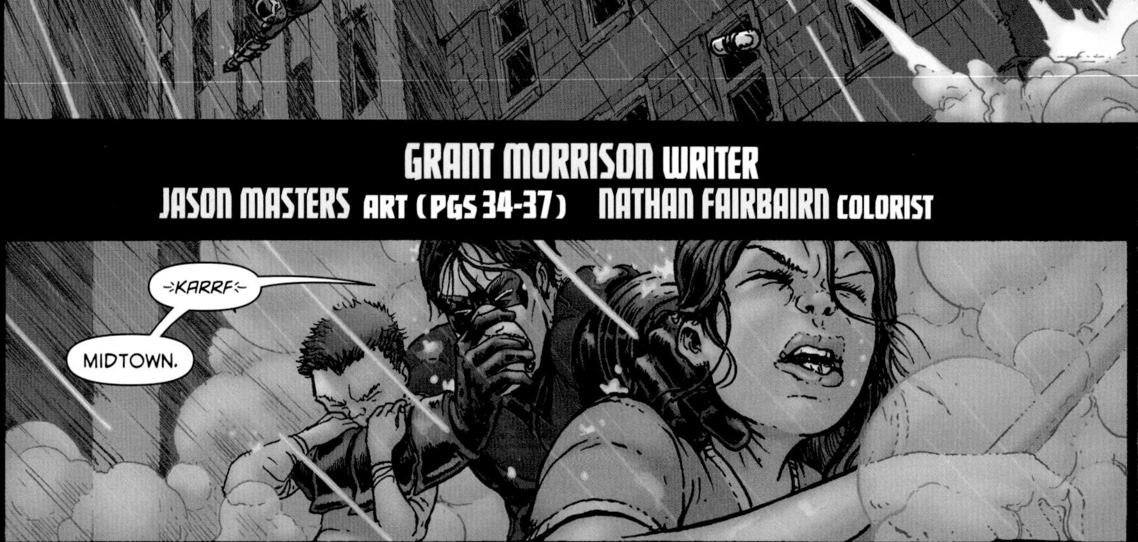
-KARRF-
MIDTOWN.

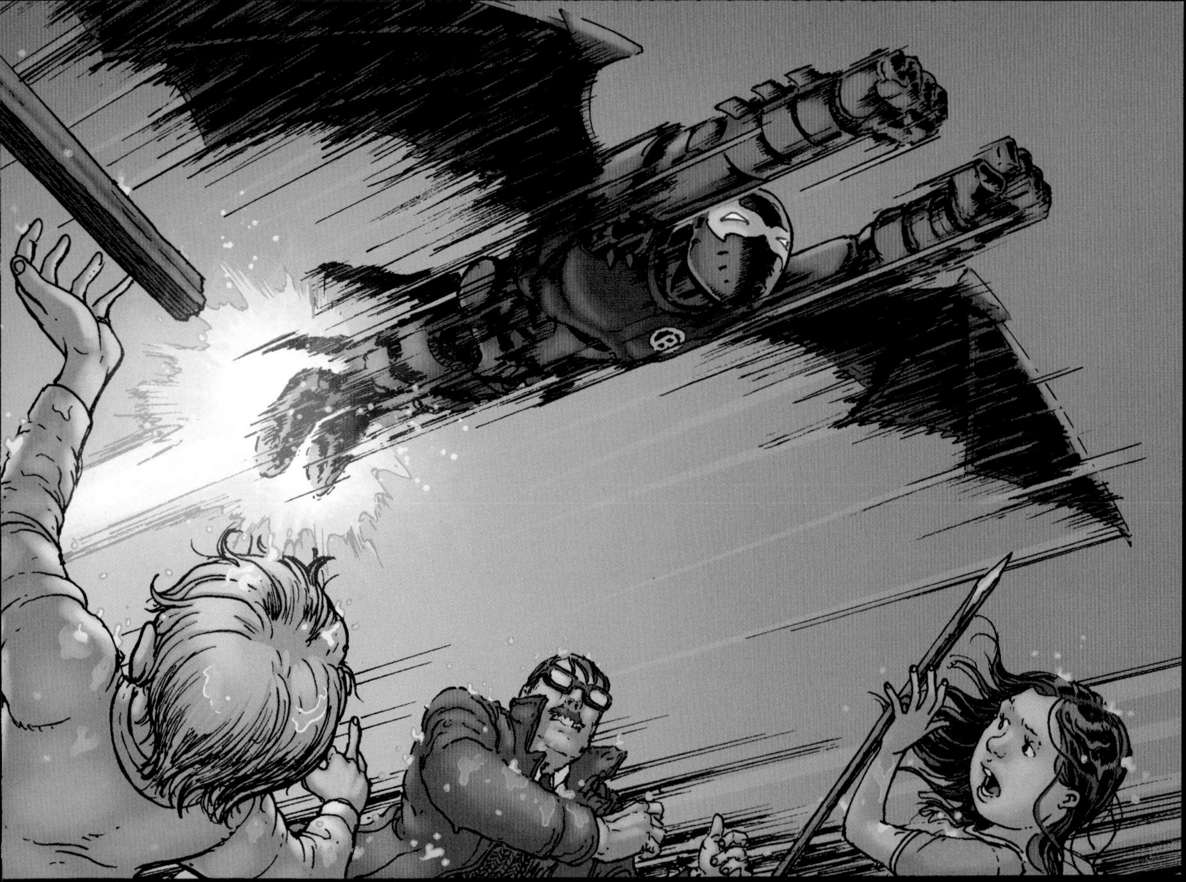

RETURNS

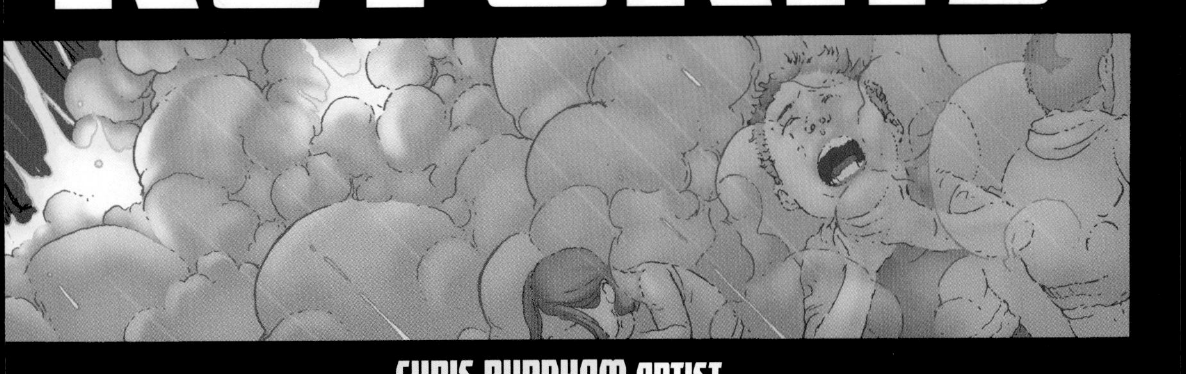

CHRIS BURNHAM ARTIST
TAYLOR ESPOSITO LETTERER BURNHAM WITH FAIRBAIRN COVER

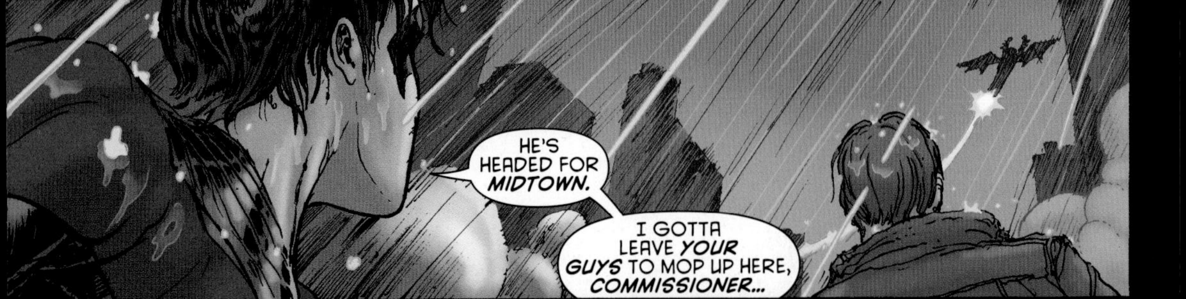
HE'S HEADED FOR *MIDTOWN.*
I GOTTA LEAVE *YOUR GUYS* TO MOP UP HERE, *COMMISSIONER...*

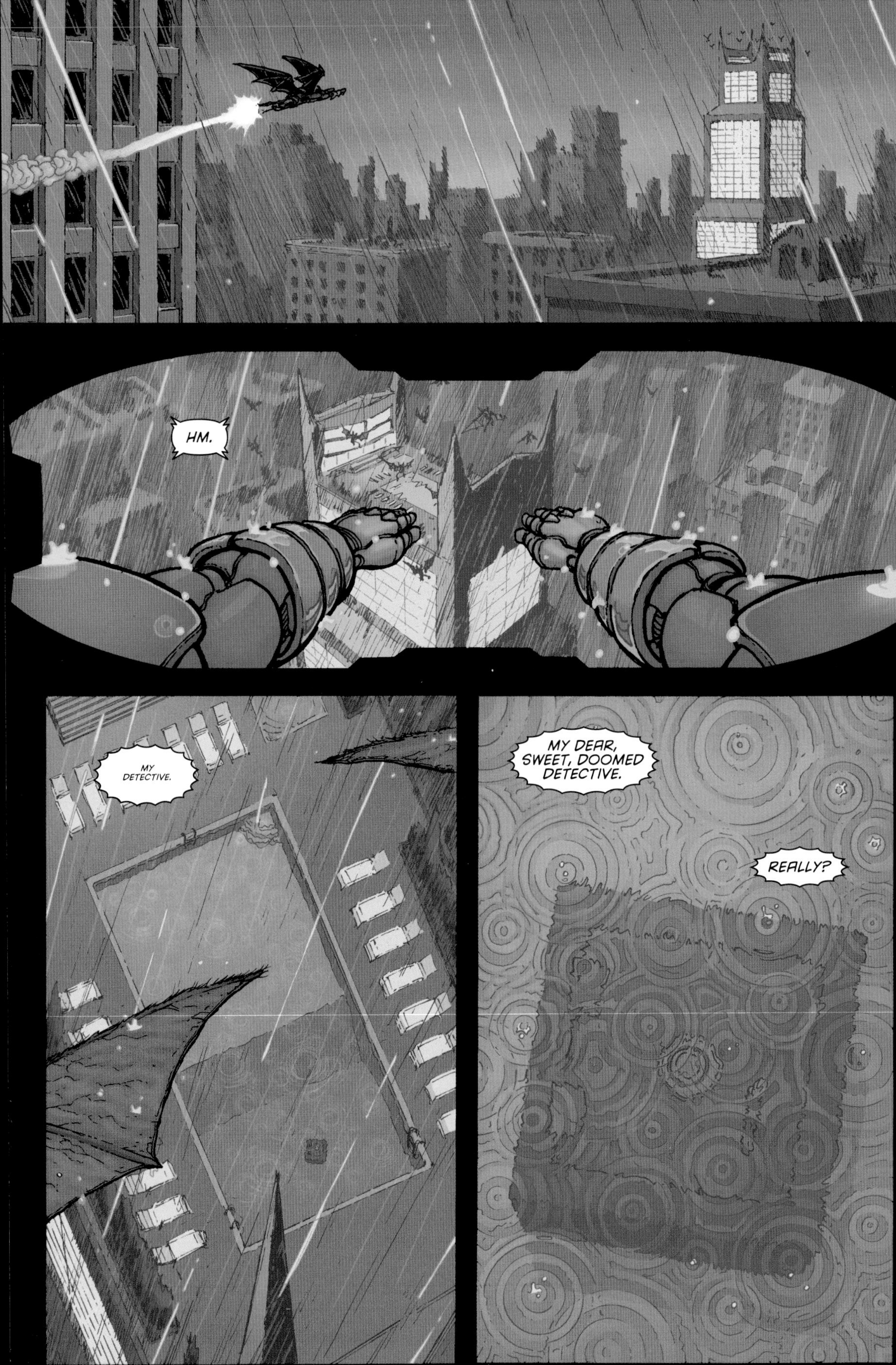
HM.
MY DETECTIVE.
MY DEAR, SWEET, DOOMED DETECTIVE.
REALLY?

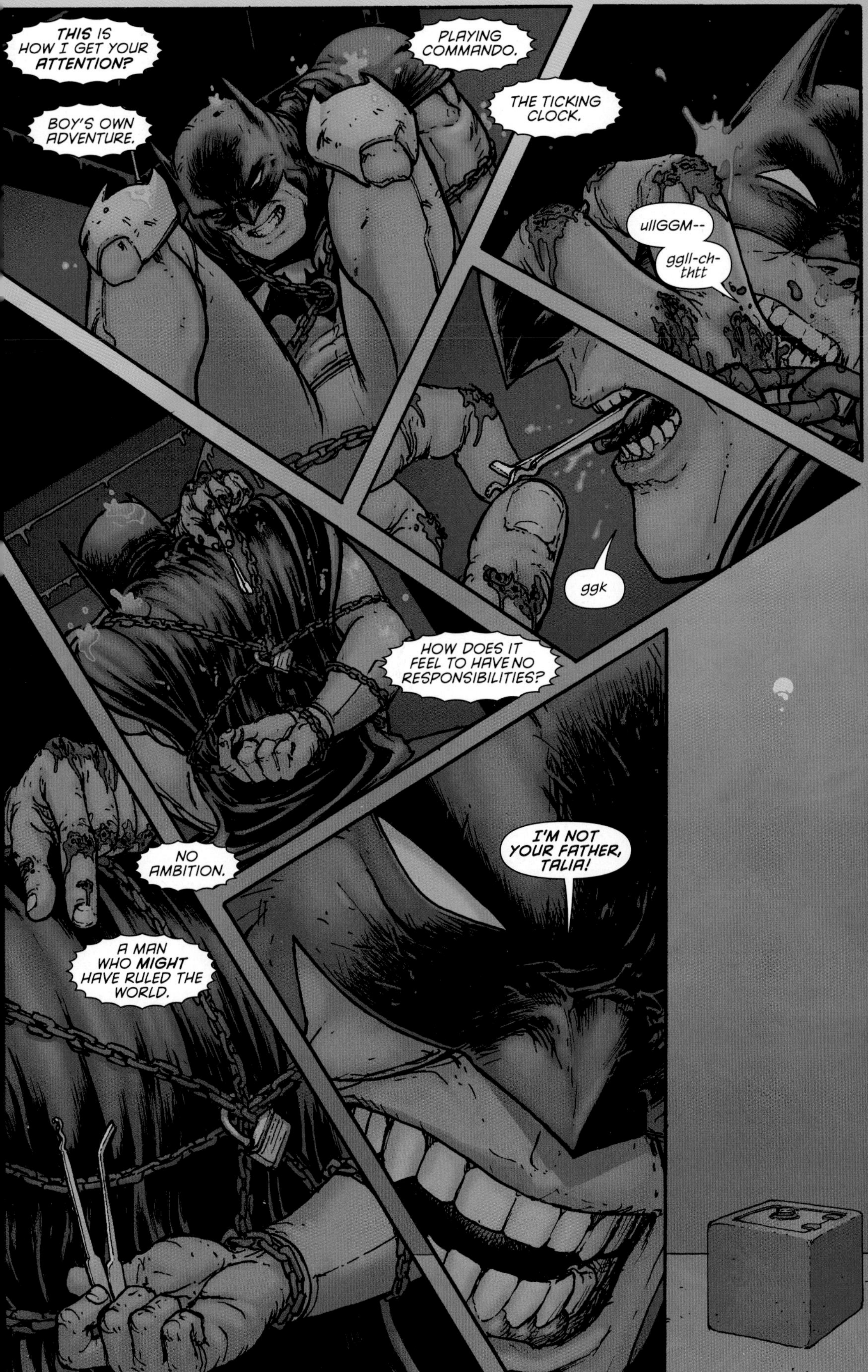

THIS IS HOW I GET YOUR ATTENTION?
PLAYING COMMANDO.
BOY'S OWN ADVENTURE.
THE TICKING CLOCK.
ullGGM--
ggll-ch-thtt
ggk
HOW DOES IT FEEL TO HAVE NO RESPONSIBILITIES?
NO AMBITION.
A MAN WHO MIGHT HAVE RULED THE WORLD.
I'M NOT YOUR FATHER, TALIA!

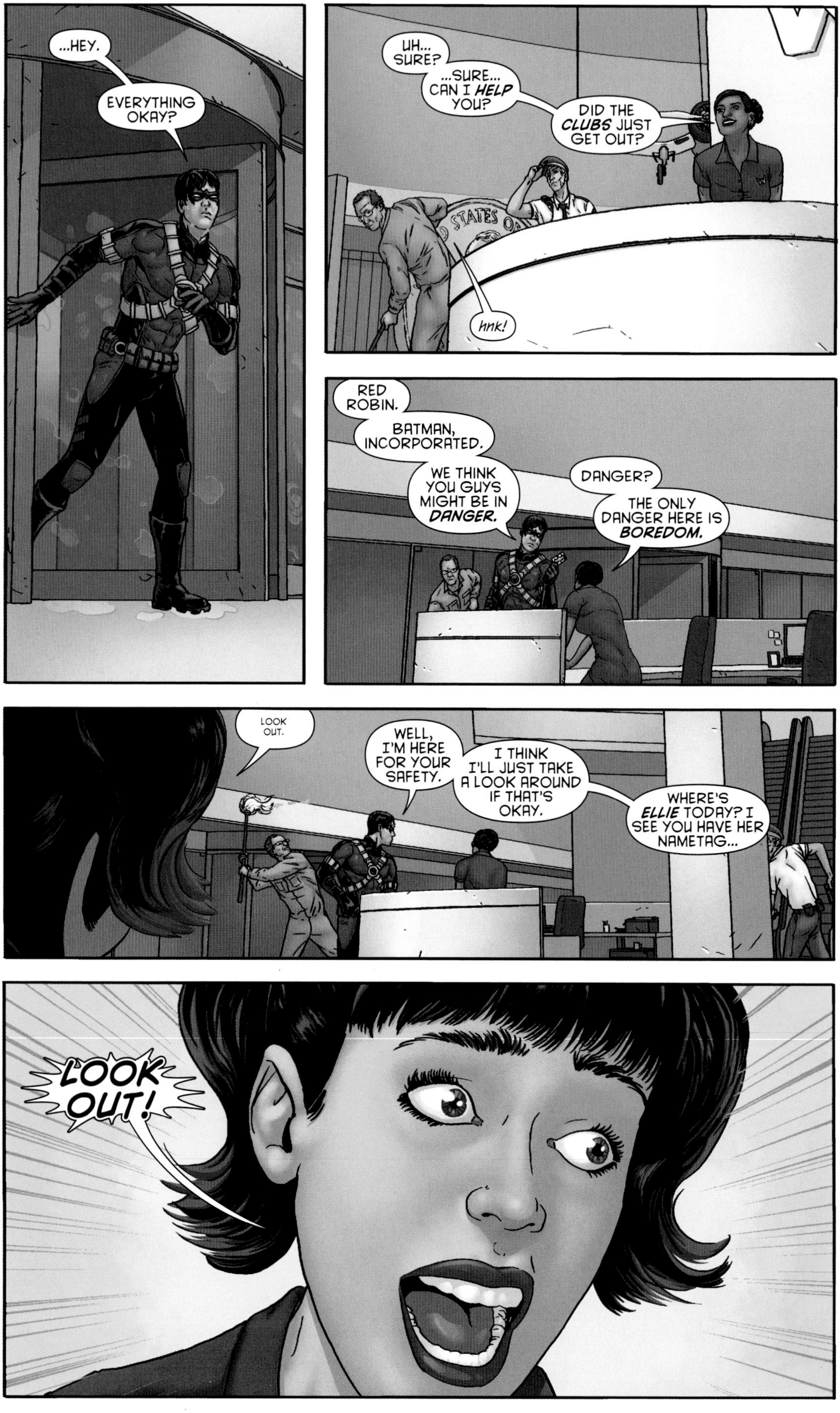
...HEY.
EVERYTHING OKAY?
UH... SURE?
...SURE... CAN I HELP YOU?
DID THE CLUBS JUST GET OUT?
hnk!
RED ROBIN.
BATMAN, INCORPORATED.
WE THINK YOU GUYS MIGHT BE IN DANGER.
DANGER?
THE ONLY DANGER HERE IS BOREDOM.
LOOK OUT.
WELL, I'M HERE FOR YOUR SAFETY.
I THINK I'LL JUST TAKE A LOOK AROUND IF THAT'S OKAY.
WHERE'S ELLIE TODAY? I SEE YOU HAVE HER NAMETAG...
LOOK OUT!

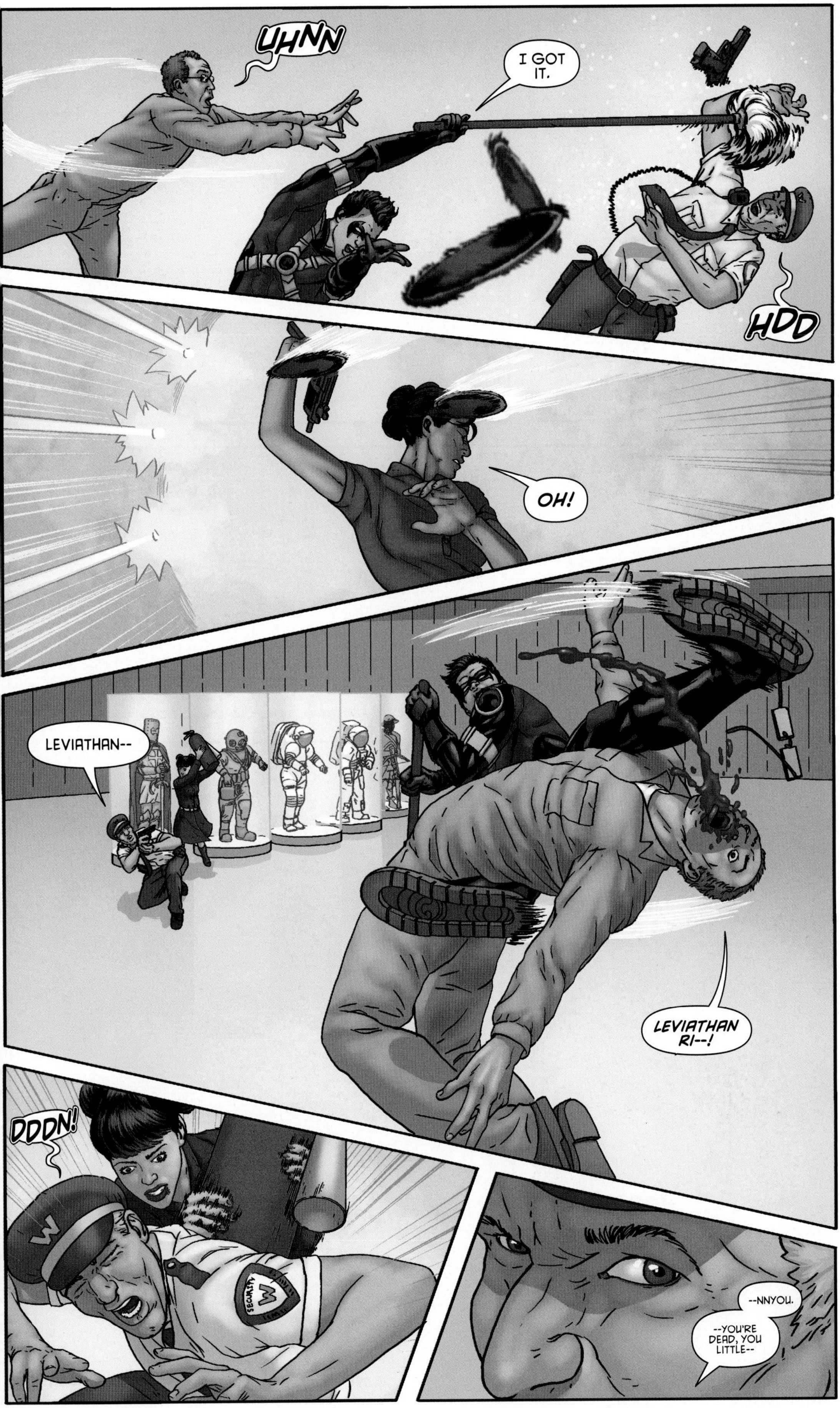
UHNN
I GOT IT.
HDD
OH!
LEVIATHAN--
LEVIATHAN RI--!
DDDN!
--NNYOU.
--YOU'RE DEAD, YOU LITTLE--

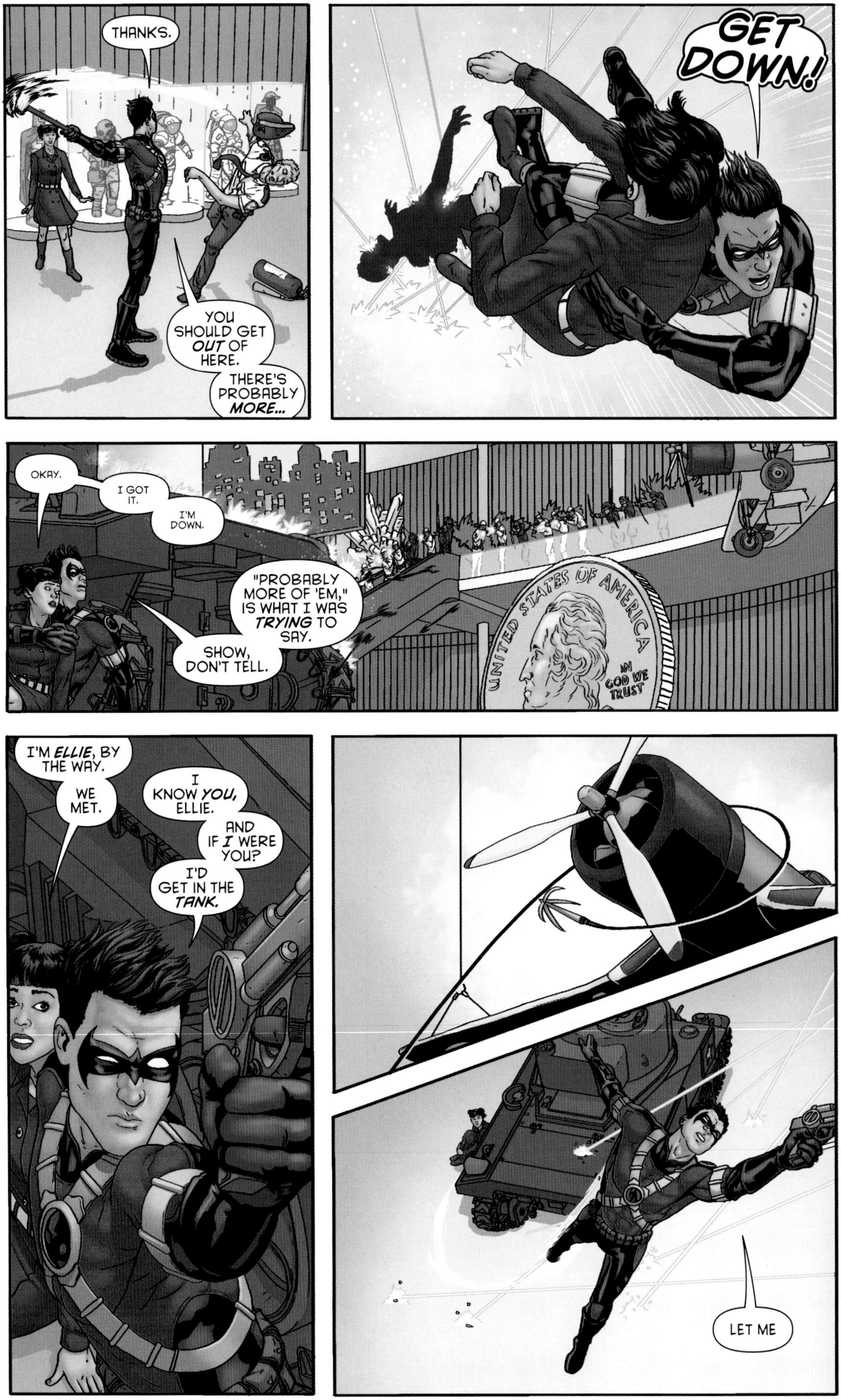

THANKS.
YOU SHOULD GET *OUT* OF HERE.
THERE'S PROBABLY *MORE...*
GET DOWN!
OKAY.
I GOT IT.
I'M DOWN.
"PROBABLY MORE OF 'EM," IS WHAT I WAS *TRYING* TO SAY.
SHOW, DON'T TELL.
UNITED STATES OF AMERICA
IN GOD WE TRUST
I'M *ELLIE*, BY THE WAY.
WE MET.
I KNOW *YOU,* ELLIE.
AND IF *I* WERE YOU?
I'D GET IN THE *TANK.*
LET ME

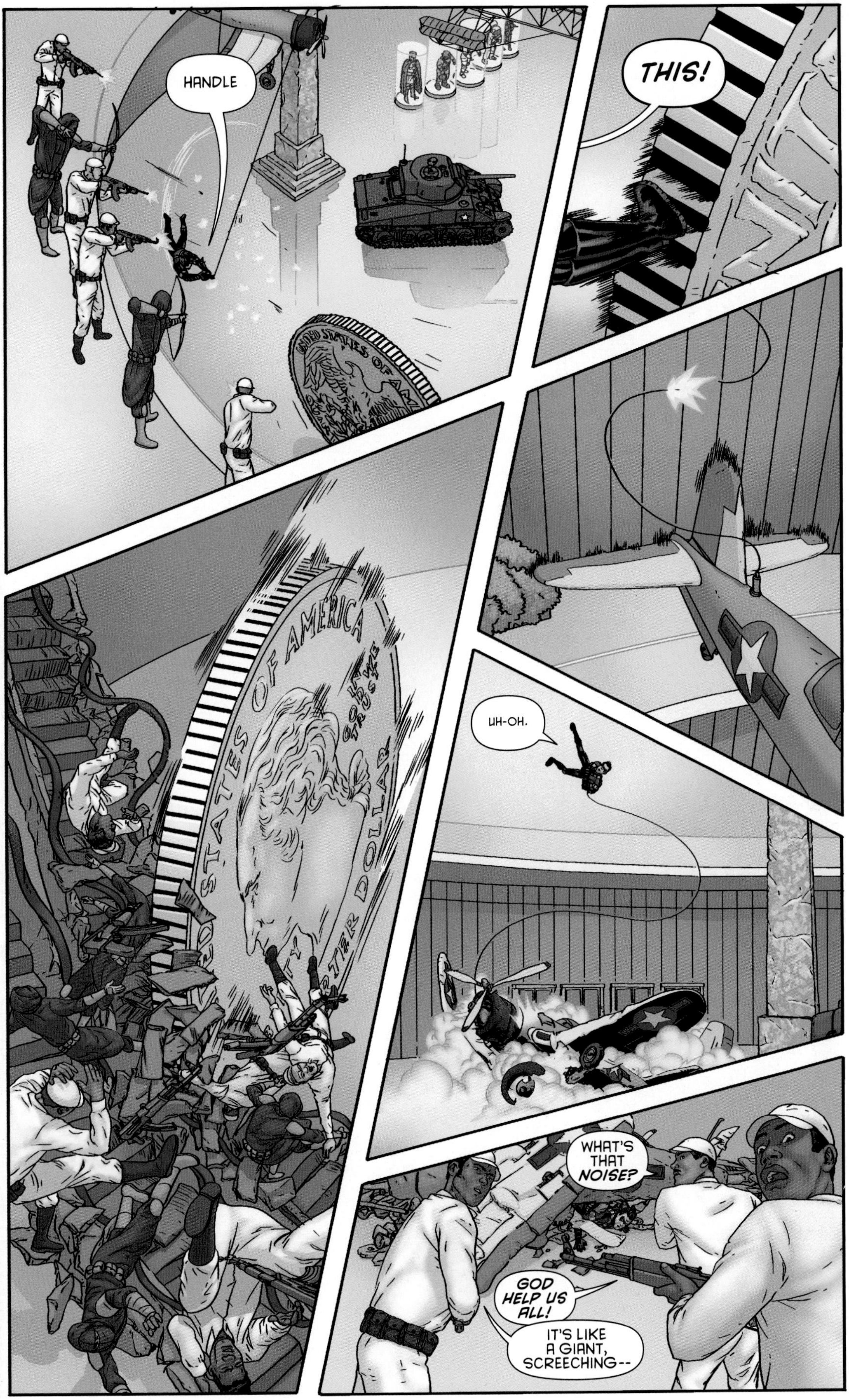
HANDLE
THIS!
UH-OH.
WHAT'S THAT NOISE?
GOD HELP US ALL!
IT'S LIKE A GIANT, SCREECHING--

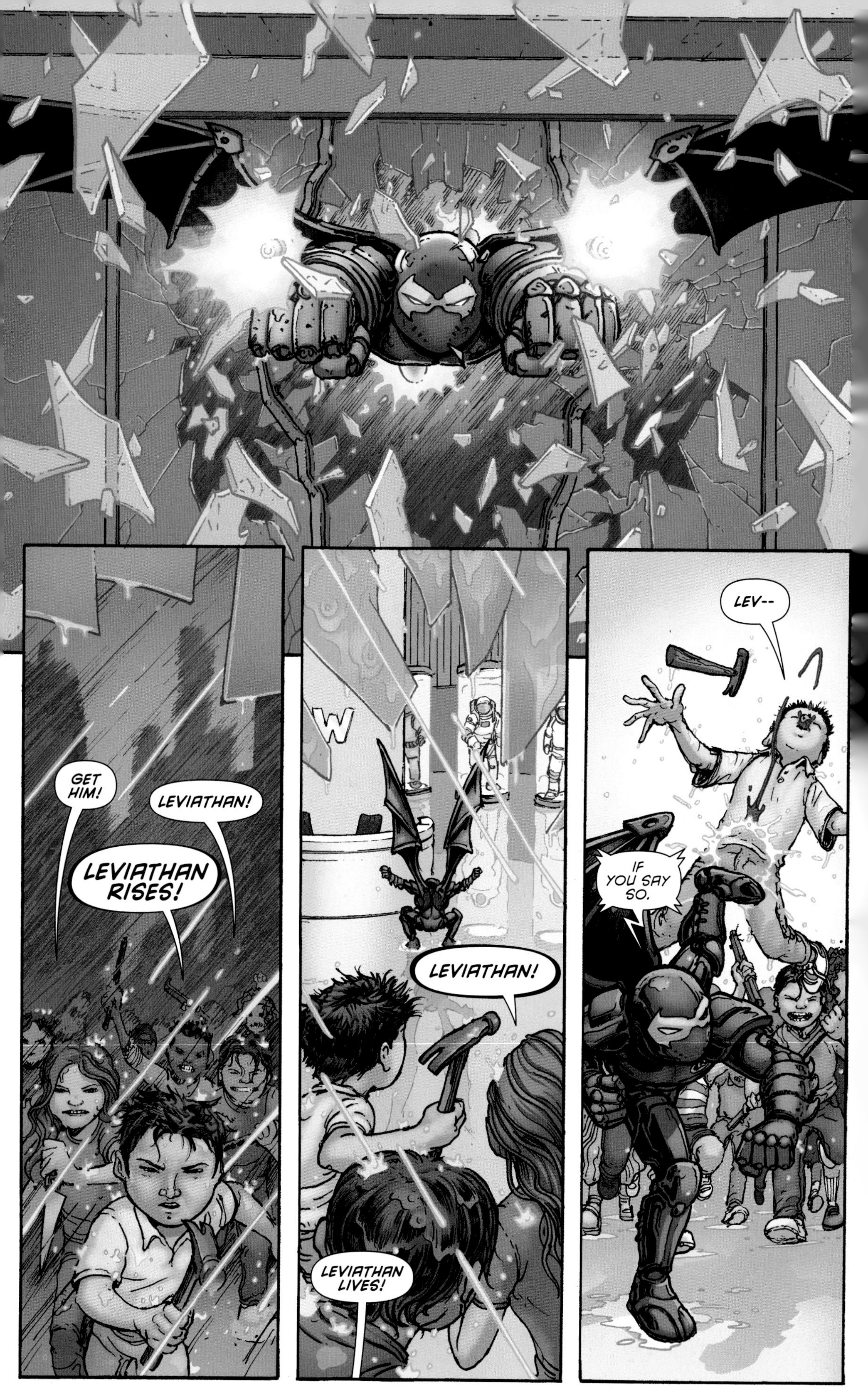
GET HIM!
LEVIATHAN!
LEVIATHAN RISES!
LEVIATHAN!
LEVIATHAN LIVES!
LEV--
IF YOU SAY SO.

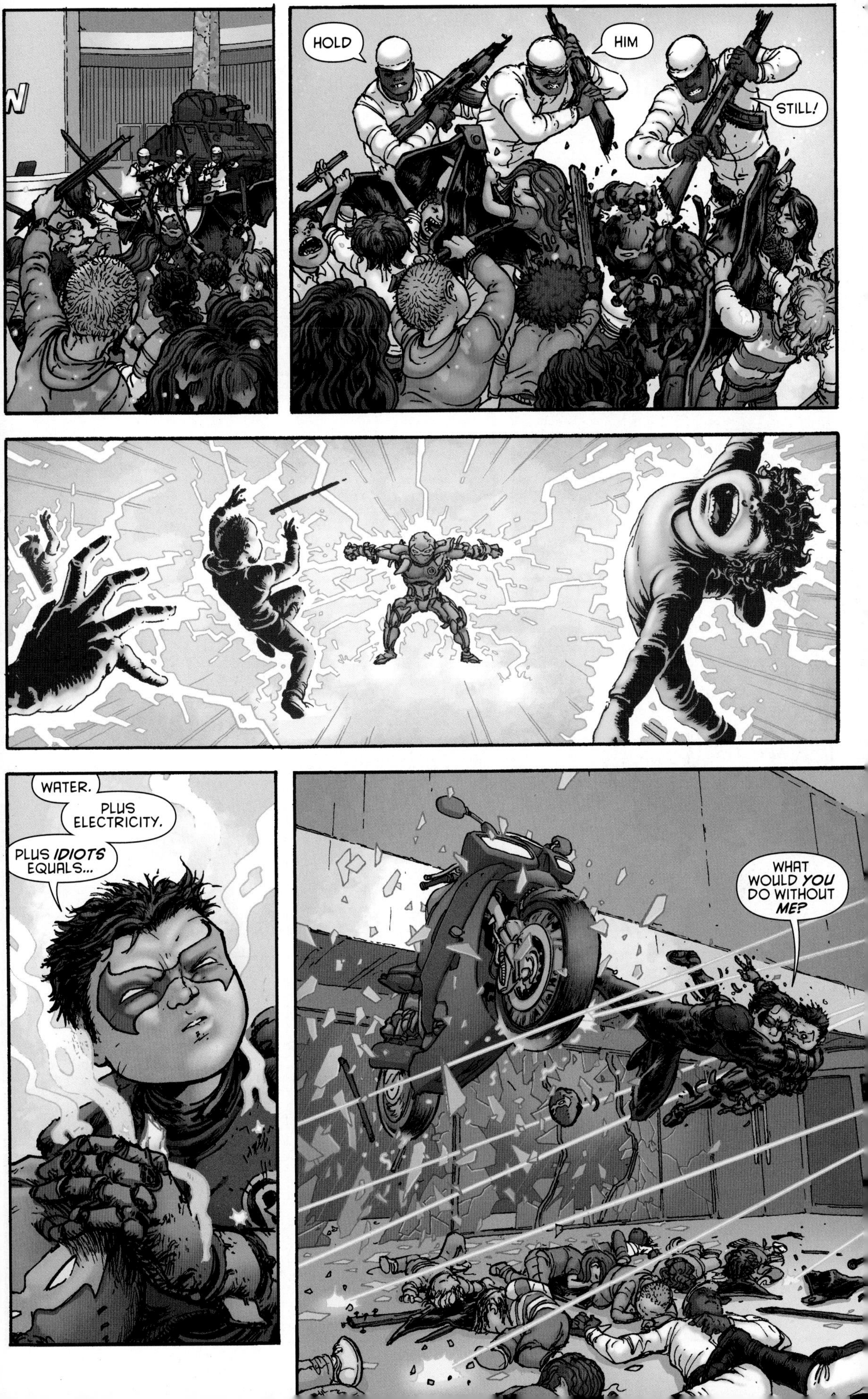
HOLD
HIM
STILL!
WATER.
PLUS ELECTRICITY.
PLUS *IDIOTS* EQUALS...
WHAT WOULD *YOU* DO WITHOUT *ME?*

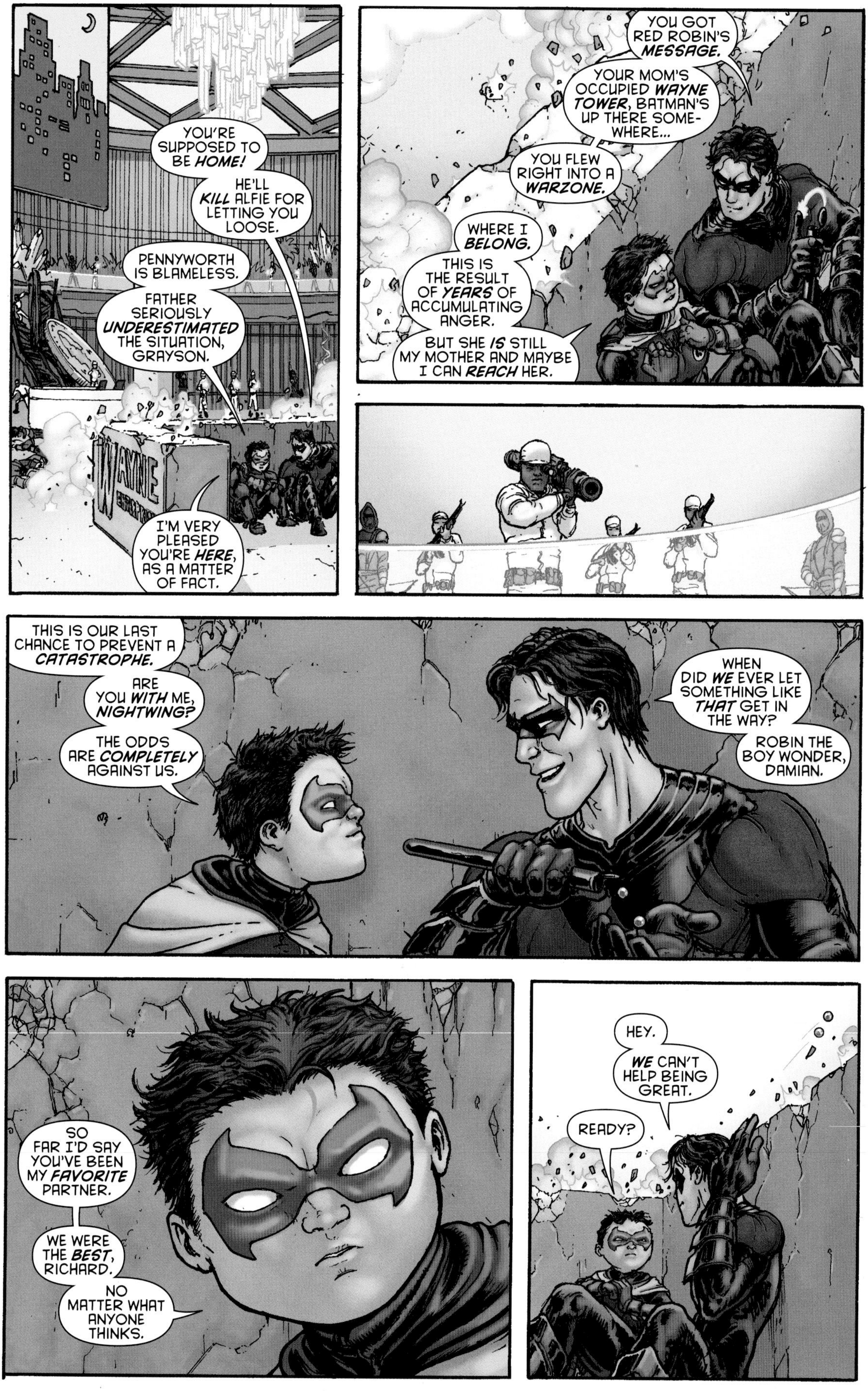

YOU'RE SUPPOSED TO BE HOME!
HE'LL KILL ALFIE FOR LETTING YOU LOOSE.
PENNYWORTH IS BLAMELESS.
FATHER SERIOUSLY UNDERESTIMATED THE SITUATION, GRAYSON.
I'M VERY PLEASED YOU'RE HERE, AS A MATTER OF FACT.
YOU GOT RED ROBIN'S MESSAGE.
YOUR MOM'S OCCUPIED WAYNE TOWER, BATMAN'S UP THERE SOME-WHERE...
YOU FLEW RIGHT INTO A WARZONE.
WHERE I BELONG.
THIS IS THE RESULT OF YEARS OF ACCUMULATING ANGER.
BUT SHE IS STILL MY MOTHER AND MAYBE I CAN REACH HER.
THIS IS OUR LAST CHANCE TO PREVENT A CATASTROPHE.
ARE YOU WITH ME, NIGHTWING?
THE ODDS ARE COMPLETELY AGAINST US.
WHEN DID WE EVER LET SOMETHING LIKE THAT GET IN THE WAY?
ROBIN THE BOY WONDER, DAMIAN.
SO FAR I'D SAY YOU'VE BEEN MY FAVORITE PARTNER.
WE WERE THE BEST, RICHARD.
NO MATTER WHAT ANYONE THINKS.
HEY.
WE CAN'T HELP BEING GREAT.
READY?

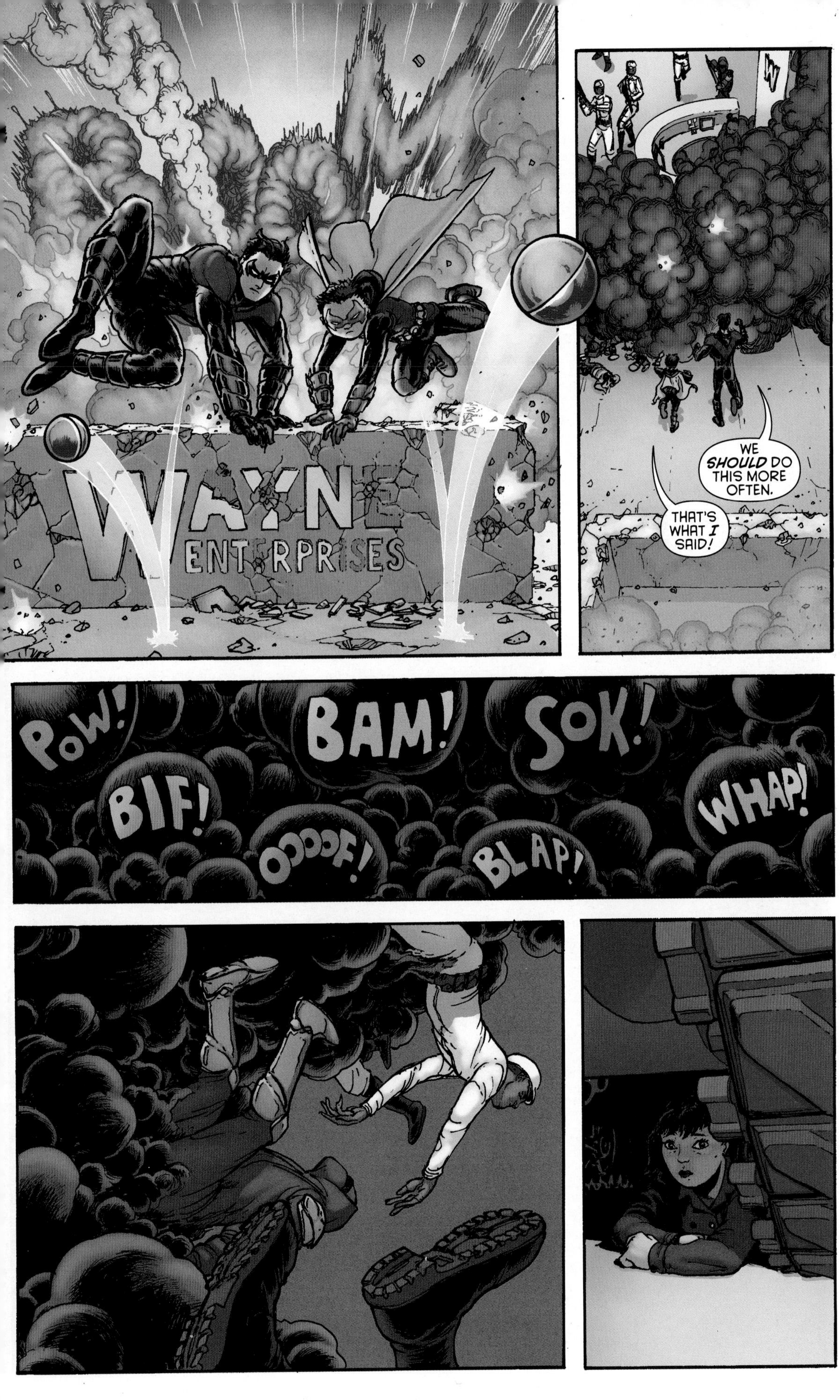
WAYNE ENTERPRISES
WE SHOULD DO THIS MORE OFTEN.
THAT'S WHAT I SAID!
POW!
BAM!
SOK!
BIF!
WHAP!
OOOOF!
BLAP!

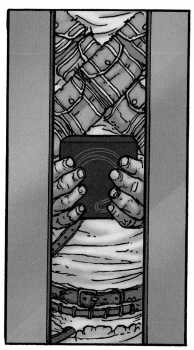

AND DON'T GET COCKY!

SAYS YOU.

?

THAT WORKED OUT.

ROBIN.

GET OUT OF HERE, NOW!

GTTT

LEAVE HIM ALONE!

LOOK AT ME!

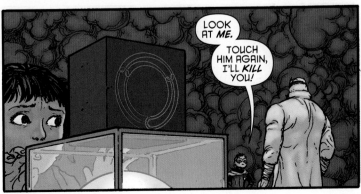

LOOK AT ME.

TOUCH HIM AGAIN, I'LL KILL YOU!

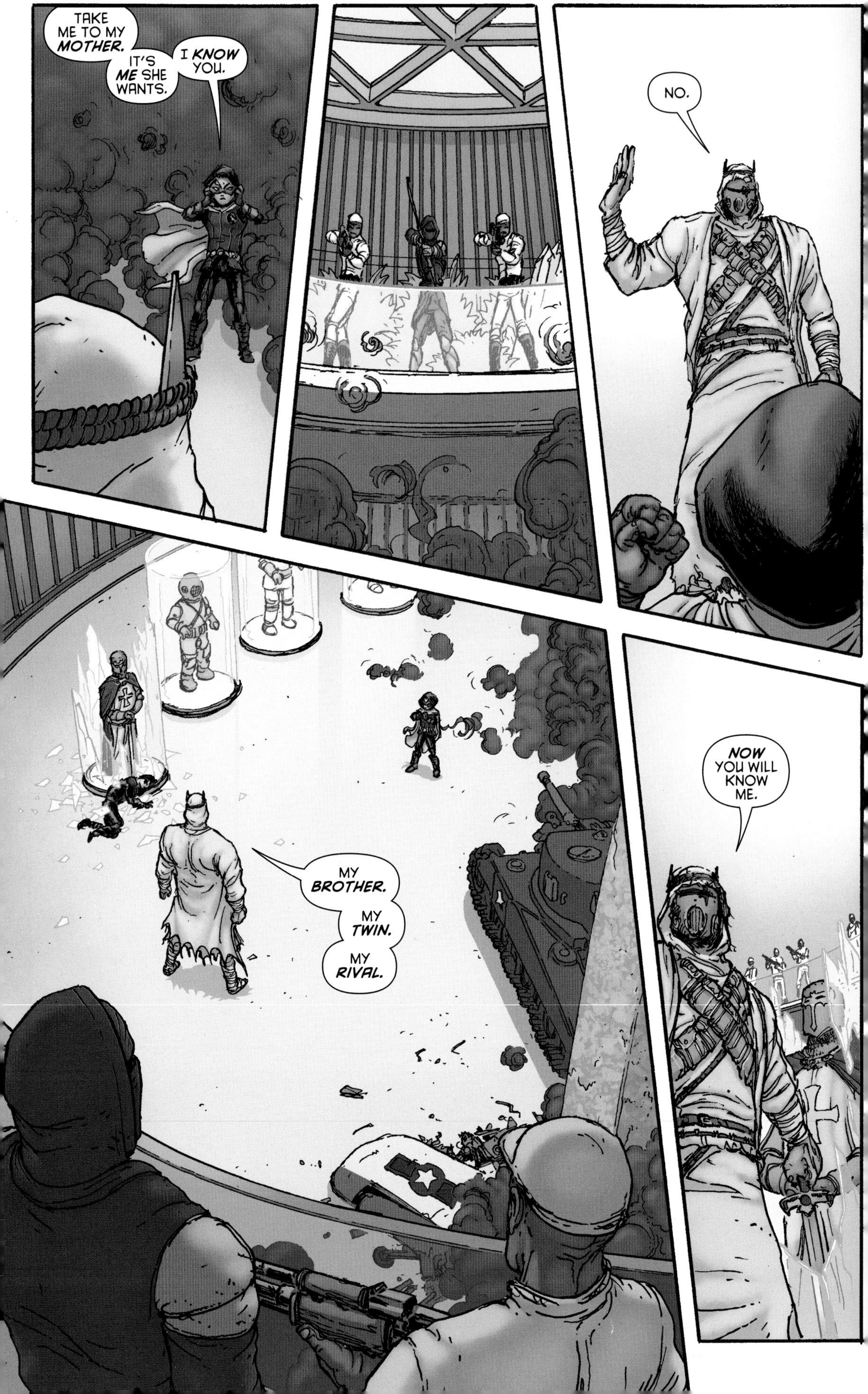
TAKE ME TO MY *MOTHER.*
IT'S *ME* SHE WANTS.
I *KNOW* YOU.
NO.
MY *BROTHER.*
MY *TWIN.*
MY *RIVAL.*
NOW YOU WILL KNOW ME.

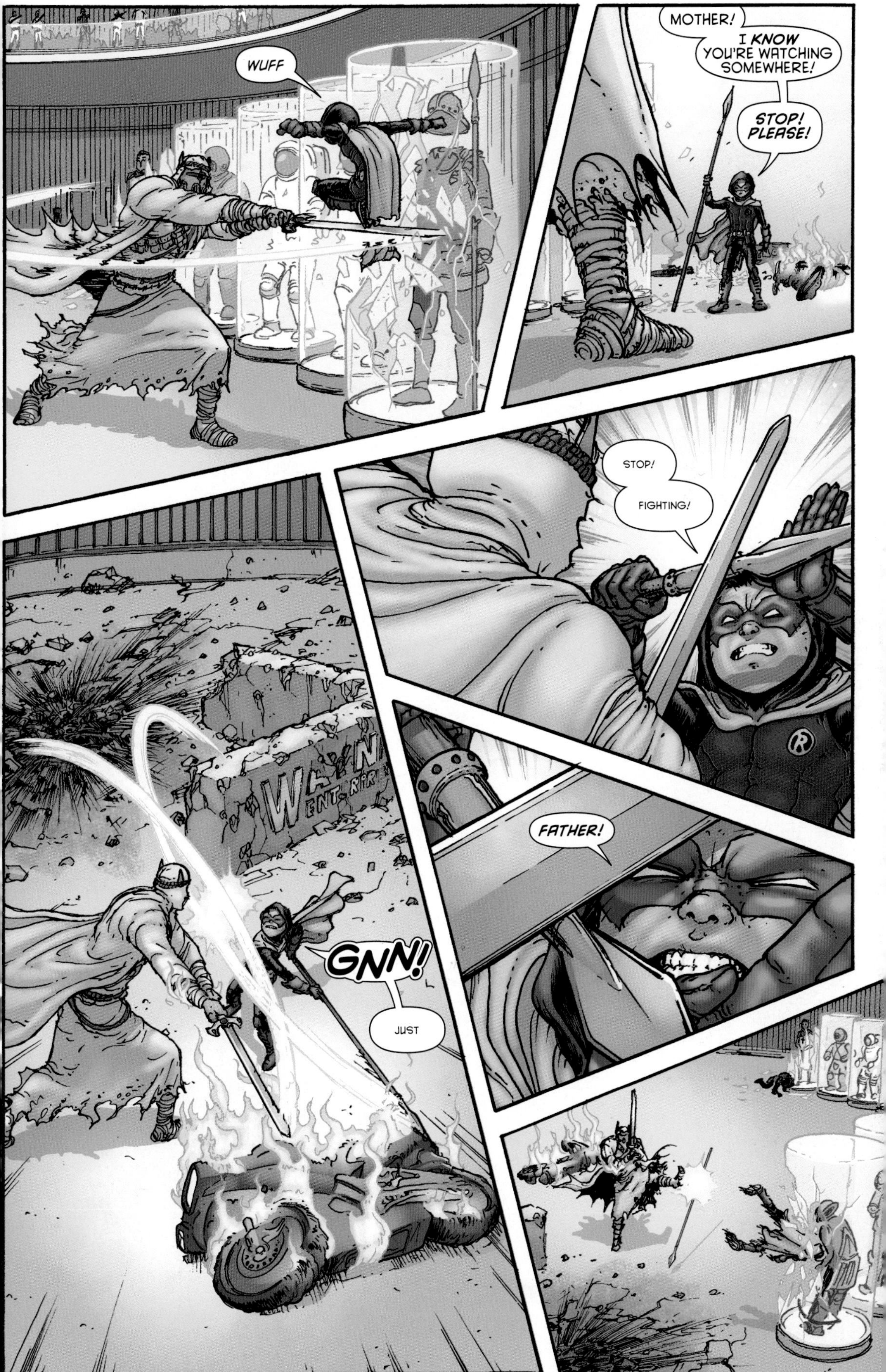
WUFF
MOTHER!
I KNOW YOU'RE WATCHING SOMEWHERE!
STOP! PLEASE!
GNN!
JUST
STOP!
FIGHTING!
FATHER!

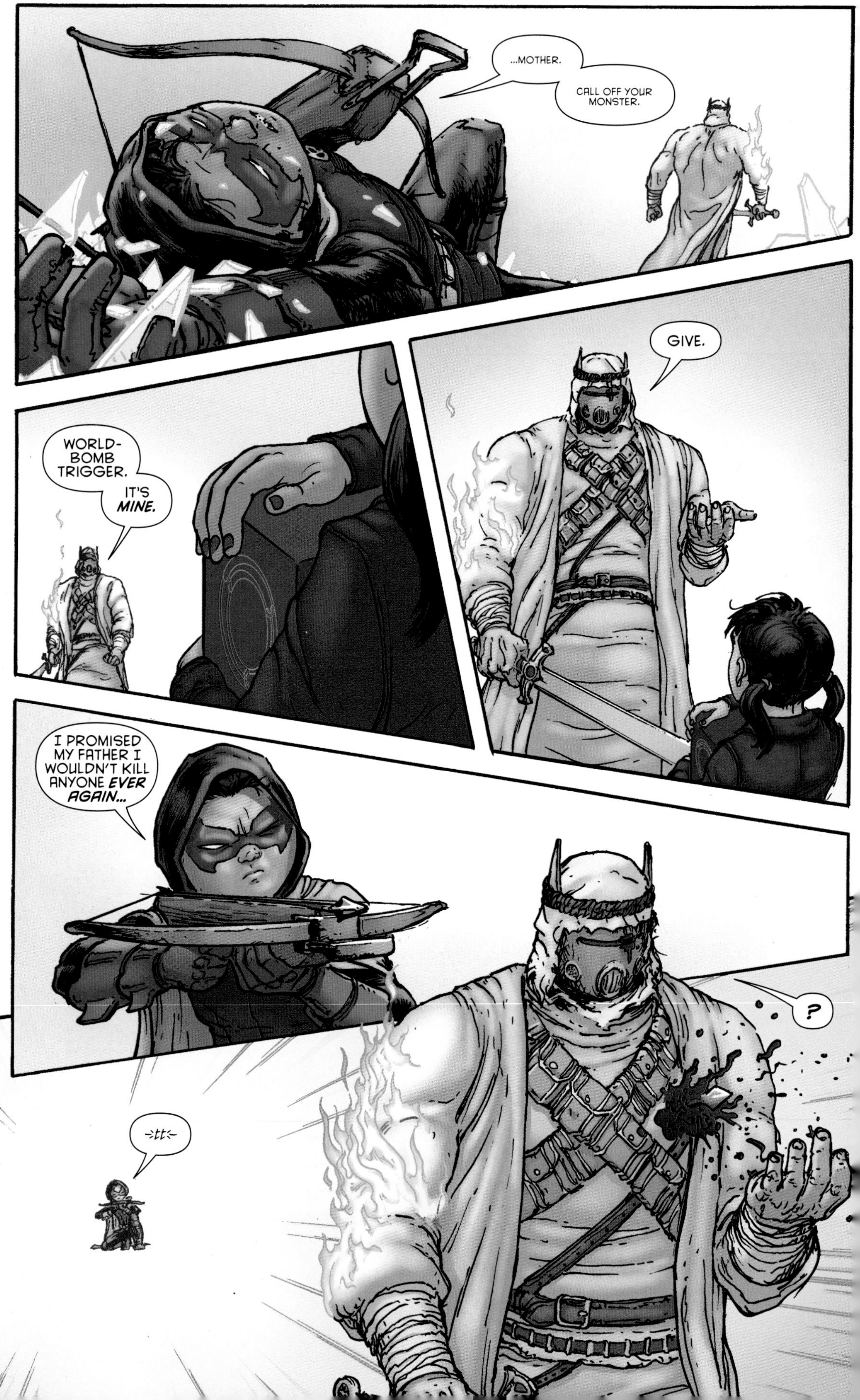

...MOTHER.
CALL OFF YOUR MONSTER.
GIVE.
WORLD-BOMB TRIGGER.
IT'S *MINE.*
I PROMISED MY FATHER I WOULDN'T KILL ANYONE *EVER AGAIN...*
?
-tt-

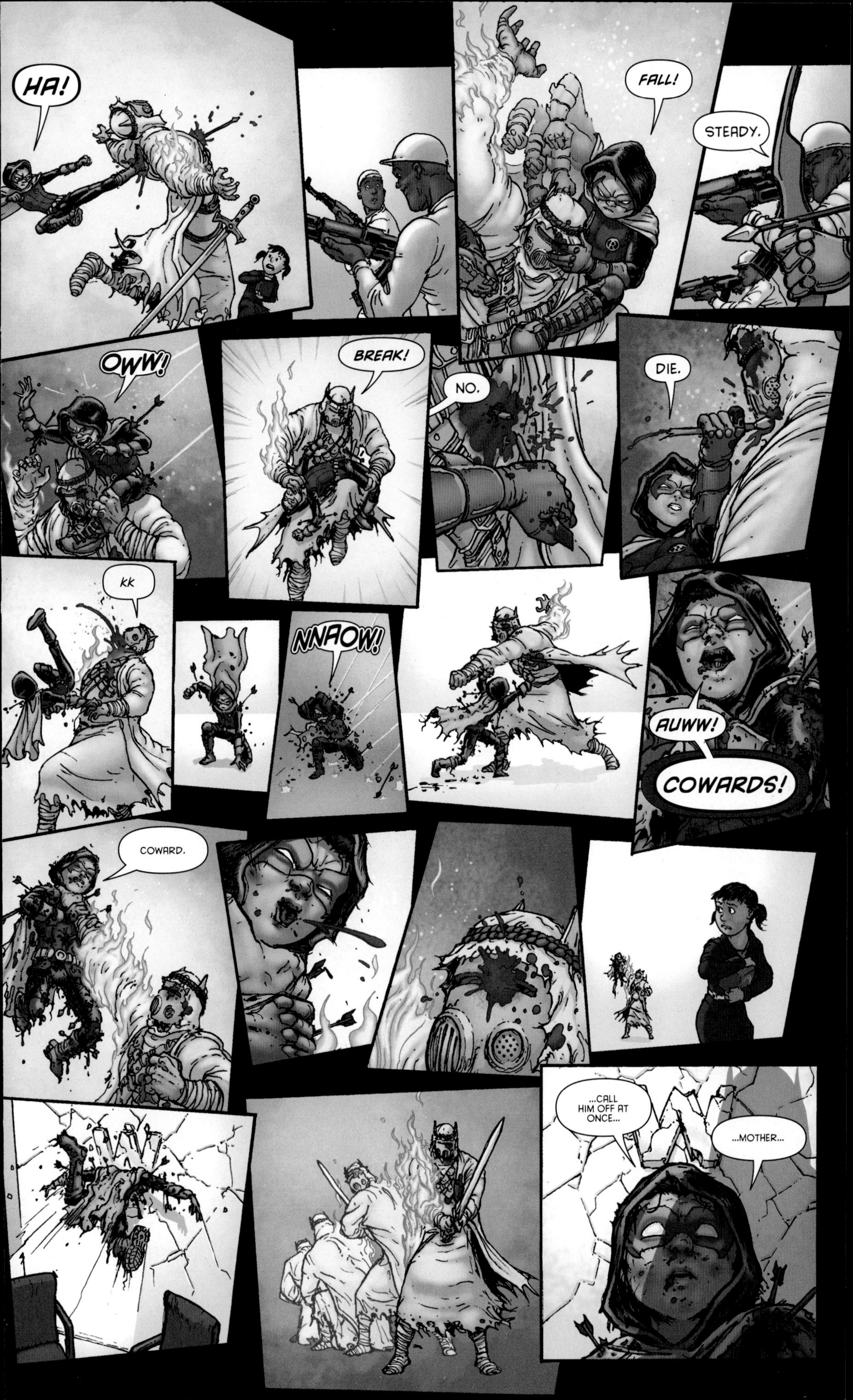
HA!
FALL!
STEADY.
OWW!
BREAK!
NO.
DIE.
KK
NNAOW!
AUWW!
COWARDS!
COWARD.
...CALL HIM OFF AT ONCE...
...MOTHER...

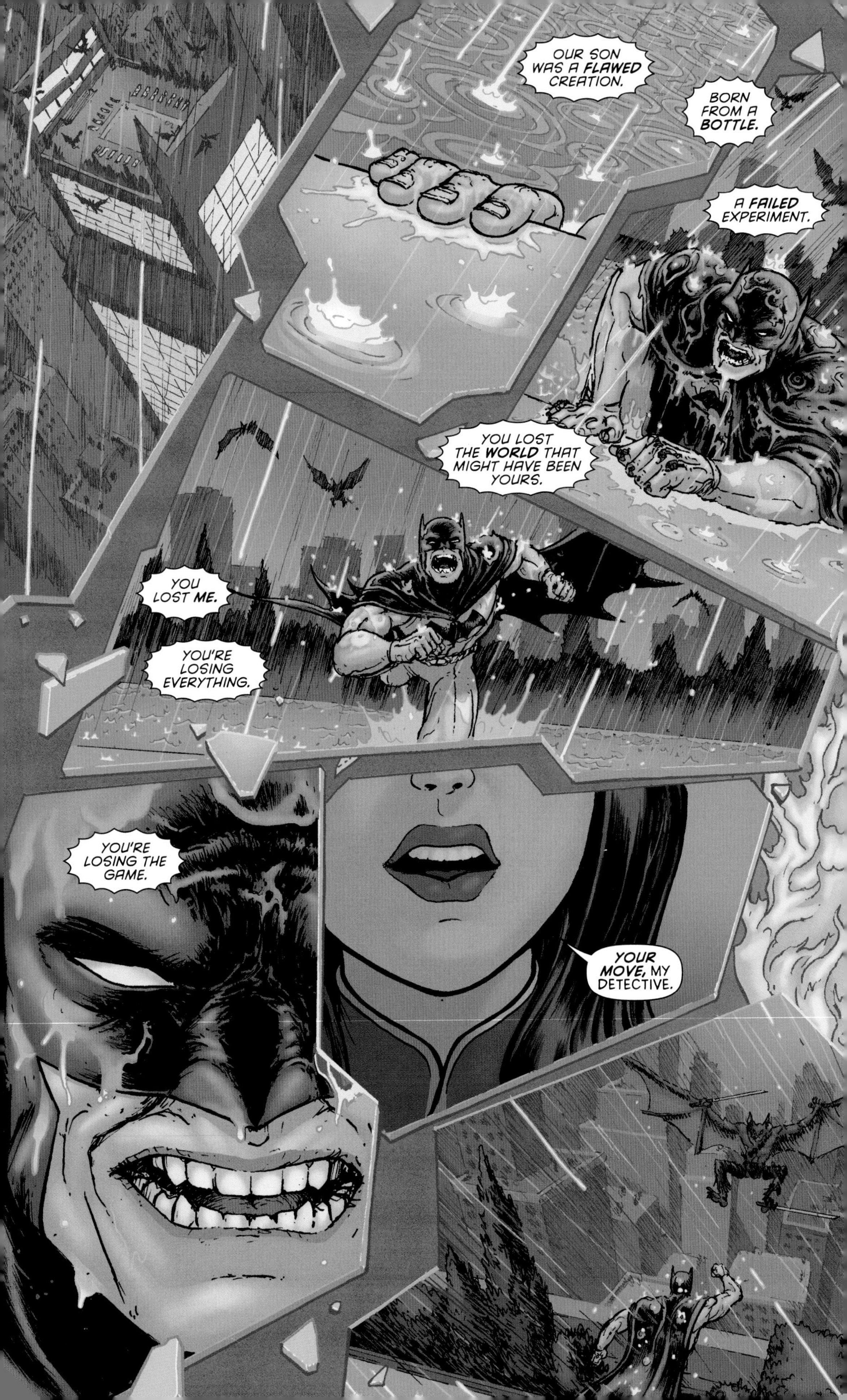
OUR SON WAS A FLAWED CREATION.
BORN FROM A BOTTLE.
A FAILED EXPERIMENT.
YOU LOST THE WORLD THAT MIGHT HAVE BEEN YOURS.
YOU LOST ME.
YOU'RE LOSING EVERYTHING.
YOU'RE LOSING THE GAME.
YOUR MOVE, MY DETECTIVE.

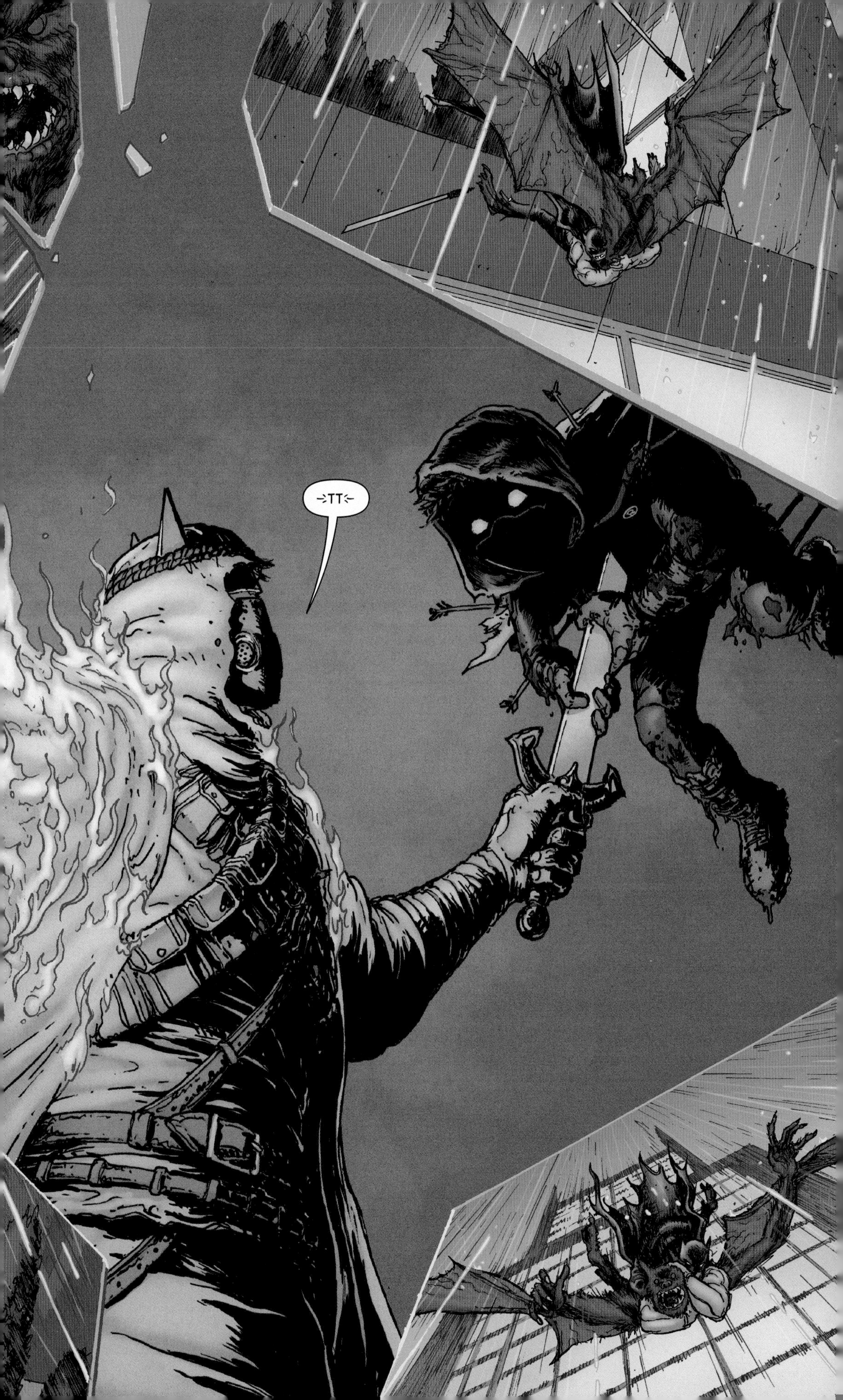

-TT-

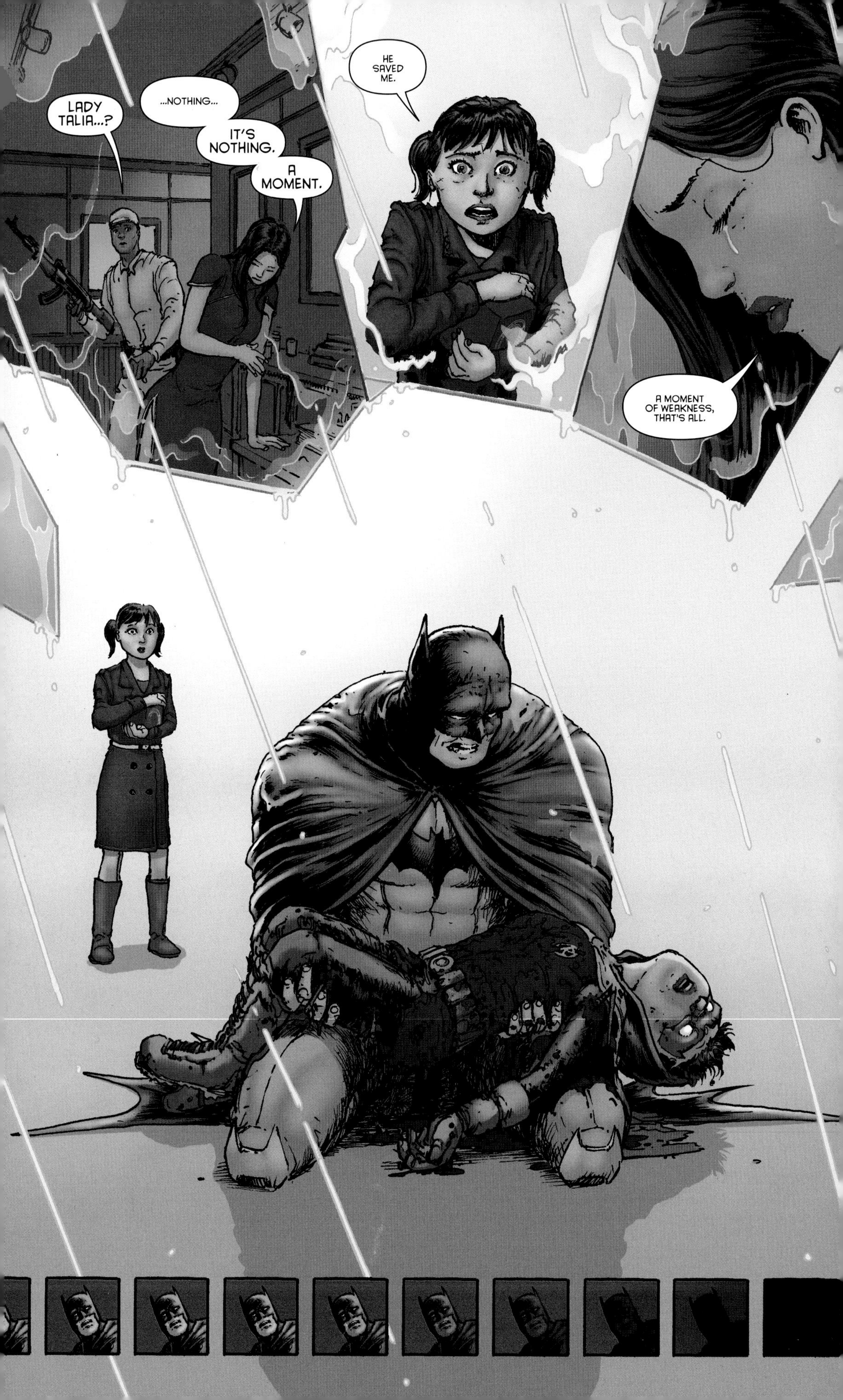
LADY TALIA...?
...NOTHING...
IT'S NOTHING.
A MOMENT.
HE SAVED ME.
A MOMENT OF WEAKNESS, THAT'S ALL.

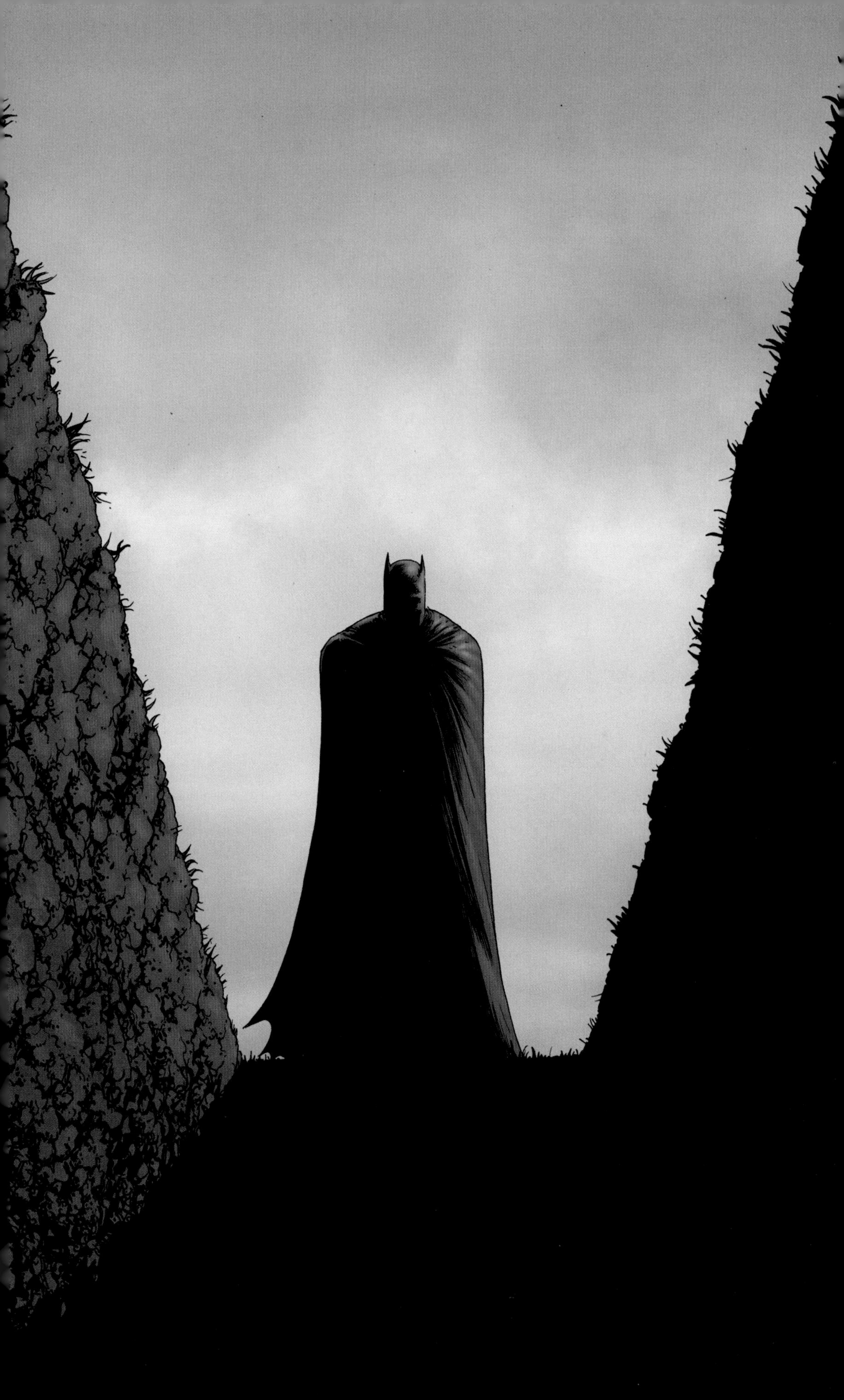

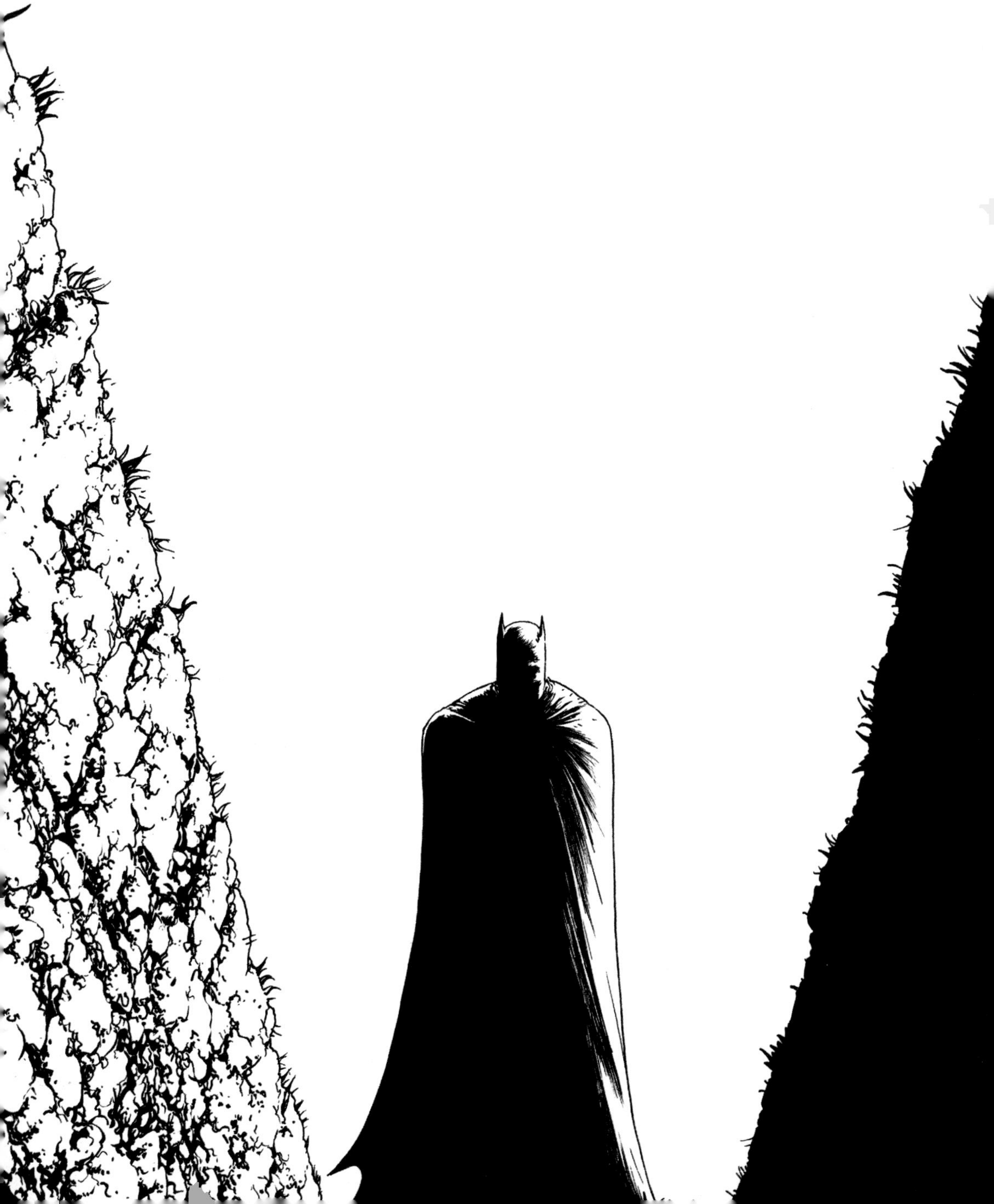

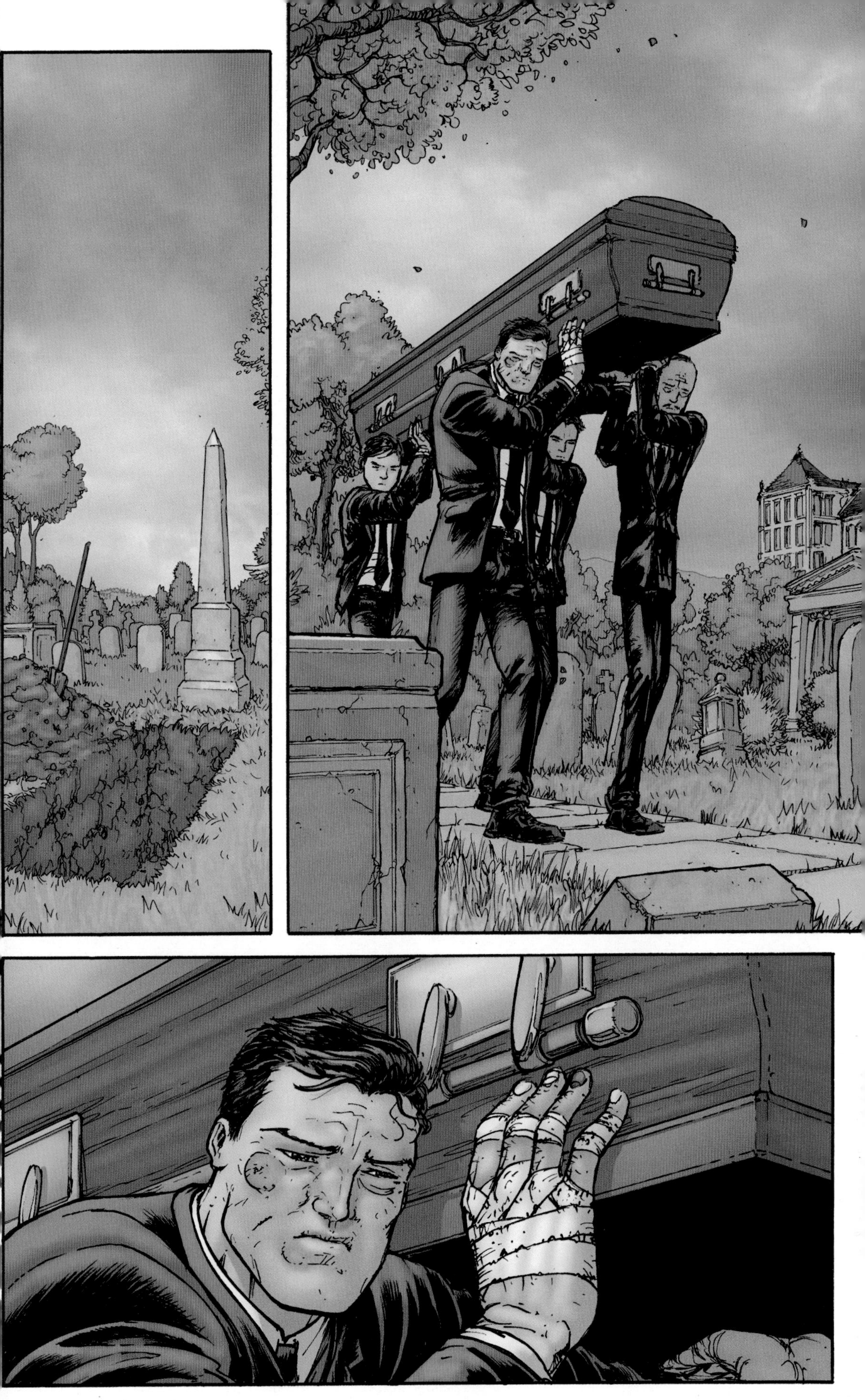

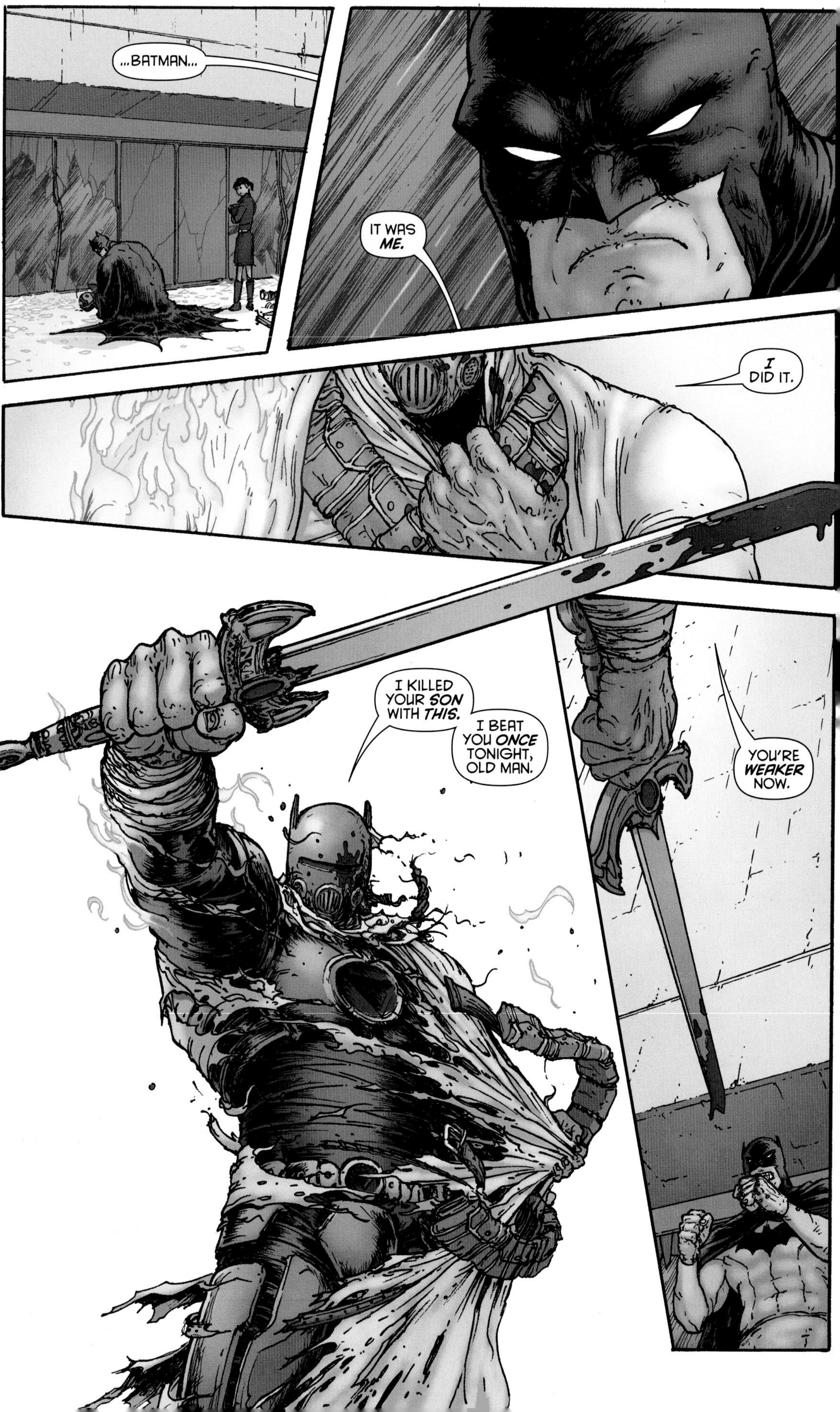
...BATMAN...
IT WAS ME.
I DID IT.
I KILLED YOUR SON WITH THIS.
I BEAT YOU ONCE TONIGHT, OLD MAN.
YOU'RE WEAKER NOW.

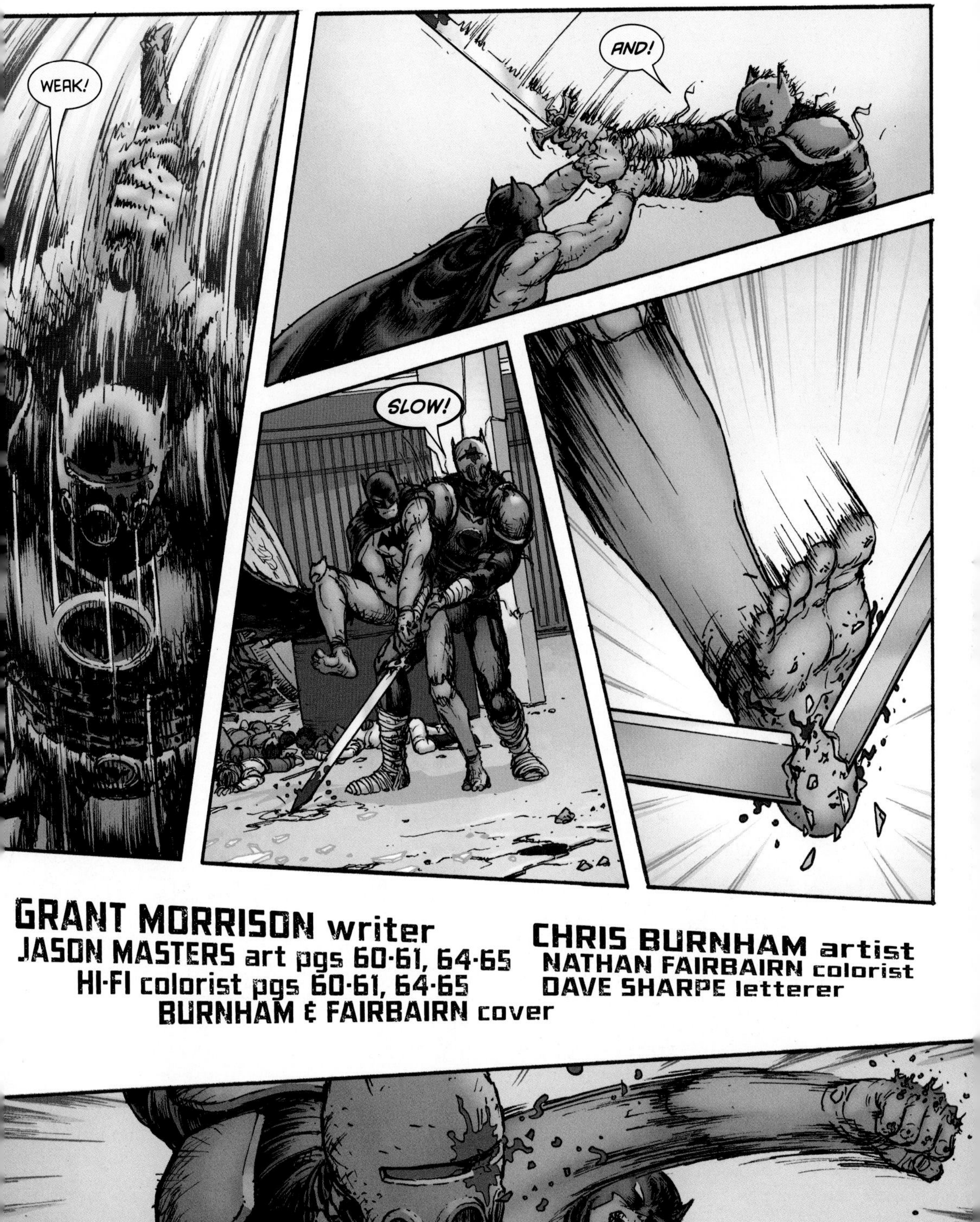
WEAK!
AND!
SLOW!

GRANT MORRISON writer
JASON MASTERS art pgs 60-61, 64-65
HI-FI colorist pgs 60-61, 64-65
BURNHAM & FAIRBAIRN cover
CHRIS BURNHAM artist
NATHAN FAIRBAIRN colorist
DAVE SHARPE letterer

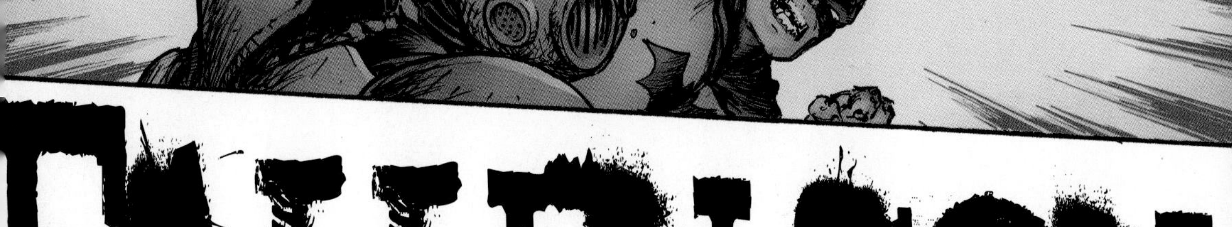

FALLEN SON

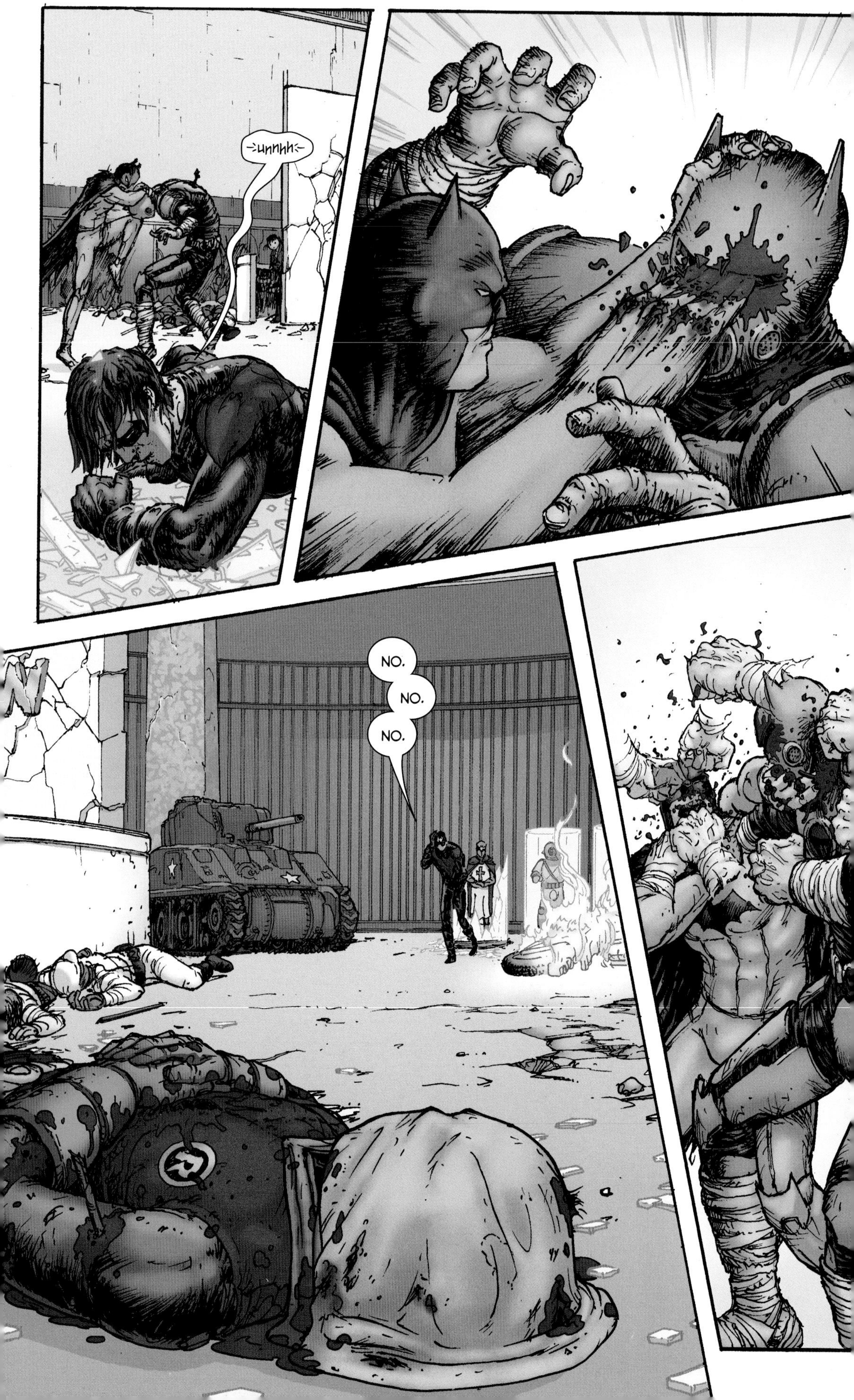
unnhh
NO.
NO.
NO.

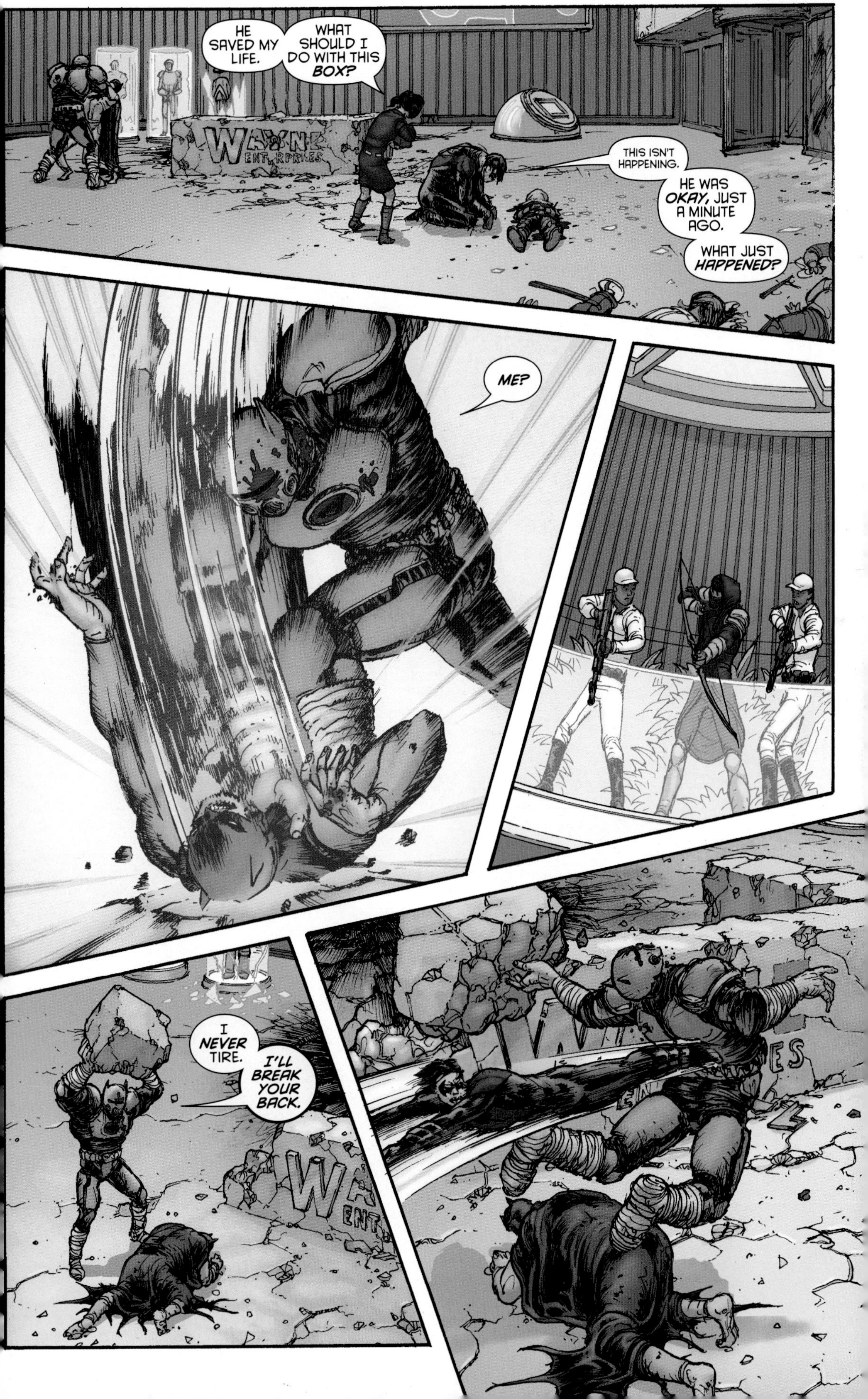
HE SAVED MY LIFE.
WHAT SHOULD I DO WITH THIS BOX?
WAYNE ENTERPRISES
THIS ISN'T HAPPENING.
HE WAS OKAY, JUST A MINUTE AGO.
WHAT JUST HAPPENED?
ME?
I NEVER TIRE.
I'LL BREAK YOUR BACK.

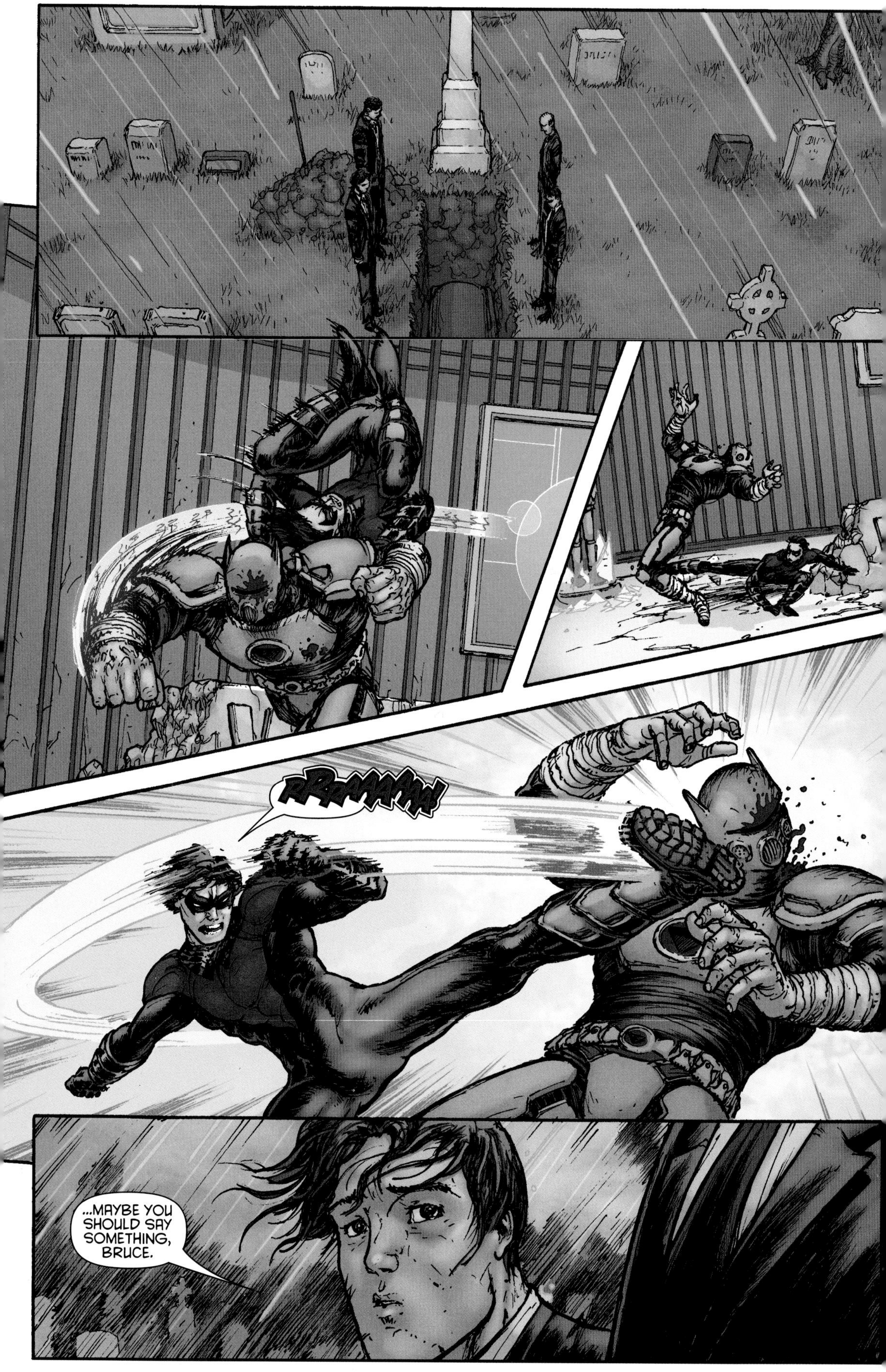
RRAAAAAA!
...MAYBE YOU SHOULD SAY SOMETHING, BRUCE.

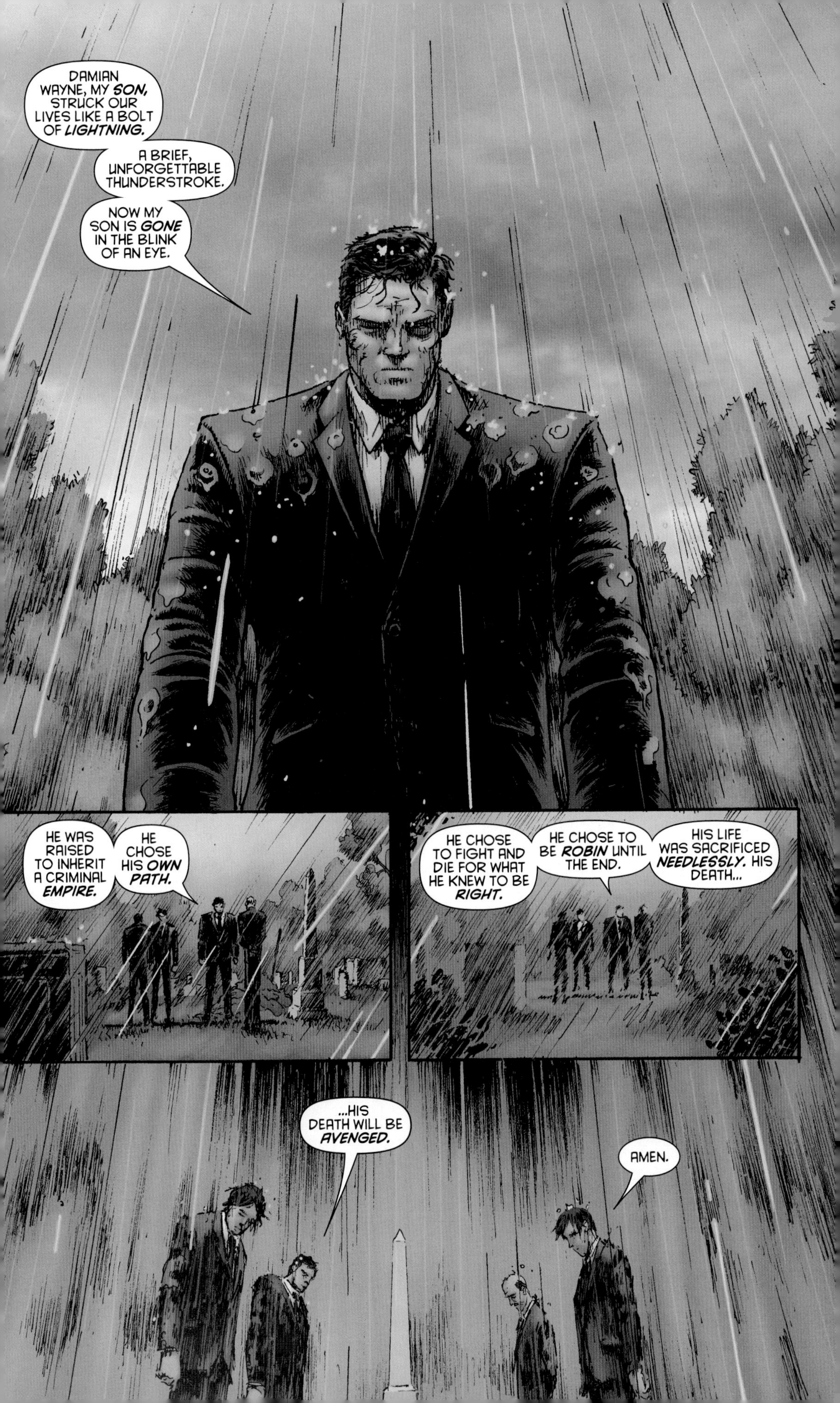
DAMIAN WAYNE, MY SON, STRUCK OUR LIVES LIKE A BOLT OF LIGHTNING.
A BRIEF, UNFORGETTABLE THUNDERSTROKE.
NOW MY SON IS GONE IN THE BLINK OF AN EYE.
HE WAS RAISED TO INHERIT A CRIMINAL EMPIRE.
HE CHOSE HIS OWN PATH.
HE CHOSE TO FIGHT AND DIE FOR WHAT HE KNEW TO BE RIGHT.
HE CHOSE TO BE ROBIN UNTIL THE END.
HIS LIFE WAS SACRIFICED NEEDLESSLY. HIS DEATH...
...HIS DEATH WILL BE AVENGED.
AMEN.

...THE KNIGHT'S COFFIN WAS *ACCOMPANIED* DOWN THE *MALL* BY OFFICERS OF THE *ROYAL HORSE GUARDS.*

PEOPLE FROM ALL CLASSES AND WALKS OF LIFE GATHERED TO SAY *FAREWELL* TO ONE OF THE NATION'S MOST *BELOVED* FIGURES.

EVEN THE *COMMONWEALTH* WAS REPRESENTED--

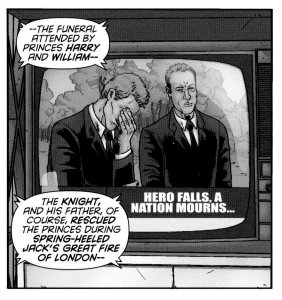

--THE FUNERAL ATTENDED BY PRINCES *HARRY* AND *WILLIAM*--

HERO FALLS, A NATION MOURNS...

THE *KNIGHT,* AND HIS FATHER, OF COURSE, *RESCUED* THE PRINCES DURING *SPRING-HEELED JACK'S GREAT FIRE* OF LONDON--

HAVE A CUPPA, BERYL.

GO ON, LOVE.

BLAMING YOURSELF WON'T BRING CYRIL BACK.

HERO FALLS, A NATION MOURNS...

--HIS PARTNER, THE *SQUIRE,* WAS NOWHERE TO BE SEEN--

NO.

I'VE BEEN *THINKING.*

I'VE HAD AN *IDEA,* MUM.

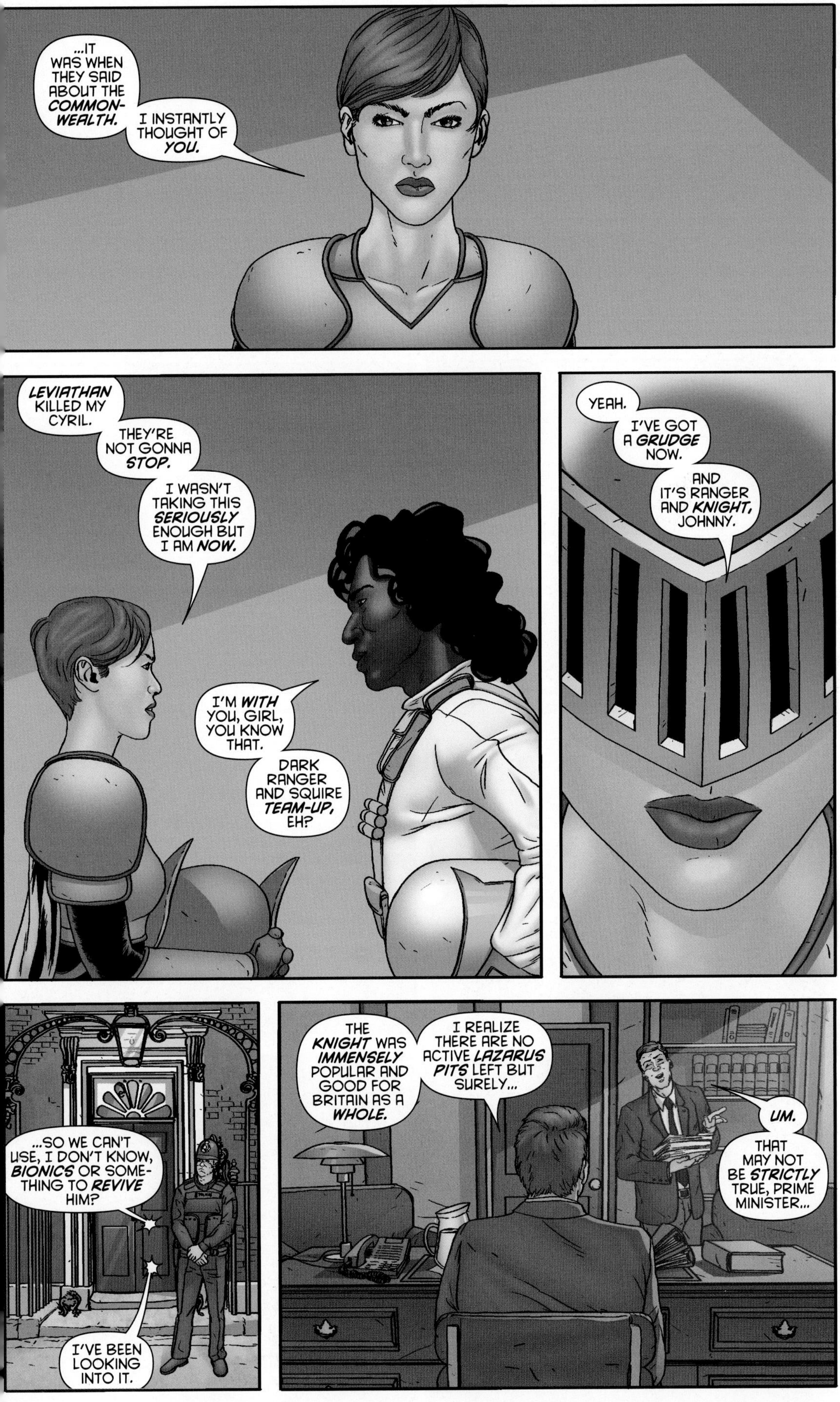

...IT WAS WHEN THEY SAID ABOUT THE COMMON-WEALTH.
I INSTANTLY THOUGHT OF YOU.
LEVIATHAN KILLED MY CYRIL.
THEY'RE NOT GONNA STOP.
I WASN'T TAKING THIS SERIOUSLY ENOUGH BUT I AM NOW.
I'M WITH YOU, GIRL, YOU KNOW THAT.
DARK RANGER AND SQUIRE TEAM-UP, EH?
YEAH.
I'VE GOT A GRUDGE NOW.
AND IT'S RANGER AND KNIGHT, JOHNNY.
...SO WE CAN'T USE, I DON'T KNOW, BIONICS OR SOME-THING TO REVIVE HIM?
I'VE BEEN LOOKING INTO IT.
THE KNIGHT WAS IMMENSELY POPULAR AND GOOD FOR BRITAIN AS A WHOLE.
I REALIZE THERE ARE NO ACTIVE LAZARUS PITS LEFT BUT SURELY...
UM.
THAT MAY NOT BE STRICTLY TRUE, PRIME MINISTER...

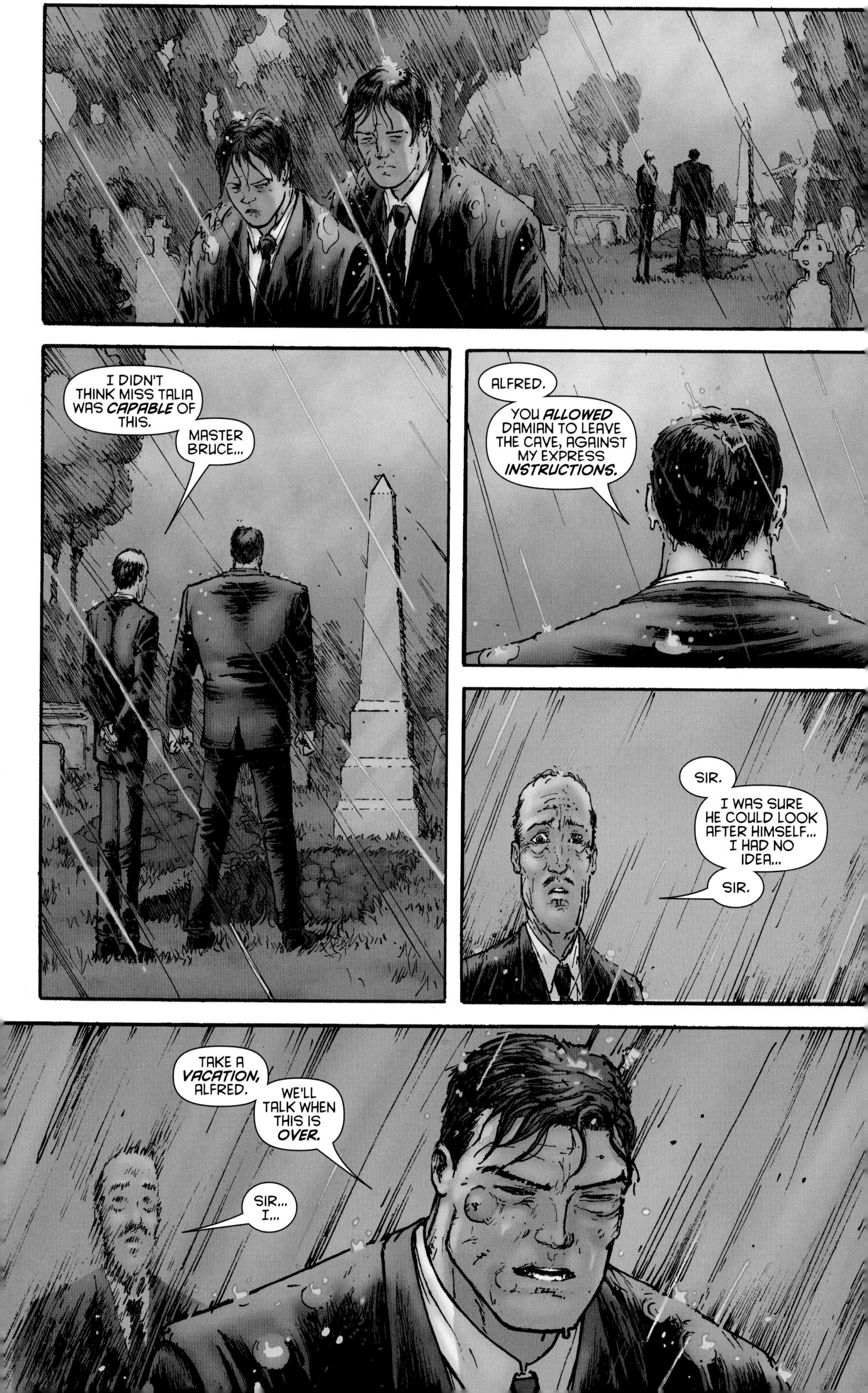
I DIDN'T THINK MISS TALIA WAS CAPABLE OF THIS.
MASTER BRUCE...
ALFRED.
YOU ALLOWED DAMIAN TO LEAVE THE CAVE, AGAINST MY EXPRESS INSTRUCTIONS.
SIR.
I WAS SURE HE COULD LOOK AFTER HIMSELF... I HAD NO IDEA...
SIR.
TAKE A VACATION, ALFRED.
WE'LL TALK WHEN THIS IS OVER.
SIR... I...

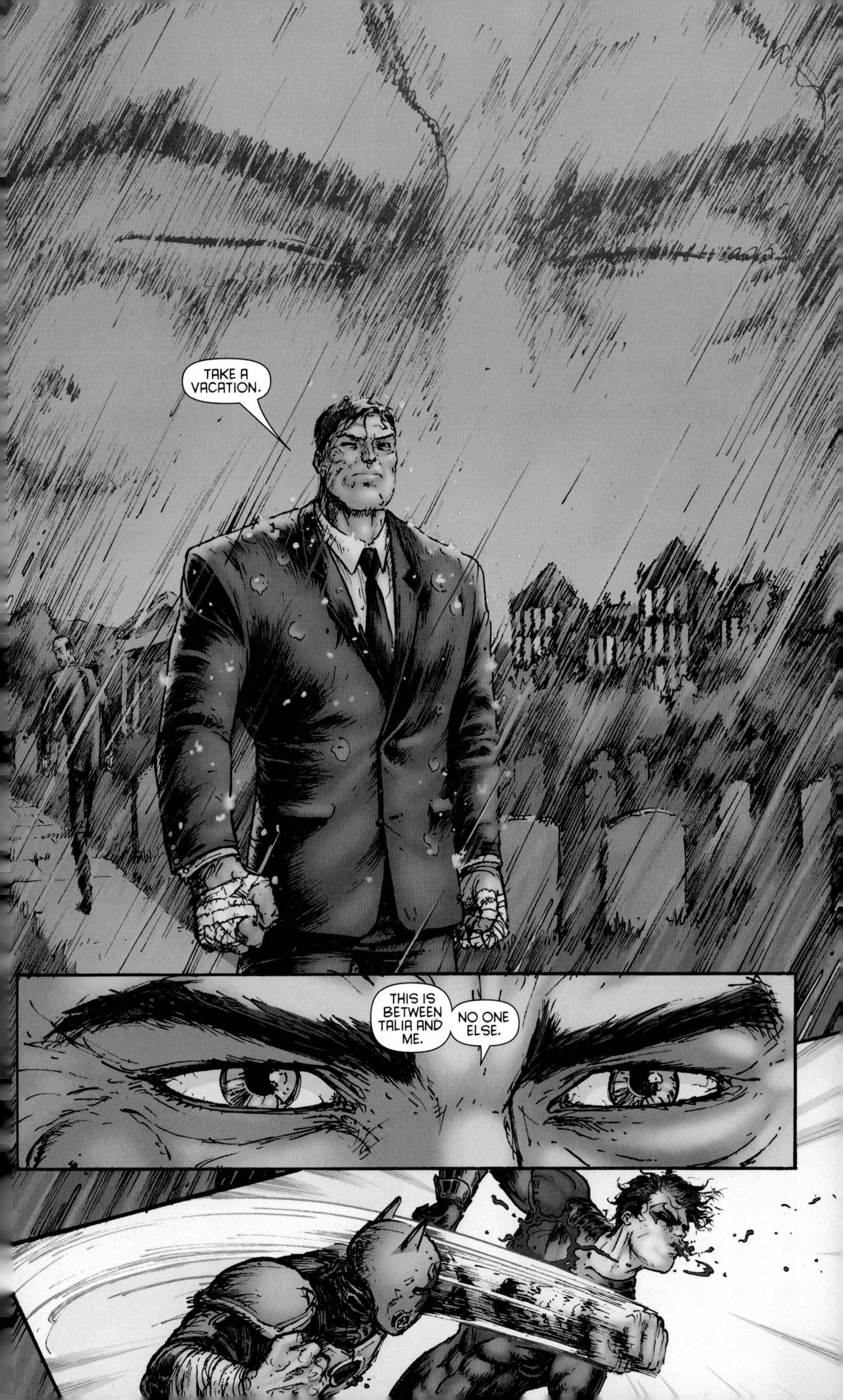
TAKE A VACATION.
THIS IS BETWEEN TALIA AND ME.
NO ONE ELSE.

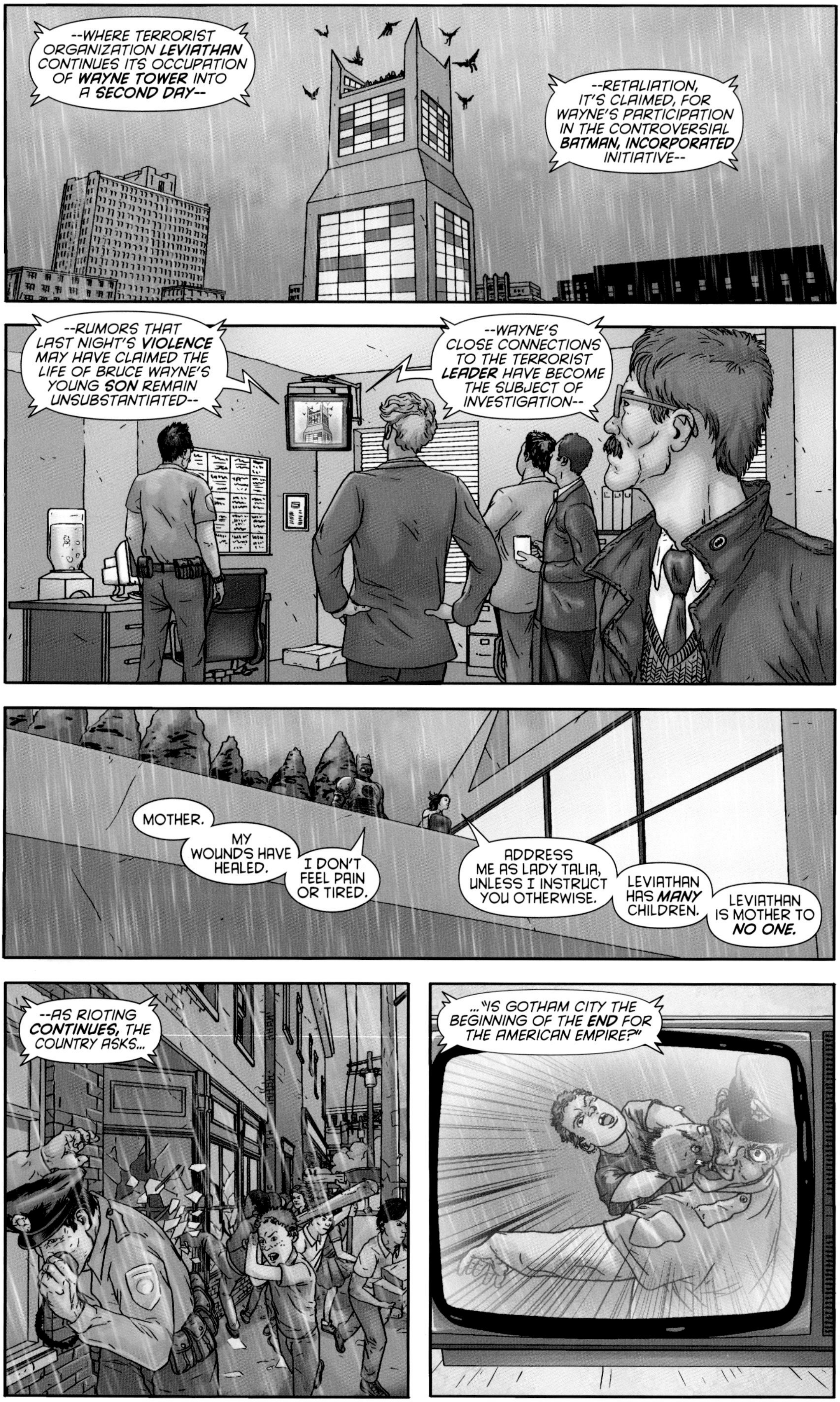
--WHERE TERRORIST ORGANIZATION LEVIATHAN CONTINUES ITS OCCUPATION OF WAYNE TOWER INTO A SECOND DAY--
--RETALIATION, IT'S CLAIMED, FOR WAYNE'S PARTICIPATION IN THE CONTROVERSIAL BATMAN, INCORPORATED INITIATIVE--
--RUMORS THAT LAST NIGHT'S VIOLENCE MAY HAVE CLAIMED THE LIFE OF BRUCE WAYNE'S YOUNG SON REMAIN UNSUBSTANTIATED--
--WAYNE'S CLOSE CONNECTIONS TO THE TERRORIST LEADER HAVE BECOME THE SUBJECT OF INVESTIGATION--
MOTHER.
MY WOUNDS HAVE HEALED.
I DON'T FEEL PAIN OR TIRED.
ADDRESS ME AS LADY TALIA, UNLESS I INSTRUCT YOU OTHERWISE.
LEVIATHAN HAS MANY CHILDREN.
LEVIATHAN IS MOTHER TO NO ONE.
--AS RIOTING CONTINUES, THE COUNTRY ASKS...
..."IS GOTHAM CITY THE BEGINNING OF THE END FOR THE AMERICAN EMPIRE?"

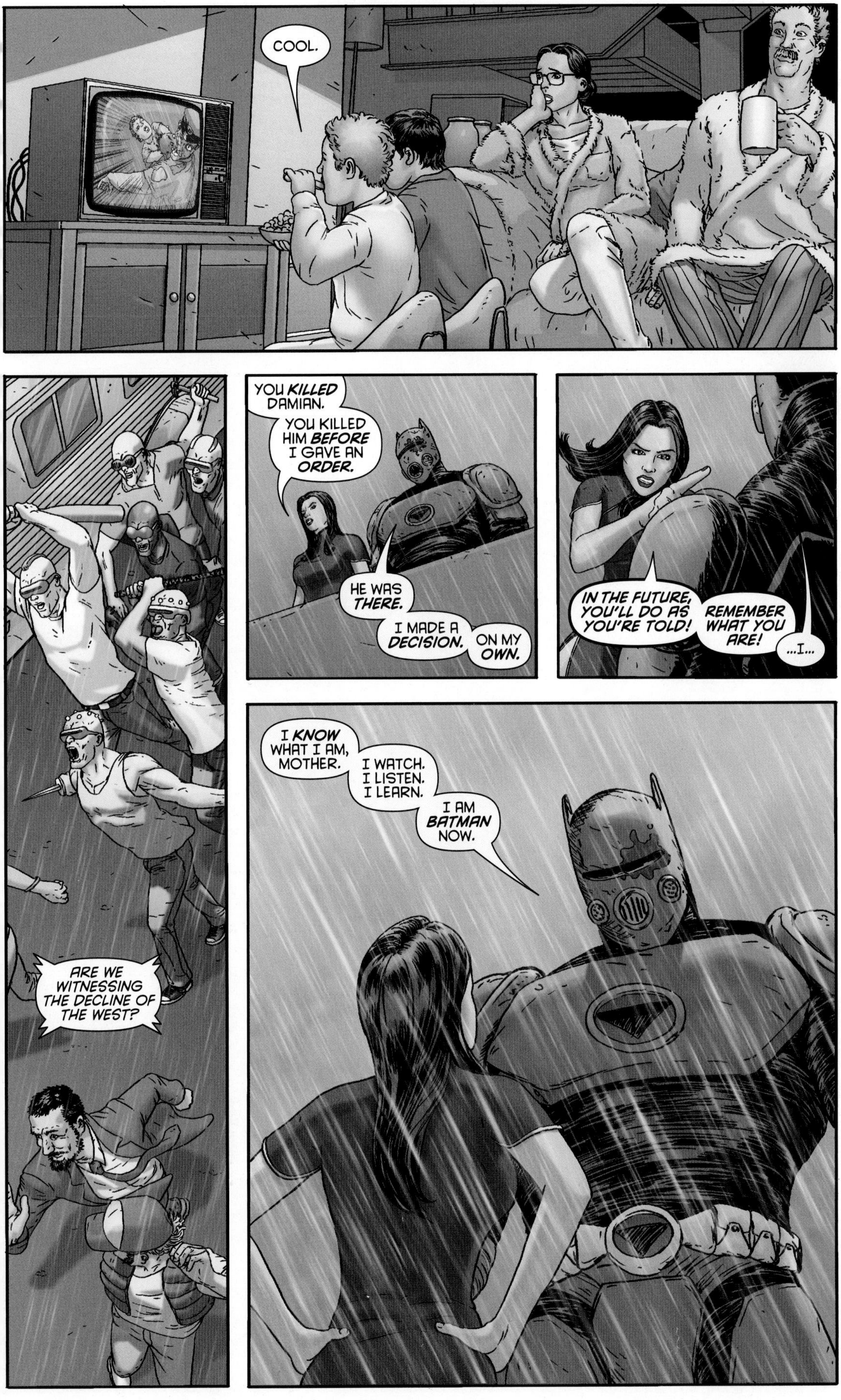
COOL.
ARE WE WITNESSING THE DECLINE OF THE WEST?
YOU KILLED DAMIAN.
YOU KILLED HIM BEFORE I GAVE AN ORDER.
HE WAS THERE.
I MADE A DECISION.
ON MY OWN.
IN THE FUTURE, YOU'LL DO AS YOU'RE TOLD!
REMEMBER WHAT YOU ARE!
...I...
I KNOW WHAT I AM, MOTHER.
I WATCH. I LISTEN. I LEARN.
I AM BATMAN NOW.

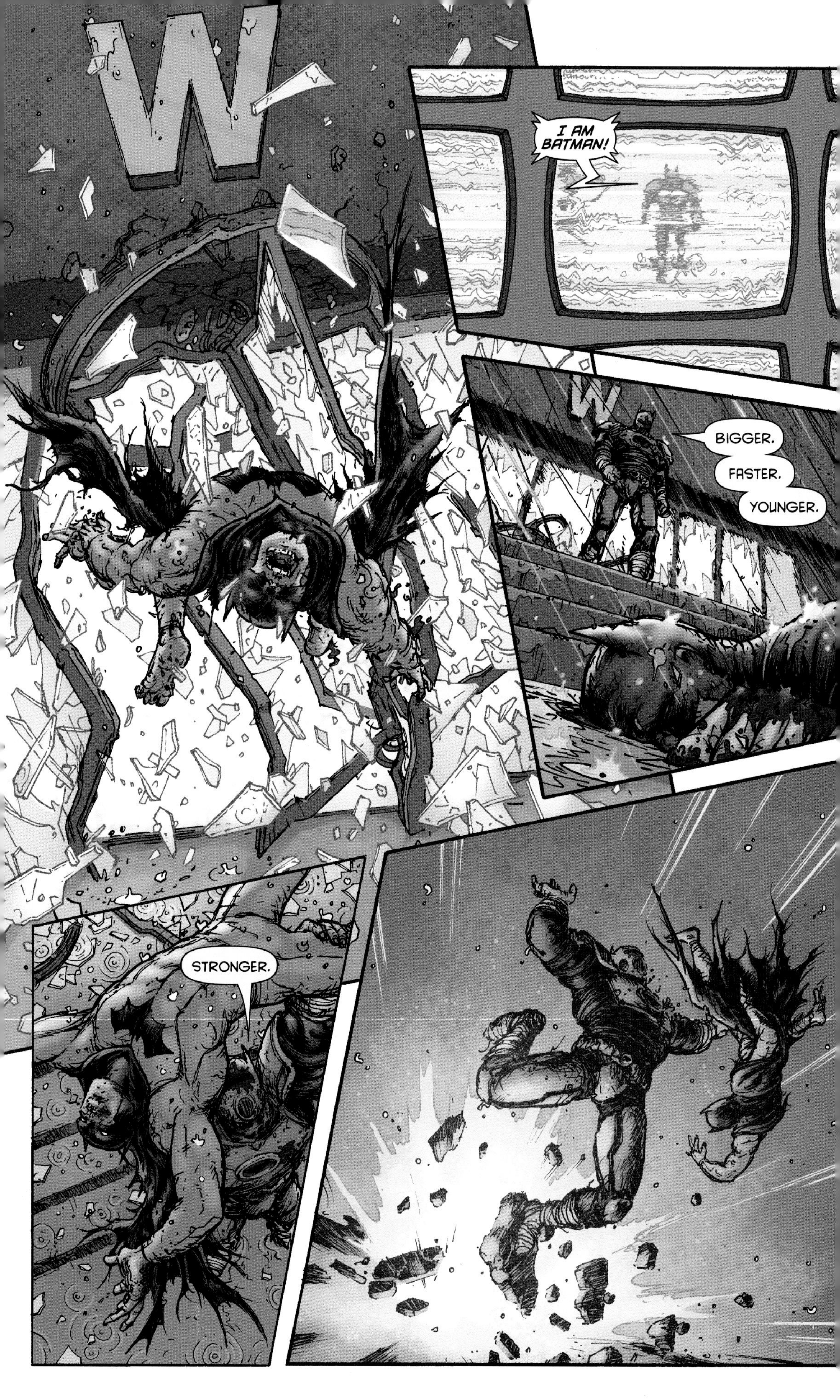
W
I AM BATMAN!
BIGGER.
FASTER.
YOUNGER.
STRONGER.

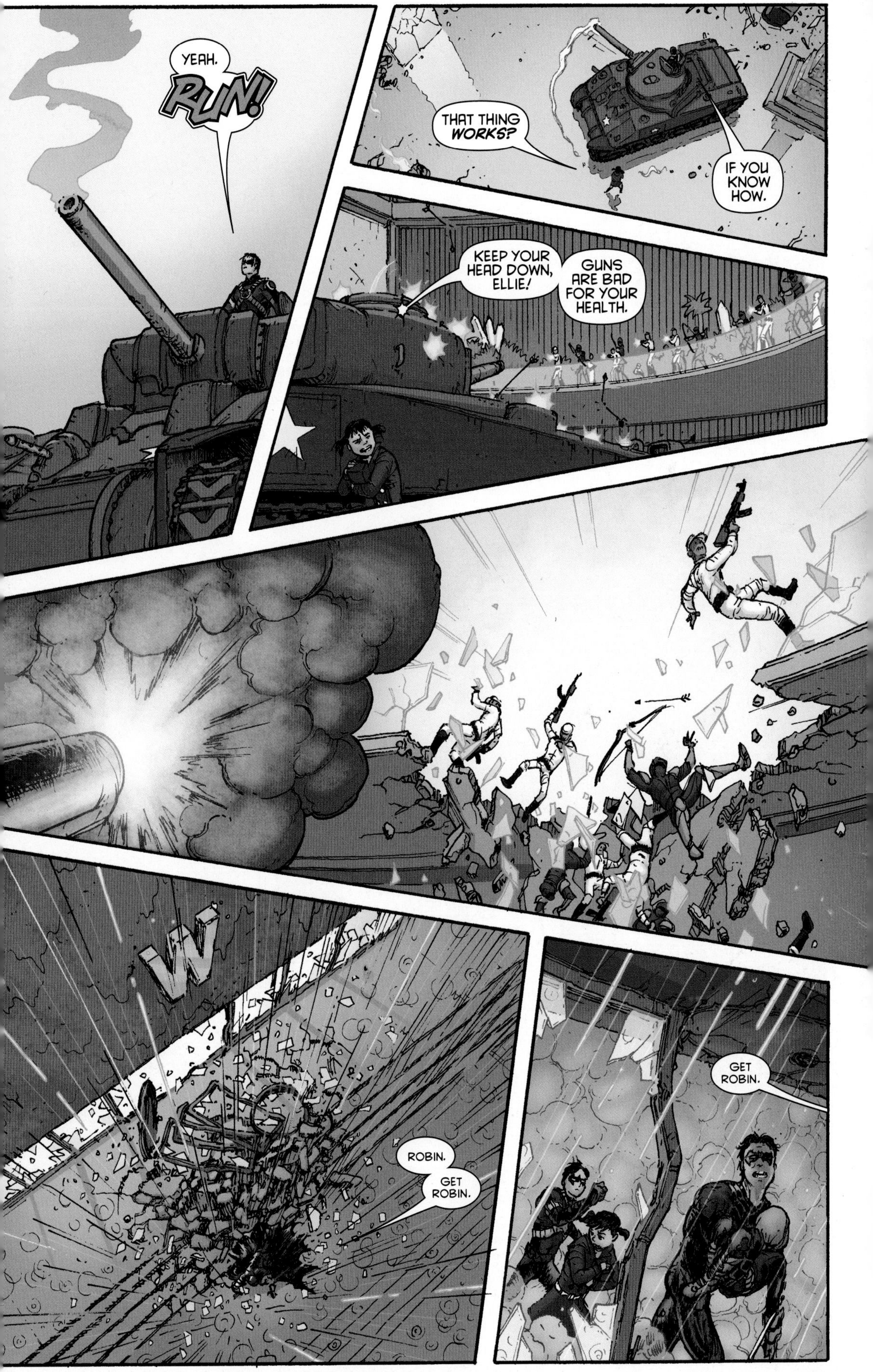
YEAH.
RUN!
THAT THING WORKS?
IF YOU KNOW HOW.
KEEP YOUR HEAD DOWN, ELLIE!
GUNS ARE BAD FOR YOUR HEALTH.
ROBIN.
GET ROBIN.
GET ROBIN.

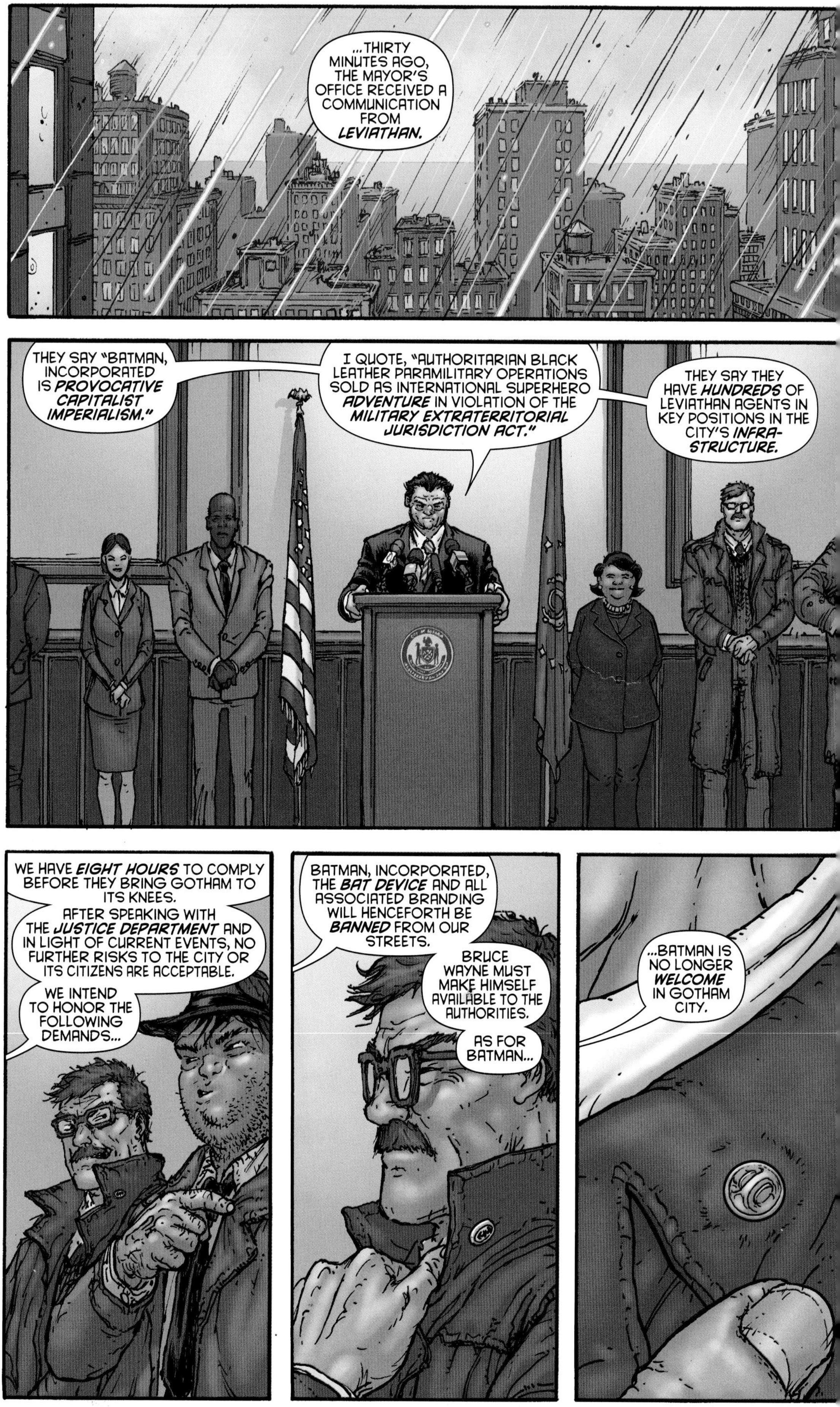

...THIRTY MINUTES AGO, THE MAYOR'S OFFICE RECEIVED A COMMUNICATION FROM LEVIATHAN.
THEY SAY "BATMAN, INCORPORATED IS PROVOCATIVE CAPITALIST IMPERIALISM."
I QUOTE, "AUTHORITARIAN BLACK LEATHER PARAMILITARY OPERATIONS SOLD AS INTERNATIONAL SUPERHERO ADVENTURE IN VIOLATION OF THE MILITARY EXTRATERRITORIAL JURISDICTION ACT."
THEY SAY THEY HAVE HUNDREDS OF LEVIATHAN AGENTS IN KEY POSITIONS IN THE CITY'S INFRA-STRUCTURE.
WE HAVE EIGHT HOURS TO COMPLY BEFORE THEY BRING GOTHAM TO ITS KNEES.
AFTER SPEAKING WITH THE JUSTICE DEPARTMENT AND IN LIGHT OF CURRENT EVENTS, NO FURTHER RISKS TO THE CITY OR ITS CITIZENS ARE ACCEPTABLE.
WE INTEND TO HONOR THE FOLLOWING DEMANDS...
BATMAN, INCORPORATED, THE BAT DEVICE AND ALL ASSOCIATED BRANDING WILL HENCEFORTH BE BANNED FROM OUR STREETS.
BRUCE WAYNE MUST MAKE HIMSELF AVAILABLE TO THE AUTHORITIES.
AS FOR BATMAN...
...BATMAN IS NO LONGER WELCOME IN GOTHAM CITY.

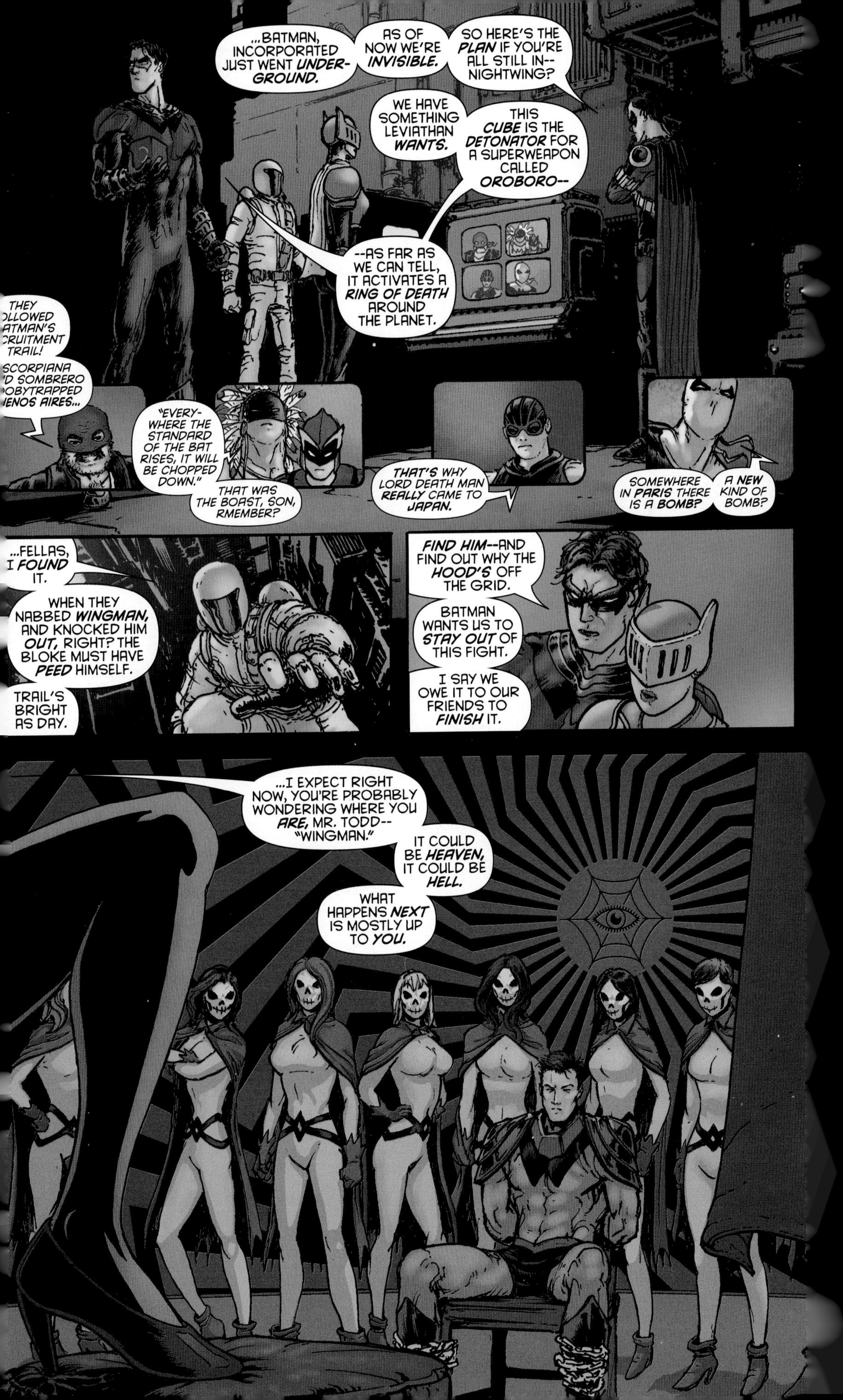

...BATMAN, INCORPORATED JUST WENT UNDER-GROUND.
AS OF NOW WE'RE INVISIBLE.
SO HERE'S THE PLAN IF YOU'RE ALL STILL IN-- NIGHTWING?
WE HAVE SOMETHING LEVIATHAN WANTS.
THIS CUBE IS THE DETONATOR FOR A SUPERWEAPON CALLED OROBORO--
--AS FAR AS WE CAN TELL, IT ACTIVATES A RING OF DEATH AROUND THE PLANET.
THEY OLLOWED ATMAN'S CRUITMENT TRAIL!
SCORPIANA 'D SOMBRERO OOBYTRAPPED UENOS AIRES...
"EVERY-WHERE THE STANDARD OF THE BAT RISES, IT WILL BE CHOPPED DOWN."
THAT WAS THE BOAST, SON, RMEMBER?
THAT'S WHY LORD DEATH MAN REALLY CAME TO JAPAN.
SOMEWHERE IN PARIS THERE IS A BOMB?
A NEW KIND OF BOMB?
...FELLAS, I FOUND IT.
WHEN THEY NABBED WINGMAN, AND KNOCKED HIM OUT, RIGHT? THE BLOKE MUST HAVE PEED HIMSELF.
TRAIL'S BRIGHT AS DAY.
FIND HIM--AND FIND OUT WHY THE HOOD'S OFF THE GRID.
BATMAN WANTS US TO STAY OUT OF THIS FIGHT.
I SAY WE OWE IT TO OUR FRIENDS TO FINISH IT.
...I EXPECT RIGHT NOW, YOU'RE PROBABLY WONDERING WHERE YOU ARE, MR. TODD-- "WINGMAN."
IT COULD BE HEAVEN, IT COULD BE HELL.
WHAT HAPPENS NEXT IS MOSTLY UP TO YOU.

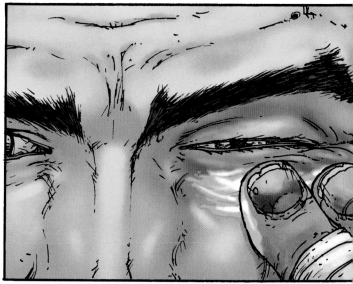

AGENT DECEASED

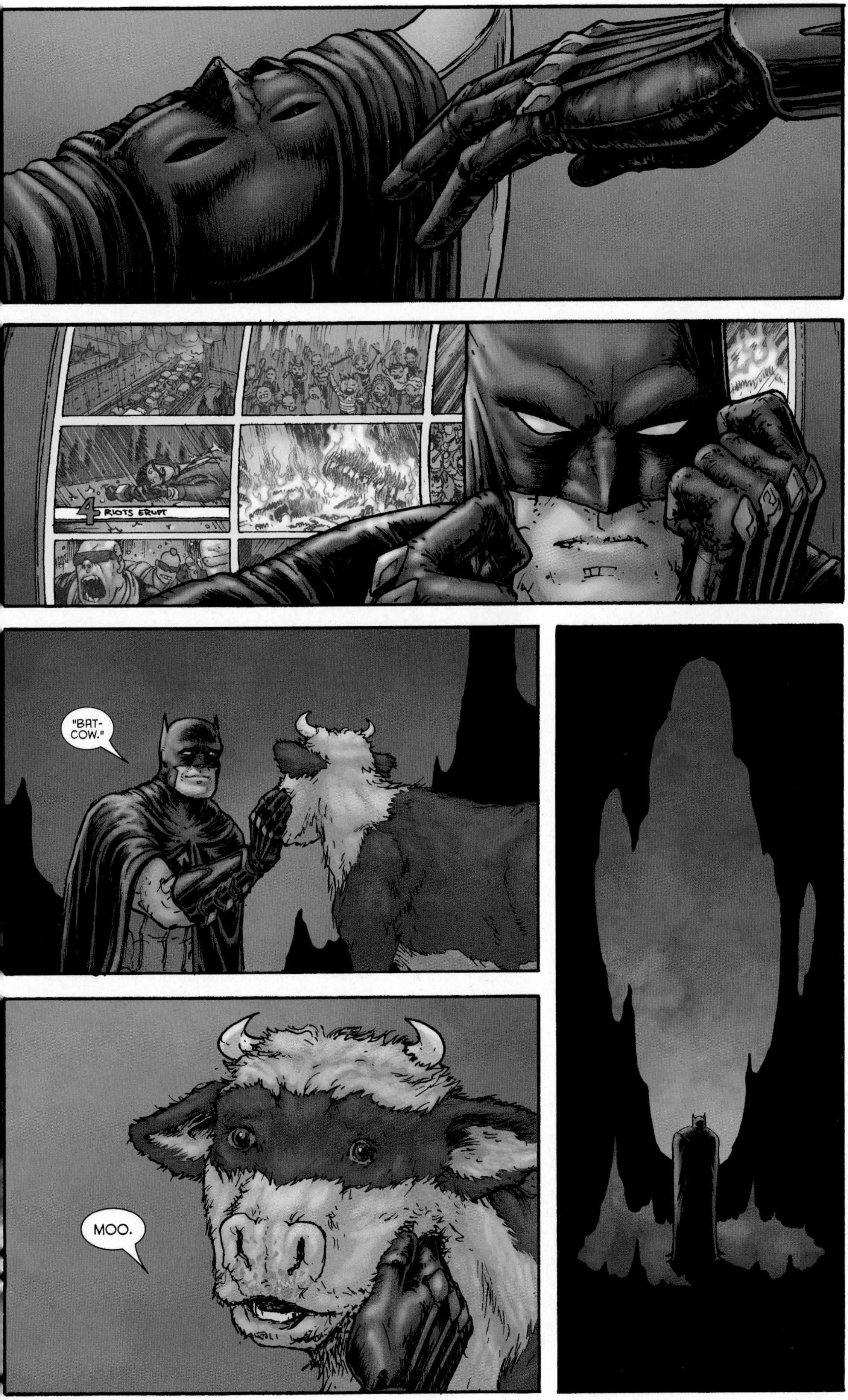
4 RIOTS ERUPT
"BAT-COW."
MOO.

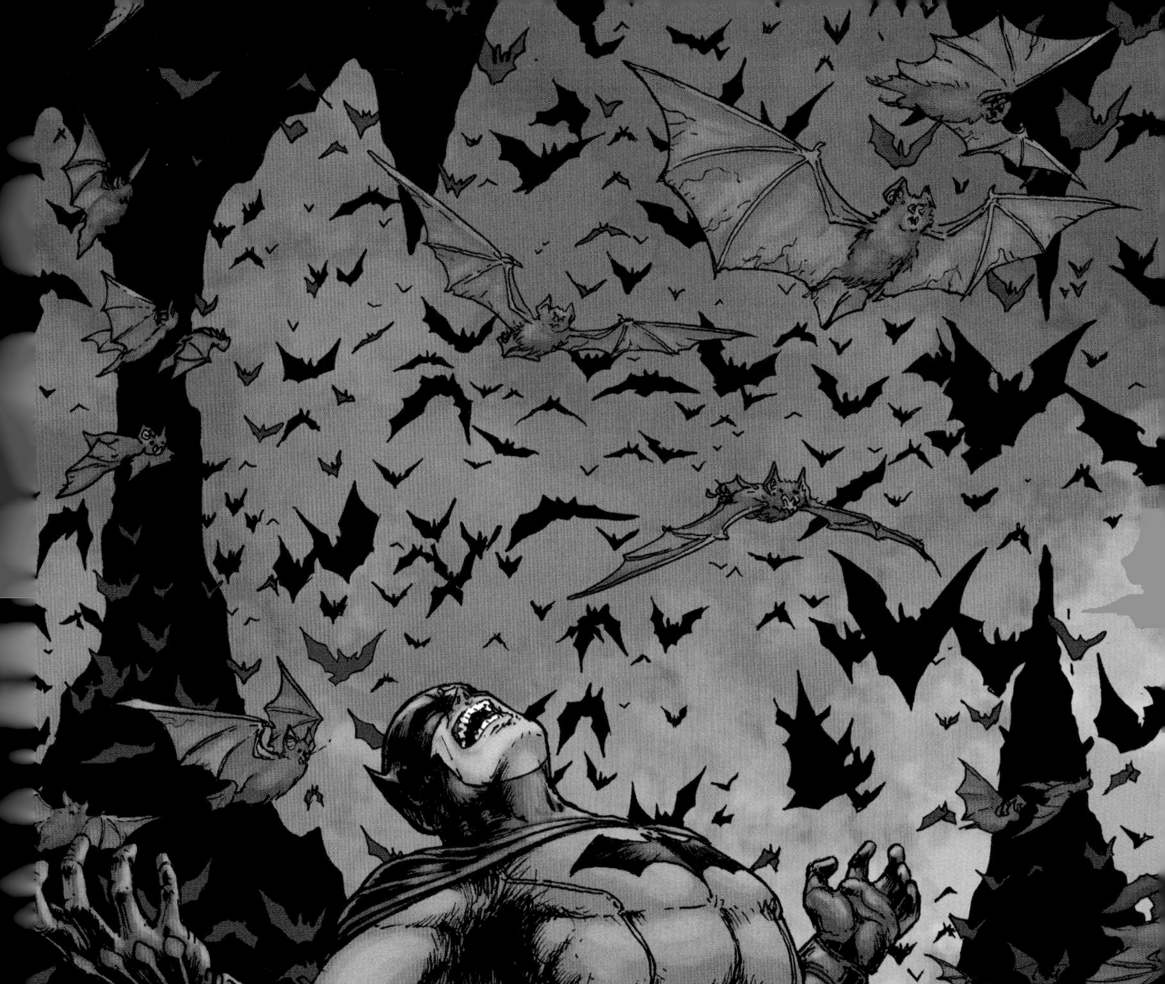

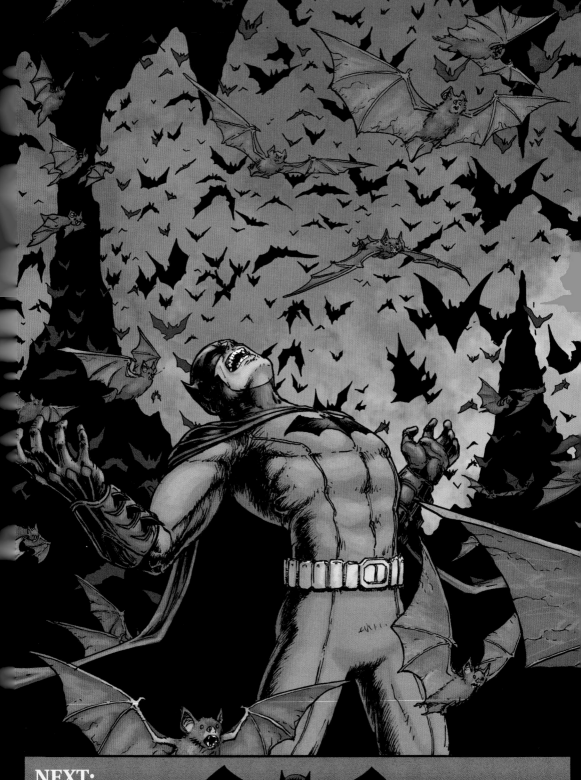

NEXT:

GOTHAM'S MOST WANTED

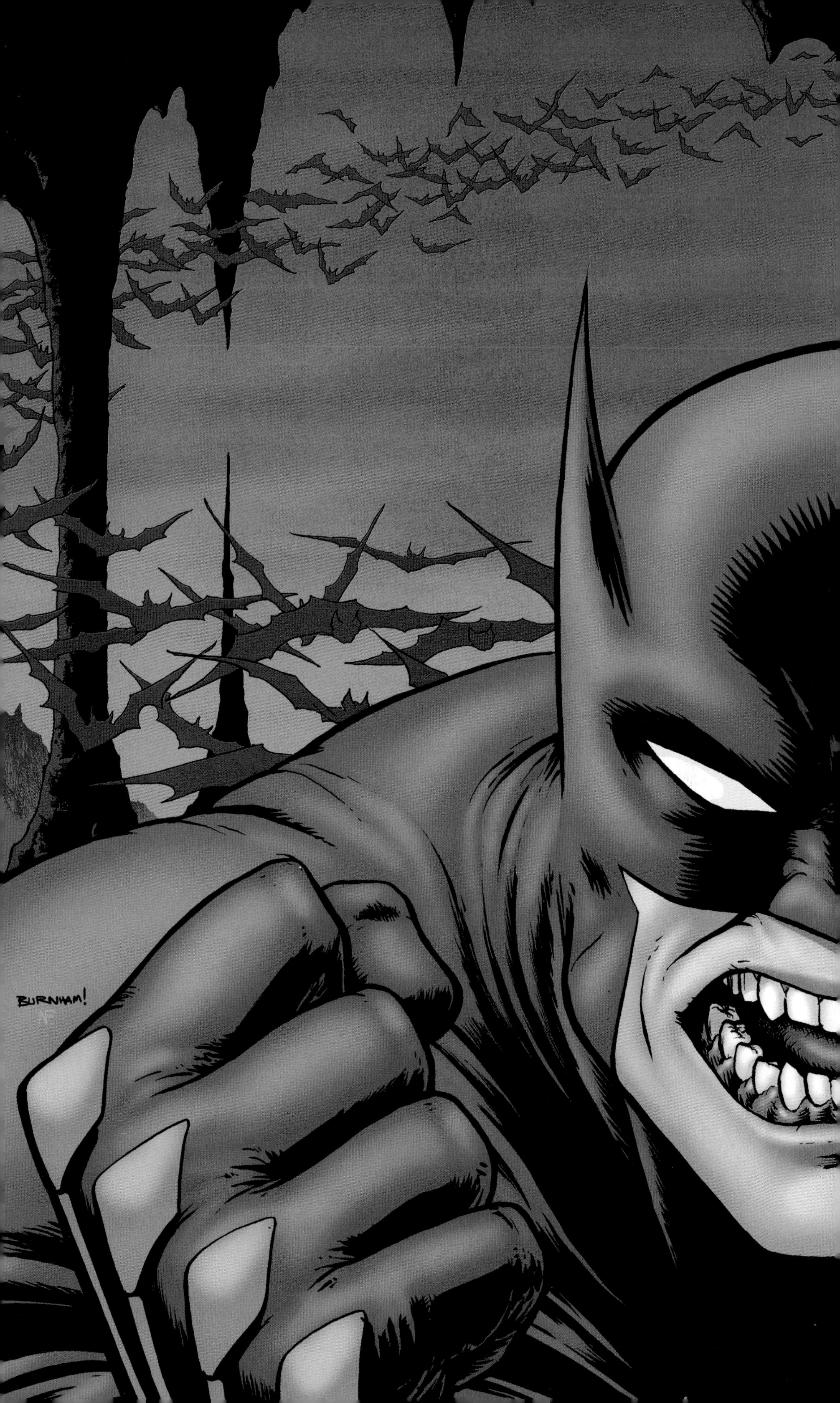
BURNHAM!
NF

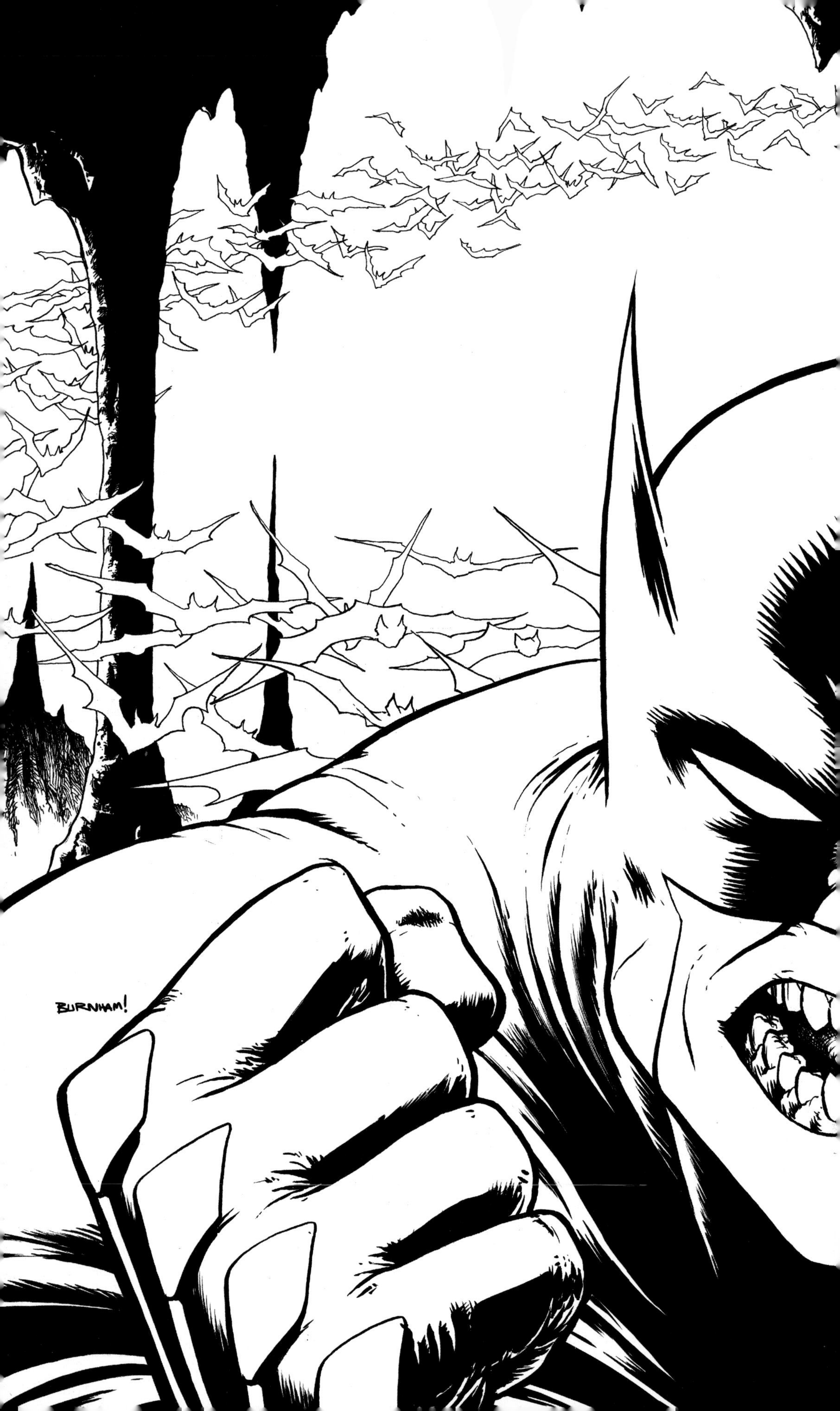
BURNHAM!

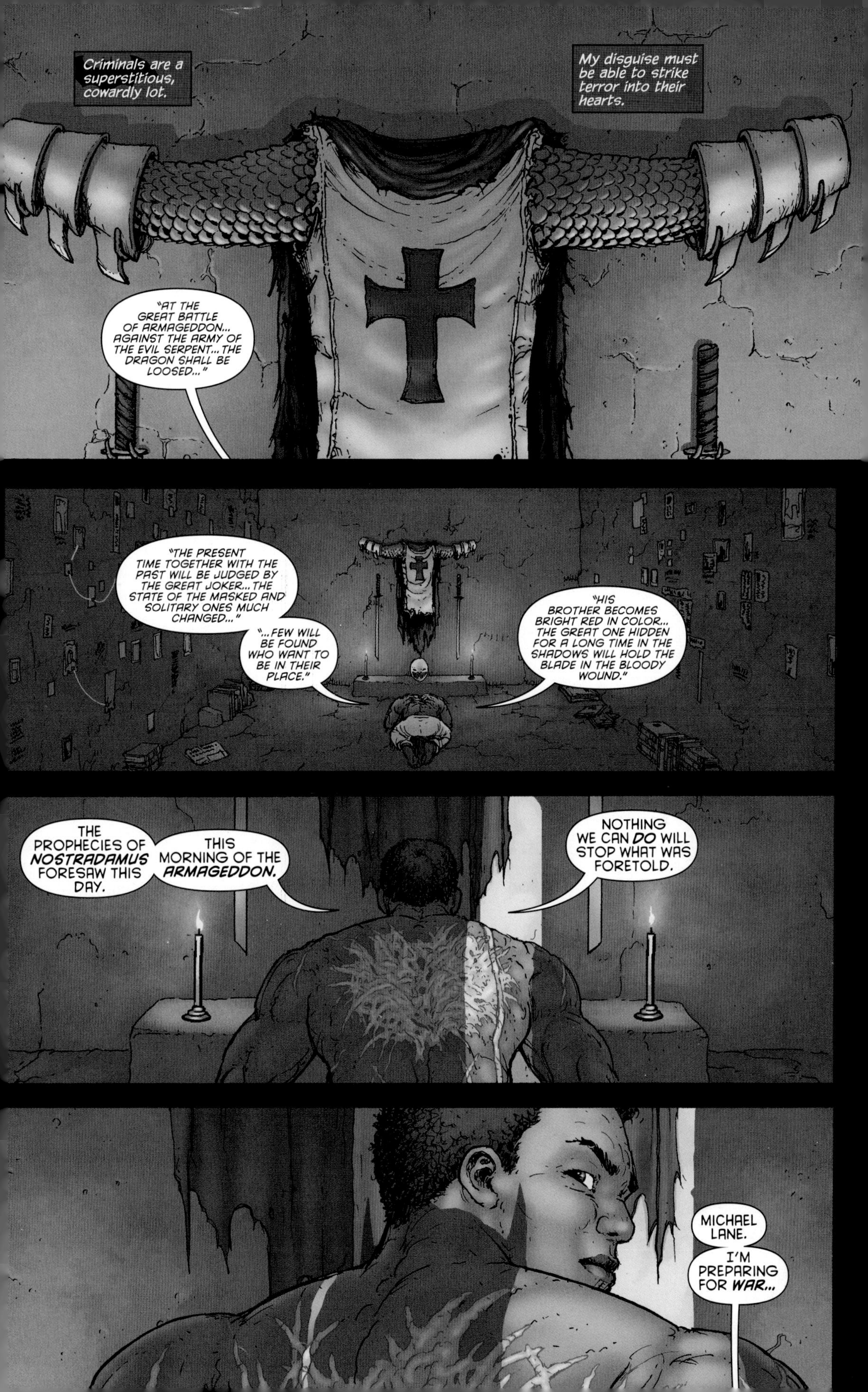
Criminals are a superstitious, cowardly lot.
My disguise must be able to strike terror into their hearts.
"AT THE GREAT BATTLE OF ARMAGEDDON... AGAINST THE ARMY OF THE EVIL SERPENT... THE DRAGON SHALL BE LOOSED..."
"THE PRESENT TIME TOGETHER WITH THE PAST WILL BE JUDGED BY THE GREAT JOKER... THE STATE OF THE MASKED AND SOLITARY ONES MUCH CHANGED..."
"...FEW WILL BE FOUND WHO WANT TO BE IN THEIR PLACE."
"HIS BROTHER BECOMES BRIGHT RED IN COLOR... THE GREAT ONE HIDDEN FOR A LONG TIME IN THE SHADOWS WILL HOLD THE BLADE IN THE BLOODY WOUND."
THE PROPHECIES OF NOSTRADAMUS FORESAW THIS DAY.
THIS MORNING OF THE ARMAGEDDON.
NOTHING WE CAN DO WILL STOP WHAT WAS FORETOLD.
MICHAEL LANE.
I'M PREPARING FOR WAR...

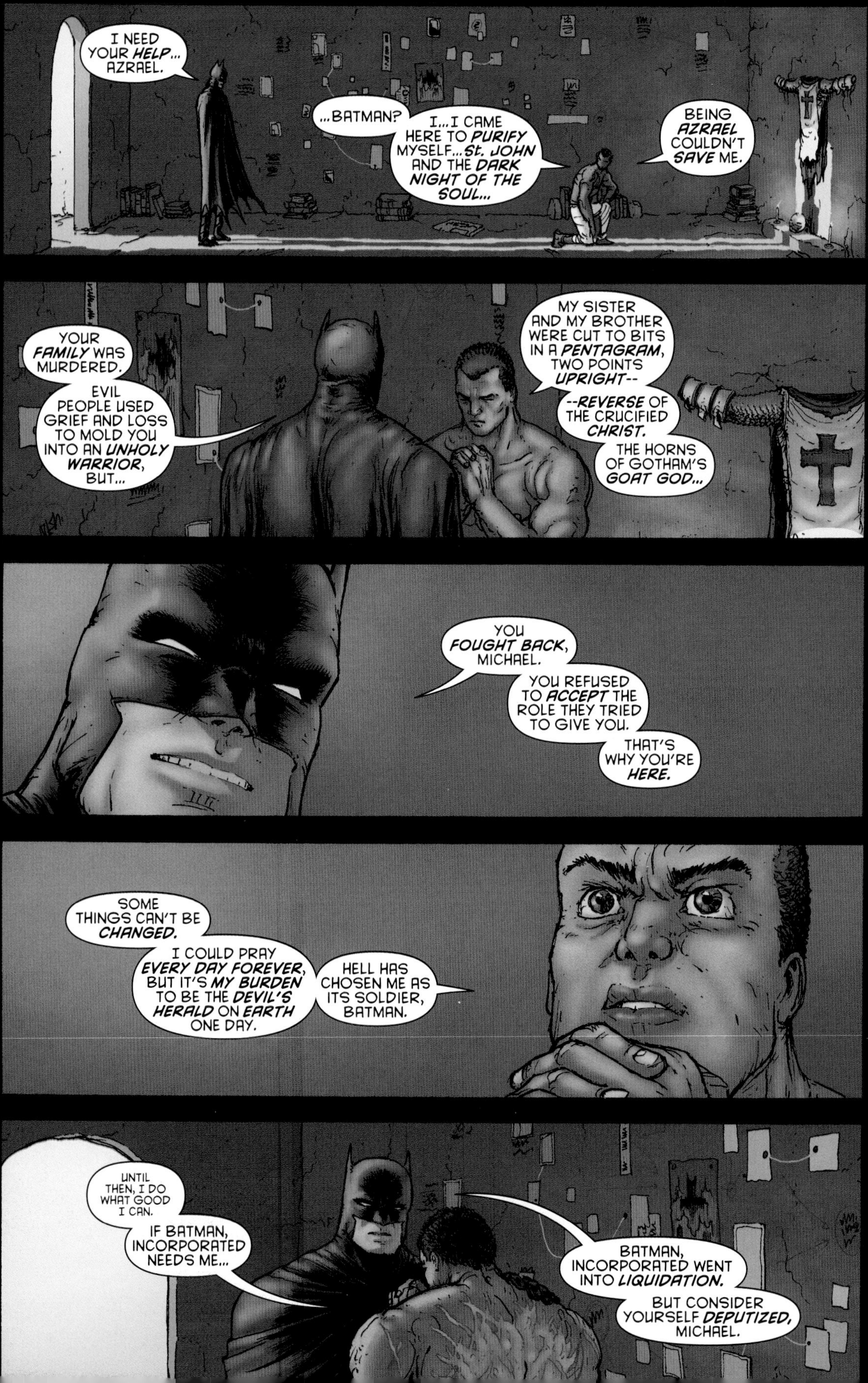
I NEED YOUR HELP... AZRAEL.
...BATMAN?
I...I CAME HERE TO PURIFY MYSELF...St. JOHN AND THE DARK NIGHT OF THE SOUL...
BEING AZRAEL COULDN'T SAVE ME.
YOUR FAMILY WAS MURDERED.
EVIL PEOPLE USED GRIEF AND LOSS TO MOLD YOU INTO AN UNHOLY WARRIOR, BUT...
MY SISTER AND MY BROTHER WERE CUT TO BITS IN A PENTAGRAM, TWO POINTS UPRIGHT--
--REVERSE OF THE CRUCIFIED CHRIST.
THE HORNS OF GOTHAM'S GOAT GOD...
YOU FOUGHT BACK, MICHAEL.
YOU REFUSED TO ACCEPT THE ROLE THEY TRIED TO GIVE YOU.
THAT'S WHY YOU'RE HERE.
SOME THINGS CAN'T BE CHANGED.
I COULD PRAY EVERY DAY FOREVER, BUT IT'S MY BURDEN TO BE THE DEVIL'S HERALD ON EARTH ONE DAY.
HELL HAS CHOSEN ME AS ITS SOLDIER, BATMAN.
UNTIL THEN, I DO WHAT GOOD I CAN.
IF BATMAN, INCORPORATED NEEDS ME...
BATMAN, INCORPORATED WENT INTO LIQUIDATION.
BUT CONSIDER YOURSELF DEPUTIZED, MICHAEL.

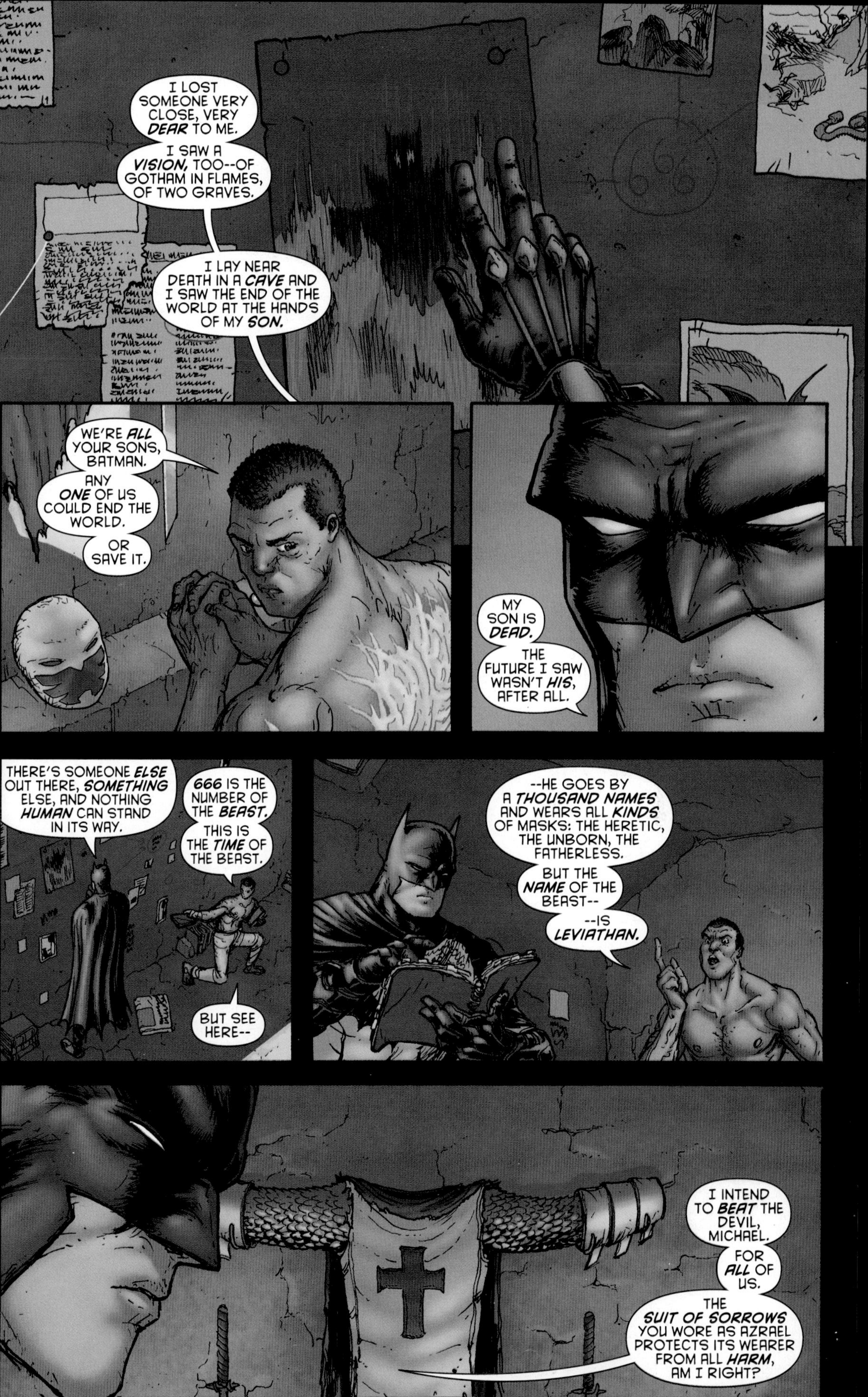

I LOST SOMEONE VERY CLOSE, VERY DEAR TO ME.
I SAW A VISION, TOO--OF GOTHAM IN FLAMES, OF TWO GRAVES.
I LAY NEAR DEATH IN A CAVE AND I SAW THE END OF THE WORLD AT THE HANDS OF MY SON.
WE'RE ALL YOUR SONS, BATMAN.
ANY ONE OF US COULD END THE WORLD.
OR SAVE IT.
MY SON IS DEAD.
THE FUTURE I SAW WASN'T HIS, AFTER ALL.
THERE'S SOMEONE ELSE OUT THERE, SOMETHING ELSE, AND NOTHING HUMAN CAN STAND IN ITS WAY.
666 IS THE NUMBER OF THE BEAST.
THIS IS THE TIME OF THE BEAST.
BUT SEE HERE--
--HE GOES BY A THOUSAND NAMES AND WEARS ALL KINDS OF MASKS: THE HERETIC, THE UNBORN, THE FATHERLESS.
BUT THE NAME OF THE BEAST--
--IS LEVIATHAN.
I INTEND TO BEAT THE DEVIL, MICHAEL.
FOR ALL OF US.
THE SUIT OF SORROWS YOU WORE AS AZRAEL PROTECTS ITS WEARER FROM ALL HARM, AM I RIGHT?

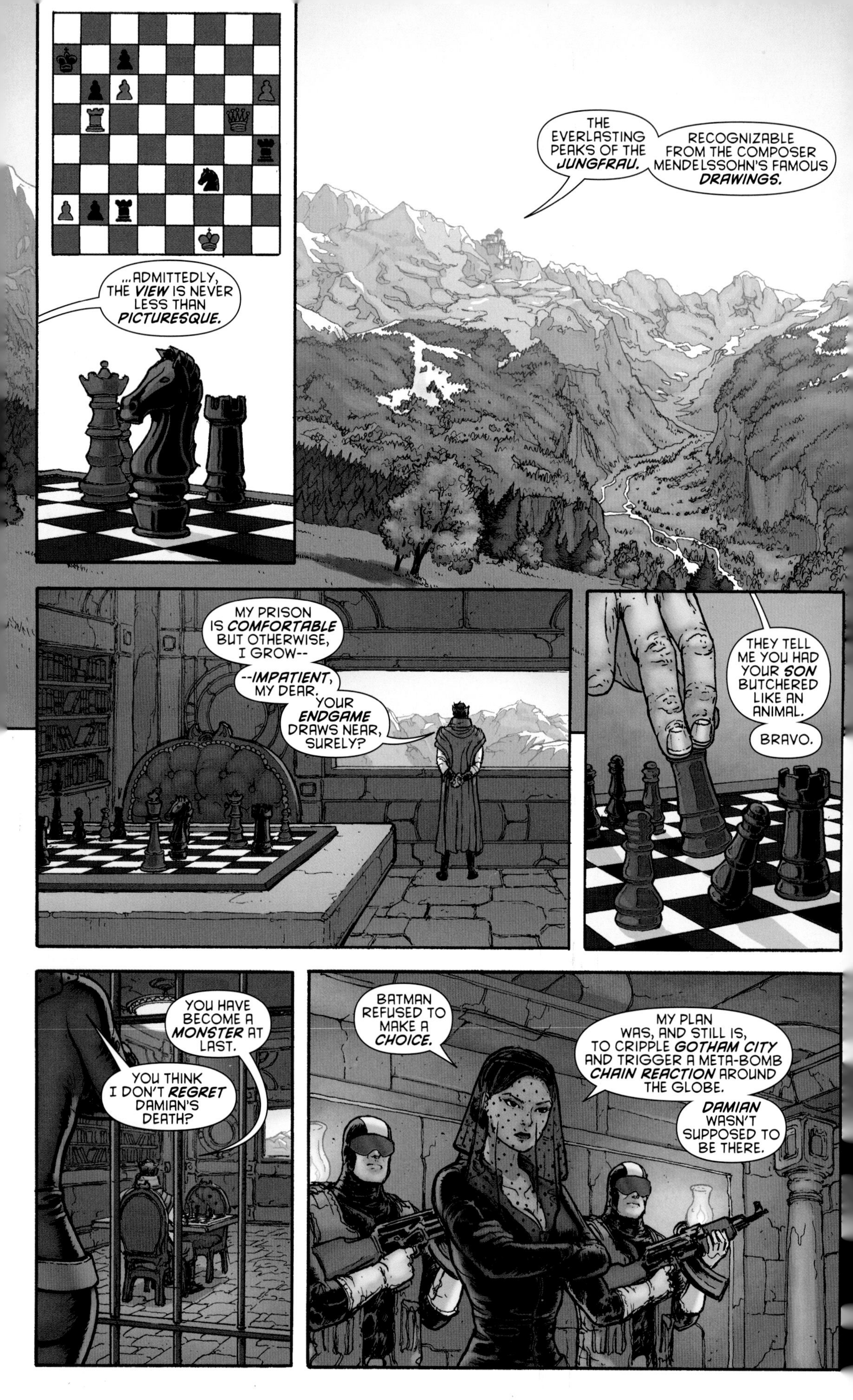
...ADMITTEDLY, THE VIEW IS NEVER LESS THAN PICTURESQUE.
THE EVERLASTING PEAKS OF THE JUNGFRAU.
RECOGNIZABLE FROM THE COMPOSER MENDELSSOHN'S FAMOUS DRAWINGS.
MY PRISON IS COMFORTABLE BUT OTHERWISE, I GROW--
--IMPATIENT, MY DEAR.
YOUR ENDGAME DRAWS NEAR, SURELY?
THEY TELL ME YOU HAD YOUR SON BUTCHERED LIKE AN ANIMAL.
BRAVO.
YOU HAVE BECOME A MONSTER AT LAST.
YOU THINK I DON'T REGRET DAMIAN'S DEATH?
BATMAN REFUSED TO MAKE A CHOICE.
MY PLAN WAS, AND STILL IS, TO CRIPPLE GOTHAM CITY AND TRIGGER A META-BOMB CHAIN REACTION AROUND THE GLOBE.
DAMIAN WASN'T SUPPOSED TO BE THERE.

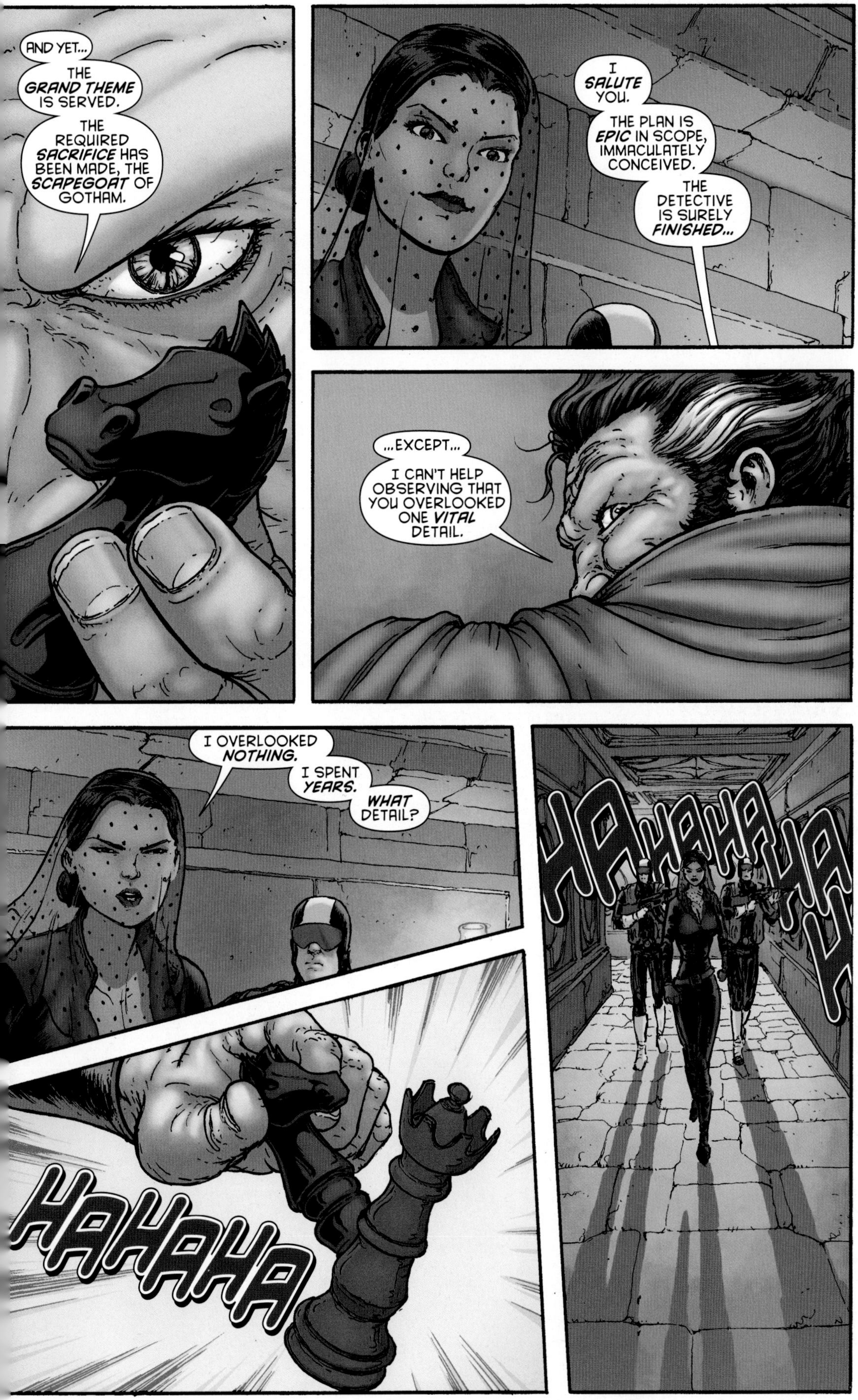

AND YET...
THE GRAND THEME IS SERVED.
THE REQUIRED SACRIFICE HAS BEEN MADE, THE SCAPEGOAT OF GOTHAM.
I SALUTE YOU.
THE PLAN IS EPIC IN SCOPE, IMMACULATELY CONCEIVED.
THE DETECTIVE IS SURELY FINISHED...
...EXCEPT...
I CAN'T HELP OBSERVING THAT YOU OVERLOOKED ONE VITAL DETAIL.
I OVERLOOKED NOTHING.
I SPENT YEARS.
WHAT DETAIL?
HAHAHAHA
HAHAHAHAHAHA

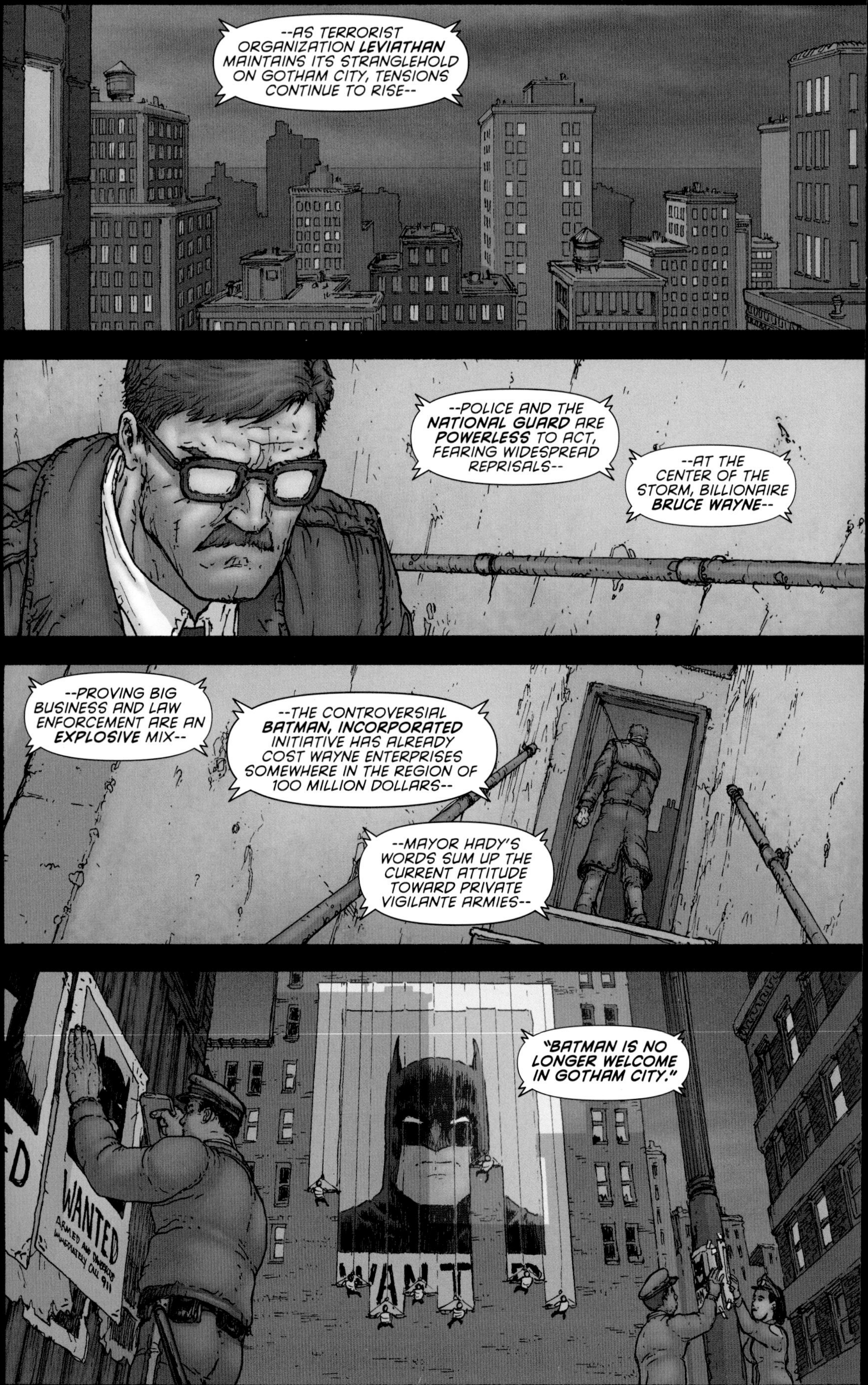
--AS TERRORIST ORGANIZATION LEVIATHAN MAINTAINS ITS STRANGLEHOLD ON GOTHAM CITY, TENSIONS CONTINUE TO RISE--
--POLICE AND THE NATIONAL GUARD ARE POWERLESS TO ACT, FEARING WIDESPREAD REPRISALS--
--AT THE CENTER OF THE STORM, BILLIONAIRE BRUCE WAYNE--
--PROVING BIG BUSINESS AND LAW ENFORCEMENT ARE AN EXPLOSIVE MIX--
--THE CONTROVERSIAL BATMAN, INCORPORATED INITIATIVE HAS ALREADY COST WAYNE ENTERPRISES SOMEWHERE IN THE REGION OF 100 MILLION DOLLARS--
--MAYOR HADY'S WORDS SUM UP THE CURRENT ATTITUDE TOWARD PRIVATE VIGILANTE ARMIES--
"BATMAN IS NO LONGER WELCOME IN GOTHAM CITY."
WANTED

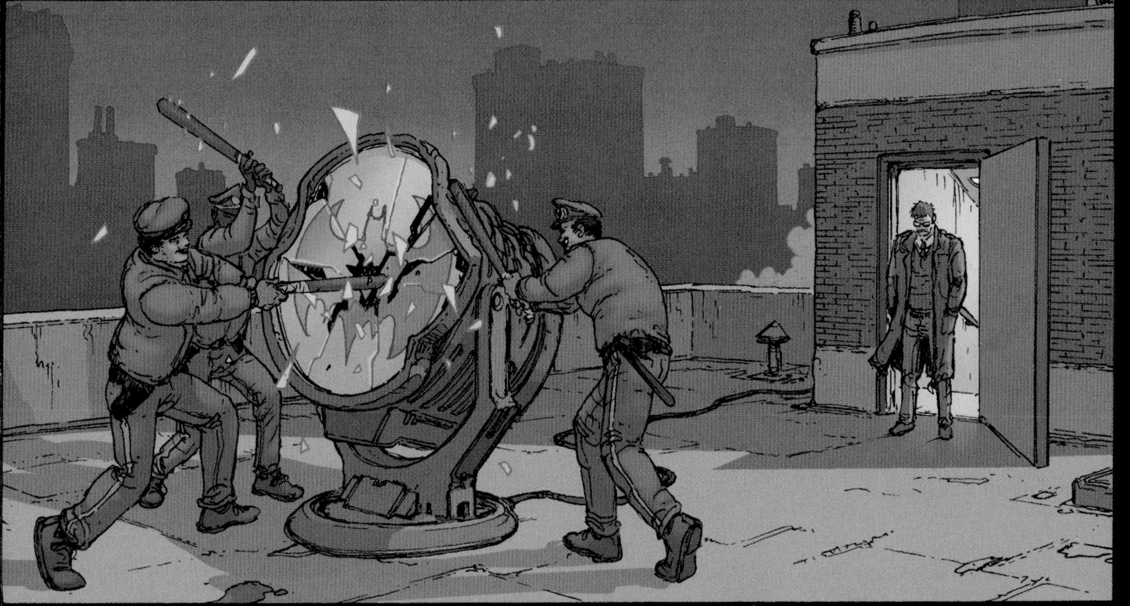

GOTHAM'S MOST WANTED

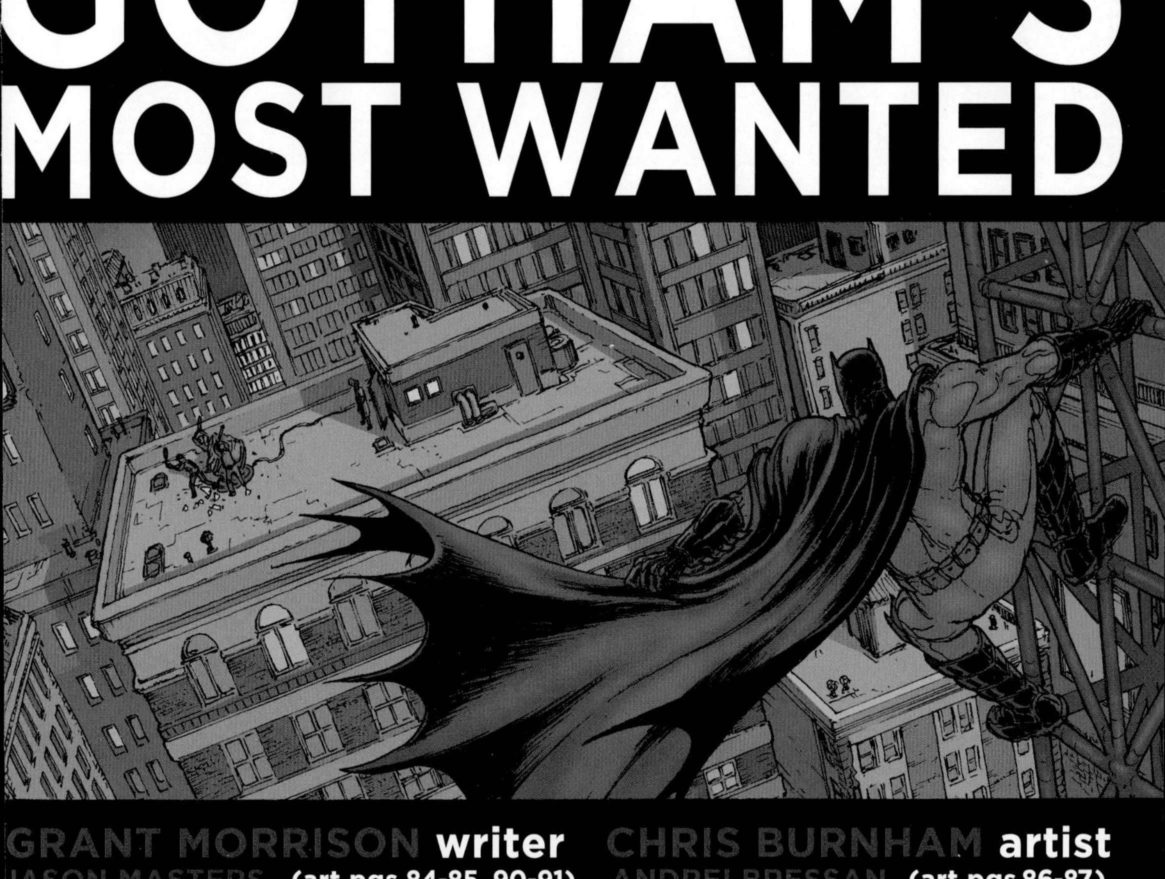

GRANT MORRISON **writer** CHRIS BURNHAM **artist**
JASON MASTERS **(art pgs 84-85, 90-91)** ANDREI BRESSAN **(art pgs 86-87)**
NATHAN FAIRBAIRN **colors** DC LETTERING **letters**
BURNHAM & FAIRBAIRN **cover**

...WAYNE ENTERPRISES UNDERSTANDS ALL OF YOUR CONCERNS.

WE'RE CURRENTLY DOING EVERYTHING WE CAN TO ENSURE THE SAFETY OF GOTHAM CITY AND ITS PEOPLE.

REST ASSURED, WE ARE REVISING OUR POSITION AND RECONSIDERING OUR RECENT EXPENDITURE.

AS FOR MR. WAYNE, WELL...

...I'VE BEEN ADVISED THAT BRUCE WAYNE WILL MAKE A STATEMENT SHORTLY.

4 · WAYNE ENTERPRISES' LUCIUS FOX

I HATE THE WAY I LOOK ON TV.

I THINK YOU NEED TO HIRE A MORE PHOTOGENIC SPOKESMAN, MR. WAYNE.

I'D SUGGEST YOU, BUT--

POINT TAKEN.

THEY WANT ME TO HAND MYSELF IN, LUCIUS, FOR CRIMES UNDISCLOSED.

I HAVE A LIMITED WINDOW OF OPPORTUNITY TO PUT THINGS RIGHT.

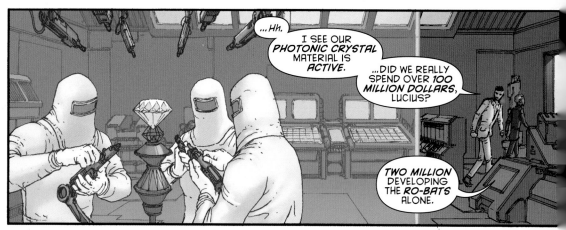

...HH.

I SEE OUR PHOTONIC CRYSTAL MATERIAL IS ACTIVE.

...DID WE REALLY SPEND OVER 100 MILLION DOLLARS, LUCIUS?

TWO MILLION DEVELOPING THE RO-BATS ALONE.

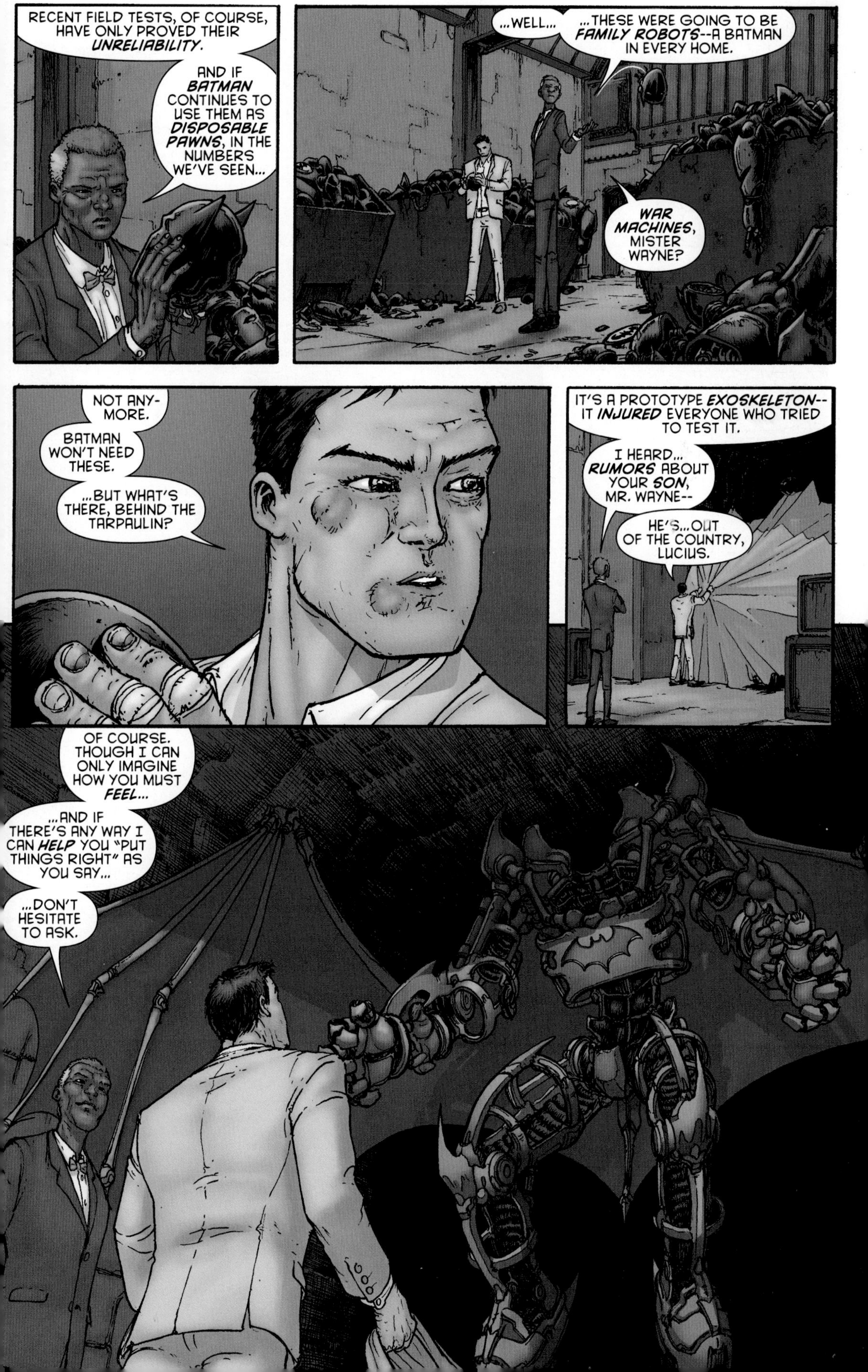
RECENT FIELD TESTS, OF COURSE, HAVE ONLY PROVED THEIR UNRELIABILITY.
AND IF BATMAN CONTINUES TO USE THEM AS DISPOSABLE PAWNS, IN THE NUMBERS WE'VE SEEN...
...WELL...
...THESE WERE GOING TO BE FAMILY ROBOTS--A BATMAN IN EVERY HOME.
WAR MACHINES, MISTER WAYNE?
NOT ANY-MORE.
BATMAN WON'T NEED THESE.
...BUT WHAT'S THERE, BEHIND THE TARPAULIN?
IT'S A PROTOTYPE EXOSKELETON--IT INJURED EVERYONE WHO TRIED TO TEST IT.
I HEARD... RUMORS ABOUT YOUR SON, MR. WAYNE--
HE'S...OUT OF THE COUNTRY, LUCIUS.
OF COURSE. THOUGH I CAN ONLY IMAGINE HOW YOU MUST FEEL...
...AND IF THERE'S ANY WAY I CAN HELP YOU "PUT THINGS RIGHT" AS YOU SAY...
...DON'T HESITATE TO ASK.

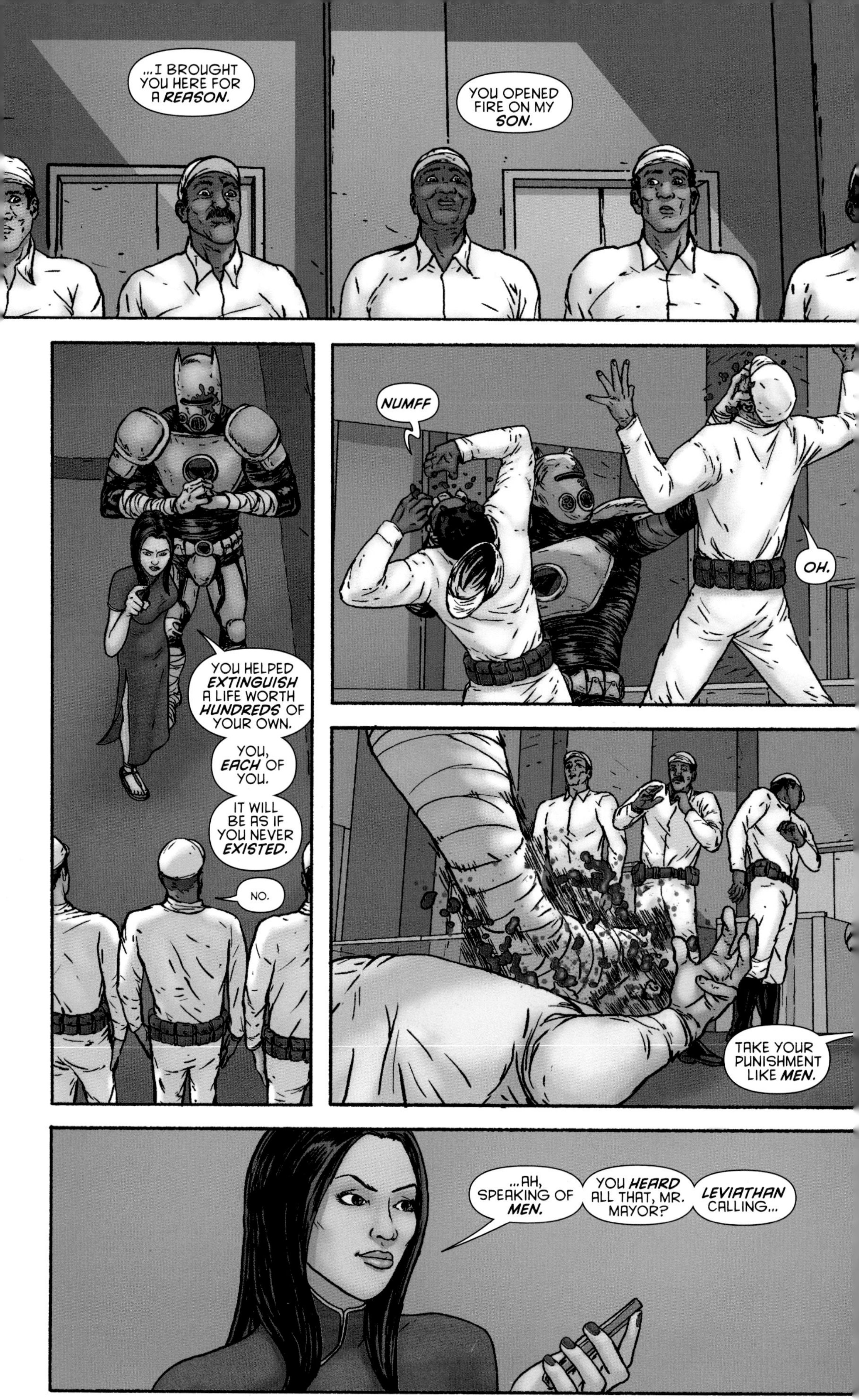
...I BROUGHT YOU HERE FOR A REASON.
YOU OPENED FIRE ON MY SON.
YOU HELPED EXTINGUISH A LIFE WORTH HUNDREDS OF YOUR OWN.
YOU, EACH OF YOU.
IT WILL BE AS IF YOU NEVER EXISTED.
NO.
NUMFF
OH.
TAKE YOUR PUNISHMENT LIKE MEN.
...AH, SPEAKING OF MEN.
YOU HEARD ALL THAT, MR. MAYOR?
LEVIATHAN CALLING...

...NO MORE **DEMANDS**, LEVIATHAN!

WE'VE DONE **EVERYTHING** YOU'VE ASKED.

PLEASE.

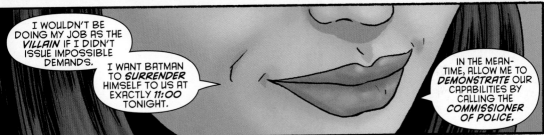

I WOULDN'T BE DOING MY JOB AS THE **VILLAIN** IF I DIDN'T ISSUE IMPOSSIBLE DEMANDS.

I WANT BATMAN TO **SURRENDER** HIMSELF TO US AT EXACTLY *11:00* TONIGHT.

IN THE MEANTIME, ALLOW ME TO **DEMONSTRATE** OUR CAPABILITIES BY CALLING THE **COMMISSIONER OF POLICE.**

...MR. MAYOR, WHAT?

I'M ON MY WAY TO A RIOT IN **COVENTRY.**

SOMEBODY HAS TO KEEP THIS DAMN CITY FROM **CONVULSING TO DEATH!**

...THEY SAID **WHAT?**

A DEMONSTRATION OF **WHAT?**

SIR.

THE CARS WON'T **START.**

THE SUPPLIERS SENT US **CONTAMINATED GAS.**

LEVIATHAN.

THEY'RE SHUTTING DOWN THE CITY'S **NERVOUS SYSTEM.**

BLOCKING ITS **CIRCULATION.**

THEY'RE **KILLING** US.

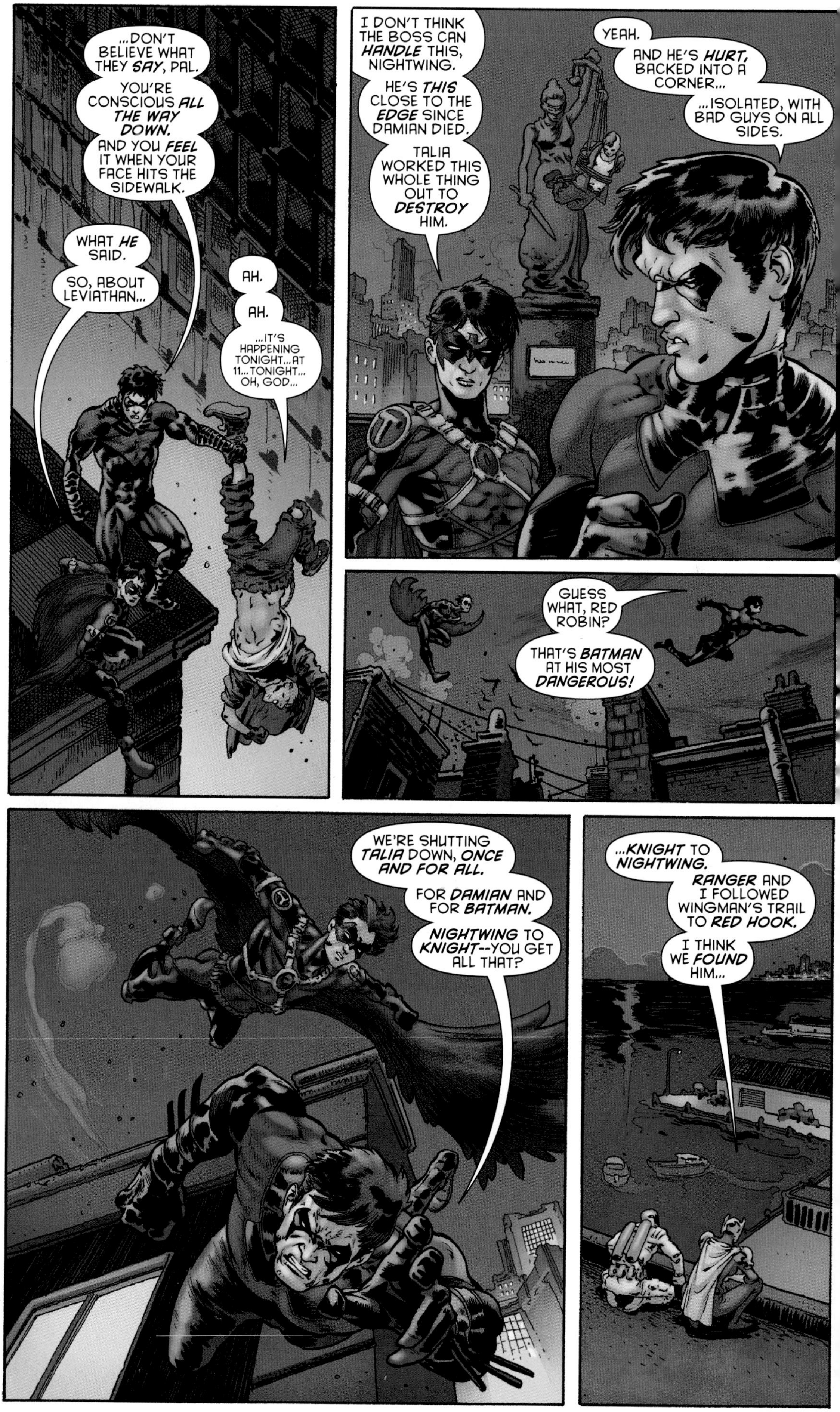
...DON'T BELIEVE WHAT THEY SAY, PAL.
YOU'RE CONSCIOUS ALL THE WAY DOWN.
AND YOU FEEL IT WHEN YOUR FACE HITS THE SIDEWALK.
WHAT HE SAID.
SO, ABOUT LEVIATHAN...
AH.
AH.
...IT'S HAPPENING TONIGHT...AT 11...TONIGHT... OH, GOD...
I DON'T THINK THE BOSS CAN HANDLE THIS, NIGHTWING.
HE'S THIS CLOSE TO THE EDGE SINCE DAMIAN DIED.
TALIA WORKED THIS WHOLE THING OUT TO DESTROY HIM.
YEAH.
AND HE'S HURT, BACKED INTO A CORNER...
...ISOLATED, WITH BAD GUYS ON ALL SIDES.
GUESS WHAT, RED ROBIN?
THAT'S BATMAN AT HIS MOST DANGEROUS!
WE'RE SHUTTING TALIA DOWN, ONCE AND FOR ALL.
FOR DAMIAN AND FOR BATMAN.
NIGHTWING TO KNIGHT--YOU GET ALL THAT?
...KNIGHT TO NIGHTWING.
RANGER AND I FOLLOWED WINGMAN'S TRAIL TO RED HOOK.
I THINK WE FOUND HIM...

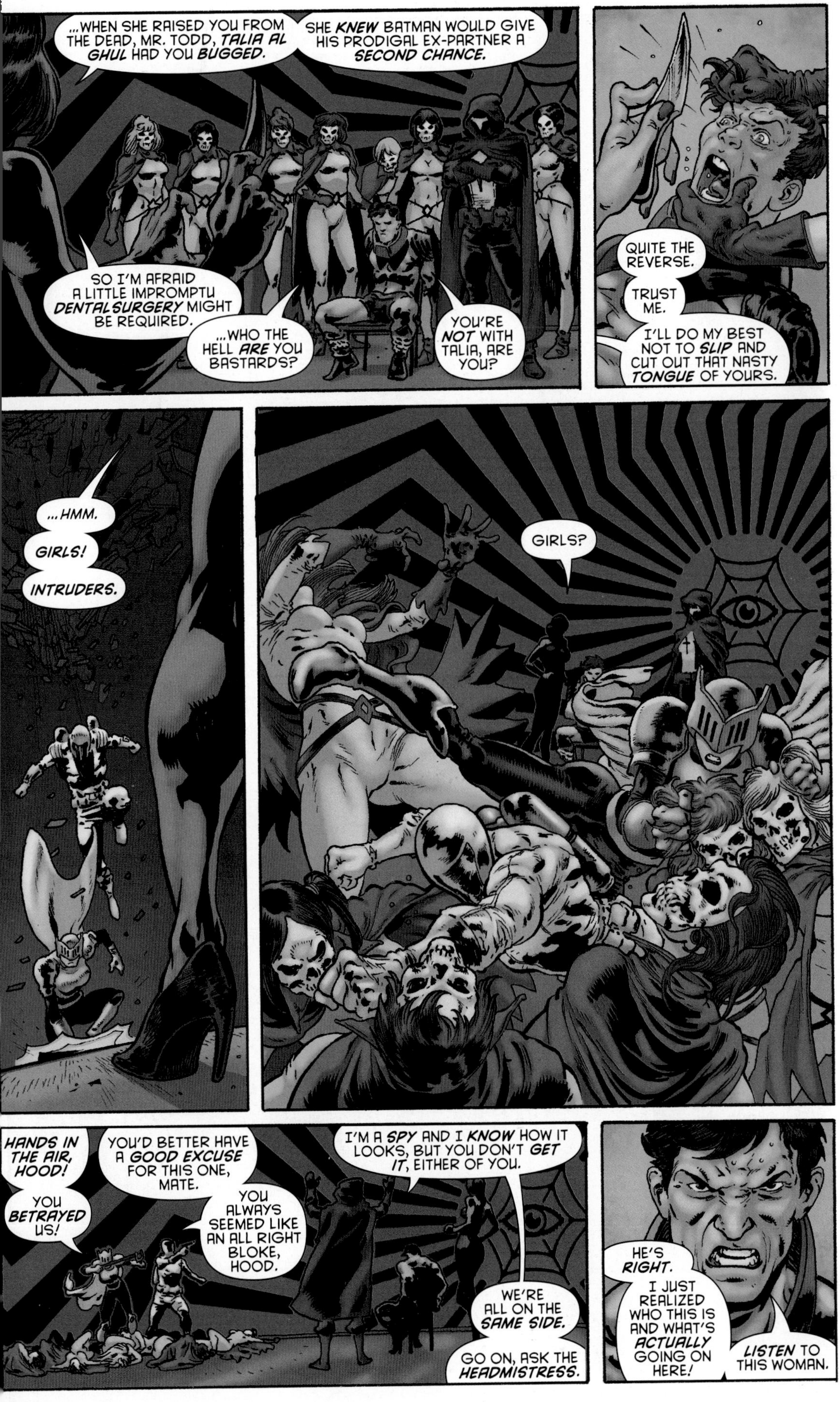
...WHEN SHE RAISED YOU FROM THE DEAD, MR. TODD, TALIA AL GHUL HAD YOU BUGGED.
SHE KNEW BATMAN WOULD GIVE HIS PRODIGAL EX-PARTNER A SECOND CHANCE.
SO I'M AFRAID A LITTLE IMPROMPTU DENTAL SURGERY MIGHT BE REQUIRED.
...WHO THE HELL ARE YOU BASTARDS?
YOU'RE NOT WITH TALIA, ARE YOU?
QUITE THE REVERSE.
TRUST ME.
I'LL DO MY BEST NOT TO SLIP AND CUT OUT THAT NASTY TONGUE OF YOURS.
...HMM.
GIRLS!
INTRUDERS.
GIRLS?
HANDS IN THE AIR, HOOD!
YOU BETRAYED US!
YOU'D BETTER HAVE A GOOD EXCUSE FOR THIS ONE, MATE.
YOU ALWAYS SEEMED LIKE AN ALL RIGHT BLOKE, HOOD.
I'M A SPY AND I KNOW HOW IT LOOKS, BUT YOU DON'T GET IT, EITHER OF YOU.
WE'RE ALL ON THE SAME SIDE.
GO ON, ASK THE HEADMISTRESS.
HE'S RIGHT.
I JUST REALIZED WHO THIS IS AND WHAT'S ACTUALLY GOING ON HERE!
LISTEN TO THIS WOMAN.

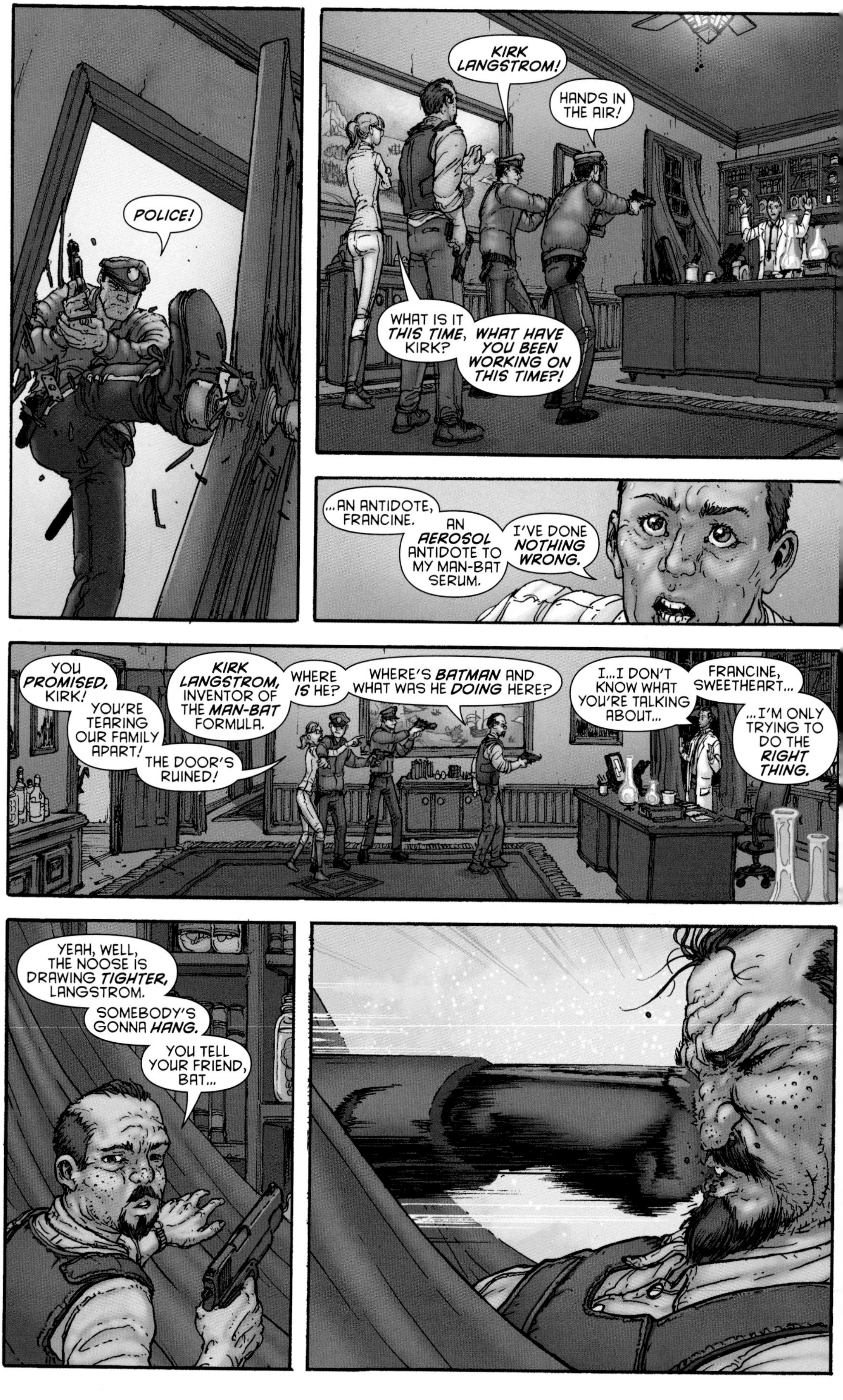
POLICE!
KIRK LANGSTROM!
HANDS IN THE AIR!
WHAT IS IT THIS TIME, KIRK?
WHAT HAVE YOU BEEN WORKING ON THIS TIME?!
...AN ANTIDOTE, FRANCINE.
AN AEROSOL ANTIDOTE TO MY MAN-BAT SERUM.
I'VE DONE NOTHING WRONG.
YOU PROMISED, KIRK!
YOU'RE TEARING OUR FAMILY APART!
KIRK LANGSTROM, INVENTOR OF THE MAN-BAT FORMULA.
THE DOOR'S RUINED!
WHERE IS HE?
WHERE'S BATMAN AND WHAT WAS HE DOING HERE?
I...I DON'T KNOW WHAT YOU'RE TALKING ABOUT...
FRANCINE, SWEETHEART...
...I'M ONLY TRYING TO DO THE RIGHT THING.
YEAH, WELL, THE NOOSE IS DRAWING TIGHTER, LANGSTROM.
SOMEBODY'S GONNA HANG.
YOU TELL YOUR FRIEND, BAT...

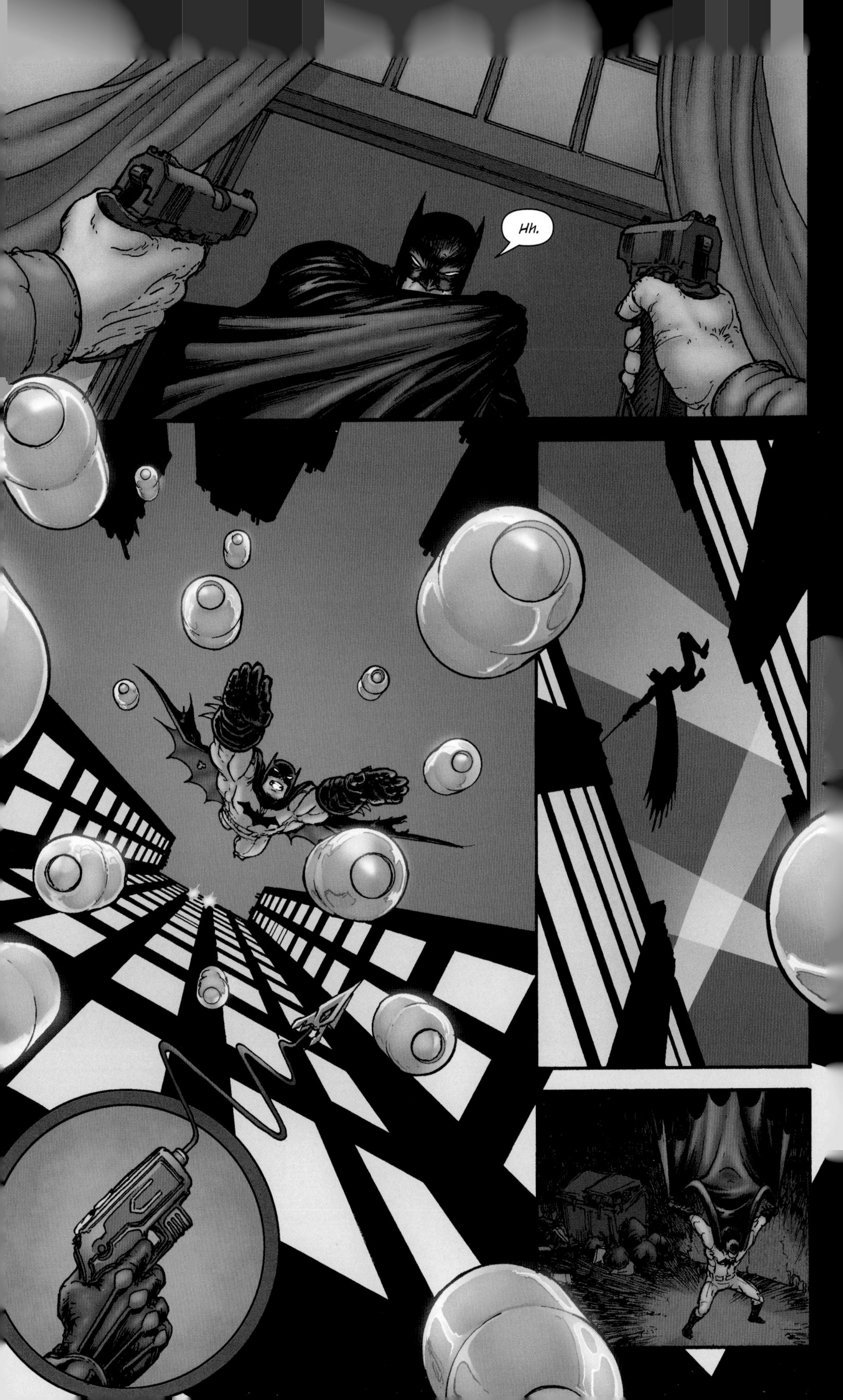
Hh.

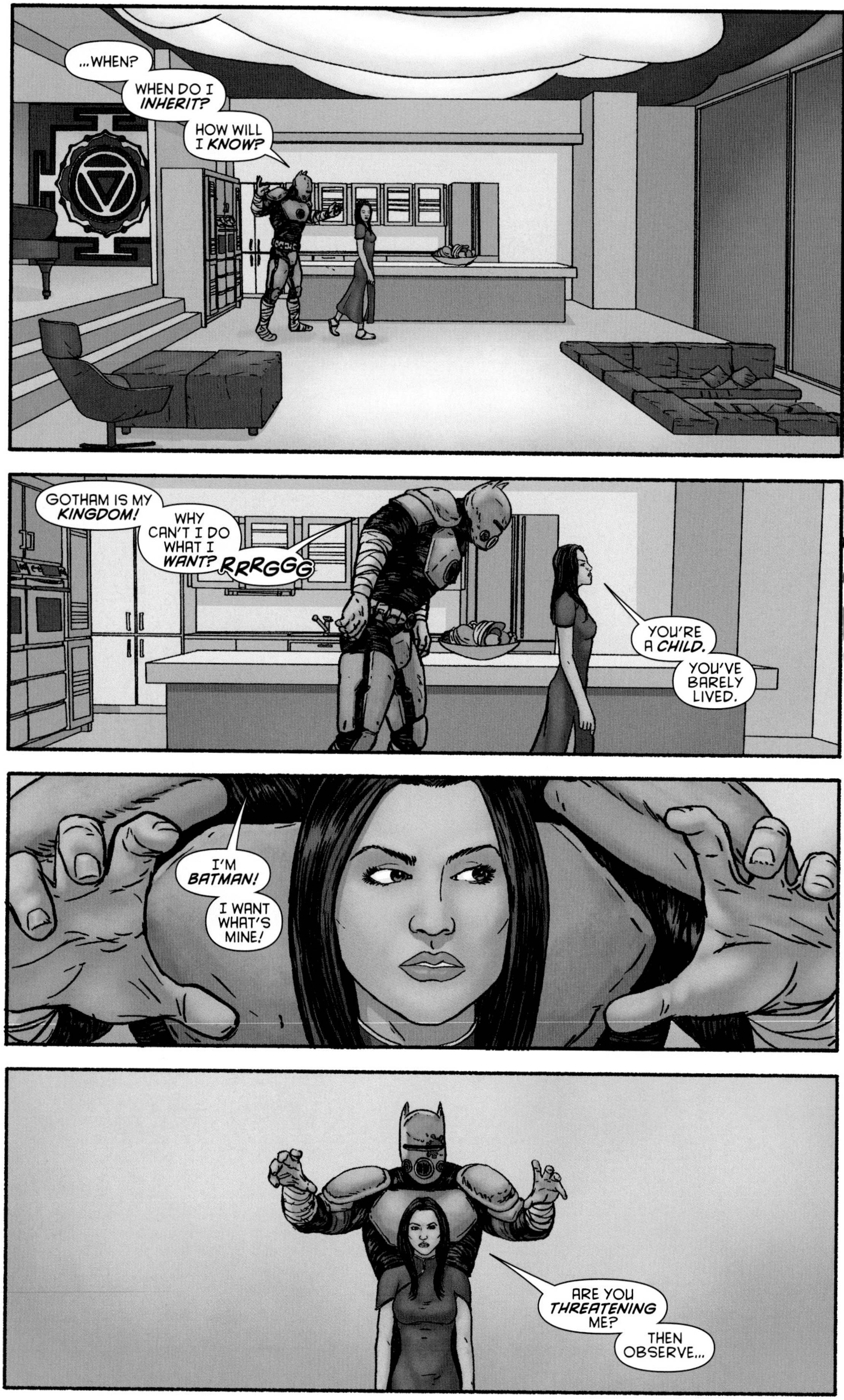
...WHEN?
WHEN DO I *INHERIT?*
HOW WILL I *KNOW?*
GOTHAM IS MY *KINGDOM!*
WHY CAN'T I DO WHAT I *WANT?* RRRGGG
YOU'RE A *CHILD.*
YOU'VE BARELY LIVED.
I'M *BATMAN!*
I WANT WHAT'S MINE!
ARE YOU *THREATENING* ME?
THEN OBSERVE...

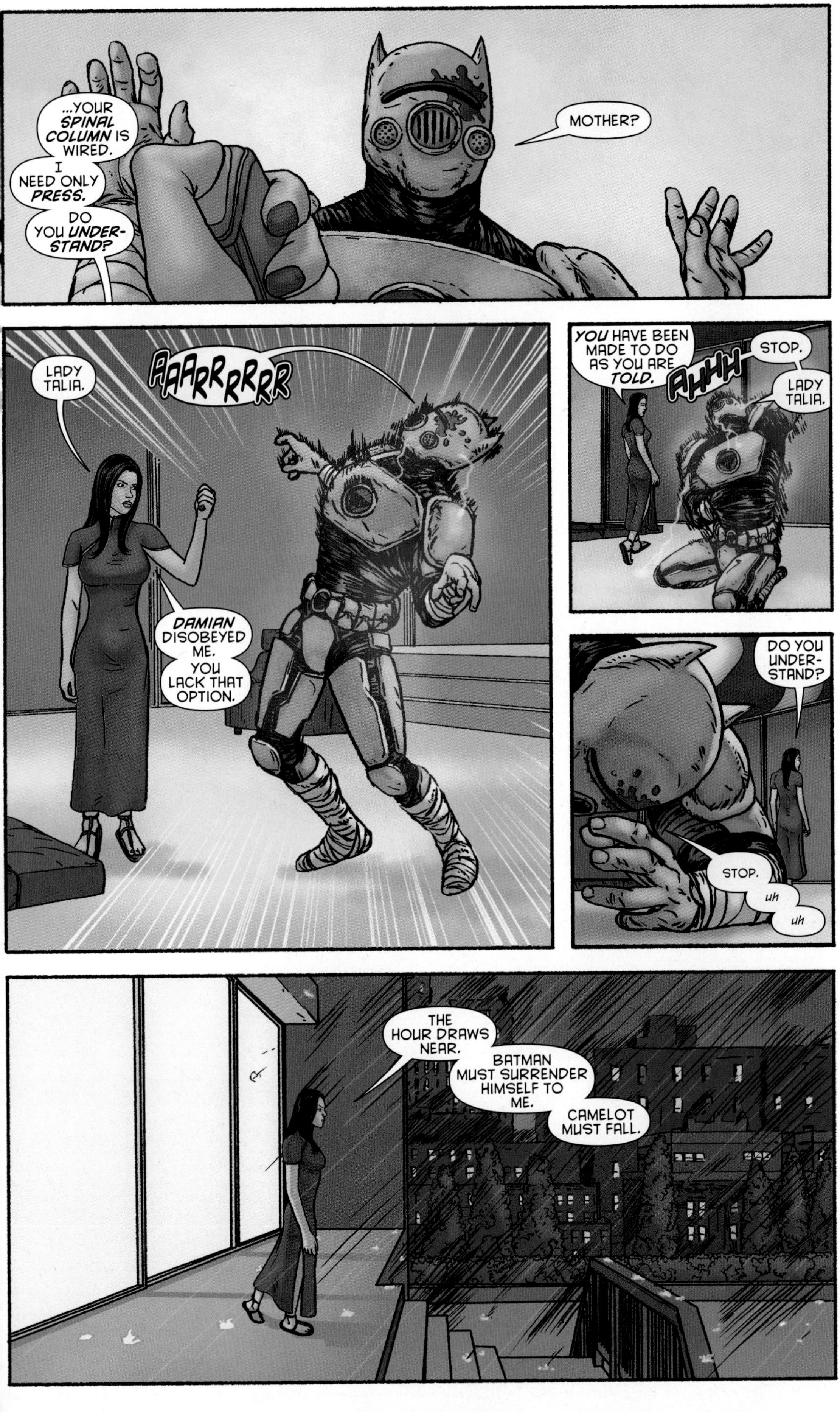
...YOUR SPINAL COLUMN IS WIRED.
I NEED ONLY PRESS.
DO YOU UNDERSTAND?
MOTHER?
LADY TALIA.
AAARRRRRR
DAMIAN DISOBEYED ME.
YOU LACK THAT OPTION.
YOU HAVE BEEN MADE TO DO AS YOU ARE TOLD.
AHHH
STOP.
LADY TALIA.
DO YOU UNDERSTAND?
STOP.
uh
uh
THE HOUR DRAWS NEAR.
BATMAN MUST SURRENDER HIMSELF TO ME.
CAMELOT MUST FALL.

Criminals are a superstitious, cowardly lot.

My disguise must be able to strike terror into their hearts.

I must be a creature of the night.

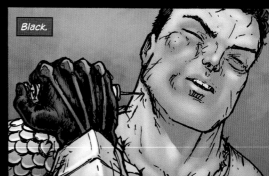

Black.

Terrible.

Yes, father.

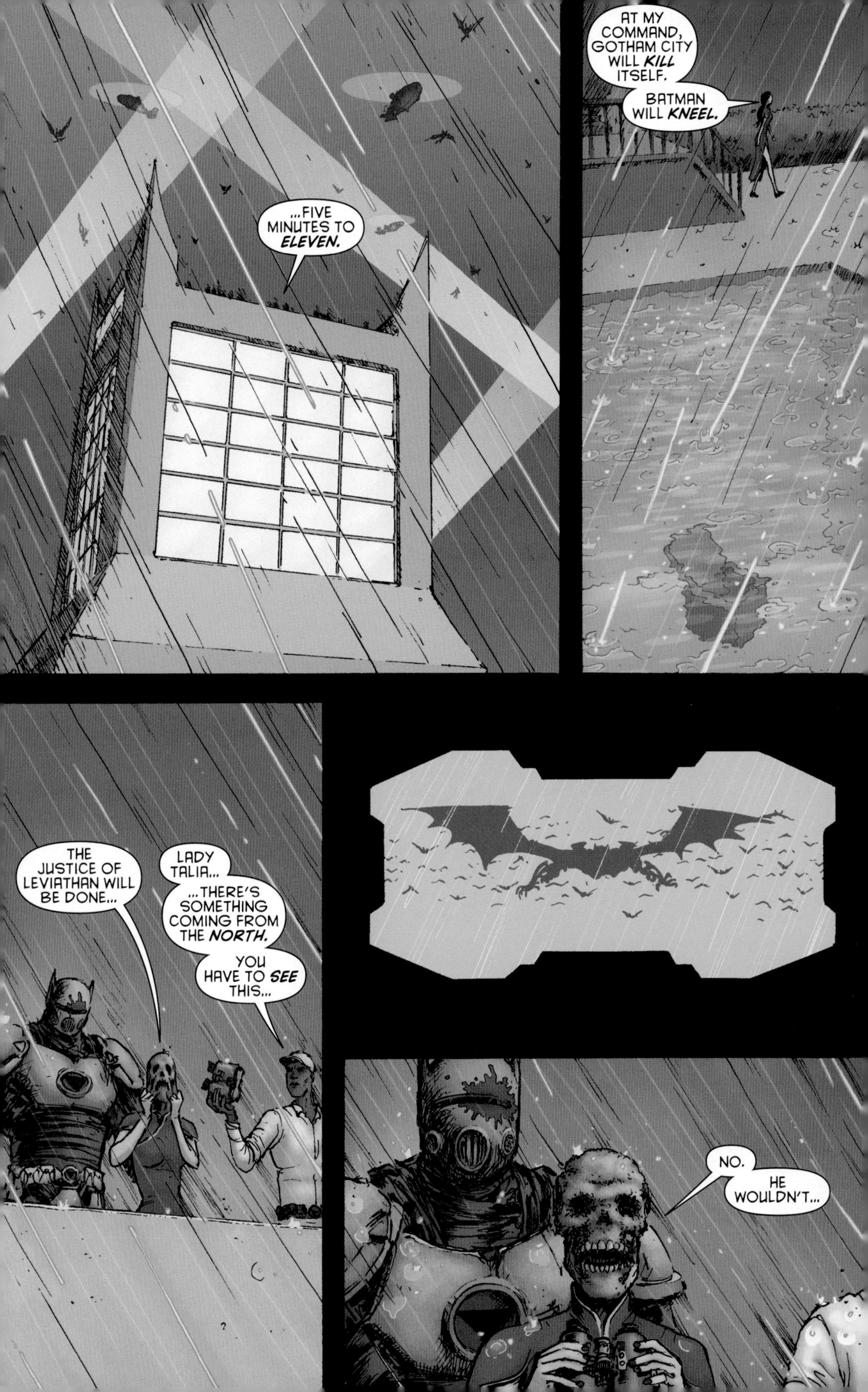
...FIVE MINUTES TO ELEVEN.
AT MY COMMAND, GOTHAM CITY WILL KILL ITSELF.
BATMAN WILL KNEEL.
THE JUSTICE OF LEVIATHAN WILL BE DONE...
LADY TALIA...
...THERE'S SOMETHING COMING FROM THE NORTH.
YOU HAVE TO SEE THIS...
NO.
HE WOULDN'T...

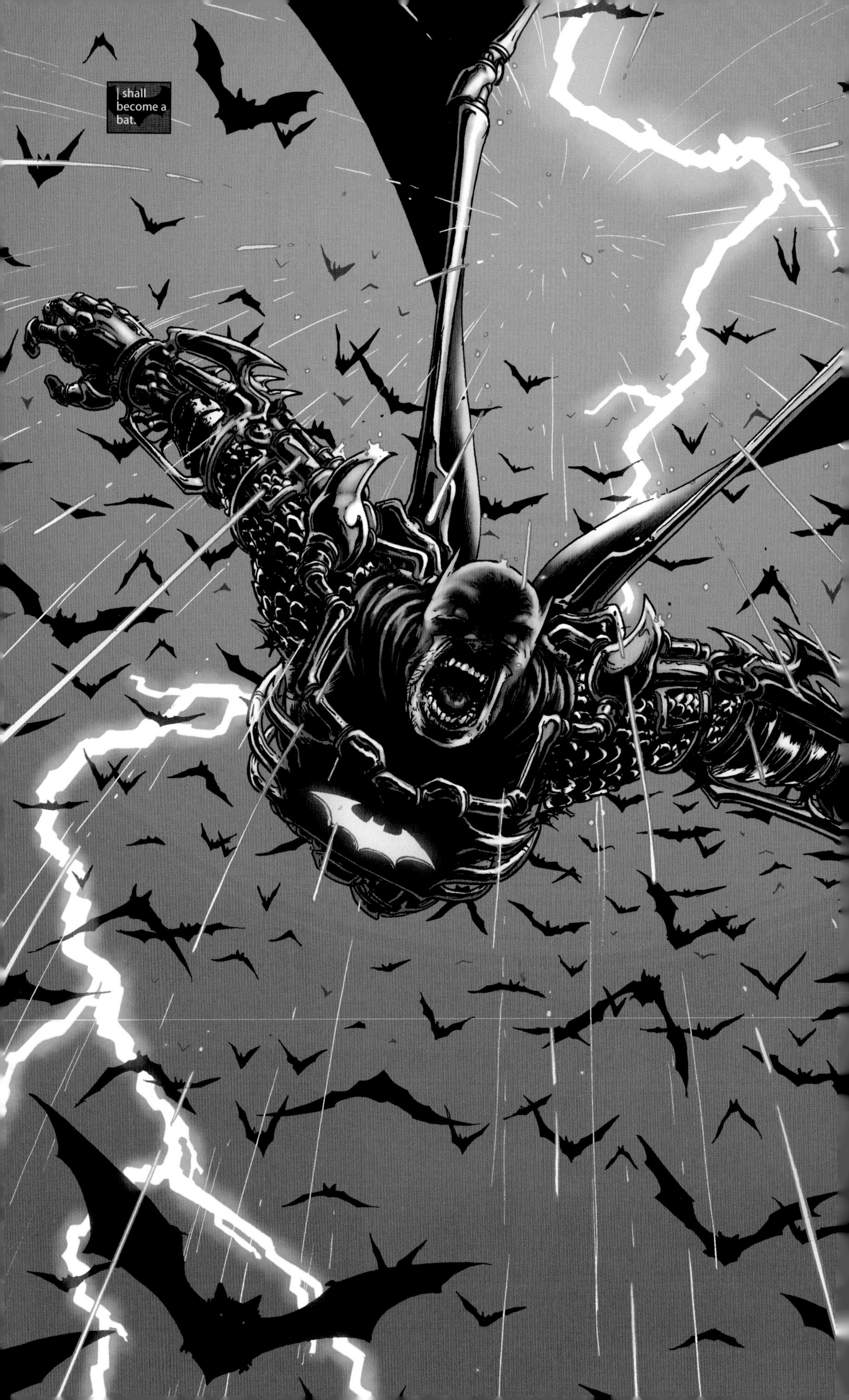
I shall become a bat.

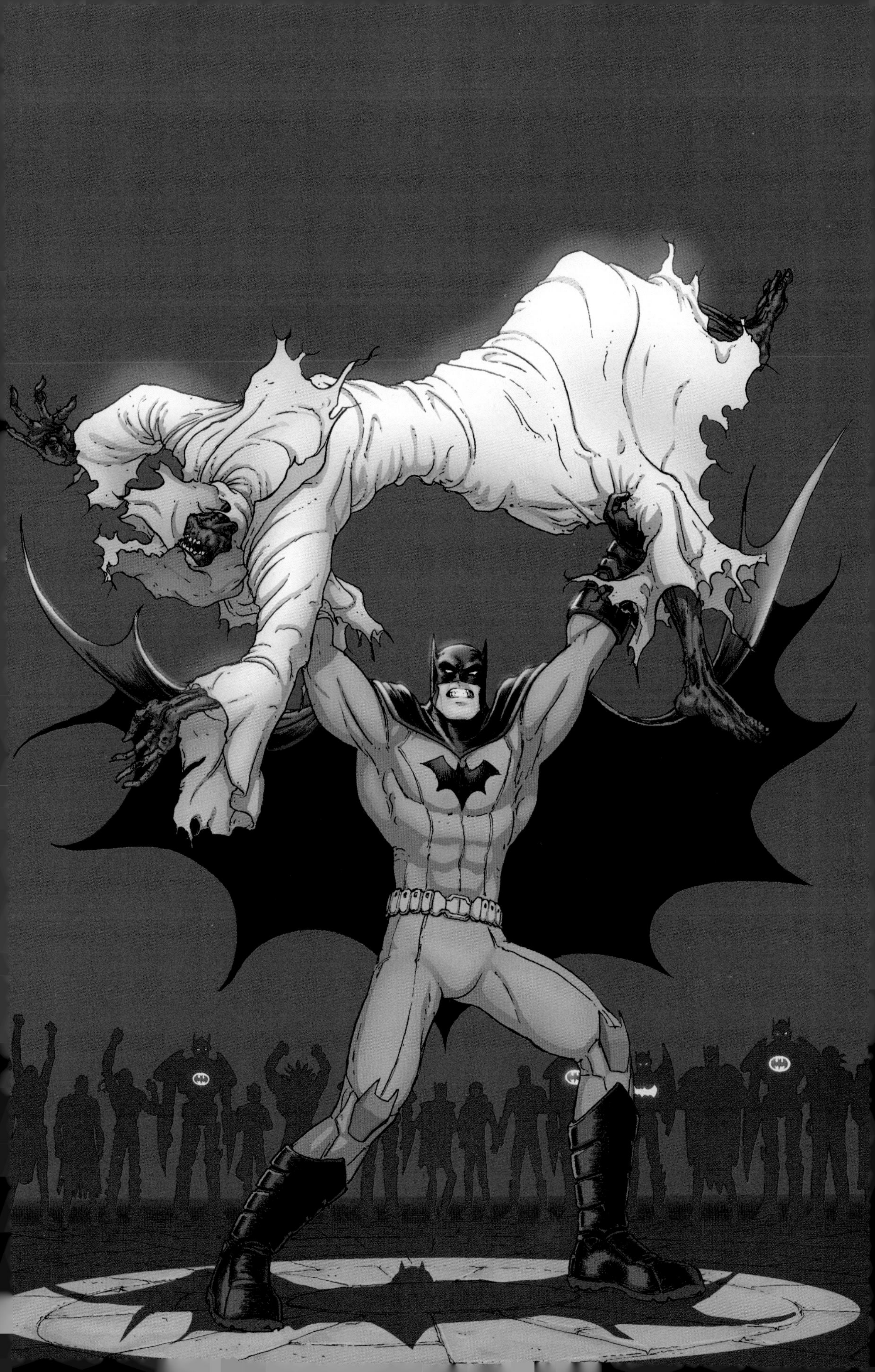

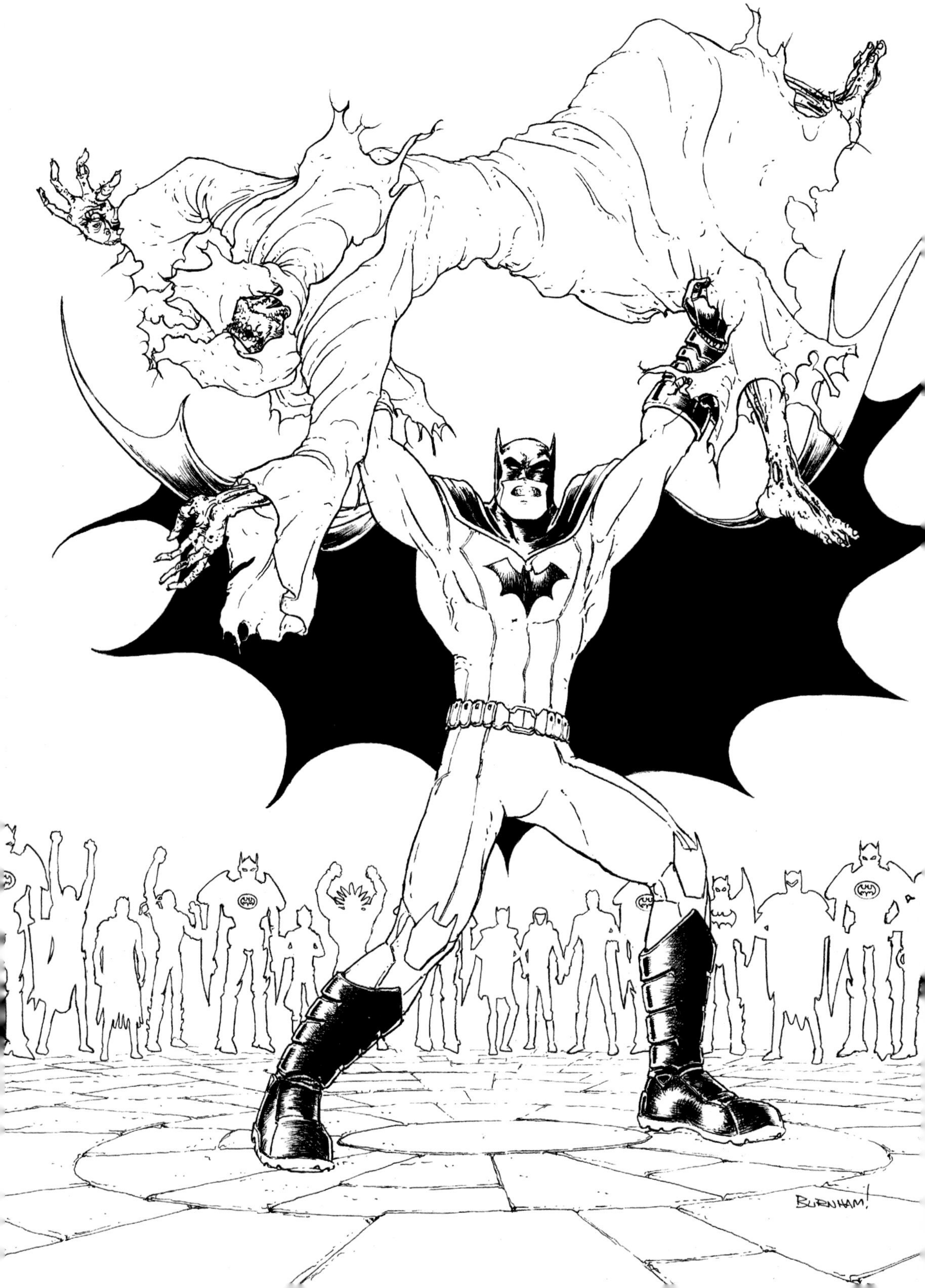
BURNHAM!

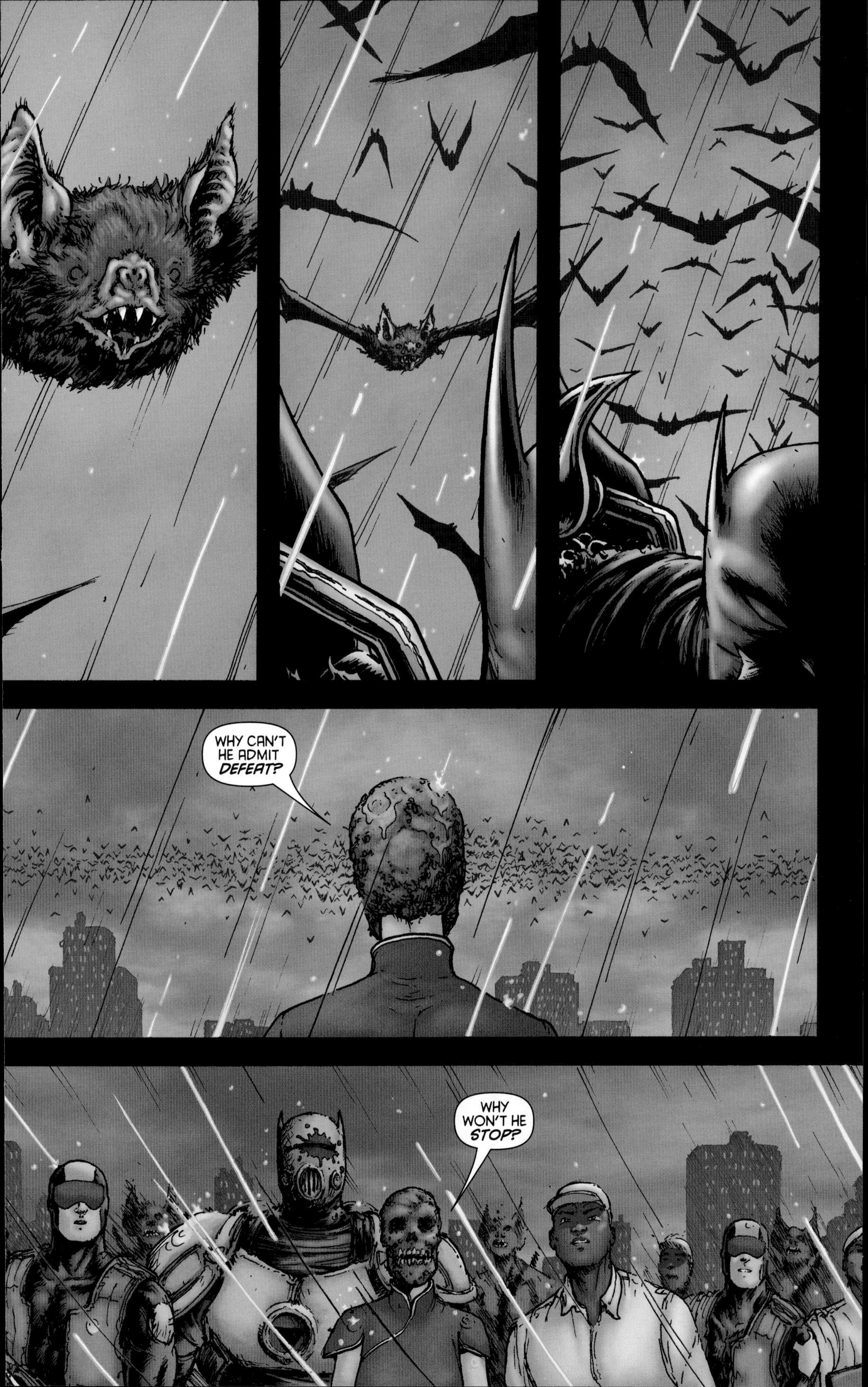
WHY CAN'T HE ADMIT DEFEAT?
WHY WON'T HE STOP?

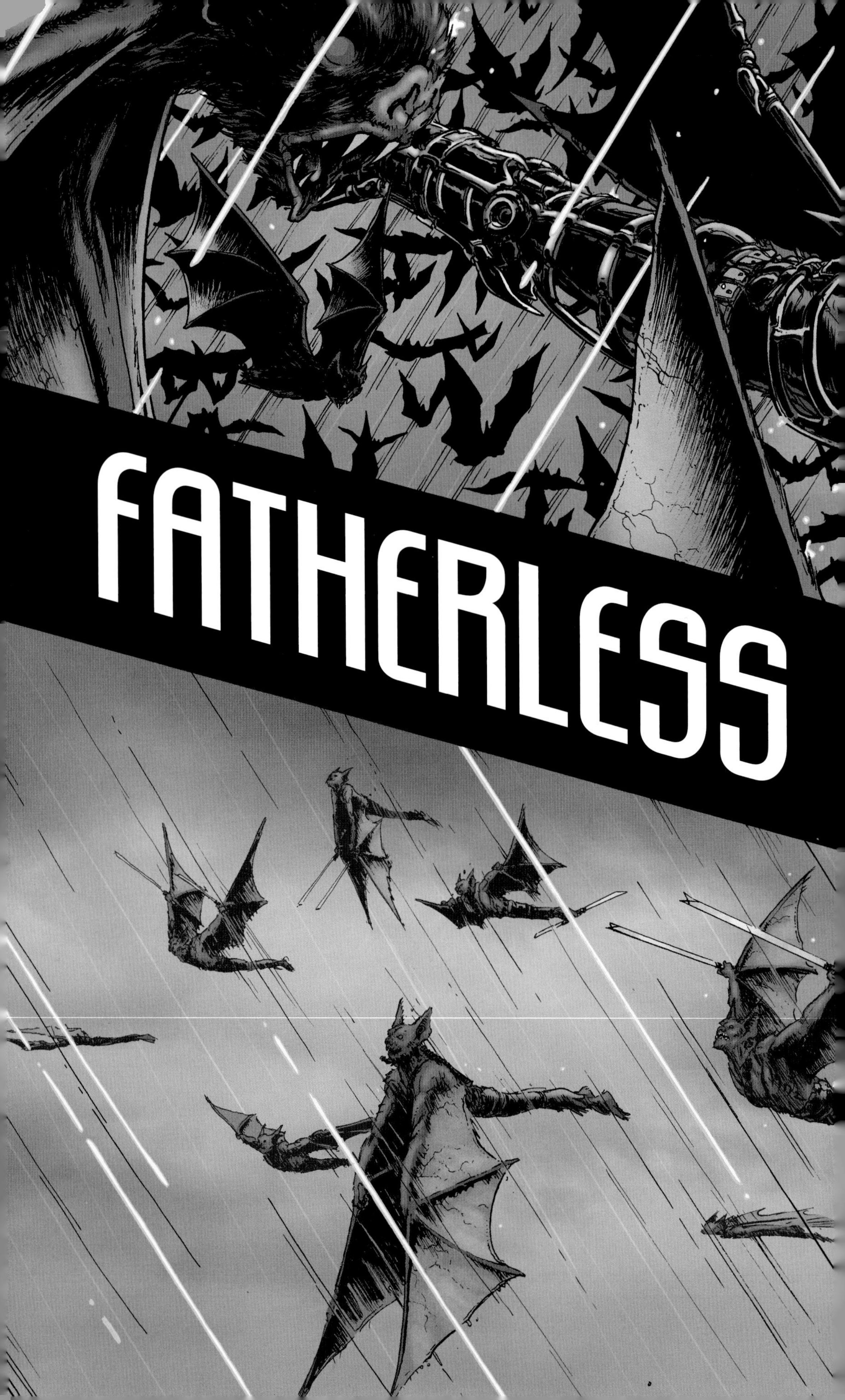
FATHERLESS

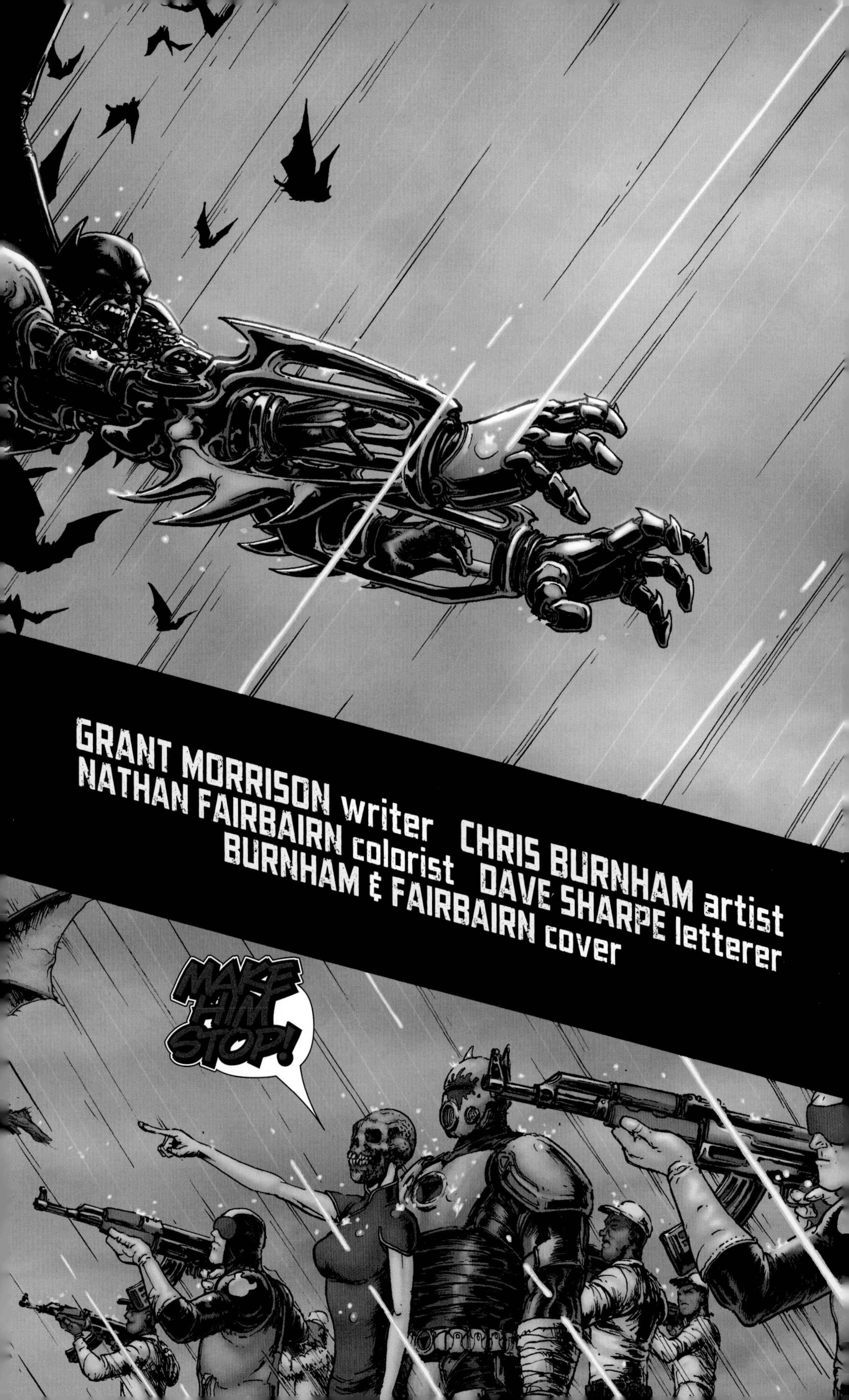
GRANT MORRISON writer CHRIS BURNHAM artist
NATHAN FAIRBAIRN colorist DAVE SHARPE letterer
BURNHAM & FAIRBAIRN cover
MAKE HIM STOP!

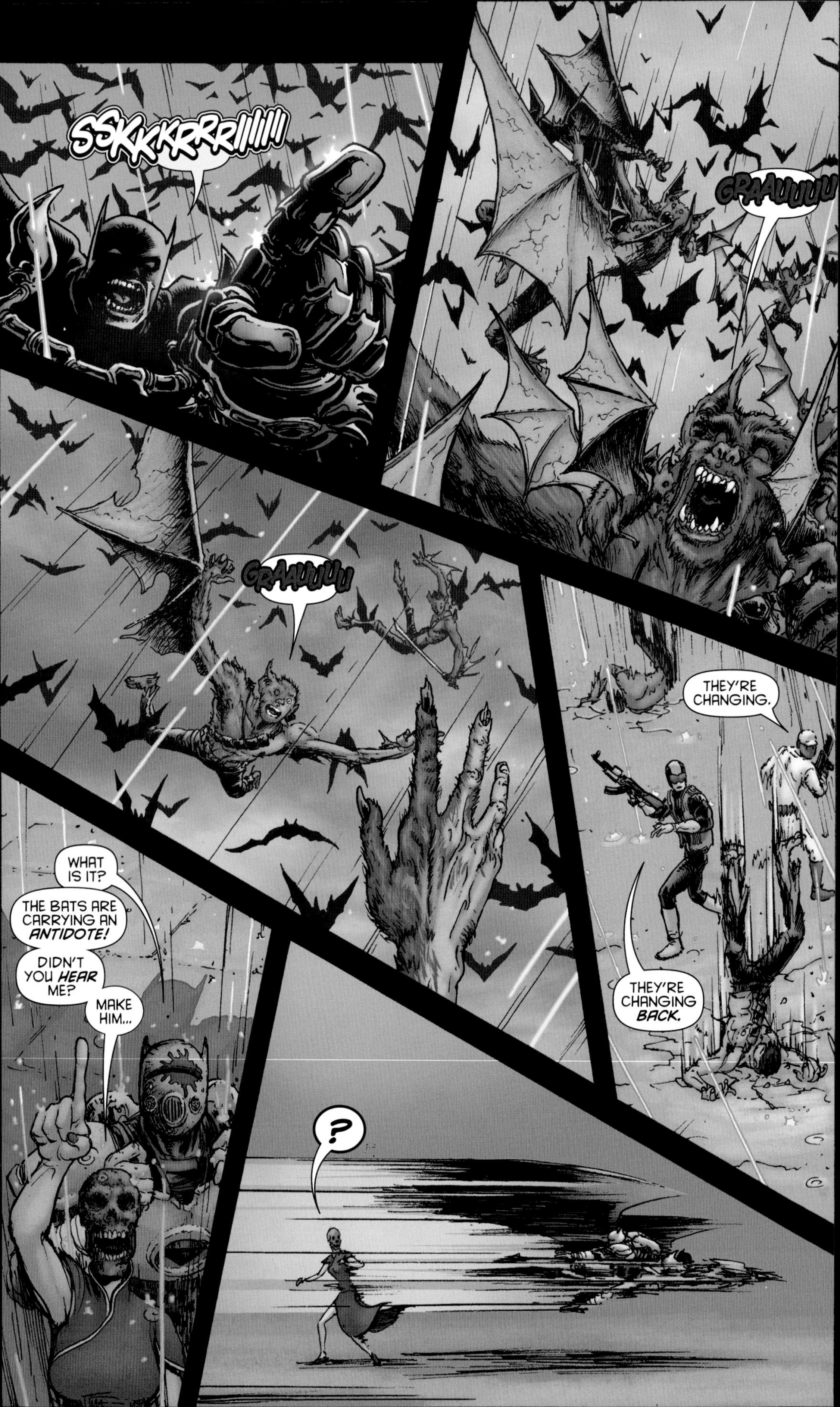

SSKKKRRR!!!!!!
GRAAUUUU
GRAAUUUU
THEY'RE CHANGING.
THEY'RE CHANGING *BACK.*
WHAT IS IT?
THE BATS ARE CARRYING AN *ANTIDOTE!*
DIDN'T YOU *HEAR* ME?
MAKE HIM...
?

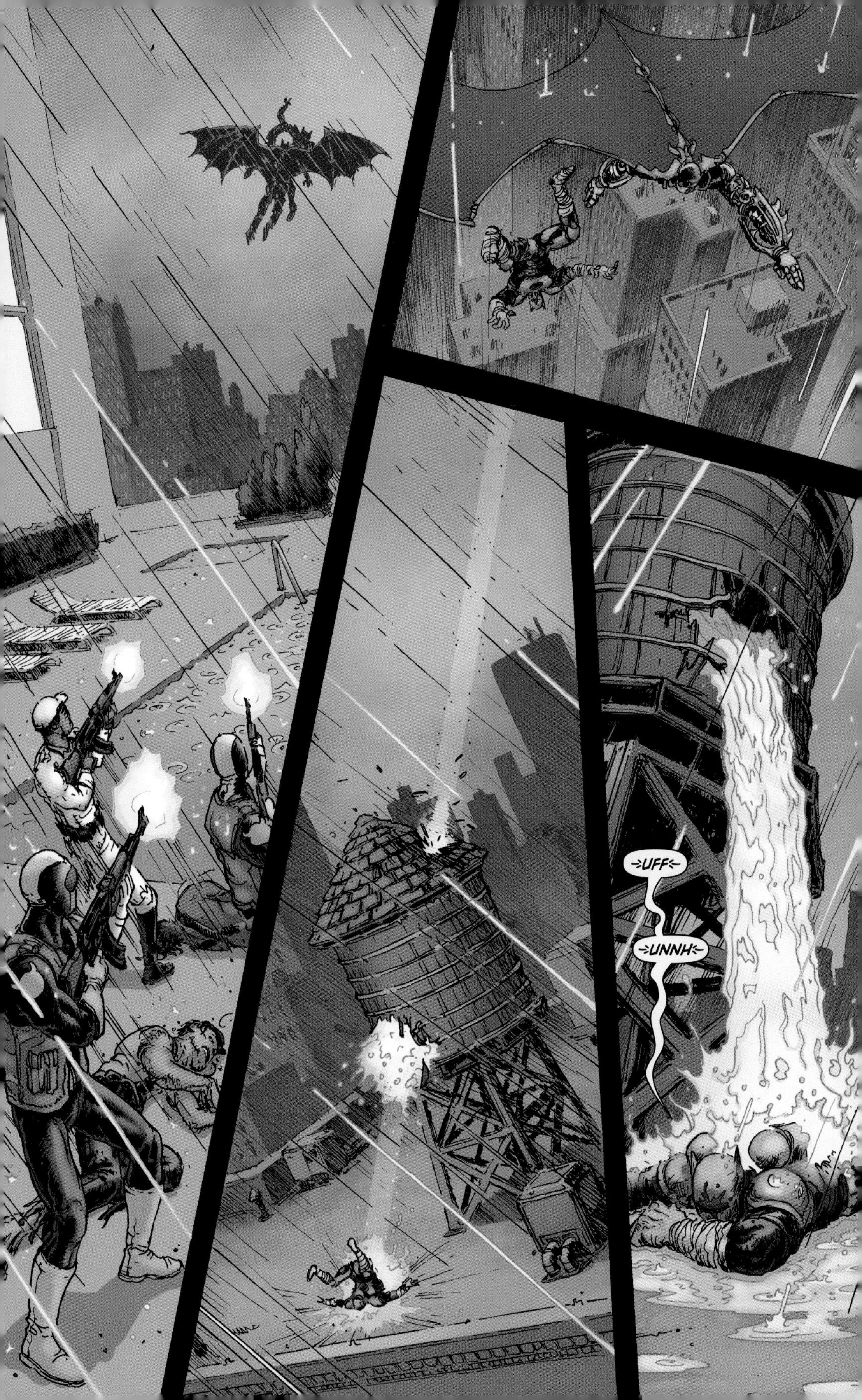
UFF
UNNH

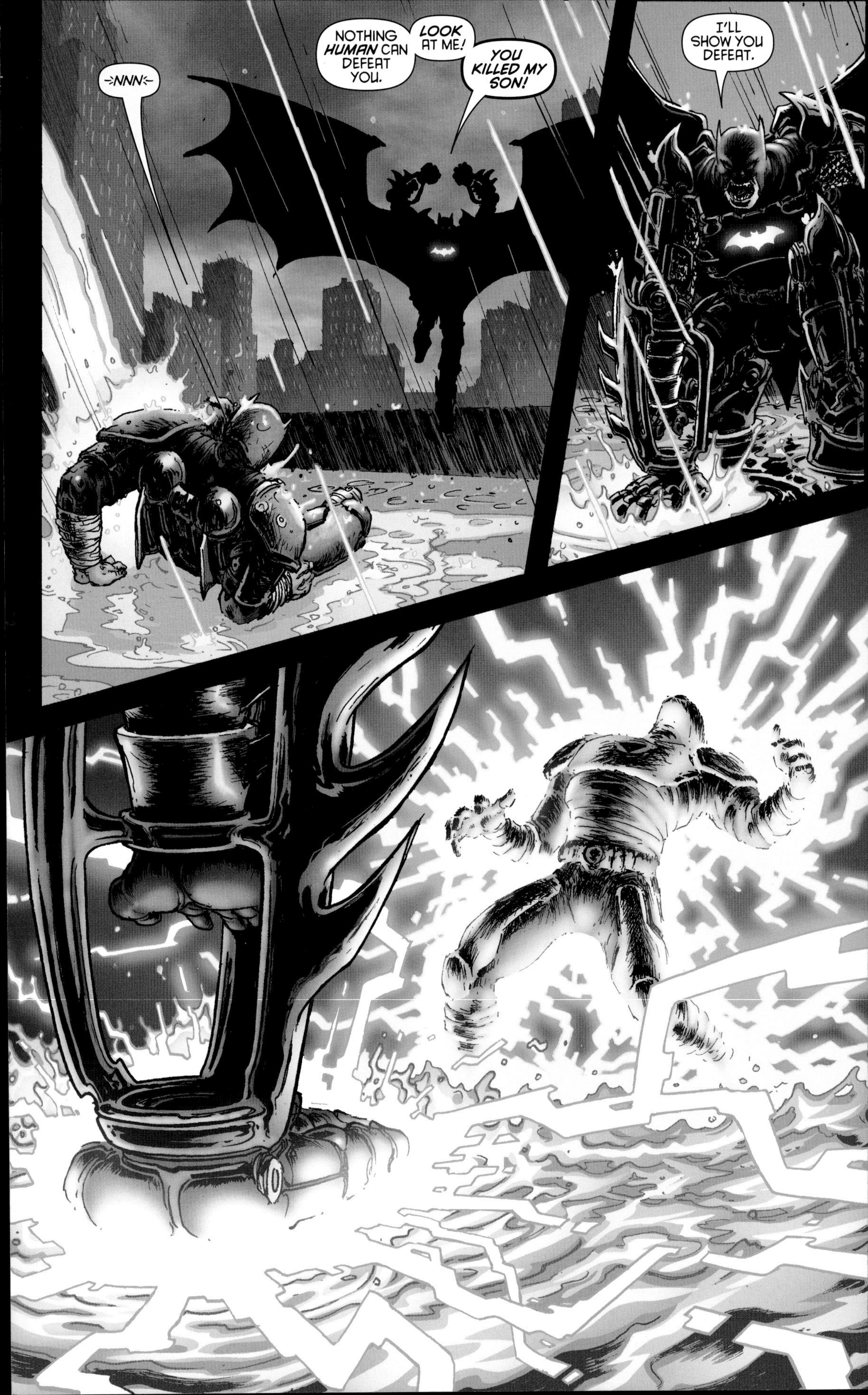

=NNN=
NOTHING HUMAN CAN DEFEAT YOU.
LOOK AT ME!
YOU KILLED MY SON!
I'LL SHOW YOU DEFEAT.

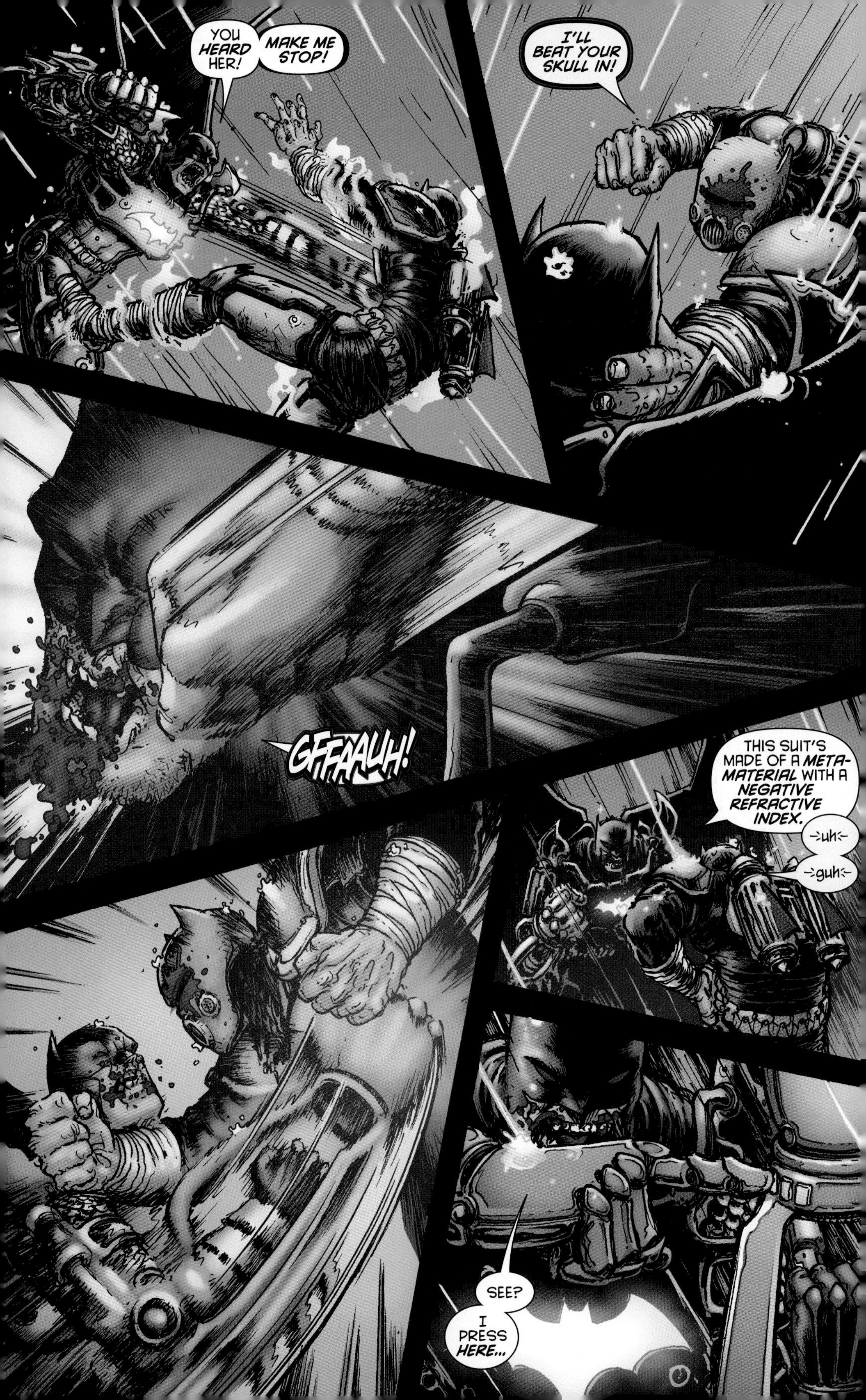

YOU HEARD HER!
MAKE ME STOP!
I'LL BEAT YOUR SKULL IN!
GFFAAUH!
THIS SUIT'S MADE OF A META-MATERIAL WITH A NEGATIVE REFRACTIVE INDEX.
uh
guh
SEE?
I PRESS HERE...

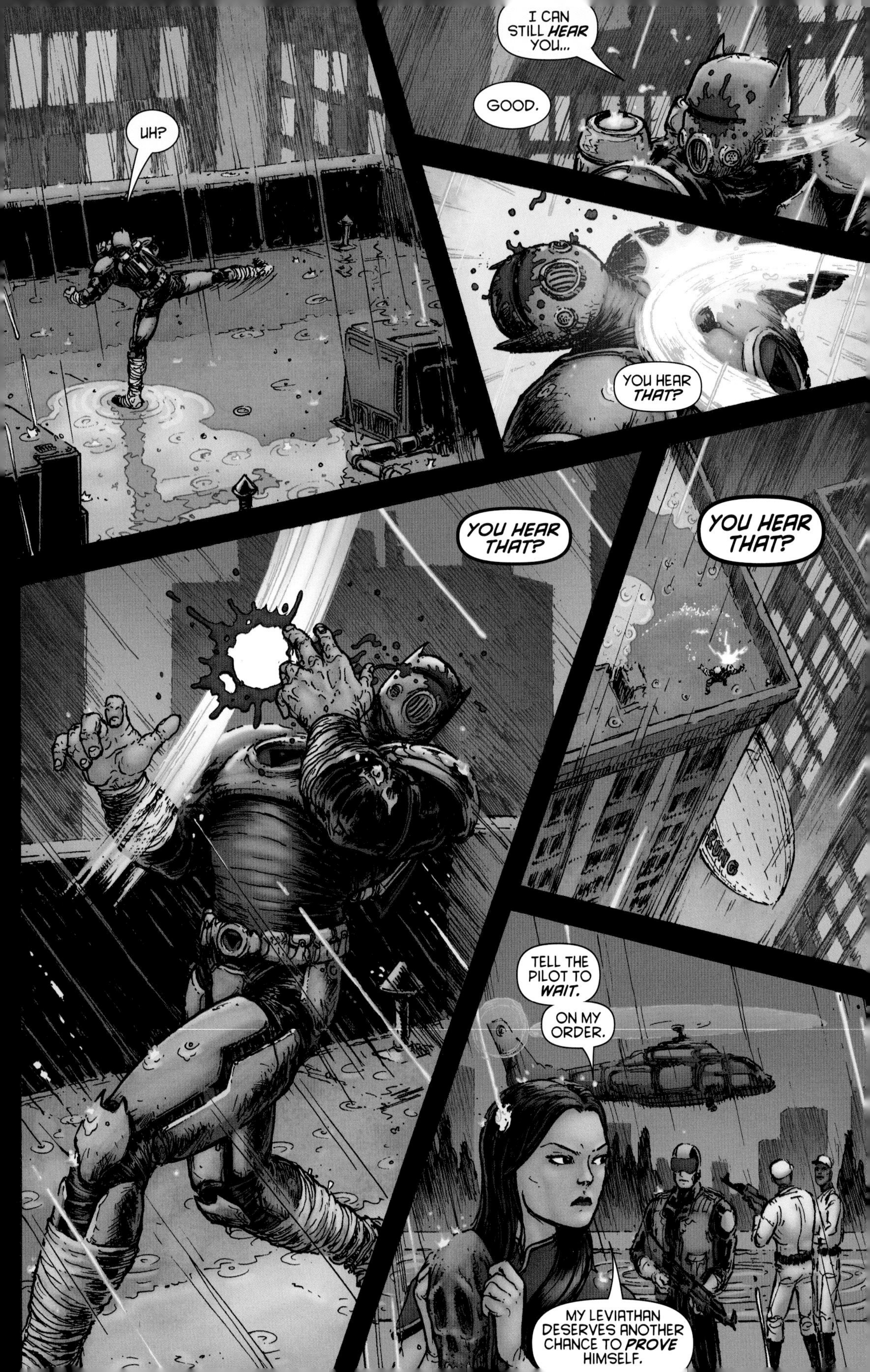
UH?
I CAN STILL *HEAR* YOU...
GOOD.
YOU HEAR *THAT?*
YOU HEAR THAT?
YOU HEAR THAT?
TELL THE PILOT TO *WAIT.*
ON MY ORDER.
MY LEVIATHAN DESERVES ANOTHER CHANCE TO *PROVE* HIMSELF.

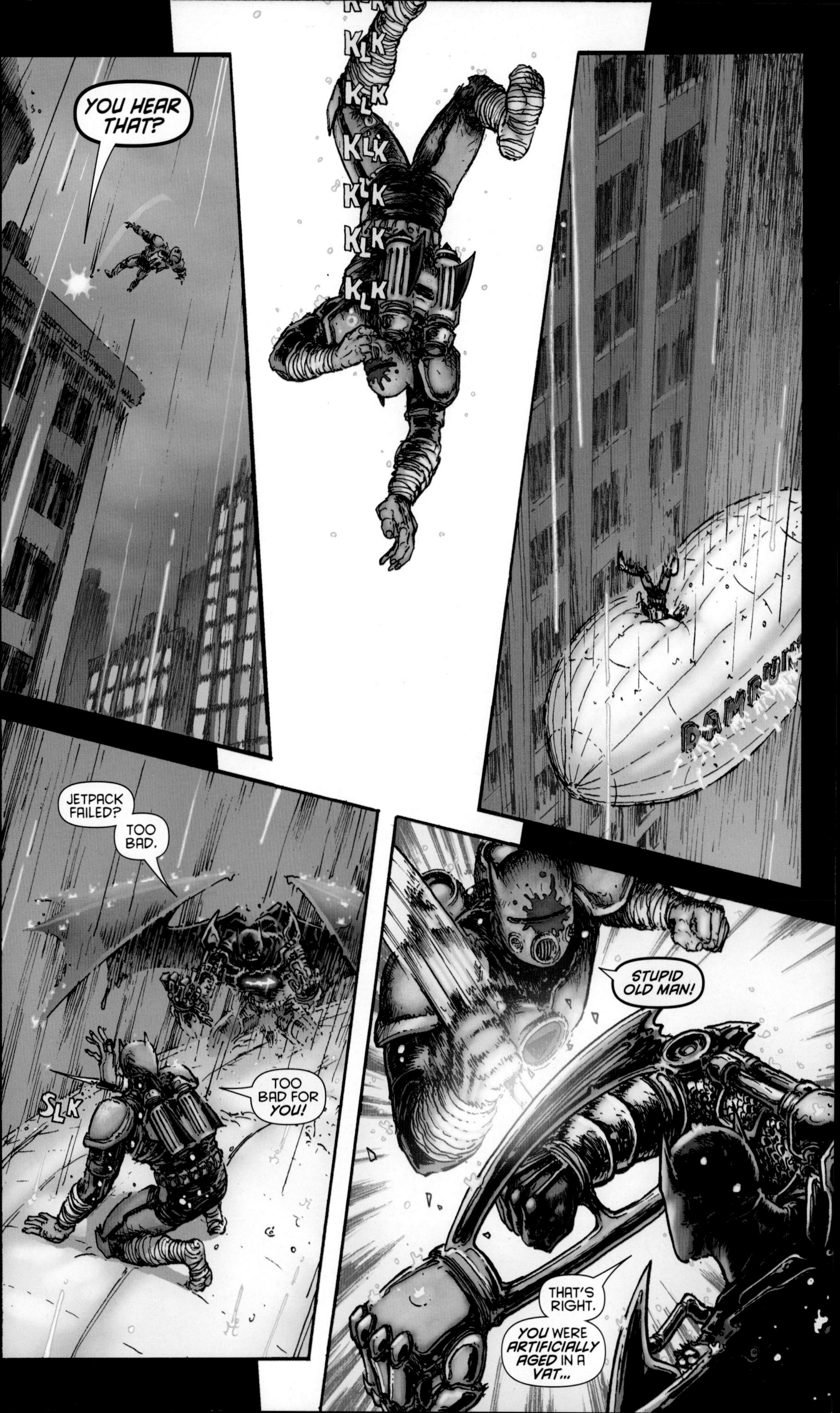
YOU HEAR THAT?
KLK
KLK
KLK
KLK
KLK
KLK
JETPACK FAILED?
TOO BAD.
SLK
TOO BAD FOR YOU!
STUPID OLD MAN!
THAT'S RIGHT.
YOU WERE ARTIFICIALLY AGED IN A VAT...

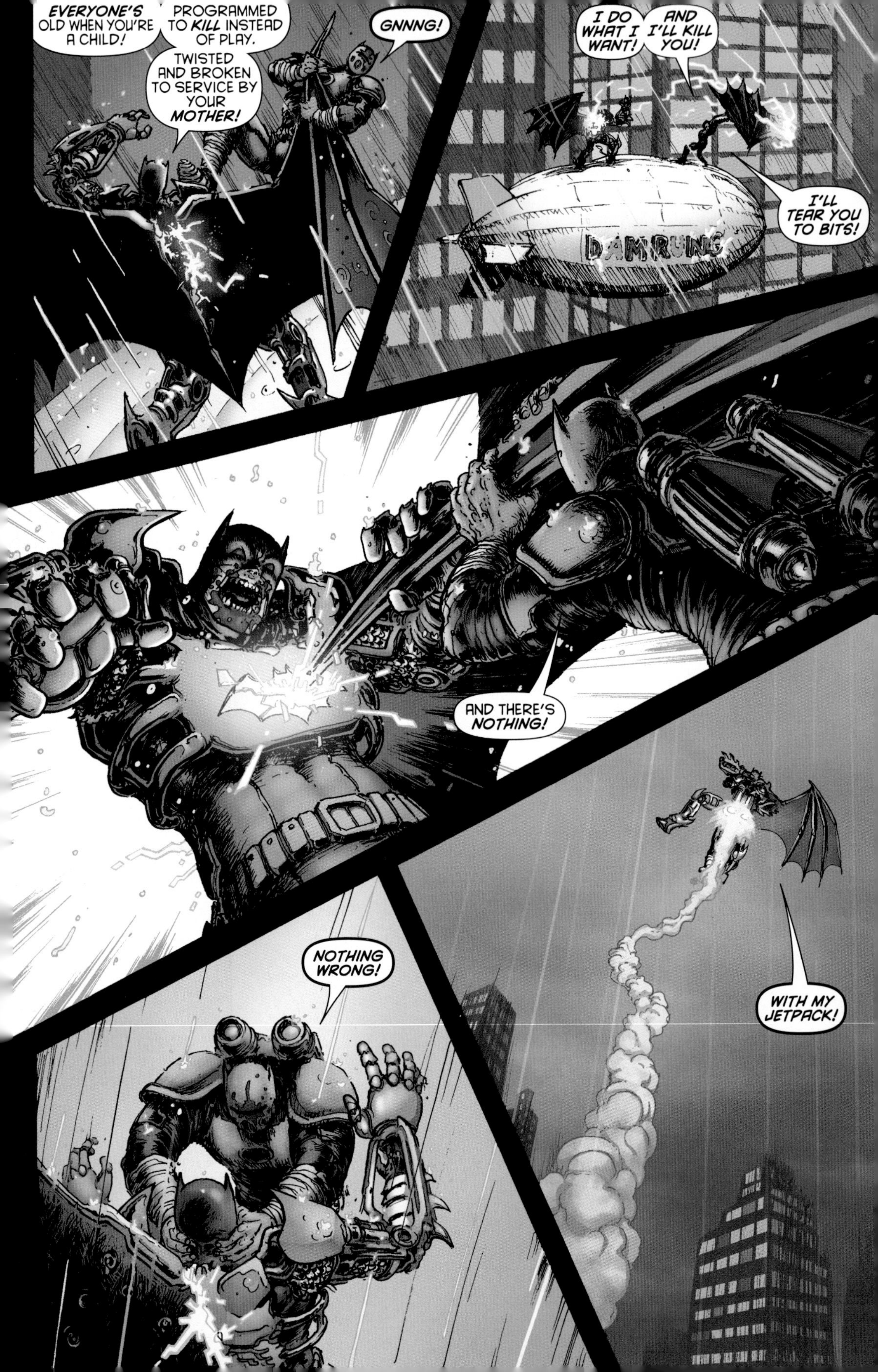
EVERYONE'S OLD WHEN YOU'RE A CHILD!
PROGRAMMED TO KILL INSTEAD OF PLAY.
TWISTED AND BROKEN TO SERVICE BY YOUR MOTHER!
GNNNG!
I DO WHAT I WANT!
AND I'LL KILL YOU!
I'LL TEAR YOU TO BITS!
DAMRUNG
AND THERE'S NOTHING!
NOTHING WRONG!
WITH MY JETPACK!

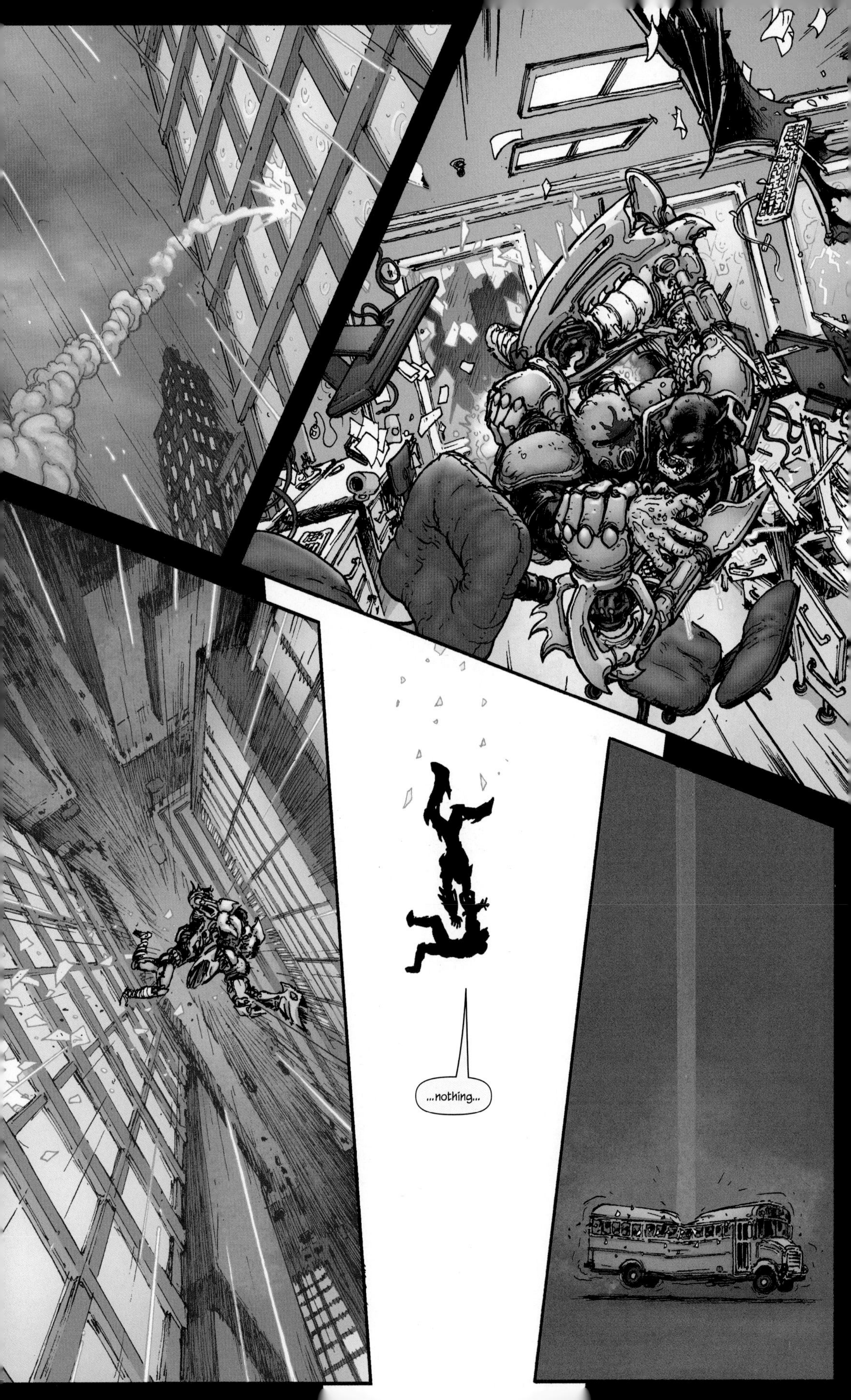
...nothing...

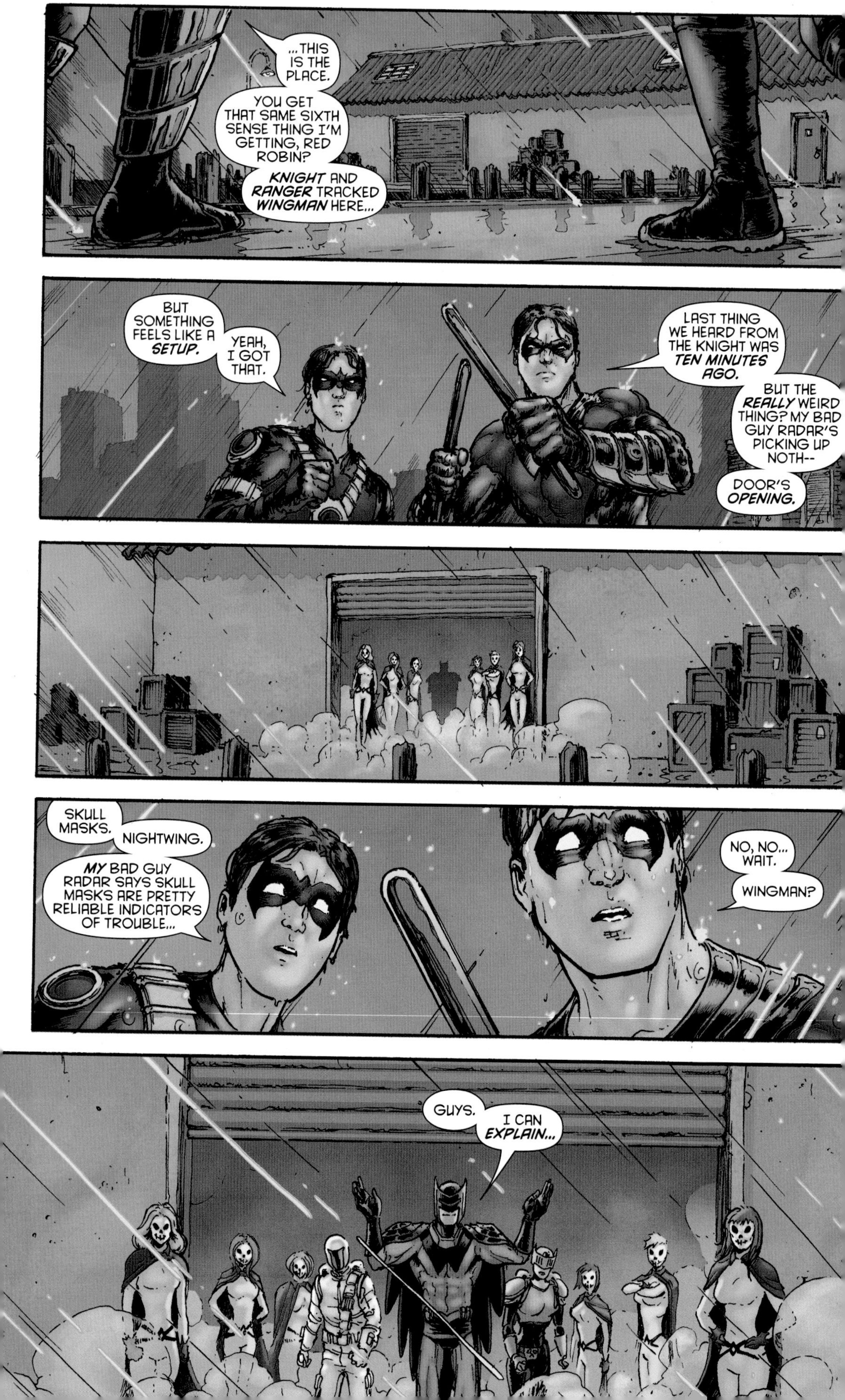
...THIS IS THE PLACE.
YOU GET THAT SAME SIXTH SENSE THING I'M GETTING, RED ROBIN?
KNIGHT AND RANGER TRACKED WINGMAN HERE...
BUT SOMETHING FEELS LIKE A SETUP.
YEAH, I GOT THAT.
LAST THING WE HEARD FROM THE KNIGHT WAS TEN MINUTES AGO.
BUT THE REALLY WEIRD THING? MY BAD GUY RADAR'S PICKING UP NOTH--
DOOR'S OPENING.
SKULL MASKS.
NIGHTWING.
MY BAD GUY RADAR SAYS SKULL MASKS ARE PRETTY RELIABLE INDICATORS OF TROUBLE...
NO, NO... WAIT.
WINGMAN?
GUYS.
I CAN EXPLAIN...

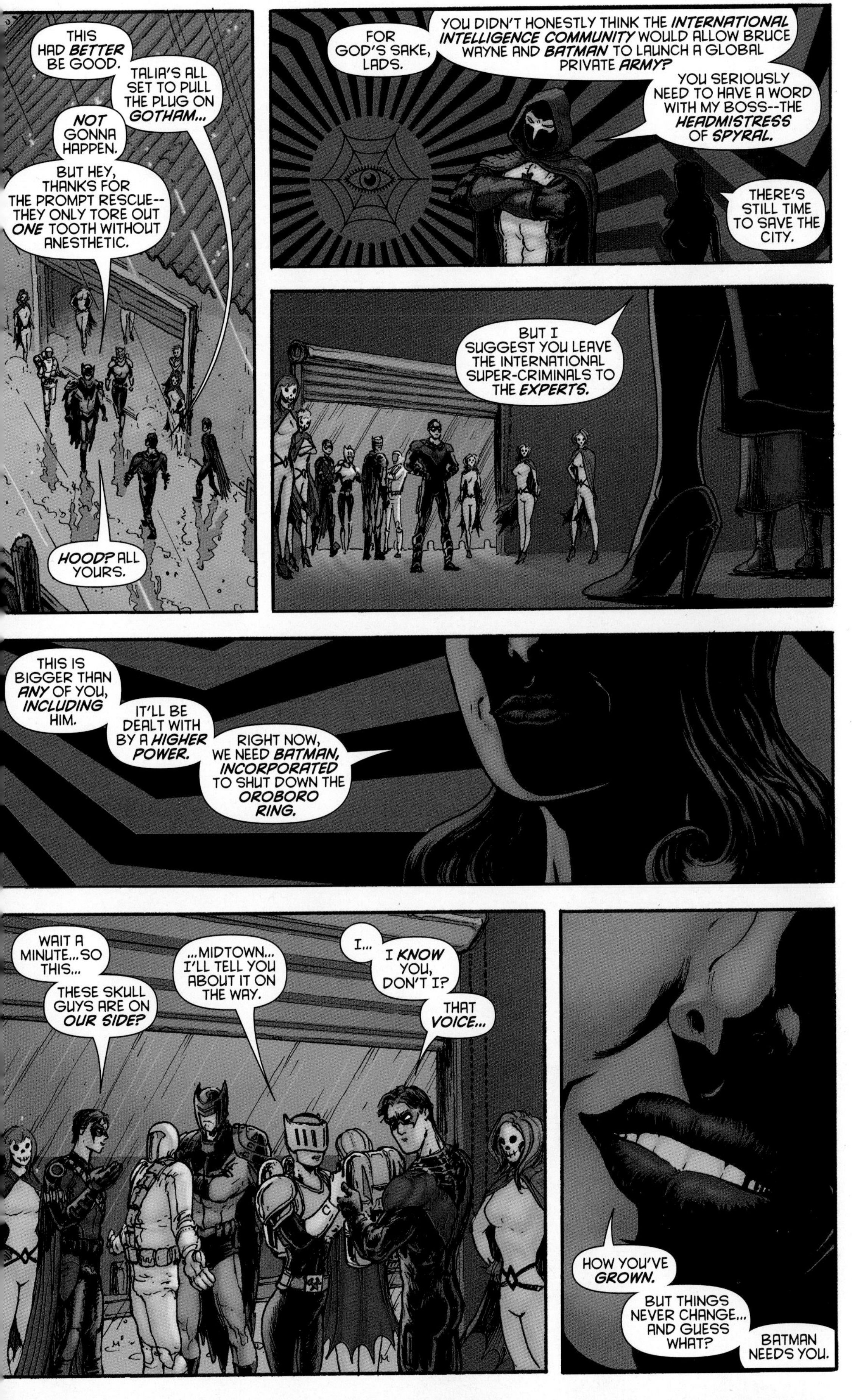
THIS HAD BETTER BE GOOD.
TALIA'S ALL SET TO PULL THE PLUG ON GOTHAM...
NOT GONNA HAPPEN.
BUT HEY, THANKS FOR THE PROMPT RESCUE-- THEY ONLY TORE OUT ONE TOOTH WITHOUT ANESTHETIC.
HOOD? ALL YOURS.
FOR GOD'S SAKE, LADS.
YOU DIDN'T HONESTLY THINK THE INTERNATIONAL INTELLIGENCE COMMUNITY WOULD ALLOW BRUCE WAYNE AND BATMAN TO LAUNCH A GLOBAL PRIVATE ARMY?
YOU SERIOUSLY NEED TO HAVE A WORD WITH MY BOSS--THE HEADMISTRESS OF SPYRAL.
THERE'S STILL TIME TO SAVE THE CITY.
BUT I SUGGEST YOU LEAVE THE INTERNATIONAL SUPER-CRIMINALS TO THE EXPERTS.
THIS IS BIGGER THAN ANY OF YOU, INCLUDING HIM.
IT'LL BE DEALT WITH BY A HIGHER POWER.
RIGHT NOW, WE NEED BATMAN, INCORPORATED TO SHUT DOWN THE OROBORO RING.
WAIT A MINUTE... SO THIS...
THESE SKULL GUYS ARE ON OUR SIDE?
...MIDTOWN... I'LL TELL YOU ABOUT IT ON THE WAY.
I...
I KNOW YOU, DON'T I?
THAT VOICE...
HOW YOU'VE GROWN.
BUT THINGS NEVER CHANGE... AND GUESS WHAT?
BATMAN NEEDS YOU.

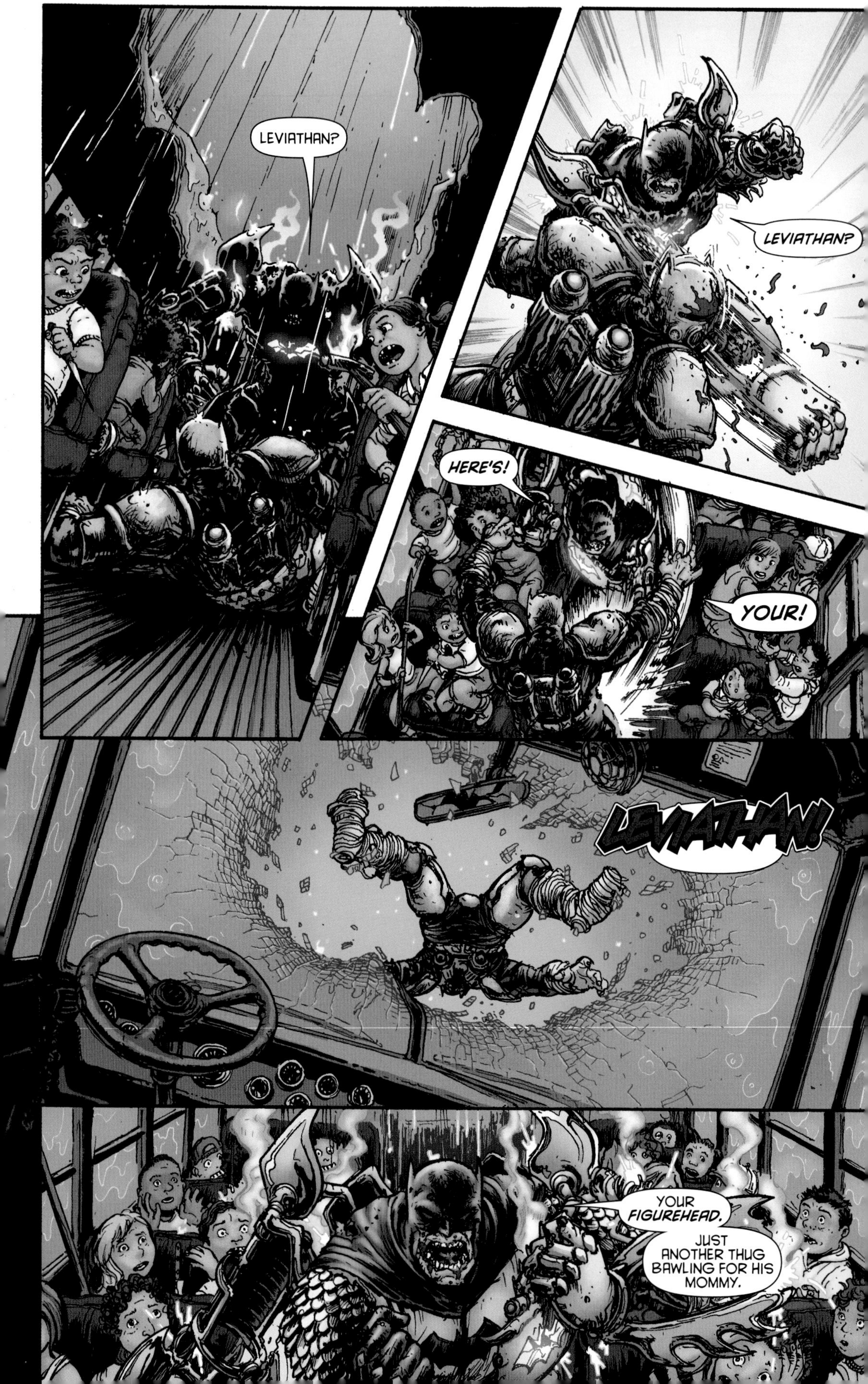
LEVIATHAN?
LEVIATHAN?
HERE'S!
YOUR!
LEVIATHAN!
YOUR FIGUREHEAD.
JUST ANOTHER THUG BAWLING FOR HIS MOMMY.

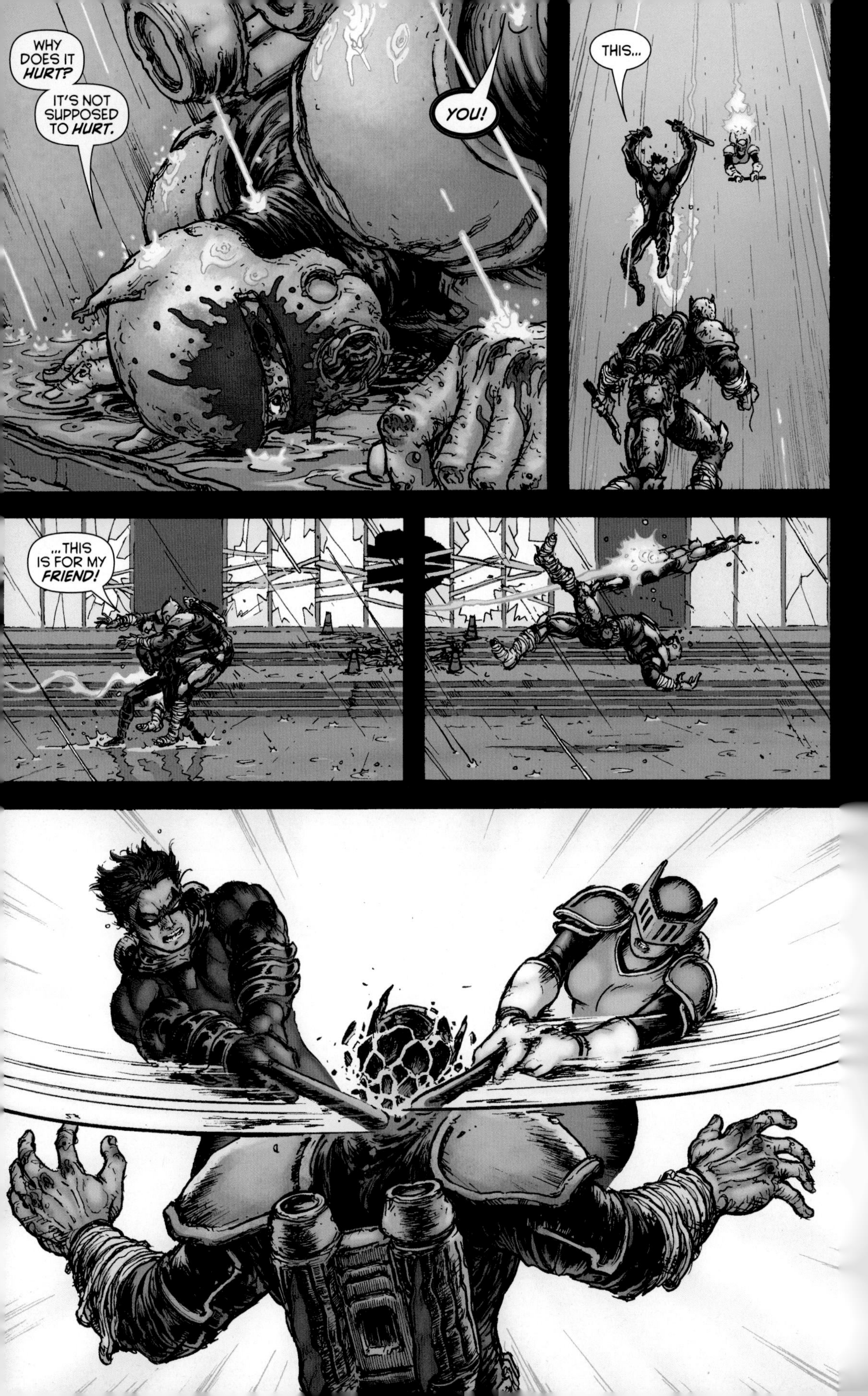
WHY DOES IT HURT? IT'S NOT SUPPOSED TO HURT.
YOU!
THIS...
...THIS IS FOR MY FRIEND!

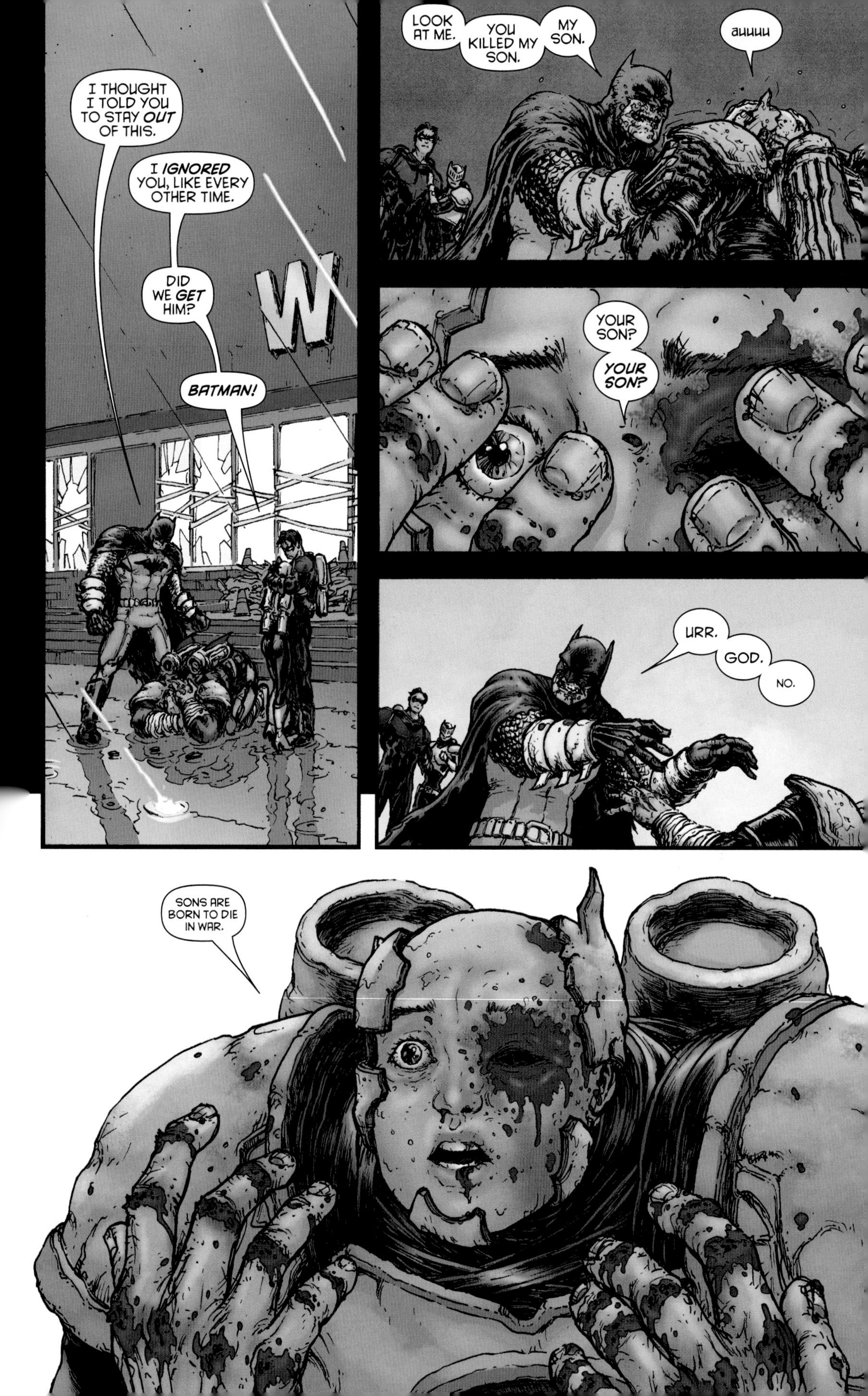
I THOUGHT I TOLD YOU TO STAY OUT OF THIS.
I IGNORED YOU, LIKE EVERY OTHER TIME.
DID WE GET HIM?
BATMAN!
W
LOOK AT ME.
YOU KILLED MY SON.
MY SON.
auuuu
YOUR SON?
YOUR SON?
URR.
GOD.
NO.
SONS ARE BORN TO DIE IN WAR.

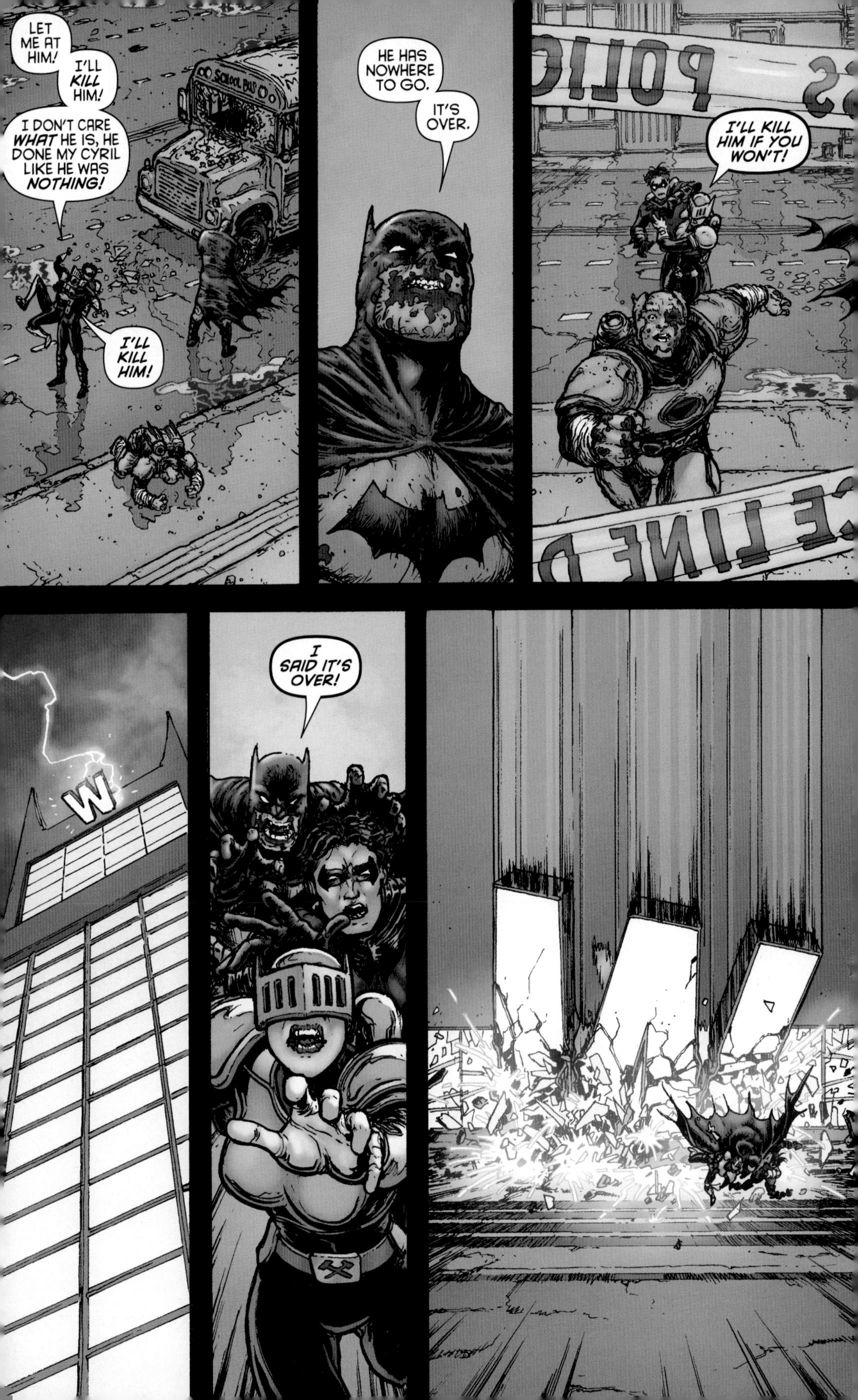

LET ME AT HIM!
I'LL KILL HIM!
I DON'T CARE WHAT HE IS, HE DONE MY CYRIL LIKE HE WAS NOTHING!
I'LL KILL HIM!
SCHOOL BUS
HE HAS NOWHERE TO GO.
IT'S OVER.
POLIC
I'LL KILL HIM IF YOU WON'T!
CE LINE D
W
I SAID IT'S OVER!

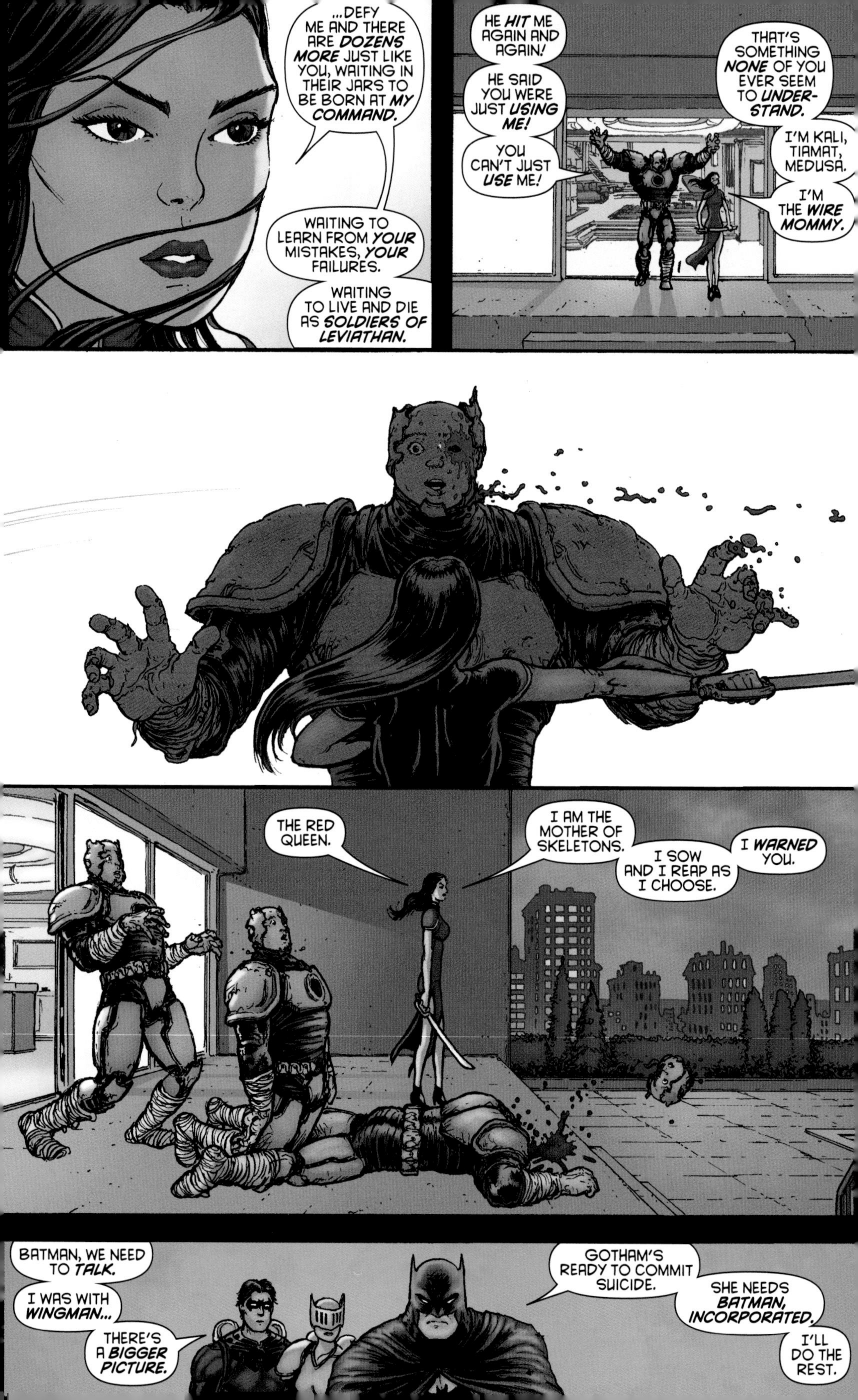
...DEFY ME AND THERE ARE DOZENS MORE JUST LIKE YOU, WAITING IN THEIR JARS TO BE BORN AT MY COMMAND.
WAITING TO LEARN FROM YOUR MISTAKES, YOUR FAILURES.
WAITING TO LIVE AND DIE AS SOLDIERS OF LEVIATHAN.
HE HIT ME AGAIN AND AGAIN!
HE SAID YOU WERE JUST USING ME!
YOU CAN'T JUST USE ME!
THAT'S SOMETHING NONE OF YOU EVER SEEM TO UNDERSTAND.
I'M KALI, TIAMAT, MEDUSA.
I'M THE WIRE MOMMY.
THE RED QUEEN.
I AM THE MOTHER OF SKELETONS.
I SOW AND I REAP AS I CHOOSE.
I WARNED YOU.
BATMAN, WE NEED TO TALK.
I WAS WITH WINGMAN...
THERE'S A BIGGER PICTURE.
GOTHAM'S READY TO COMMIT SUICIDE.
SHE NEEDS BATMAN, INCORPORATED.
I'LL DO THE REST.

GIVE THE ORDER.

KILL THE CITY.

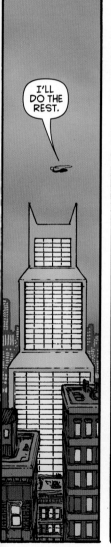

I'LL DO THE REST.

LIGHTS OUT.

LET FALL THE HOUSE OF WAYNE.

BDEEP

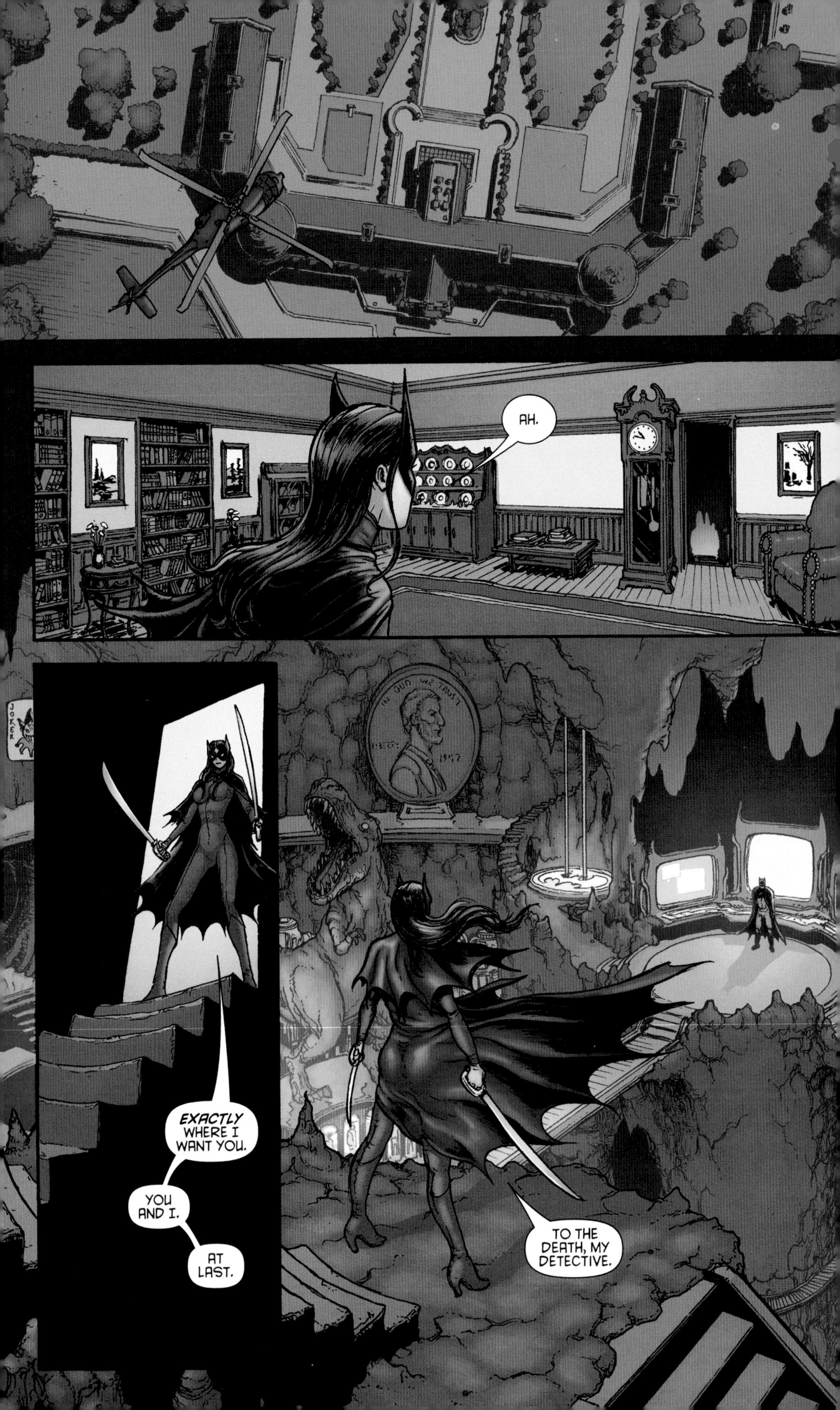

AH.
EXACTLY WHERE I WANT YOU.
YOU AND I.
AT LAST.
TO THE DEATH, MY DETECTIVE.

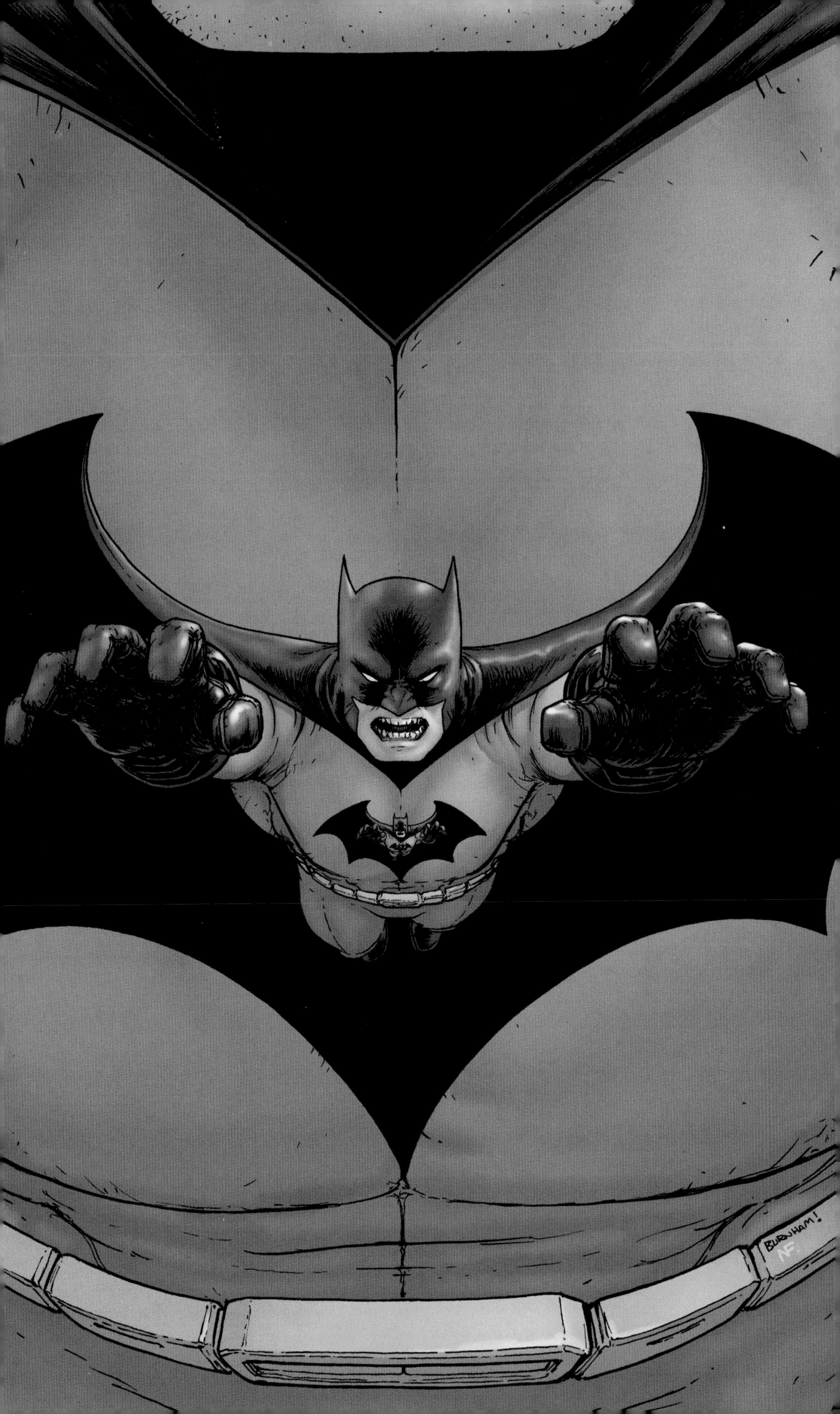
BURNHAM!
NF.

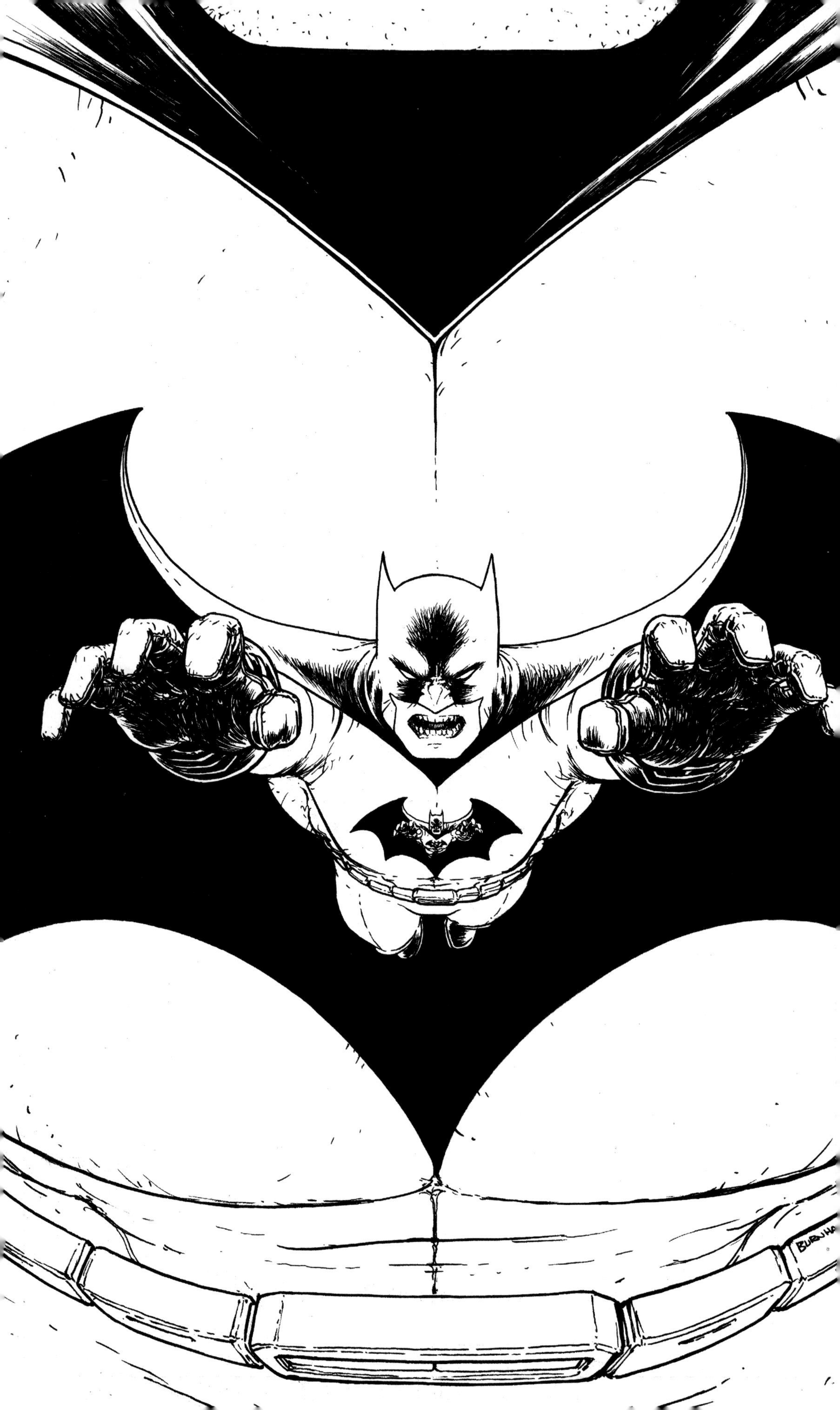

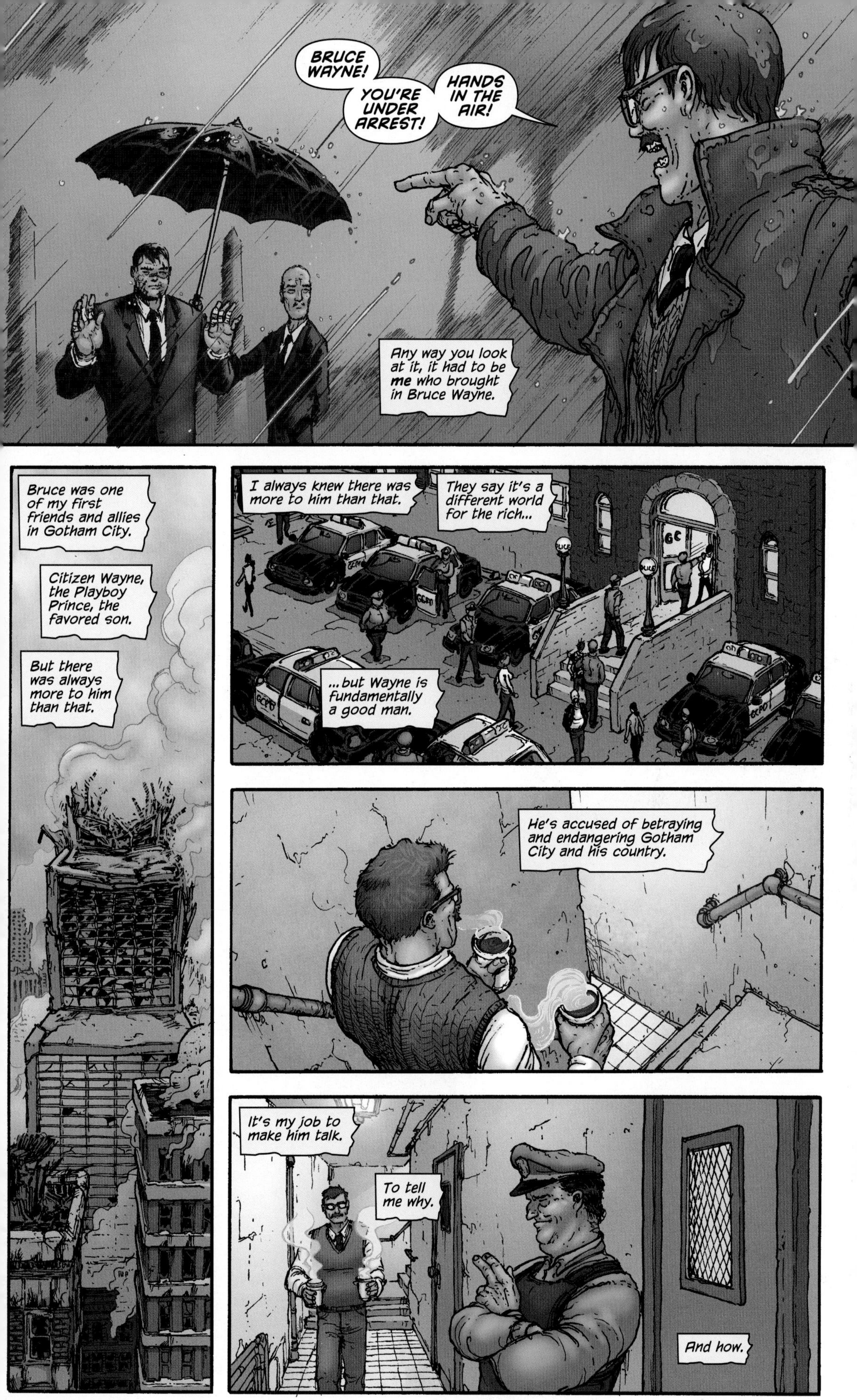

BRUCE WAYNE!
YOU'RE UNDER ARREST!
HANDS IN THE AIR!
Any way you look at it, it had to be **me** who brought in Bruce Wayne.
Bruce was one of my first friends and allies in Gotham City.
Citizen Wayne, the Playboy Prince, the favored son.
But there was always more to him than that.
I always knew there was more to him than that.
They say it's a different world for the rich...
...but Wayne is fundamentally a good man.
He's accused of betraying and endangering Gotham City and his country.
It's my job to make him talk.
To tell me why.
And how.

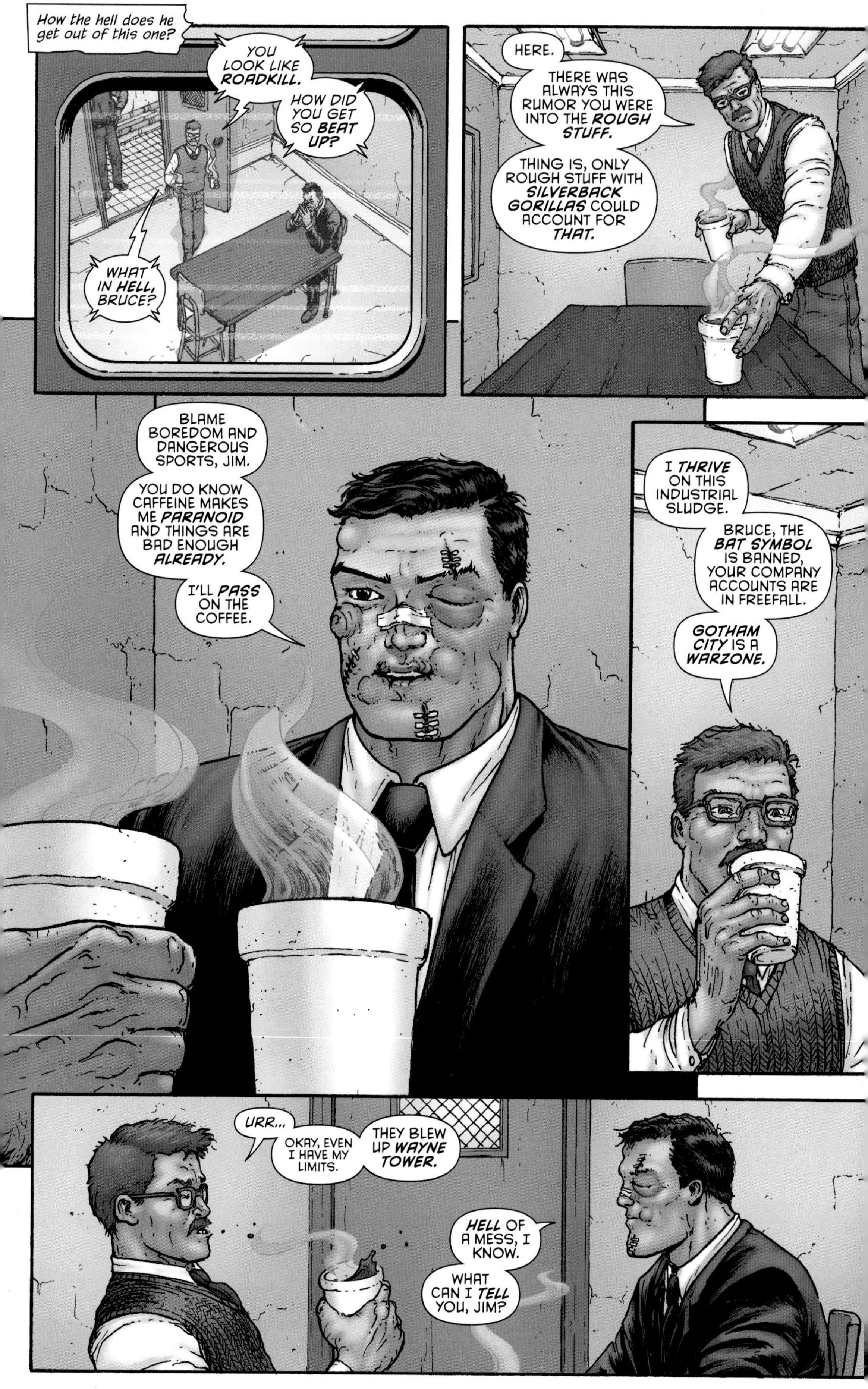
How the hell does he get out of this one?
YOU LOOK LIKE ROADKILL.
HOW DID YOU GET SO BEAT UP?
WHAT IN HELL, BRUCE?
HERE.
THERE WAS ALWAYS THIS RUMOR YOU WERE INTO THE ROUGH STUFF.
THING IS, ONLY ROUGH STUFF WITH SILVERBACK GORILLAS COULD ACCOUNT FOR THAT.
BLAME BOREDOM AND DANGEROUS SPORTS, JIM.
YOU DO KNOW CAFFEINE MAKES ME PARANOID AND THINGS ARE BAD ENOUGH ALREADY.
I'LL PASS ON THE COFFEE.
I THRIVE ON THIS INDUSTRIAL SLUDGE.
BRUCE, THE BAT SYMBOL IS BANNED, YOUR COMPANY ACCOUNTS ARE IN FREEFALL.
GOTHAM CITY IS A WARZONE.
URR...
OKAY, EVEN I HAVE MY LIMITS.
THEY BLEW UP WAYNE TOWER.
HELL OF A MESS, I KNOW.
WHAT CAN I TELL YOU, JIM?

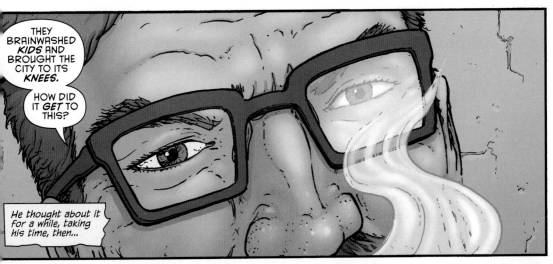

THEY BRAINWASHED *KIDS* AND BROUGHT THE CITY TO ITS *KNEES.*

HOW DID IT *GET* TO THIS?

He thought about it for a while, taking his time, then...

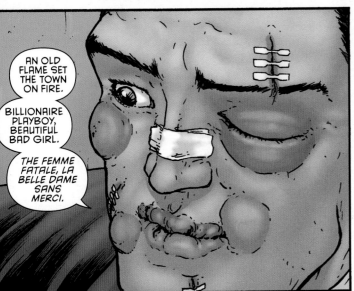

AN OLD FLAME SET THE TOWN ON FIRE.

BILLIONAIRE PLAYBOY, BEAUTIFUL BAD GIRL.

THE FEMME FATALE, LA BELLE DAME SANS MERCI.

WE HAD A *SON.*

BAD SEED.

BAD BLOOD.

I DID MY *BEST* TO RESCUE THE BOY FROM HIS MOTHER'S INFLUENCE.

I FAILED.

I TRIGGERED A KIND OF *WAR.*

SO *THAT'S* WHY YOU BUILT A PRIVATE ARMY OF INTERNATIONAL BATMEN?

DEAR GOD, BRUCE.

YOU DATED THE DAUGHTER OF *RA'S AL GHUL?*

THE WORLD'S NUMBER ONE *CRIMINAL MASTERMIND?*

My first thought was to ask: "How did Batman feel about that?"

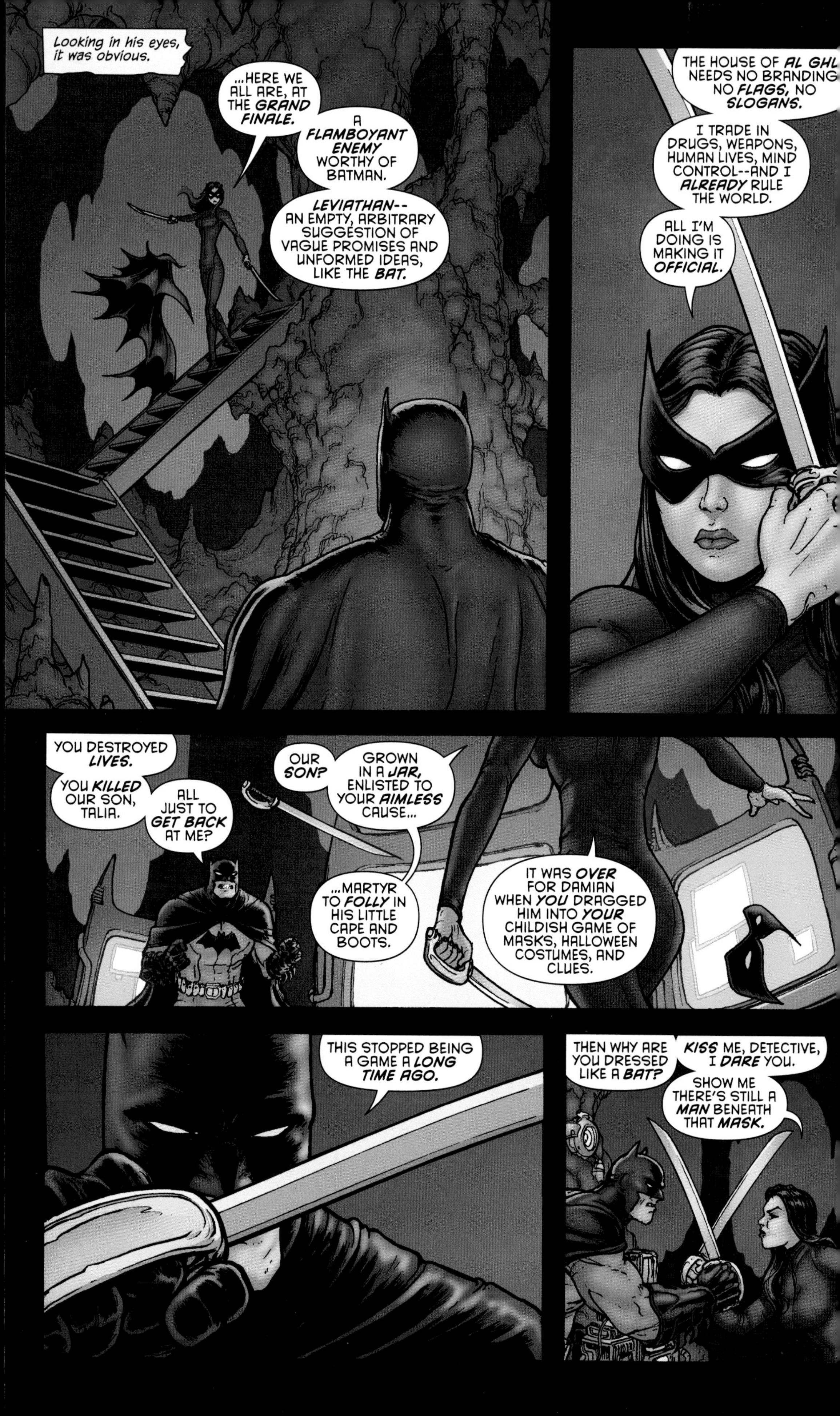

Looking in his eyes, it was obvious.
...HERE WE ALL ARE, AT THE ***GRAND FINALE.***
A ***FLAMBOYANT ENEMY*** WORTHY OF BATMAN.
LEVIATHAN-- AN EMPTY, ARBITRARY SUGGESTION OF VAGUE PROMISES AND UNFORMED IDEAS, LIKE THE ***BAT.***
THE HOUSE OF ***AL GHUL*** NEEDS NO BRANDING NO ***FLAGS,*** NO ***SLOGANS.***
I TRADE IN DRUGS, WEAPONS, HUMAN LIVES, MIND CONTROL--AND I ***ALREADY*** RULE THE WORLD.
ALL I'M DOING IS MAKING IT ***OFFICIAL.***
YOU DESTROYED ***LIVES.***
YOU ***KILLED*** OUR SON, TALIA.
ALL JUST TO ***GET BACK*** AT ME?
OUR ***SON?***
GROWN IN A ***JAR,*** ENLISTED TO YOUR ***AIMLESS*** CAUSE...
...MARTYR TO ***FOLLY*** IN HIS LITTLE CAPE AND BOOTS.
IT WAS ***OVER*** FOR DAMIAN WHEN ***YOU*** DRAGGED HIM INTO ***YOUR*** CHILDISH GAME OF MASKS, HALLOWEEN COSTUMES, AND CLUES.
THIS STOPPED BEING A GAME A ***LONG TIME AGO.***
THEN WHY ARE YOU DRESSED LIKE A ***BAT?***
KISS ME, DETECTIVE, I ***DARE*** YOU.
SHOW ME THERE'S STILL A ***MAN*** BENEATH THAT ***MASK.***

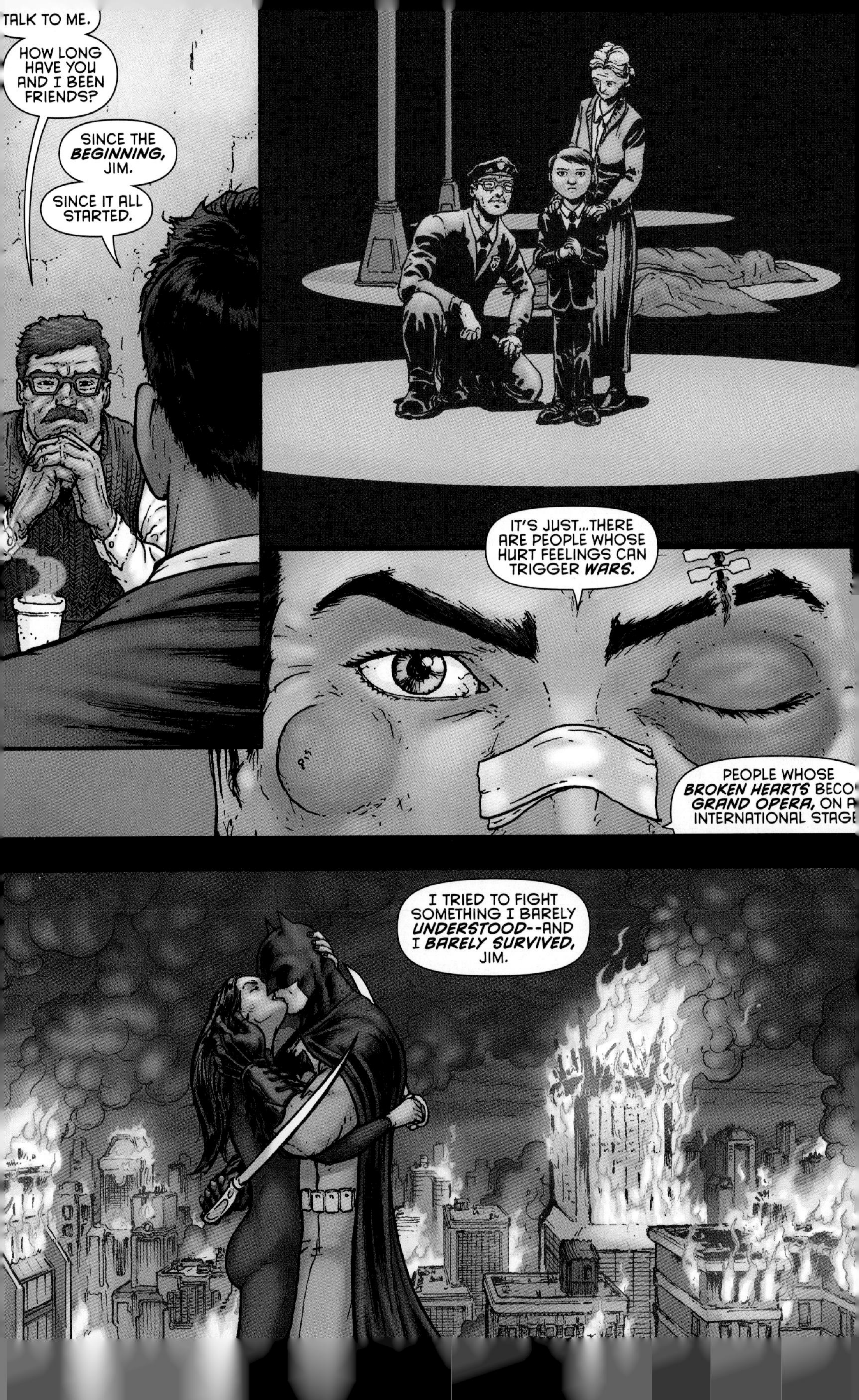
TALK TO ME.
HOW LONG HAVE YOU AND I BEEN FRIENDS?
SINCE THE *BEGINNING,* JIM.
SINCE IT ALL STARTED.
IT'S JUST...THERE ARE PEOPLE WHOSE HURT FEELINGS CAN TRIGGER *WARS.*
PEOPLE WHOSE *BROKEN HEARTS* BECO *GRAND OPERA,* ON A INTERNATIONAL STAGE
I TRIED TO FIGHT SOMETHING I BARELY *UNDERSTOOD*--AND I *BARELY SURVIVED,* JIM.

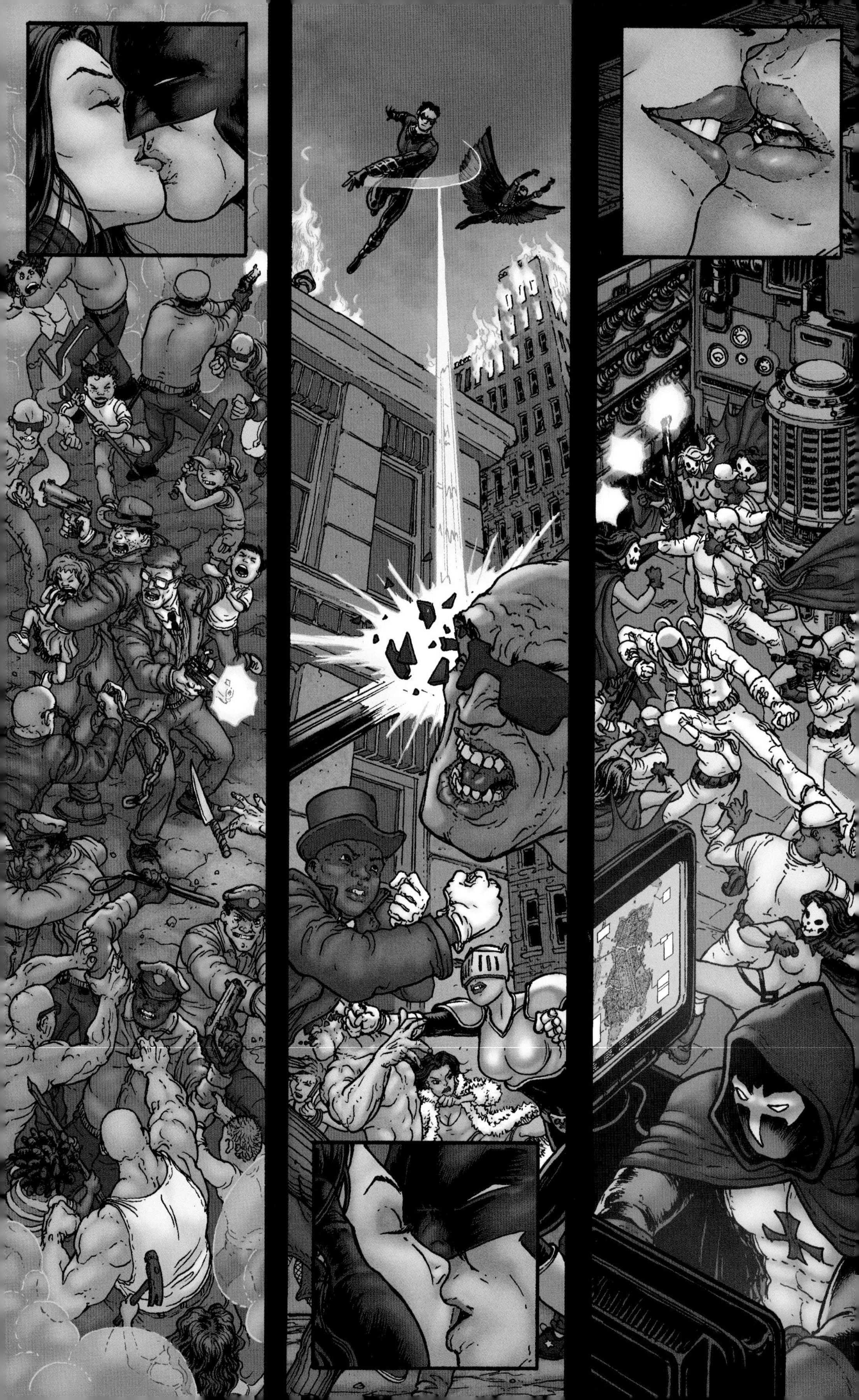

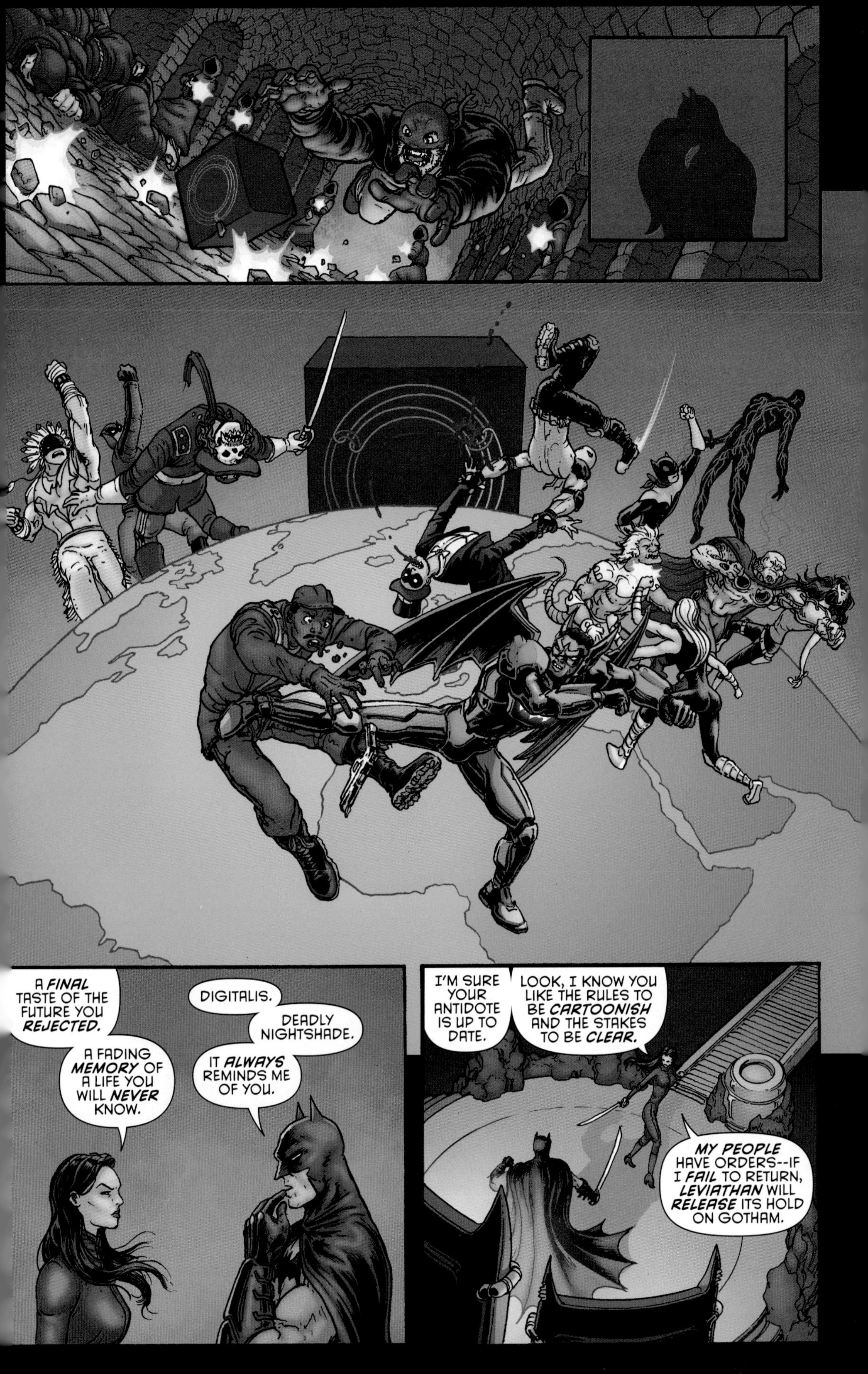
A FINAL TASTE OF THE FUTURE YOU REJECTED.
A FADING MEMORY OF A LIFE YOU WILL NEVER KNOW.
DIGITALIS.
DEADLY NIGHTSHADE.
IT ALWAYS REMINDS ME OF YOU.
I'M SURE YOUR ANTIDOTE IS UP TO DATE.
LOOK, I KNOW YOU LIKE THE RULES TO BE CARTOONISH AND THE STAKES TO BE CLEAR.
MY PEOPLE HAVE ORDERS--IF I FAIL TO RETURN, LEVIATHAN WILL RELEASE ITS HOLD ON GOTHAM.

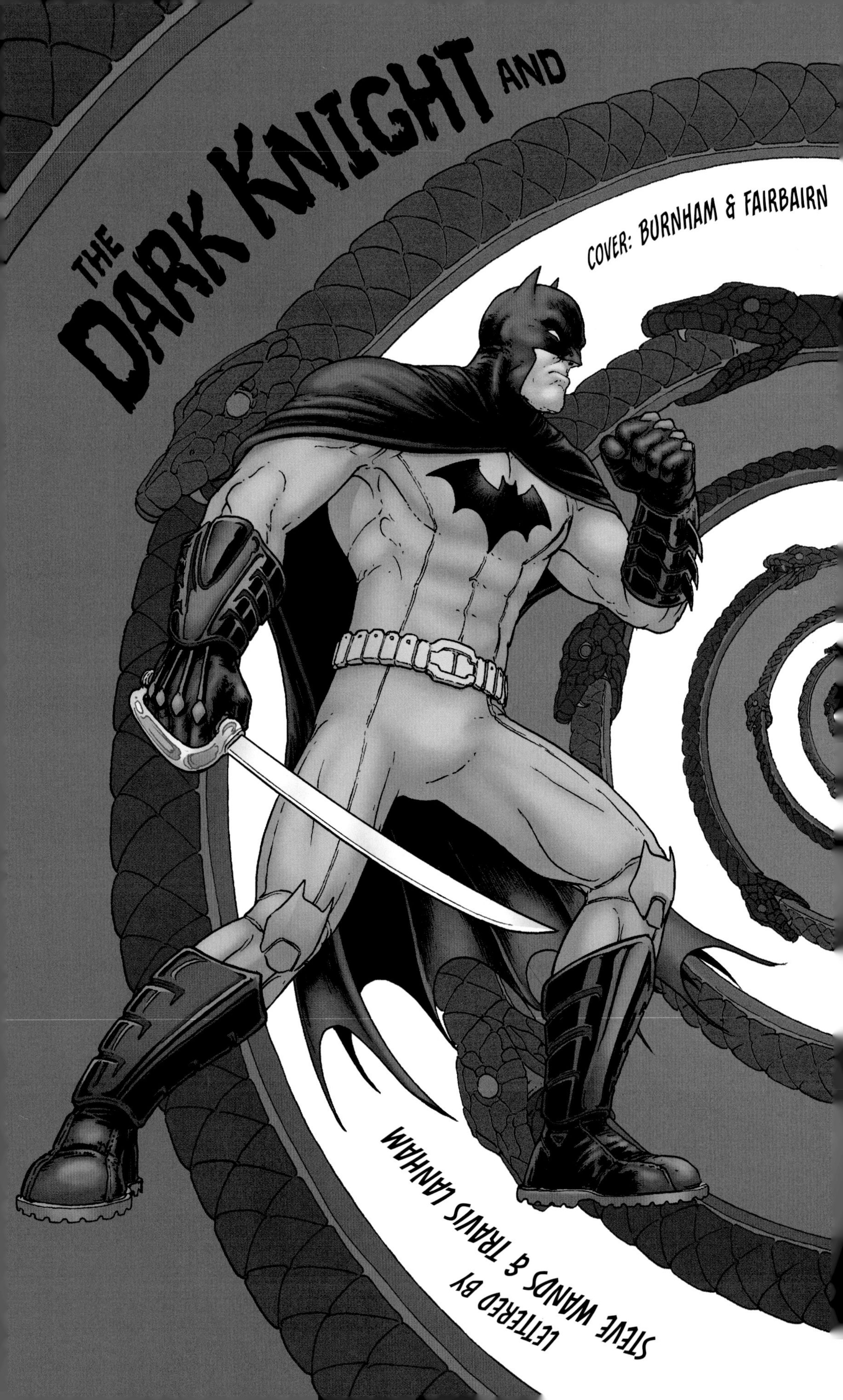

THE DARK KNIGHT AND
COVER: BURNHAM & FAIRBAIRN
LETTERED BY
STEVE WANDS & TRAVIS LANHAM

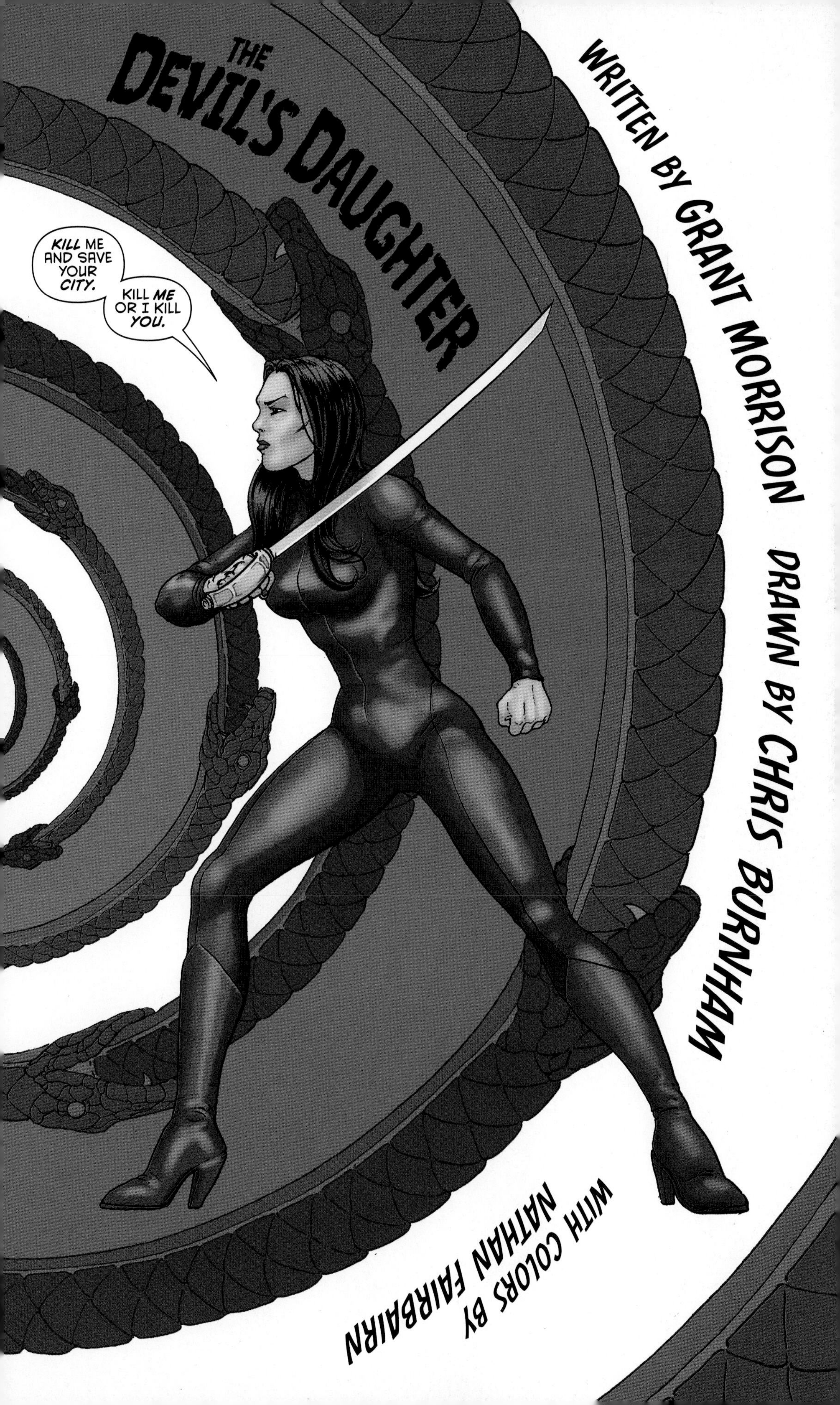
THE DEVIL'S DAUGHTER
KILL ME AND SAVE YOUR CITY.
KILL ME OR I KILL YOU.
WRITTEN BY GRANT MORRISON
DRAWN BY CHRIS BURNHAM
WITH COLORS BY NATHAN FAIRBAIRN

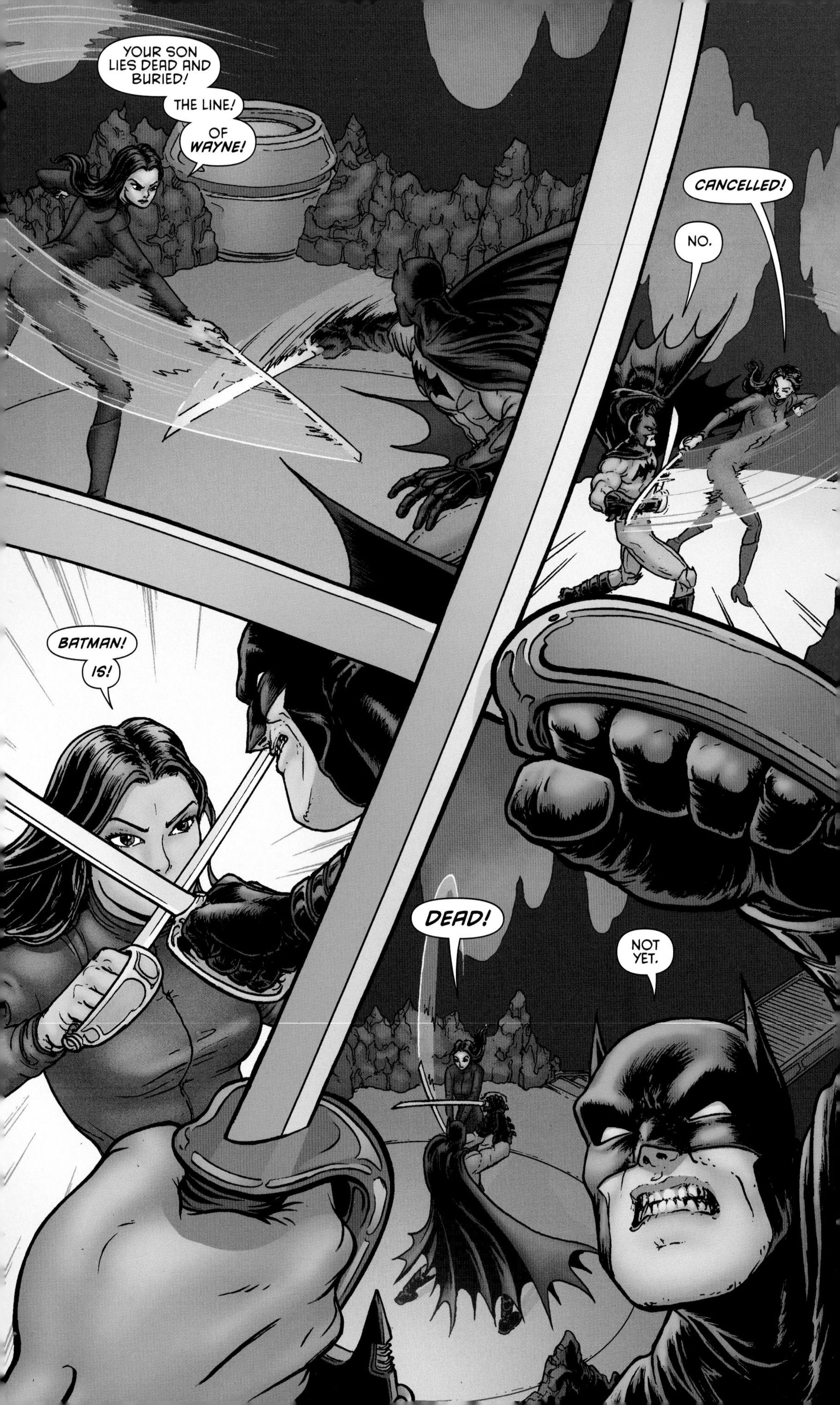
YOUR SON LIES DEAD AND BURIED!
THE LINE!
OF WAYNE!
CANCELLED!
NO.
BATMAN!
IS!
DEAD!
NOT YET.

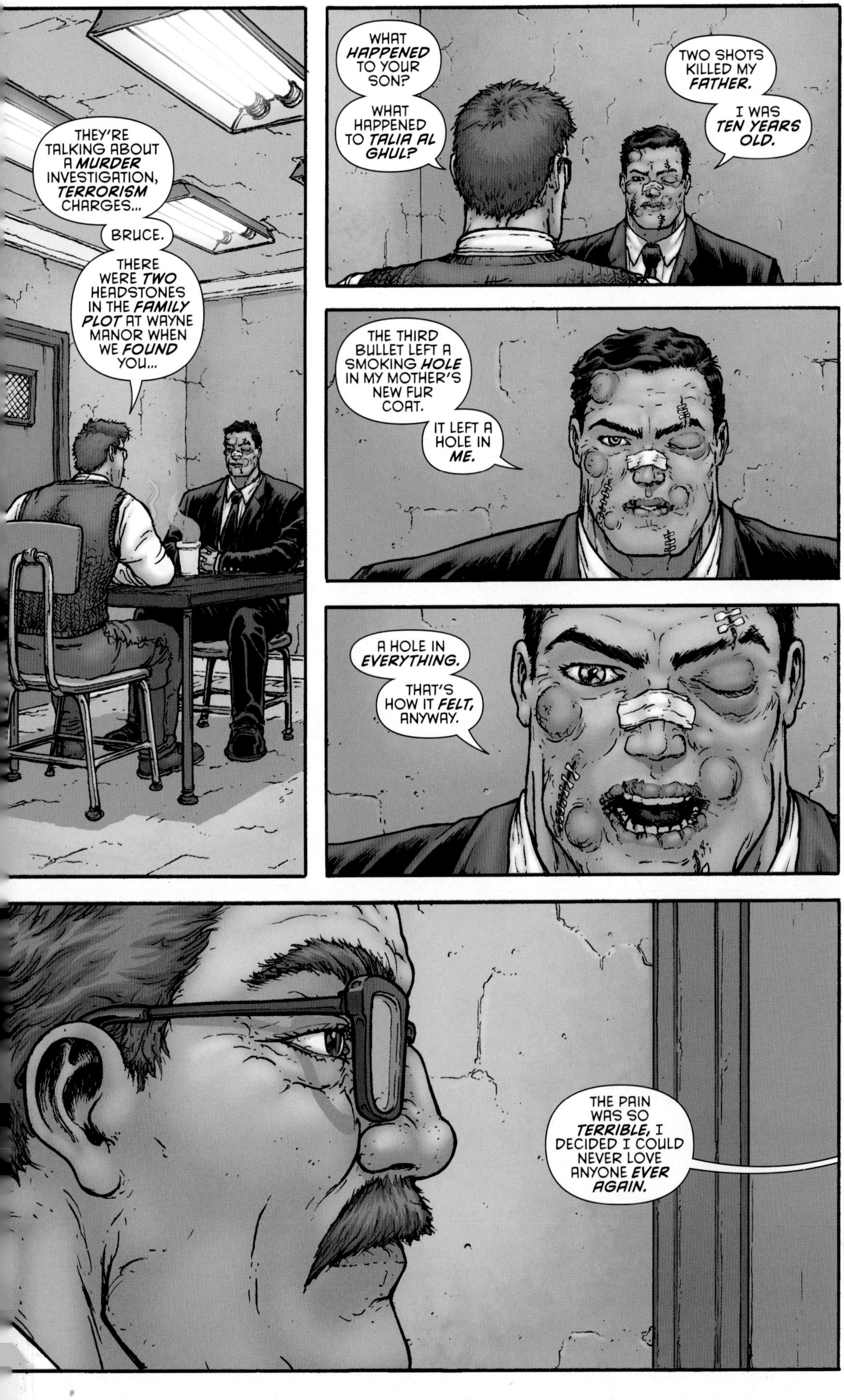

THEY'RE TALKING ABOUT A MURDER INVESTIGATION, TERRORISM CHARGES...
BRUCE.
THERE WERE TWO HEADSTONES IN THE FAMILY PLOT AT WAYNE MANOR WHEN WE FOUND YOU...
WHAT HAPPENED TO YOUR SON?
WHAT HAPPENED TO TALIA AL GHUL?
TWO SHOTS KILLED MY FATHER.
I WAS TEN YEARS OLD.
THE THIRD BULLET LEFT A SMOKING HOLE IN MY MOTHER'S NEW FUR COAT.
IT LEFT A HOLE IN ME.
A HOLE IN EVERYTHING.
THAT'S HOW IT FELT, ANYWAY.
THE PAIN WAS SO TERRIBLE, I DECIDED I COULD NEVER LOVE ANYONE EVER AGAIN.

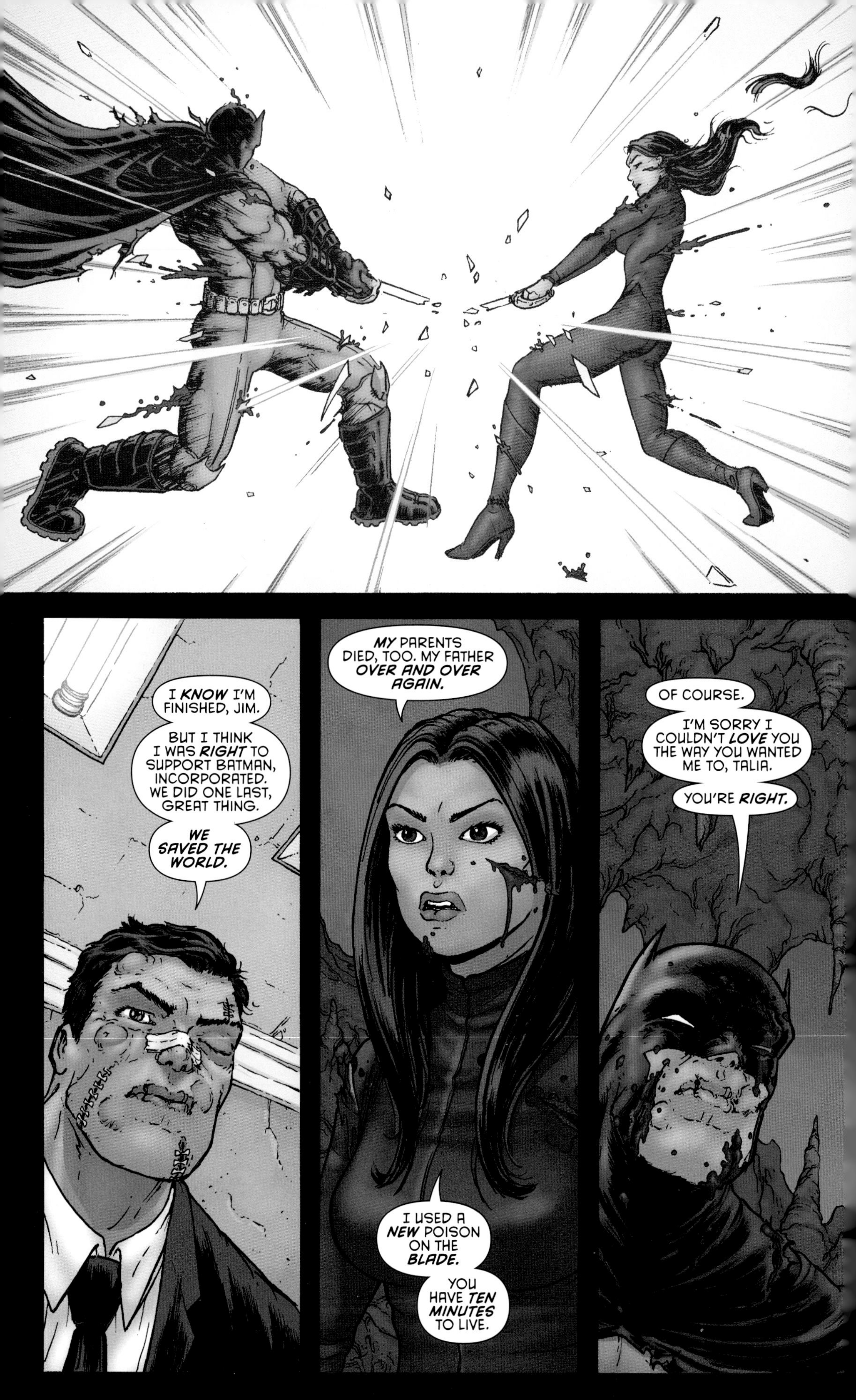
I KNOW I'M FINISHED, JIM.
BUT I THINK I WAS RIGHT TO SUPPORT BATMAN, INCORPORATED. WE DID ONE LAST, GREAT THING.
WE SAVED THE WORLD.
MY PARENTS DIED, TOO. MY FATHER OVER AND OVER AGAIN.
I USED A NEW POISON ON THE BLADE.
YOU HAVE TEN MINUTES TO LIVE.
OF COURSE.
I'M SORRY I COULDN'T LOVE YOU THE WAY YOU WANTED ME TO, TALIA.
YOU'RE RIGHT.

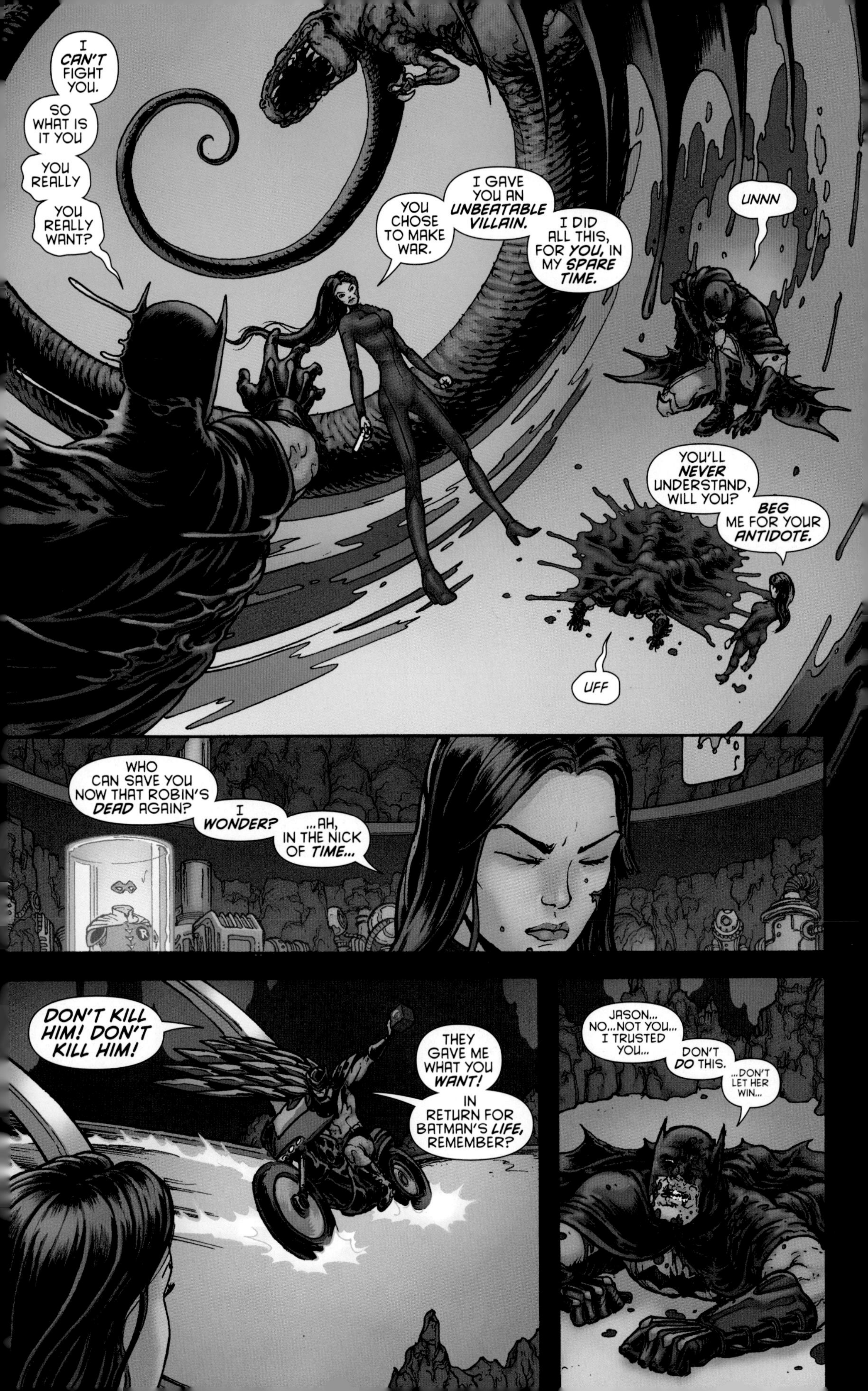

I CAN'T FIGHT YOU.
SO WHAT IS IT YOU
YOU REALLY
YOU REALLY WANT?
YOU CHOSE TO MAKE WAR.
I GAVE YOU AN UNBEATABLE VILLAIN.
I DID ALL THIS, FOR YOU, IN MY SPARE TIME.
UNNN
YOU'LL NEVER UNDERSTAND, WILL YOU?
BEG ME FOR YOUR ANTIDOTE.
UFF
WHO CAN SAVE YOU NOW THAT ROBIN'S DEAD AGAIN?
I WONDER?
...AH, IN THE NICK OF TIME...
DON'T KILL HIM! DON'T KILL HIM!
THEY GAVE ME WHAT YOU WANT!
IN RETURN FOR BATMAN'S LIFE, REMEMBER?
JASON... NO...NOT YOU... I TRUSTED YOU...
DON'T DO THIS.
...DON'T LET HER WIN...

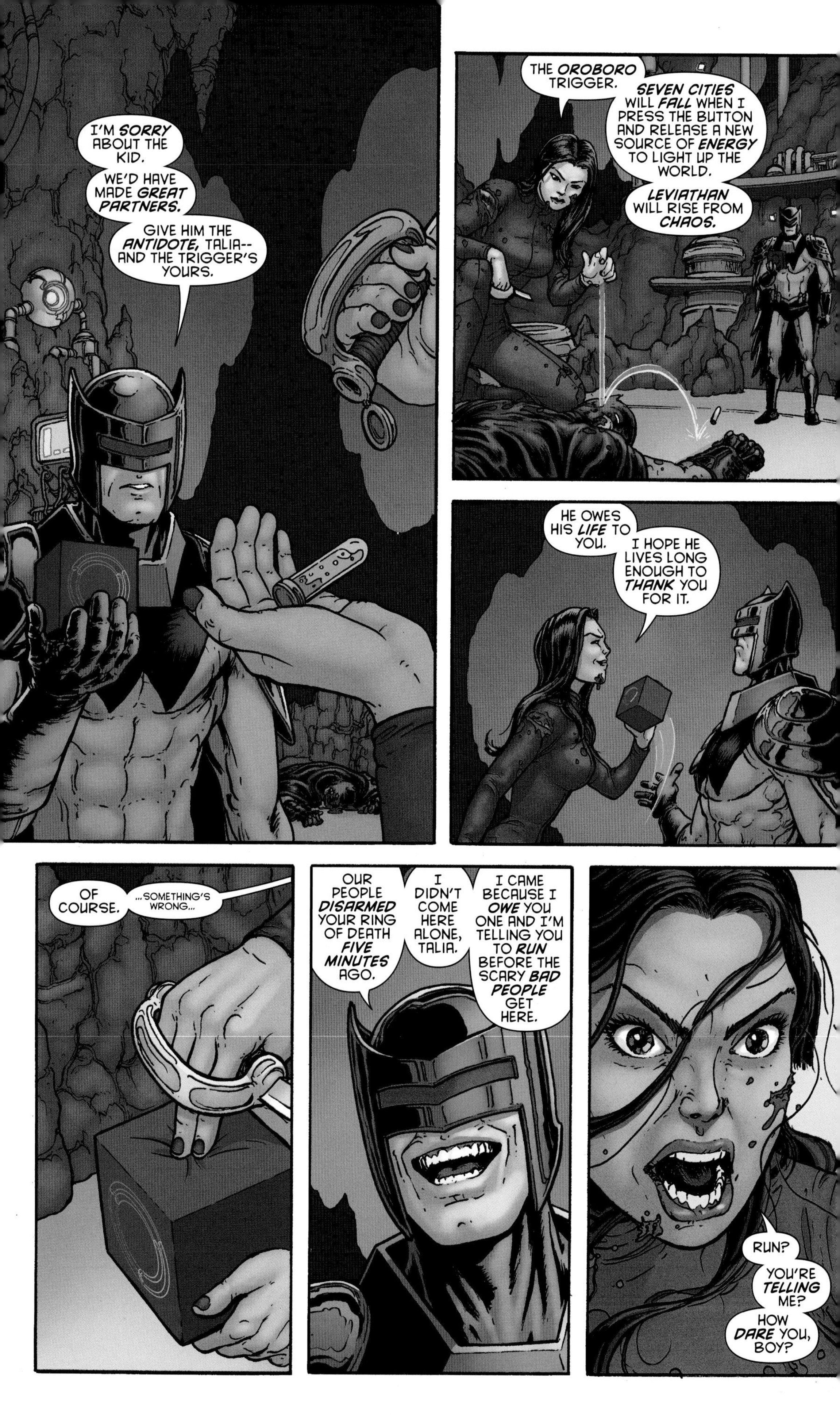
I'M SORRY ABOUT THE KID.
WE'D HAVE MADE GREAT PARTNERS.
GIVE HIM THE ANTIDOTE, TALIA-- AND THE TRIGGER'S YOURS.
THE OROBORO TRIGGER.
SEVEN CITIES WILL FALL WHEN I PRESS THE BUTTON AND RELEASE A NEW SOURCE OF ENERGY TO LIGHT UP THE WORLD.
LEVIATHAN WILL RISE FROM CHAOS.
HE OWES HIS LIFE TO YOU.
I HOPE HE LIVES LONG ENOUGH TO THANK YOU FOR IT.
OF COURSE.
...SOMETHING'S WRONG...
OUR PEOPLE DISARMED YOUR RING OF DEATH FIVE MINUTES AGO.
I DIDN'T COME HERE ALONE, TALIA.
I CAME BECAUSE I OWE YOU ONE AND I'M TELLING YOU TO RUN BEFORE THE SCARY BAD PEOPLE GET HERE.
RUN?
YOU'RE TELLING ME?
HOW DARE YOU, BOY?

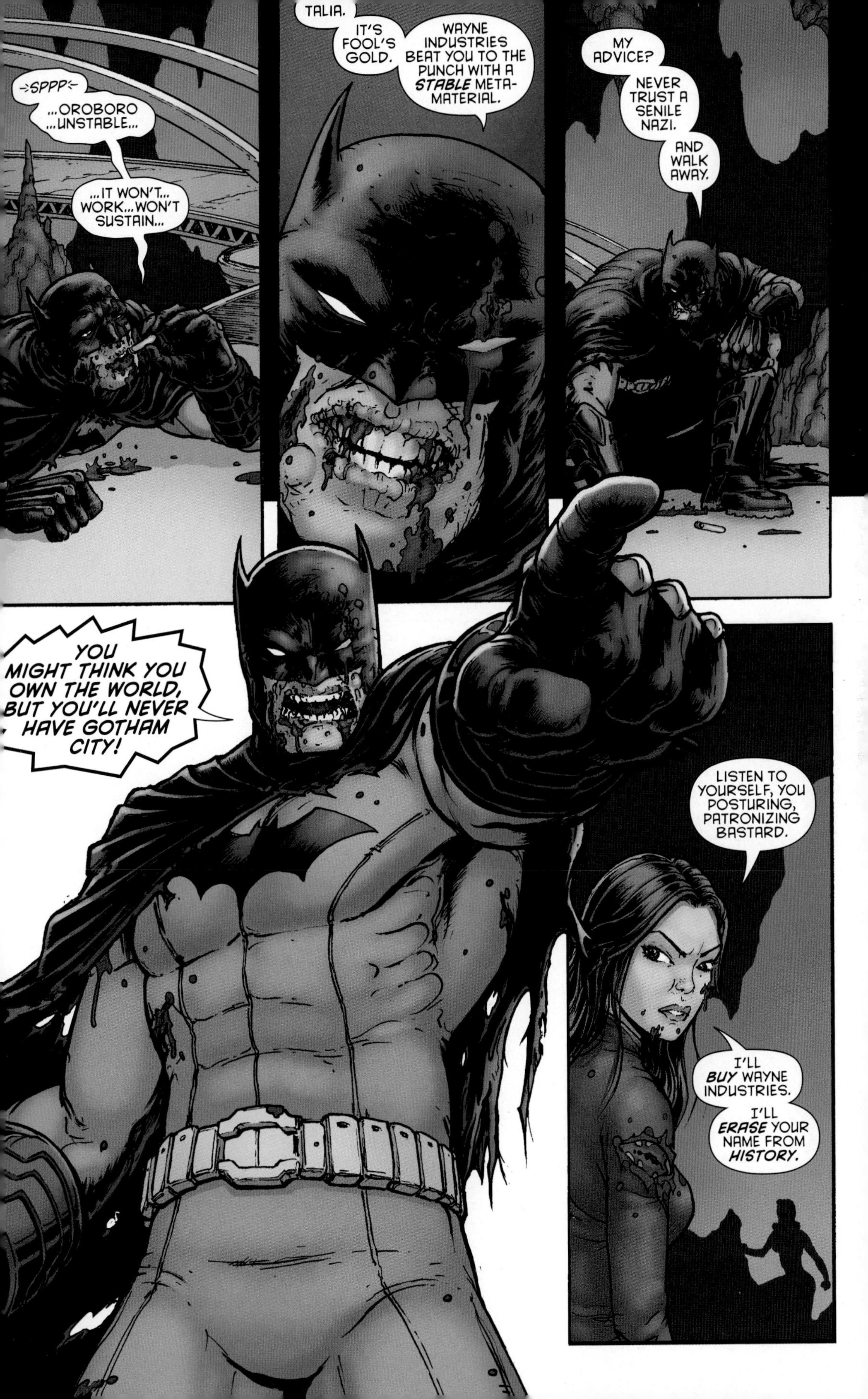

SPPP
...OROBORO ...UNSTABLE...
...IT WON'T... WORK...WON'T SUSTAIN...
TALIA.
IT'S FOOL'S GOLD.
WAYNE INDUSTRIES BEAT YOU TO THE PUNCH WITH A STABLE META-MATERIAL.
MY ADVICE?
NEVER TRUST A SENILE NAZI.
AND WALK AWAY.
YOU MIGHT THINK YOU OWN THE WORLD, BUT YOU'LL NEVER HAVE GOTHAM CITY!
LISTEN TO YOURSELF, YOU POSTURING, PATRONIZING BASTARD.
I'LL BUY WAYNE INDUSTRIES.
I'LL ERASE YOUR NAME FROM HISTORY.

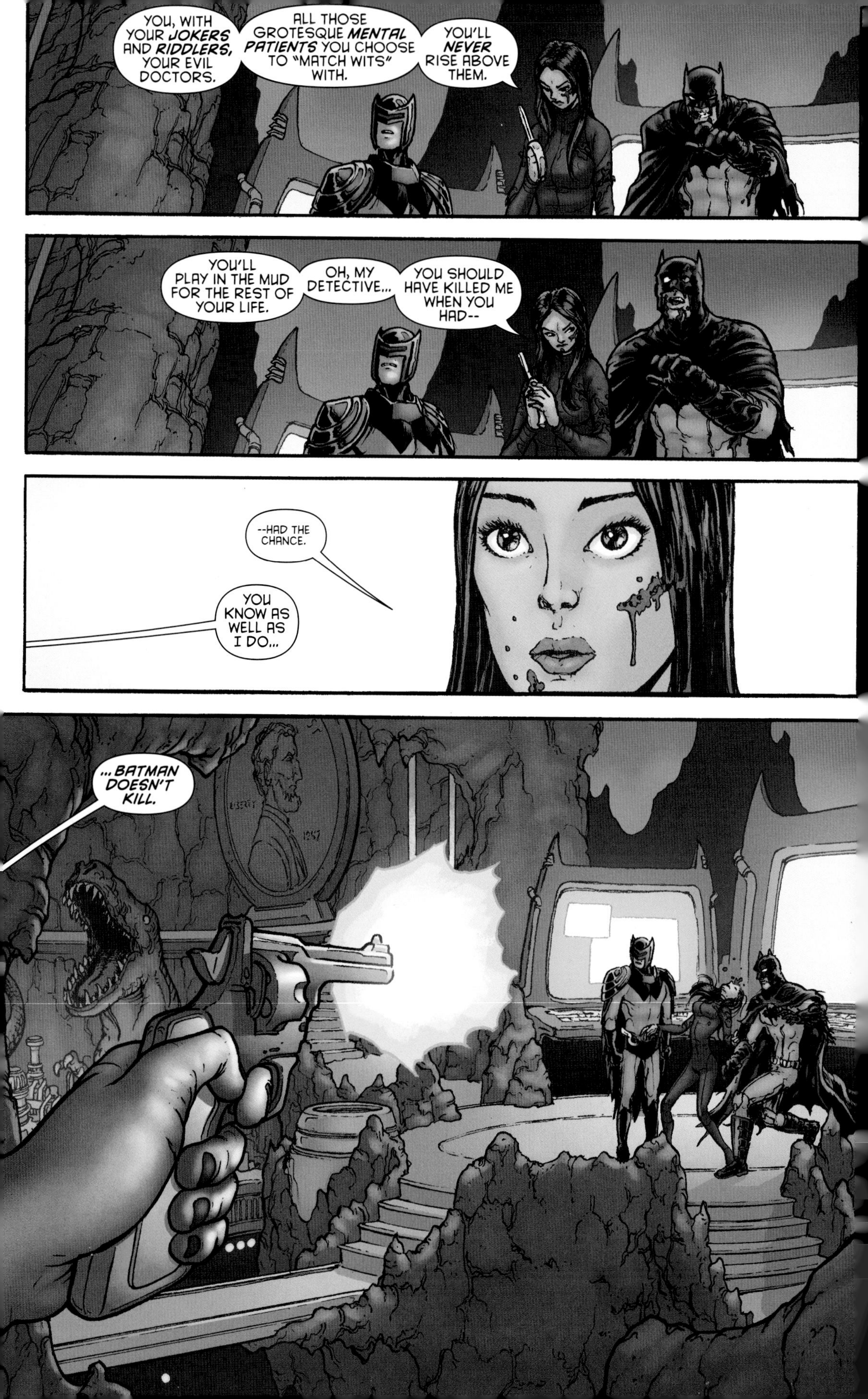
YOU, WITH YOUR JOKERS AND RIDDLERS, YOUR EVIL DOCTORS.
ALL THOSE GROTESQUE MENTAL PATIENTS YOU CHOOSE TO "MATCH WITS" WITH.
YOU'LL NEVER RISE ABOVE THEM.
YOU'LL PLAY IN THE MUD FOR THE REST OF YOUR LIFE.
OH, MY DETECTIVE...
YOU SHOULD HAVE KILLED ME WHEN YOU HAD--
--HAD THE CHANCE.
YOU KNOW AS WELL AS I DO...
...BATMAN DOESN'T KILL.

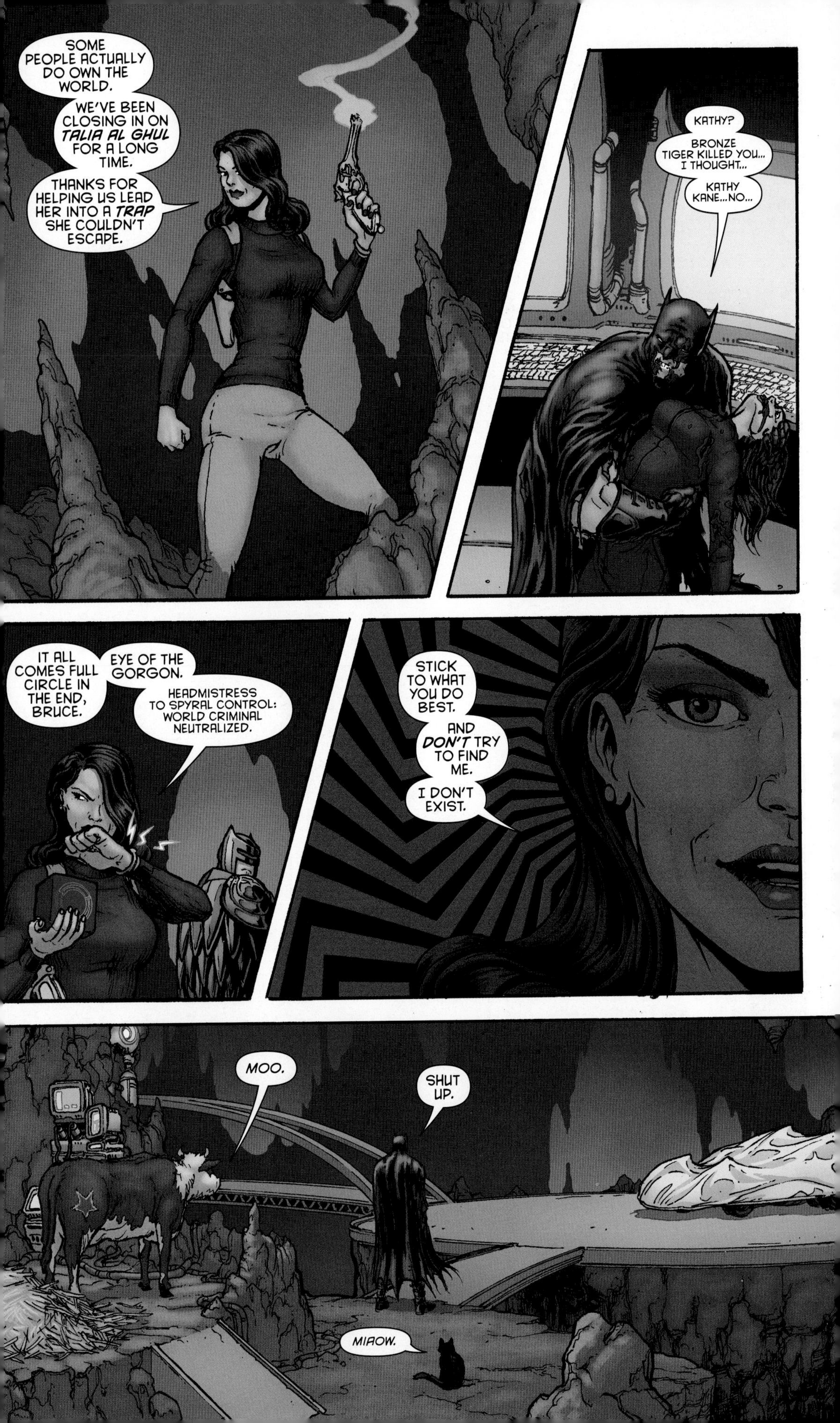
SOME PEOPLE ACTUALLY DO OWN THE WORLD.
WE'VE BEEN CLOSING IN ON *TALIA AL GHUL* FOR A LONG TIME.
THANKS FOR HELPING US LEAD HER INTO A *TRAP* SHE COULDN'T ESCAPE.
KATHY?
BRONZE TIGER KILLED YOU... I THOUGHT...
KATHY KANE... NO...
IT ALL COMES FULL CIRCLE IN THE END, BRUCE.
EYE OF THE GORGON.
HEADMISTRESS TO SPYRAL CONTROL: WORLD CRIMINAL NEUTRALIZED.
STICK TO WHAT YOU DO BEST.
AND *DON'T* TRY TO FIND ME.
I DON'T EXIST.
MOO.
SHUT UP.
MIAOW.

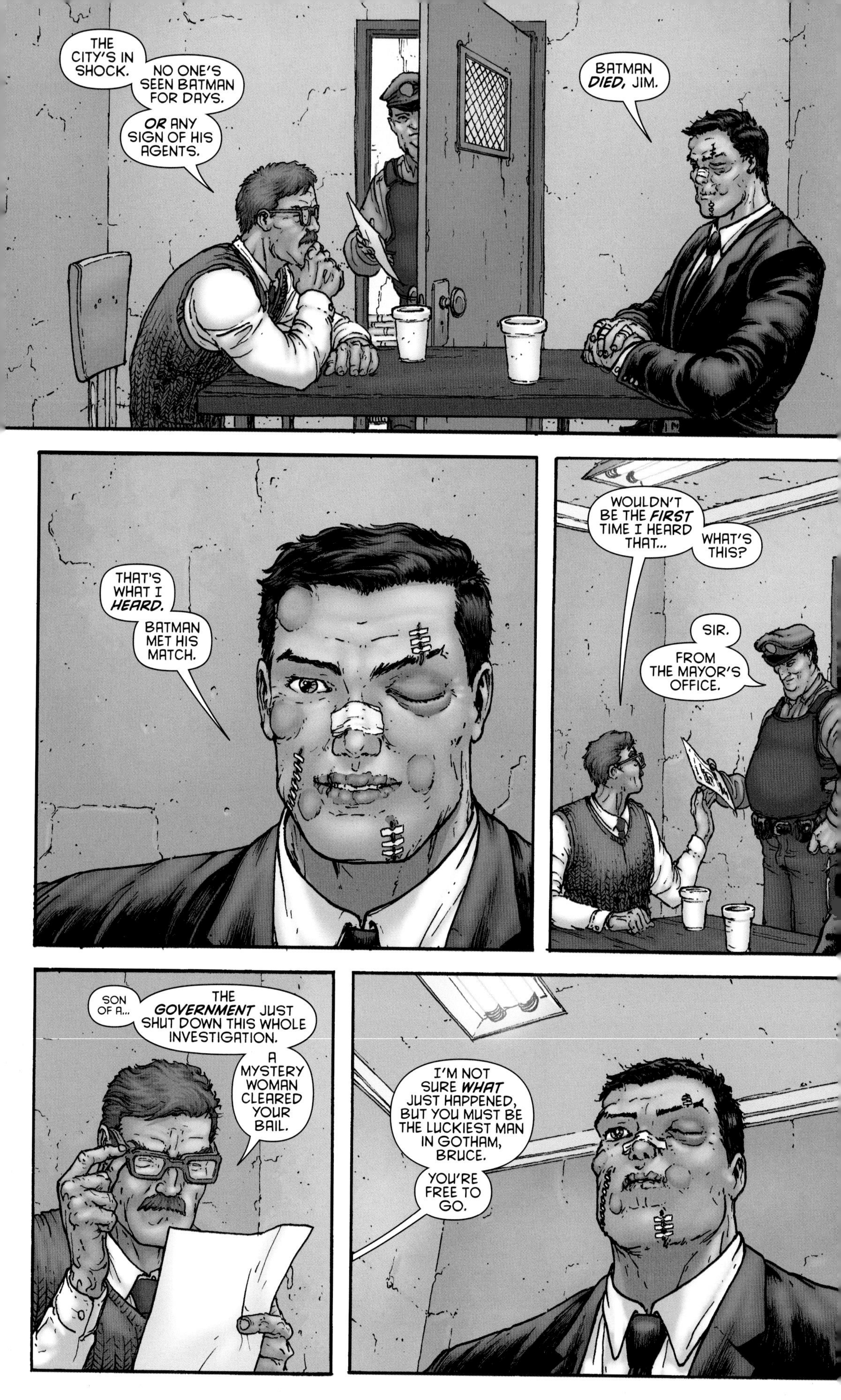
THE CITY'S IN SHOCK.
NO ONE'S SEEN BATMAN FOR DAYS.
OR ANY SIGN OF HIS AGENTS.
BATMAN DIED, JIM.
THAT'S WHAT I HEARD.
BATMAN MET HIS MATCH.
WOULDN'T BE THE FIRST TIME I HEARD THAT...
WHAT'S THIS?
SIR.
FROM THE MAYOR'S OFFICE.
SON OF A...
THE GOVERNMENT JUST SHUT DOWN THIS WHOLE INVESTIGATION.
A MYSTERY WOMAN CLEARED YOUR BAIL.
I'M NOT SURE WHAT JUST HAPPENED, BUT YOU MUST BE THE LUCKIEST MAN IN GOTHAM, BRUCE.
YOU'RE FREE TO GO.

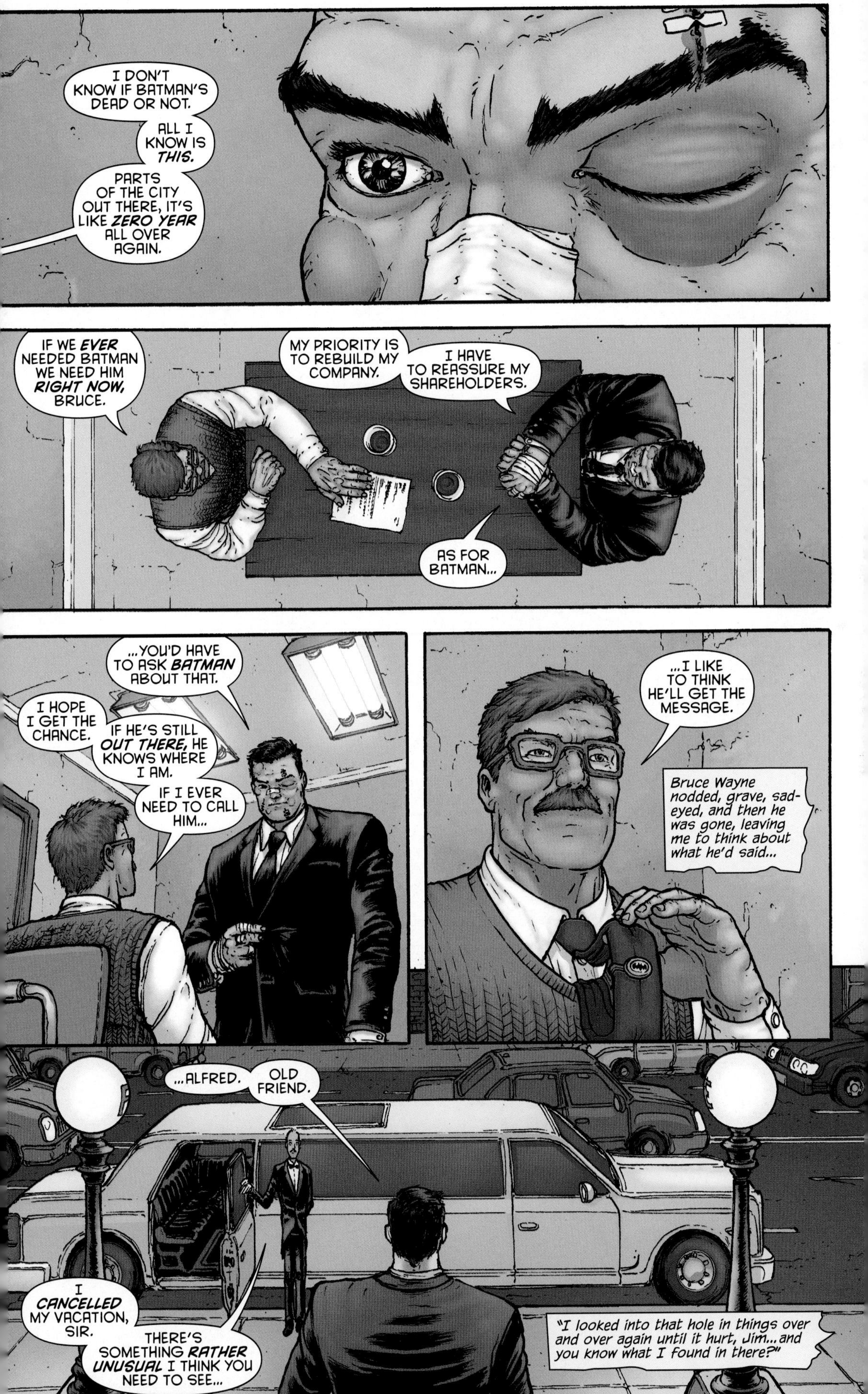
I DON'T KNOW IF BATMAN'S DEAD OR NOT.
ALL I KNOW IS *THIS.*
PARTS OF THE CITY OUT THERE, IT'S LIKE *ZERO YEAR* ALL OVER AGAIN.
IF WE *EVER* NEEDED BATMAN WE NEED HIM *RIGHT NOW,* BRUCE.
MY PRIORITY IS TO REBUILD MY COMPANY.
I HAVE TO REASSURE MY SHAREHOLDERS.
AS FOR BATMAN...
...YOU'D HAVE TO ASK *BATMAN* ABOUT THAT.
I HOPE I GET THE CHANCE.
IF HE'S STILL *OUT THERE,* HE KNOWS WHERE I AM.
IF I EVER NEED TO CALL HIM...
...I LIKE TO THINK HE'LL GET THE MESSAGE.
Bruce Wayne nodded, grave, sad-eyed, and then he was gone, leaving me to think about what he'd said...
...ALFRED.
OLD FRIEND.
I *CANCELLED* MY VACATION, SIR.
THERE'S SOMETHING *RATHER UNUSUAL* I THINK YOU NEED TO SEE...
"I looked into that hole in things over and over again until it hurt, Jim... and you know what I found in there?"

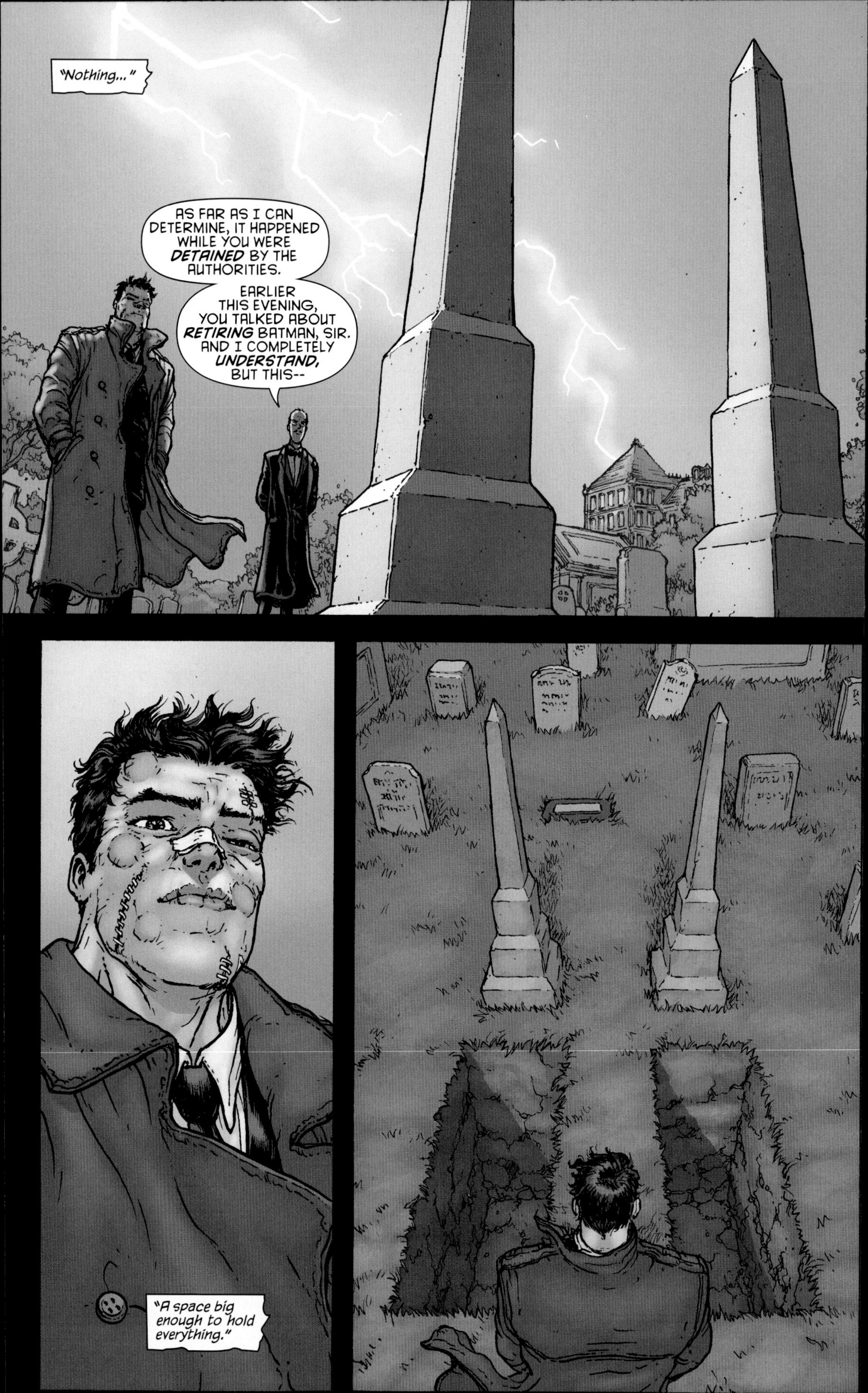
"Nothing..."
AS FAR AS I CAN DETERMINE, IT HAPPENED WHILE YOU WERE DETAINED BY THE AUTHORITIES.
EARLIER THIS EVENING, YOU TALKED ABOUT RETIRING BATMAN, SIR. AND I COMPLETELY UNDERSTAND, BUT THIS--
"A space big enough to hold everything."

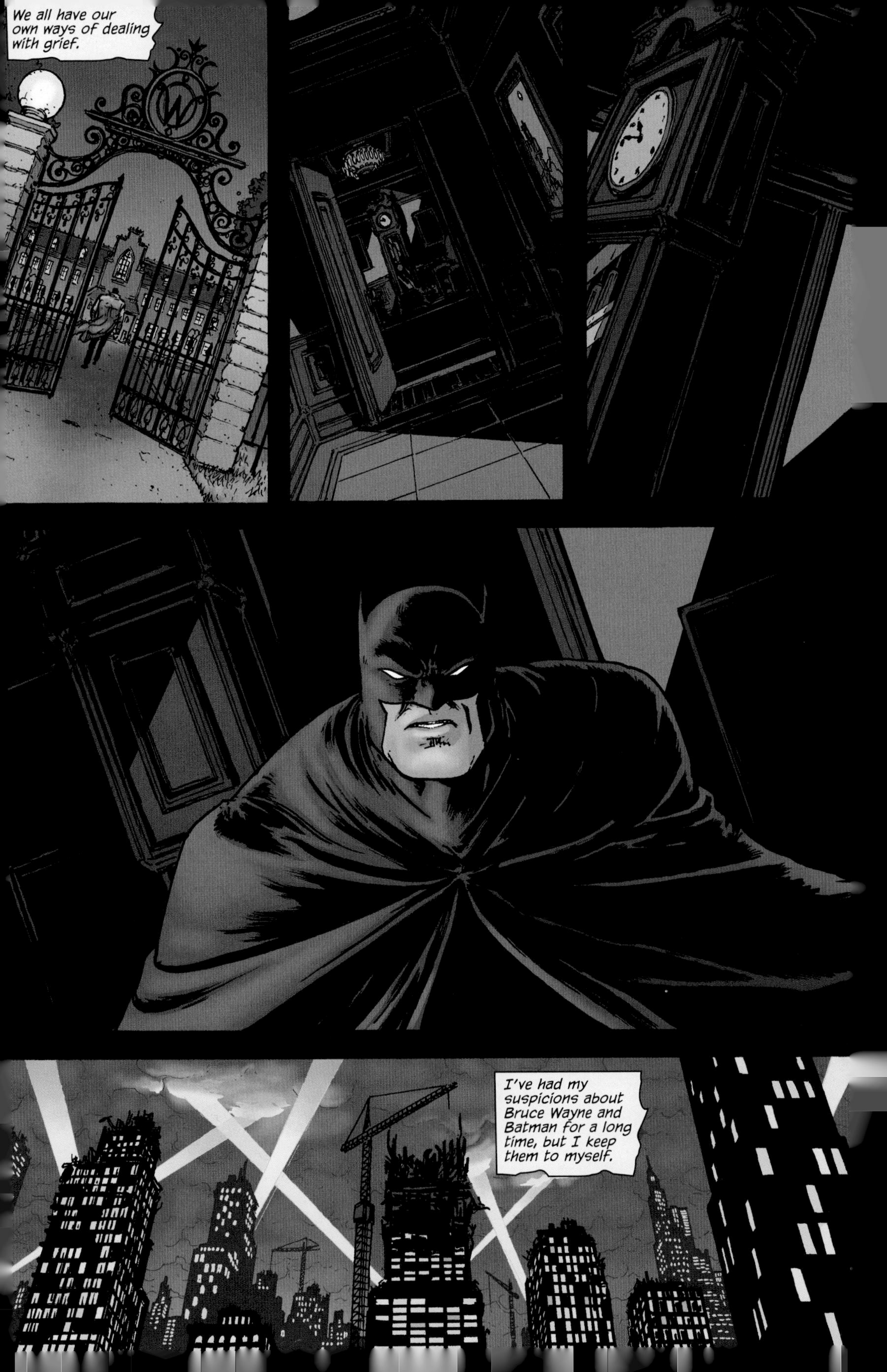
We all have our own ways of dealing with grief.
I've had my suspicions about Bruce Wayne and Batman for a long time, but I keep them to myself.

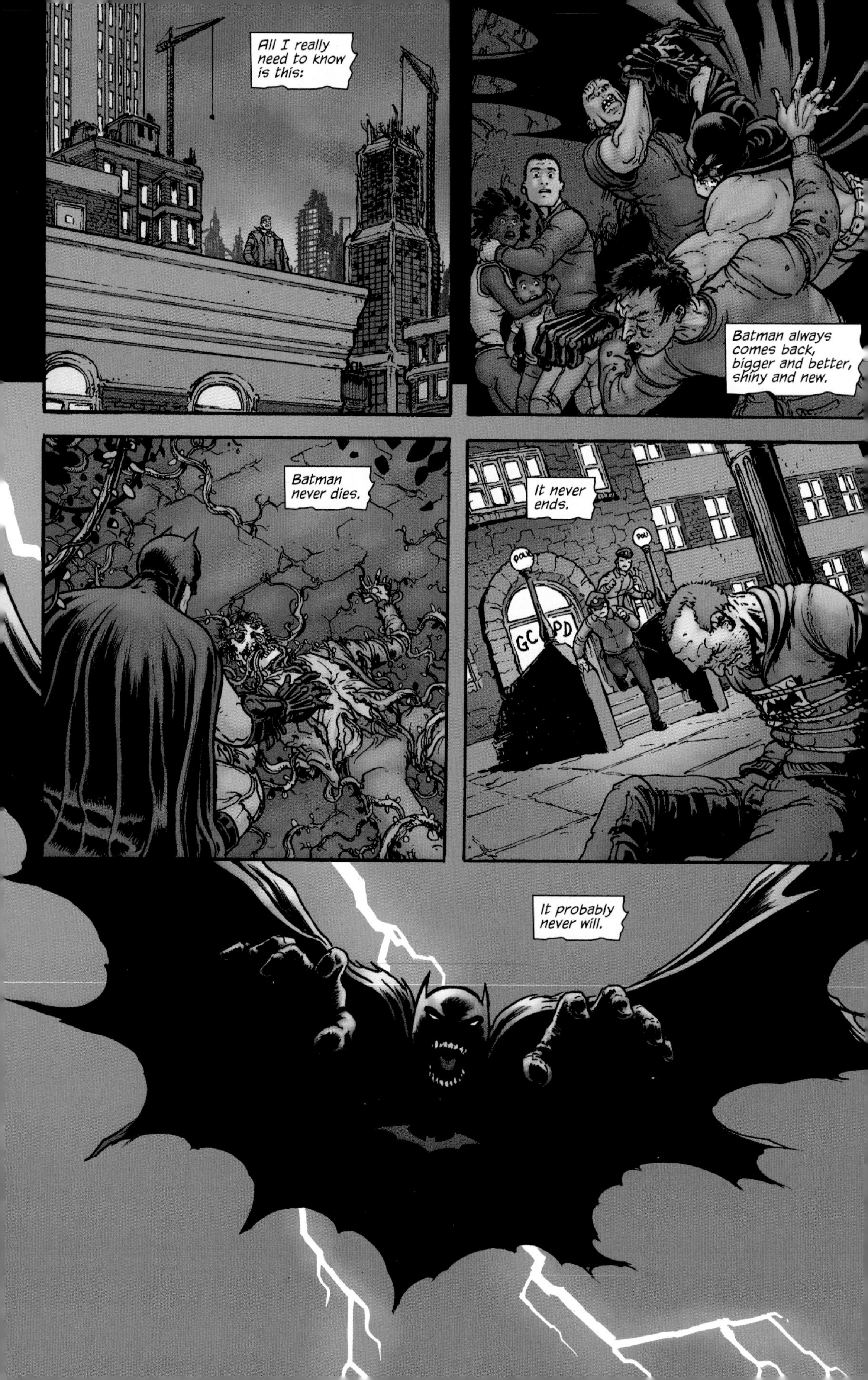
All I really need to know is this:
Batman always comes back, bigger and better, shiny and new.
Batman never dies.
It never ends.
GCPD
It probably never will.

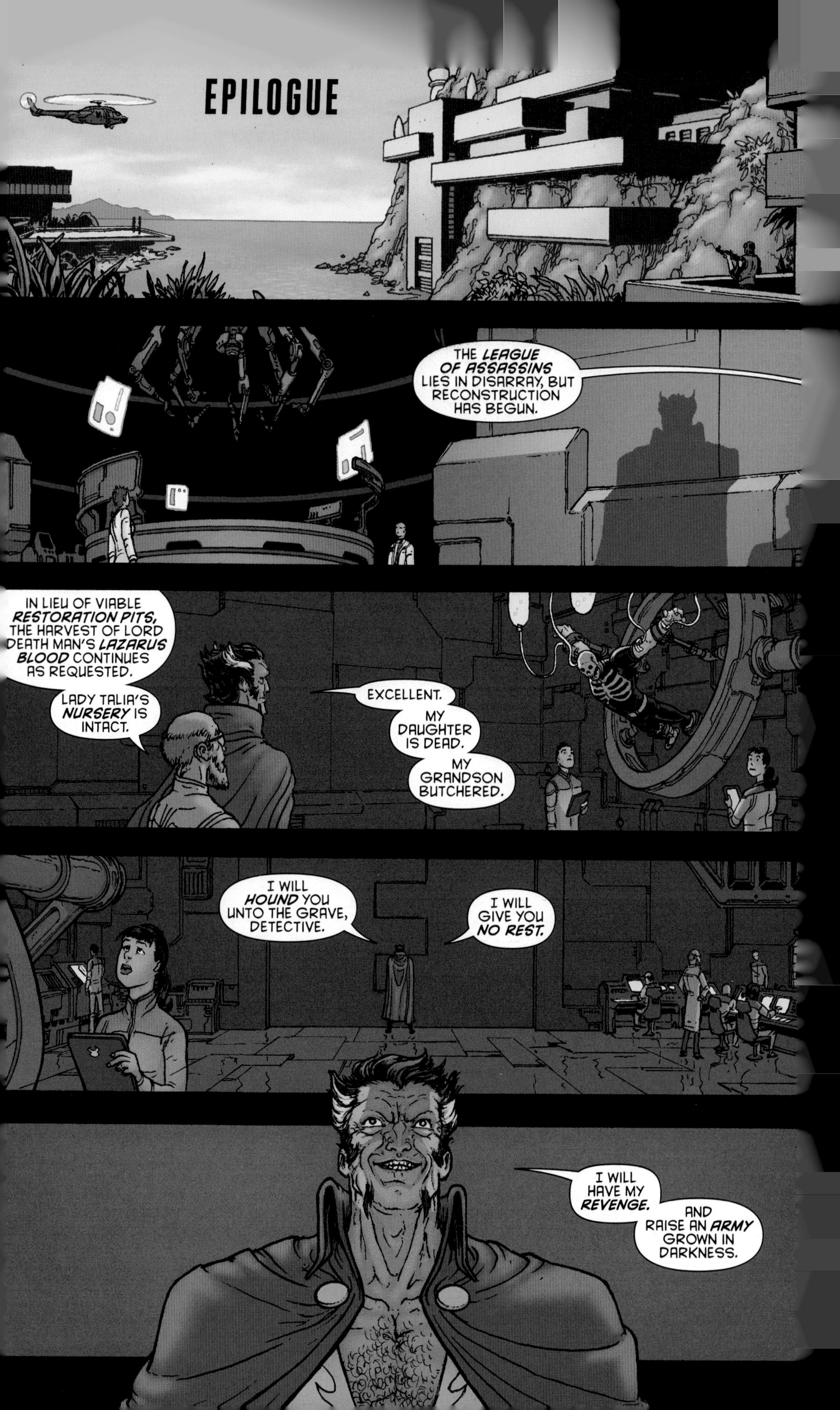
EPILOGUE
THE LEAGUE OF ASSASSINS LIES IN DISARRAY, BUT RECONSTRUCTION HAS BEGUN.
IN LIEU OF VIABLE RESTORATION PITS, THE HARVEST OF LORD DEATH MAN'S LAZARUS BLOOD CONTINUES AS REQUESTED.
LADY TALIA'S NURSERY IS INTACT.
EXCELLENT.
MY DAUGHTER IS DEAD.
MY GRANDSON BUTCHERED.
I WILL HOUND YOU UNTO THE GRAVE, DETECTIVE.
I WILL GIVE YOU NO REST.
I WILL HAVE MY REVENGE.
AND RAISE AN ARMY GROWN IN DARKNESS.

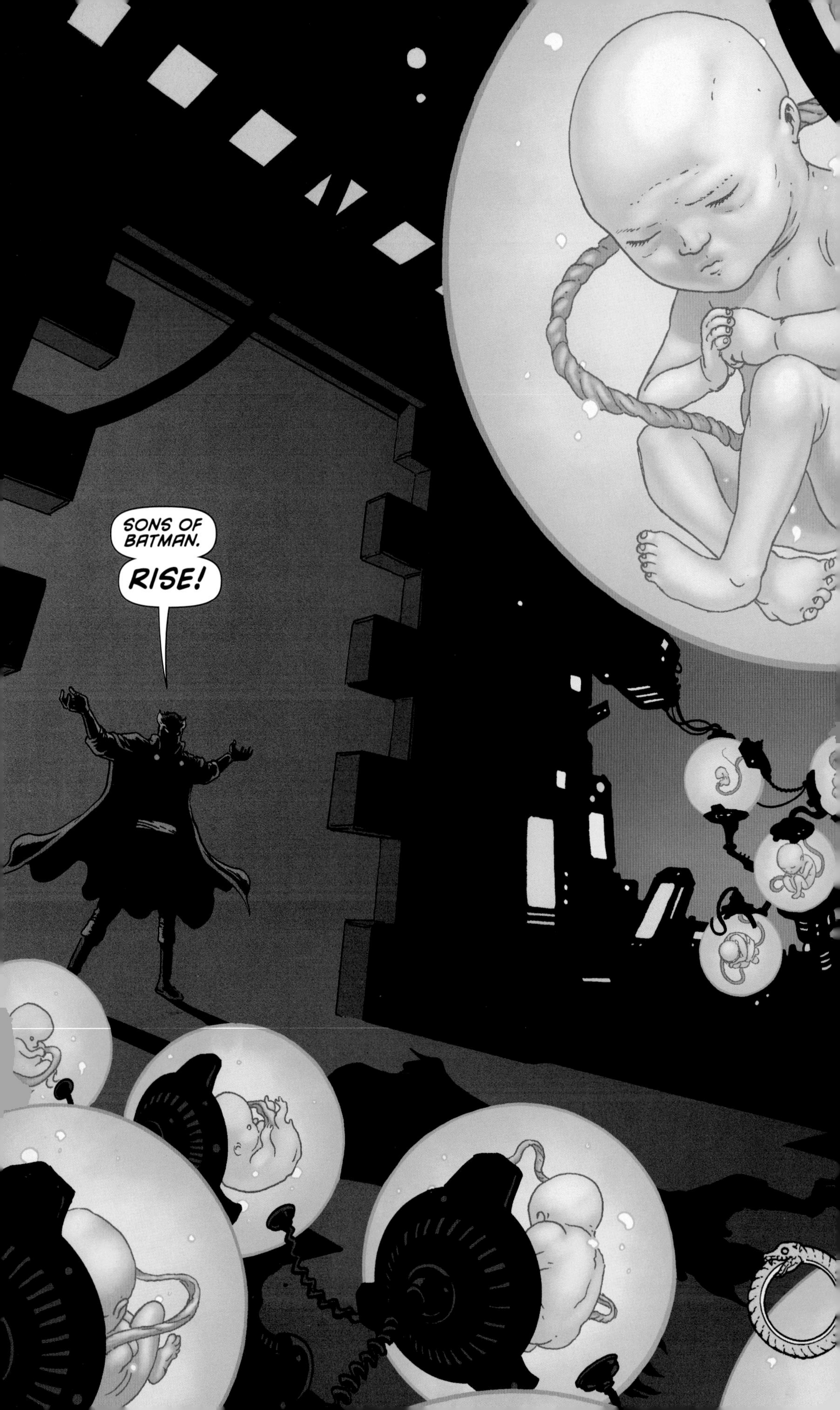
SONS OF BATMAN.
RISE!

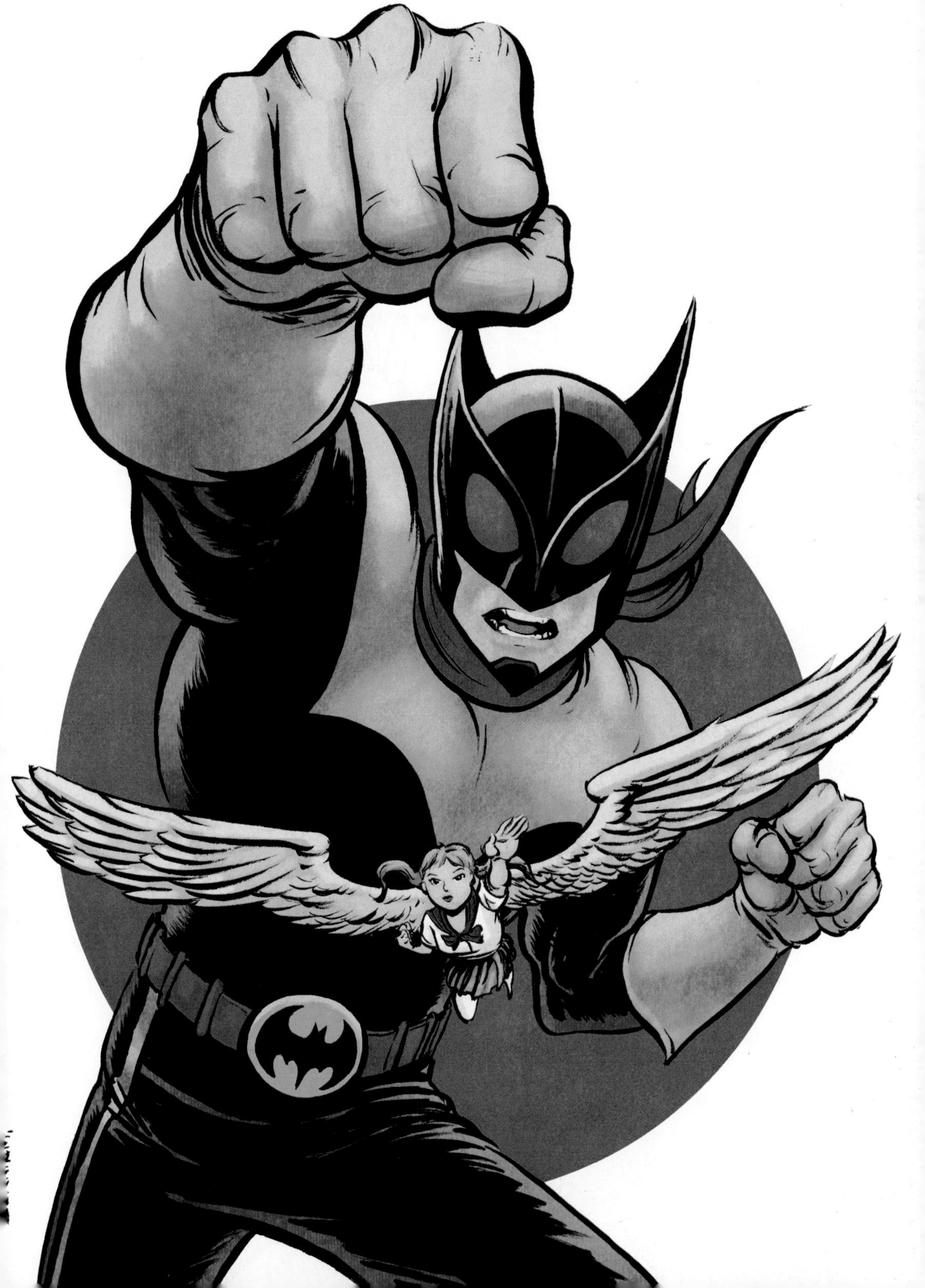

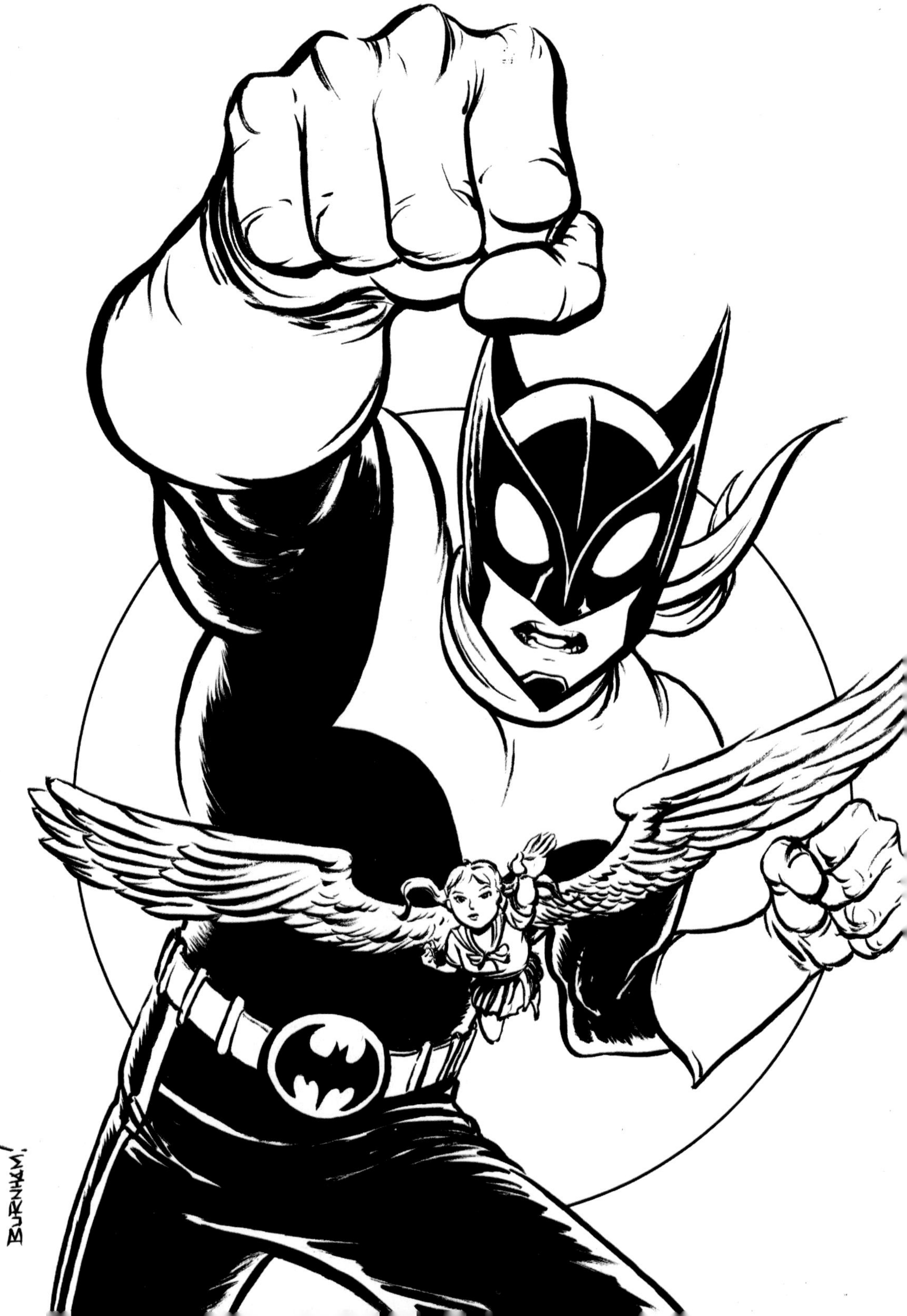
BURNHAM!

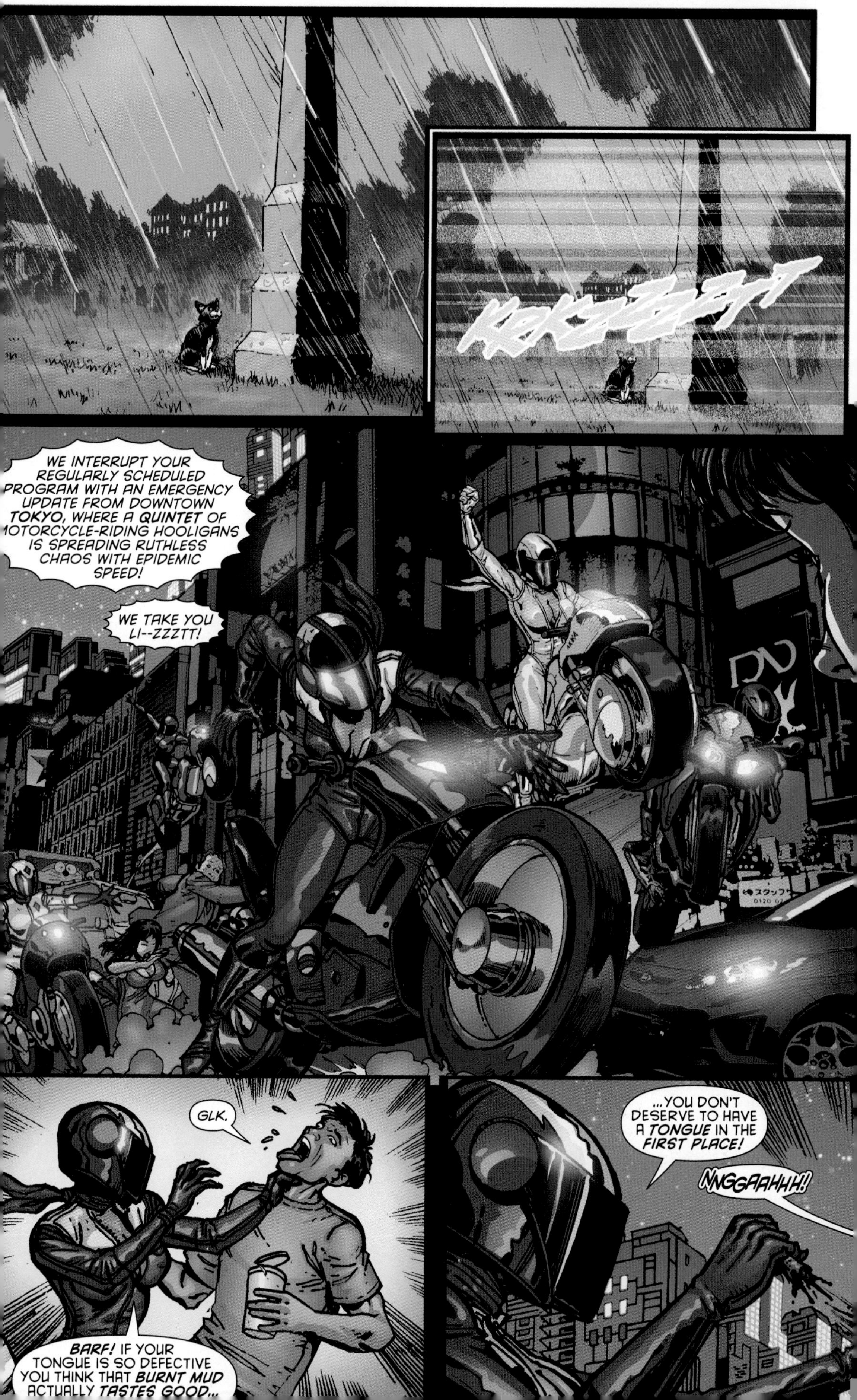
KRKZZZZZT
WE INTERRUPT YOUR REGULARLY SCHEDULED PROGRAM WITH AN EMERGENCY UPDATE FROM DOWNTOWN TOKYO, WHERE A QUINTET OF MOTORCYCLE-RIDING HOOLIGANS IS SPREADING RUTHLESS CHAOS WITH EPIDEMIC SPEED!
WE TAKE YOU LI--ZZZTT!
GLK.
BARF! IF YOUR TONGUE IS SO DEFECTIVE YOU THINK THAT BURNT MUD ACTUALLY TASTES GOOD...
...YOU DON'T DESERVE TO HAVE A TONGUE IN THE FIRST PLACE!
NNGGAAHHH!

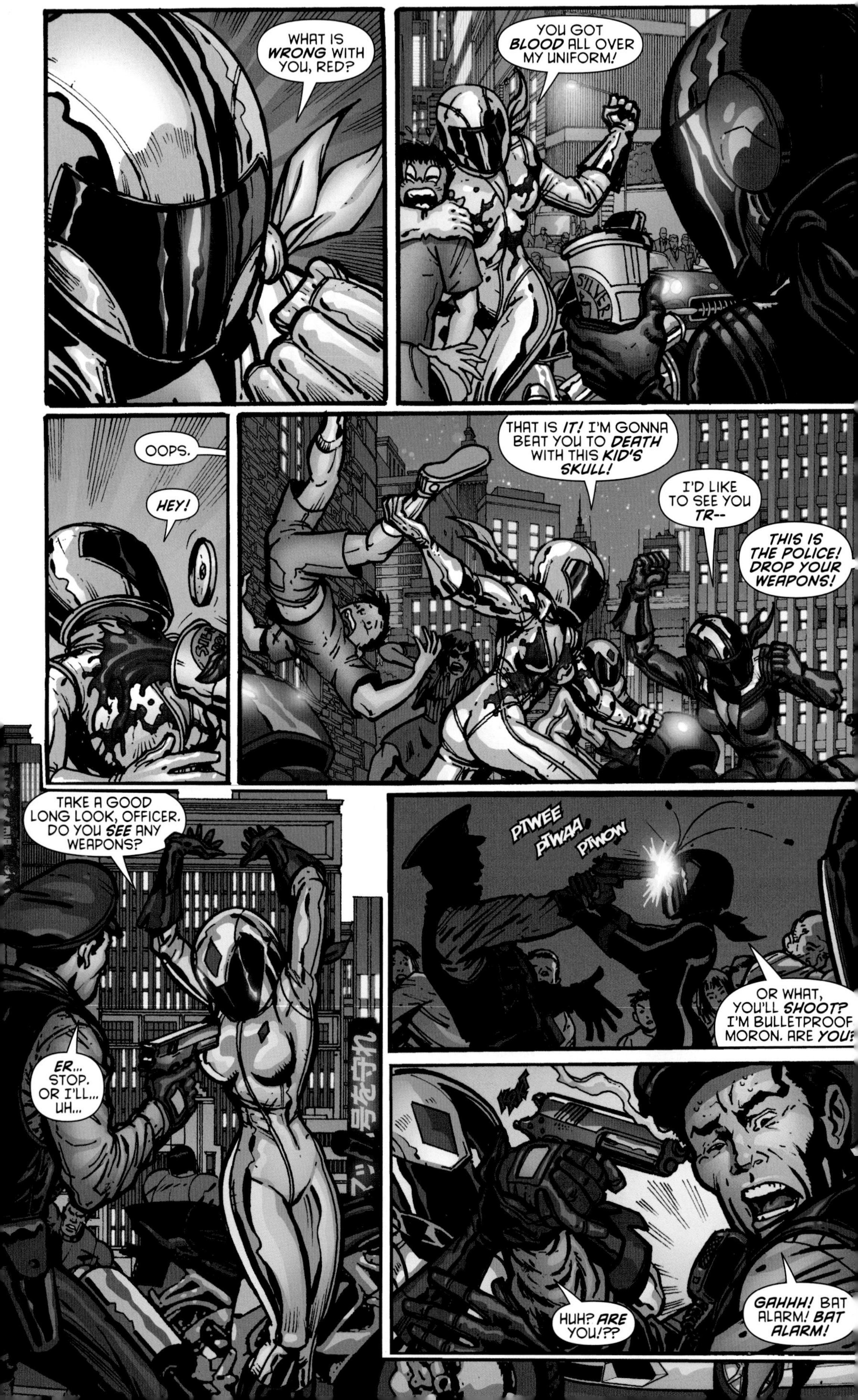
WHAT IS WRONG WITH YOU, RED?
YOU GOT BLOOD ALL OVER MY UNIFORM!
OOPS.
HEY!
THAT IS IT! I'M GONNA BEAT YOU TO DEATH WITH THIS KID'S SKULL!
I'D LIKE TO SEE YOU TR--
THIS IS THE POLICE! DROP YOUR WEAPONS!
TAKE A GOOD LONG LOOK, OFFICER. DO YOU SEE ANY WEAPONS?
ER... STOP. OR I'LL... UH...
PTWEE
PTWAA
PTWOW
OR WHAT, YOU'LL SHOOT? I'M BULLETPROOF MORON. ARE YOU?
HUH? ARE YOU!??
GAHHH! BAT ALARM! BAT ALARM!

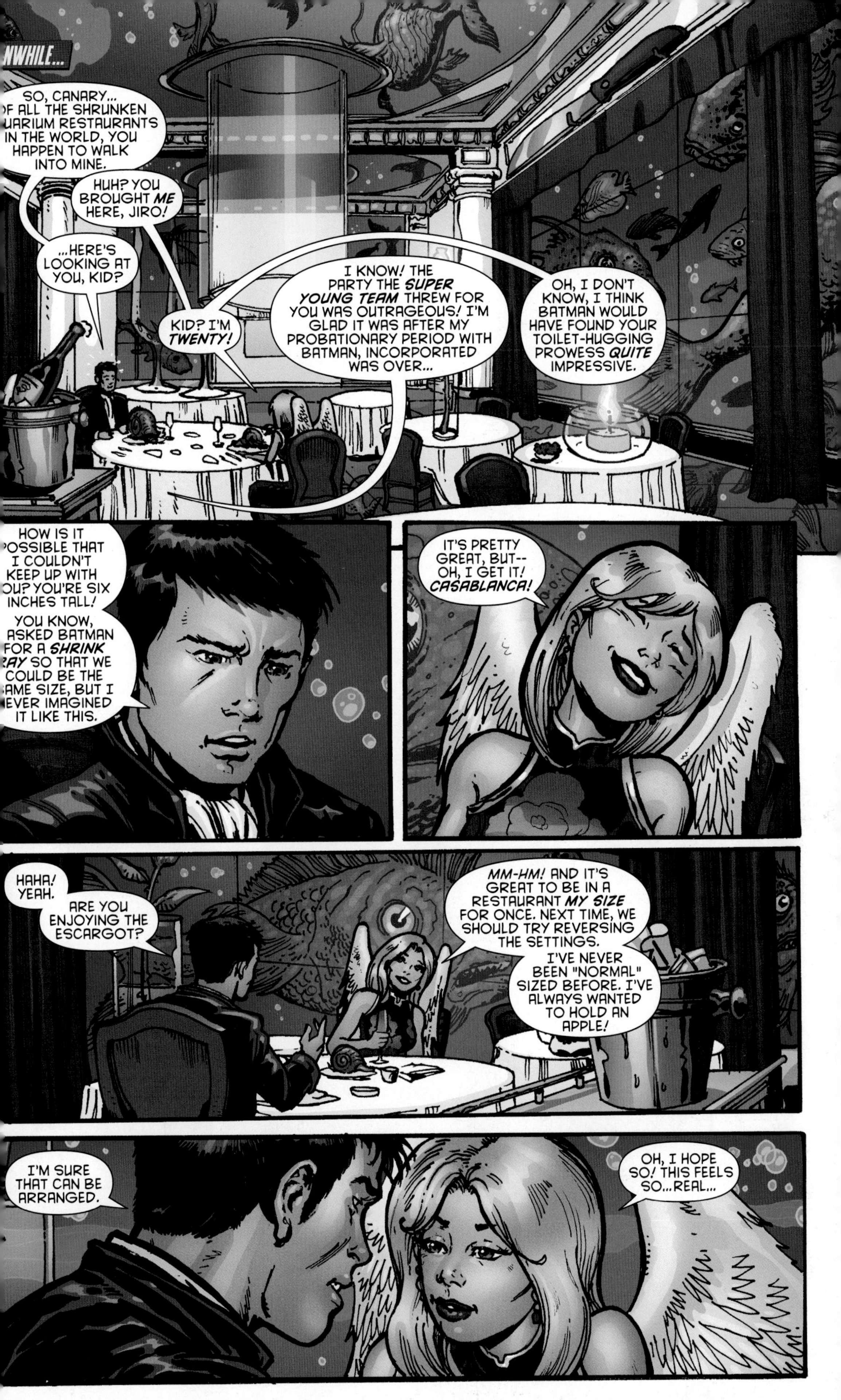
NWHILE...
SO, CANARY... OF ALL THE SHRUNKEN UARIUM RESTAURANTS IN THE WORLD, YOU HAPPEN TO WALK INTO MINE.
HUH? YOU BROUGHT ME HERE, JIRO!
...HERE'S LOOKING AT YOU, KID?
KID? I'M TWENTY!
I KNOW! THE PARTY THE SUPER YOUNG TEAM THREW FOR YOU WAS OUTRAGEOUS! I'M GLAD IT WAS AFTER MY PROBATIONARY PERIOD WITH BATMAN, INCORPORATED WAS OVER...
OH, I DON'T KNOW, I THINK BATMAN WOULD HAVE FOUND YOUR TOILET-HUGGING PROWESS QUITE IMPRESSIVE.
HOW IS IT OSSIBLE THAT I COULDN'T KEEP UP WITH OU? YOU'RE SIX INCHES TALL!
YOU KNOW, ASKED BATMAN FOR A SHRINK RAY SO THAT WE COULD BE THE AME SIZE, BUT I EVER IMAGINED IT LIKE THIS.
IT'S PRETTY GREAT, BUT-- OH, I GET IT! CASABLANCA!
HAHA! YEAH.
ARE YOU ENJOYING THE ESCARGOT?
MM-HM! AND IT'S GREAT TO BE IN A RESTAURANT MY SIZE FOR ONCE. NEXT TIME, WE SHOULD TRY REVERSING THE SETTINGS.
I'VE NEVER BEEN "NORMAL" SIZED BEFORE. I'VE ALWAYS WANTED TO HOLD AN APPLE!
I'M SURE THAT CAN BE ARRANGED.
OH, I HOPE SO! THIS FEELS SO...REAL...

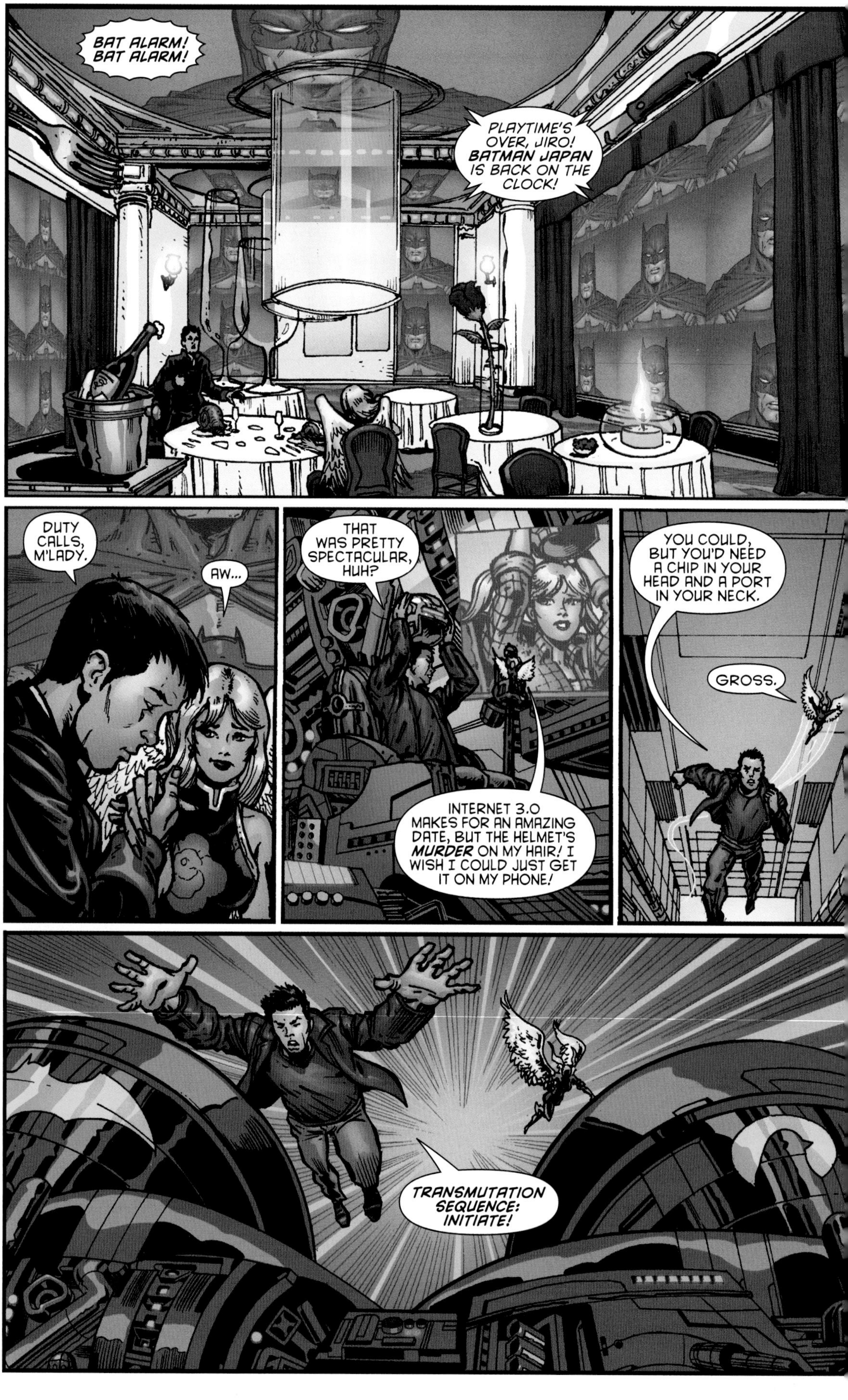
BAT ALARM! BAT ALARM!
PLAYTIME'S OVER, JIRO! BATMAN JAPAN IS BACK ON THE CLOCK!
DUTY CALLS, M'LADY.
AW...
THAT WAS PRETTY SPECTACULAR, HUH?
INTERNET 3.0 MAKES FOR AN AMAZING DATE, BUT THE HELMET'S MURDER ON MY HAIR! I WISH I COULD JUST GET IT ON MY PHONE!
YOU COULD, BUT YOU'D NEED A CHIP IN YOUR HEAD AND A PORT IN YOUR NECK.
GROSS.
TRANSMUTATION SEQUENCE: INITIATE!

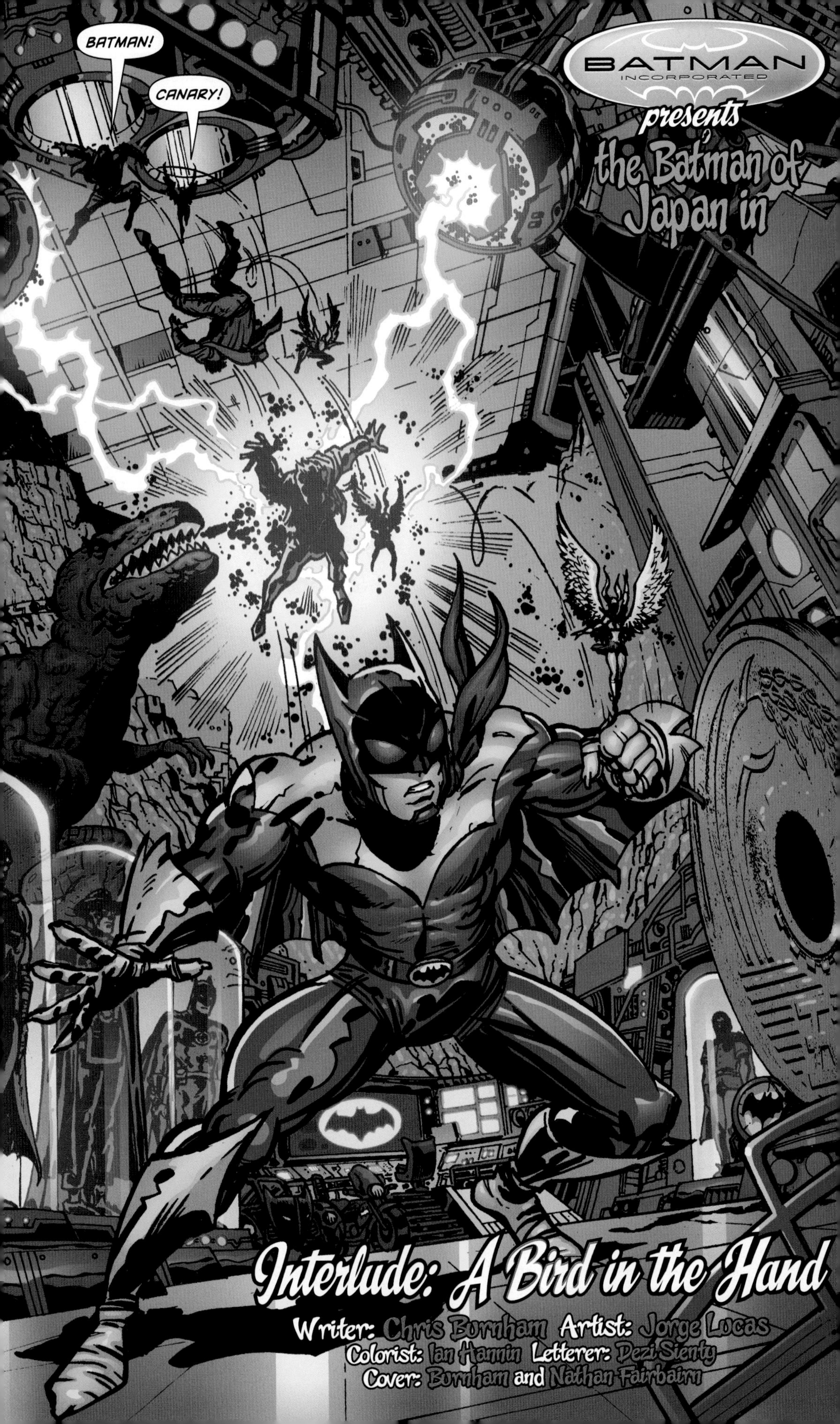
BATMAN!
CANARY!
BATMAN INCORPORATED
presents
the Batman of Japan in
Interlude: A Bird in the Hand
Writer: Chris Burnham Artist: Jorge Lucas
Colorist: Ian Hannin Letterer: Dezi Sienty
Cover: Burnham and Nathan Fairbairn

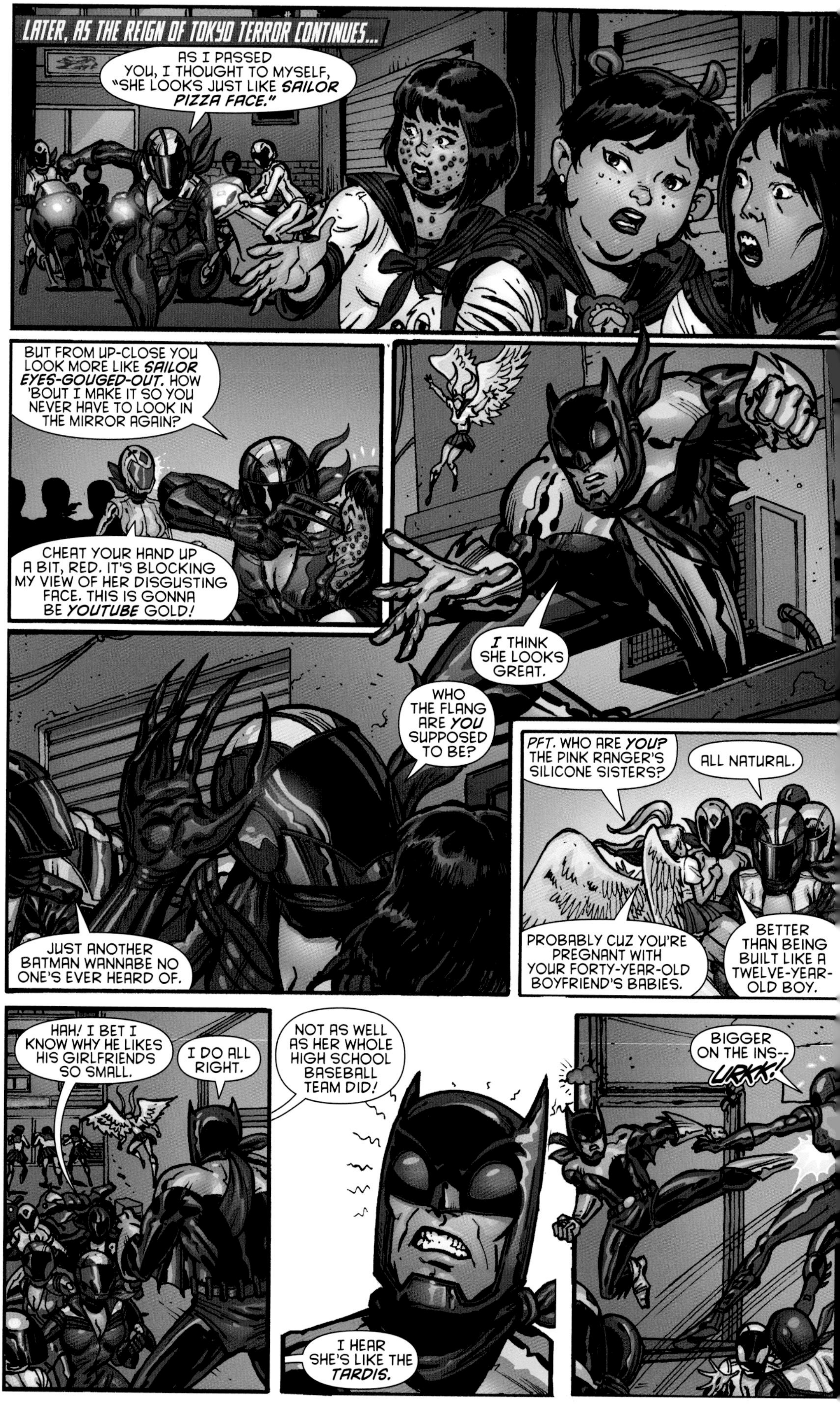
LATER, AS THE REIGN OF TOKYO TERROR CONTINUES...
AS I PASSED YOU, I THOUGHT TO MYSELF, "SHE LOOKS JUST LIKE SAILOR PIZZA FACE."
BUT FROM UP-CLOSE YOU LOOK MORE LIKE SAILOR EYES-GOUGED-OUT. HOW 'BOUT I MAKE IT SO YOU NEVER HAVE TO LOOK IN THE MIRROR AGAIN?
CHEAT YOUR HAND UP A BIT, RED. IT'S BLOCKING MY VIEW OF HER DISGUSTING FACE. THIS IS GONNA BE YOUTUBE GOLD!
I THINK SHE LOOKS GREAT.
WHO THE FLANG ARE YOU SUPPOSED TO BE?
JUST ANOTHER BATMAN WANNABE NO ONE'S EVER HEARD OF.
PFT. WHO ARE YOU? THE PINK RANGER'S SILICONE SISTERS?
ALL NATURAL.
PROBABLY CUZ YOU'RE PREGNANT WITH YOUR FORTY-YEAR-OLD BOYFRIEND'S BABIES.
BETTER THAN BEING BUILT LIKE A TWELVE-YEAR-OLD BOY.
HAH! I BET I KNOW WHY HE LIKES HIS GIRLFRIENDS SO SMALL.
I DO ALL RIGHT.
NOT AS WELL AS HER WHOLE HIGH SCHOOL BASEBALL TEAM DID!
I HEAR SHE'S LIKE THE TARDIS.
BIGGER ON THE INS--
URKK!

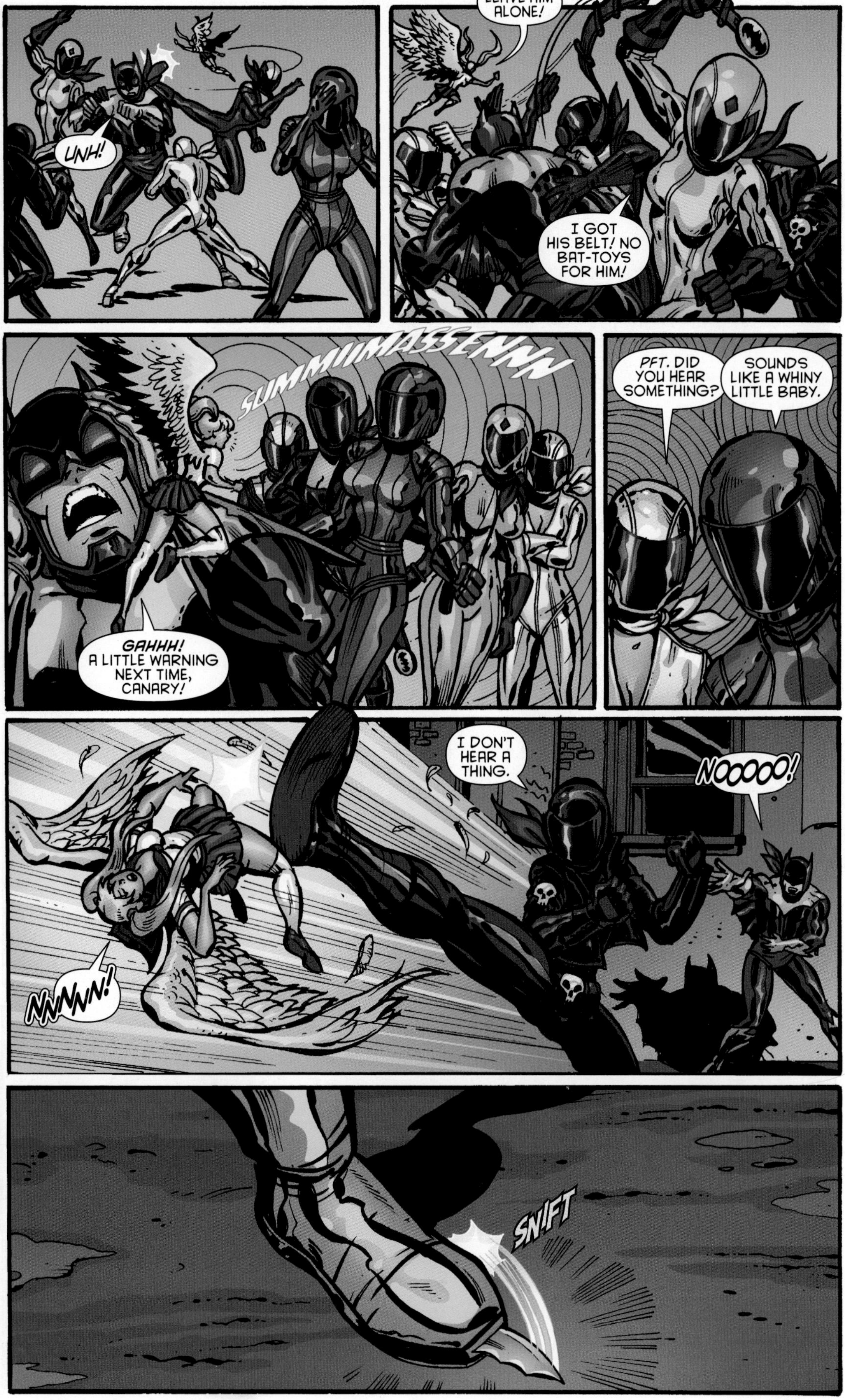
UNH!
LEAVE HIM ALONE!
I GOT HIS BELT! NO BAT-TOYS FOR HIM!
SUMMMMASSENNN
GAHHH! A LITTLE WARNING NEXT TIME, CANARY!
PFT. DID YOU HEAR SOMETHING?
SOUNDS LIKE A WHINY LITTLE BABY.
I DON'T HEAR A THING.
NOOOOO!
NNNNN!
SNIFT

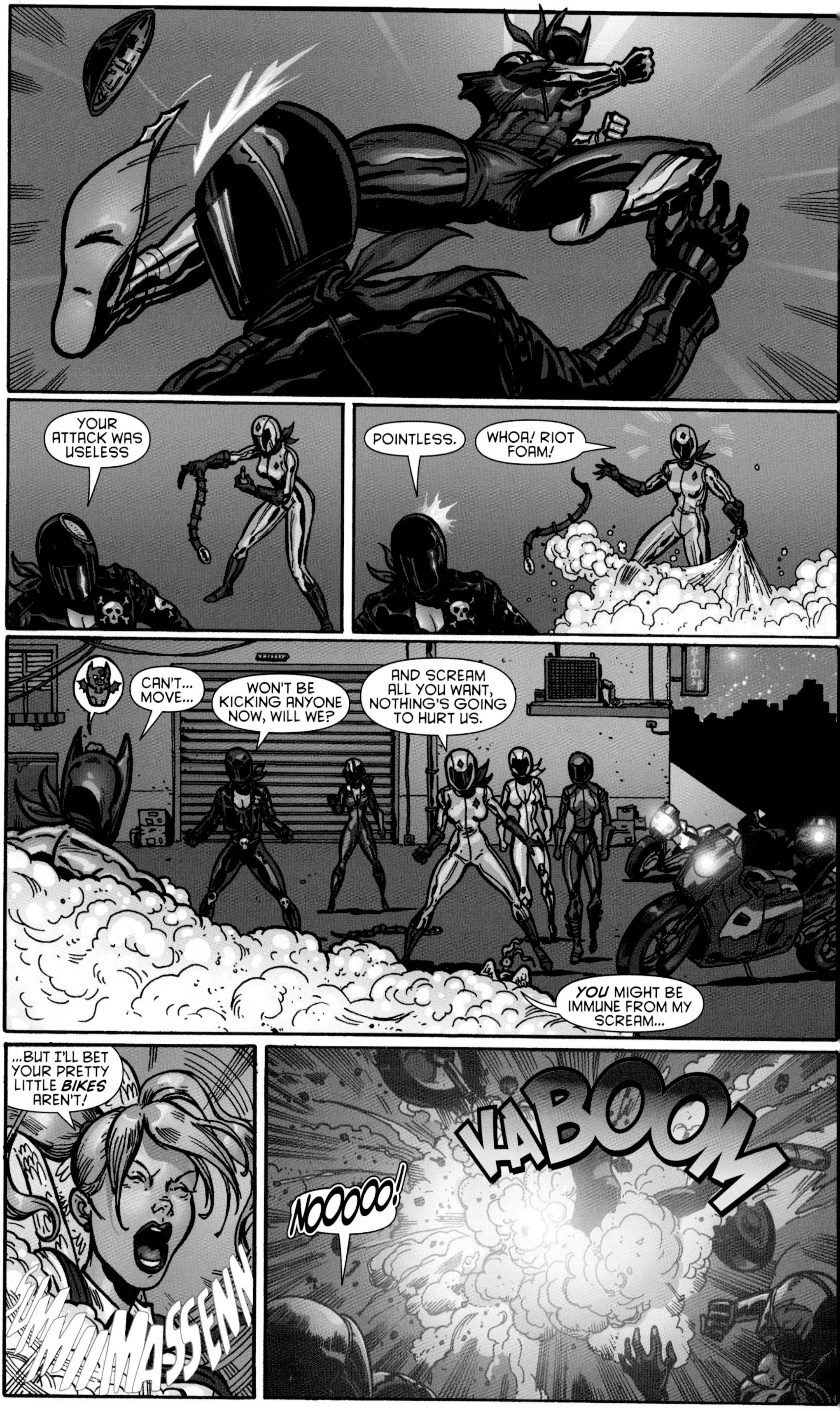
YOUR ATTACK WAS USELESS
POINTLESS.
WHOA! RIOT FOAM!
CAN'T... MOVE...
WON'T BE KICKING ANYONE NOW, WILL WE?
AND SCREAM ALL YOU WANT, NOTHING'S GOING TO HURT US.
YOU MIGHT BE IMMUNE FROM MY SCREAM...
...BUT I'LL BET YOUR PRETTY LITTLE BIKES AREN'T!
SHMMMASSENN
KABOOM
NOOOOO!

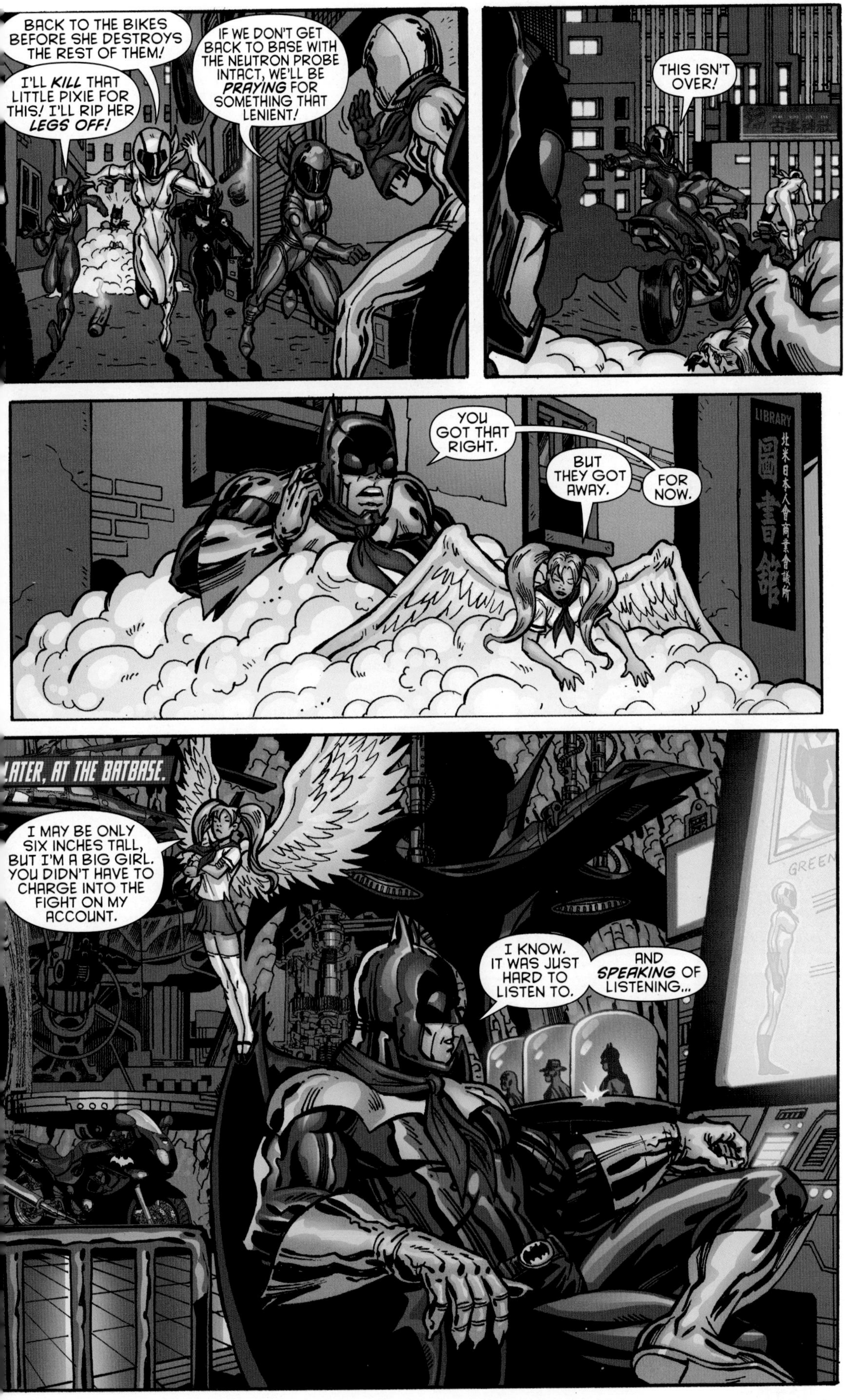

BACK TO THE BIKES BEFORE SHE DESTROYS THE REST OF THEM!
I'LL *KILL* THAT LITTLE PIXIE FOR THIS! I'LL RIP HER *LEGS OFF!*
IF WE DON'T GET BACK TO BASE WITH THE NEUTRON PROBE INTACT, WE'LL BE *PRAYING* FOR SOMETHING THAT LENIENT!
THIS ISN'T OVER!
YOU GOT THAT RIGHT.
BUT THEY GOT AWAY.
FOR NOW.
LIBRARY
圖書館
LATER, AT THE BATBASE.
I MAY BE ONLY SIX INCHES TALL, BUT I'M A BIG GIRL. YOU DIDN'T HAVE TO CHARGE INTO THE FIGHT ON MY ACCOUNT.
I KNOW. IT WAS JUST HARD TO LISTEN TO.
AND *SPEAKING* OF LISTENING...

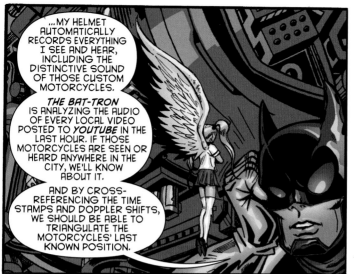

...MY HELMET AUTOMATICALLY RECORDS EVERYTHING I SEE AND HEAR, INCLUDING THE DISTINCTIVE SOUND OF THOSE CUSTOM MOTORCYCLES.

THE BAT-TRON IS ANALYZING THE AUDIO OF EVERY LOCAL VIDEO POSTED TO *YOUTUBE* IN THE LAST HOUR. IF THOSE MOTORCYCLES ARE SEEN OR HEARD ANYWHERE IN THE CITY, WE'LL KNOW ABOUT IT.

AND BY CROSS-REFERENCING THE TIME STAMPS AND DOPPLER SHIFTS, WE SHOULD BE ABLE TO TRIANGULATE THE MOTORCYCLES' LAST KNOWN POSITION.

BUT COULDN'T YOU DO ALL THAT REMOTELY FROM YOUR BAT-PHONE? WHY DID WE HAVE TO COME BACK HERE?

GOOD QUESTION.

WHAT YOU SAID BEFORE ABOUT GETTING INTERNET 3.0 ON YOUR PHONE GAVE ME AN IDEA...

OMG! THEIR HELMETS! THE WAY THE BLACK ONE HEALED ITSELF!

YEAH, I'D SAY IT'S SOME SORT OF SOPHISTICATED *NANO-TECHNOLOGY.*

THAT MIGHT EXPLAIN THEIR INCREASED STRENGTH AND REFLEXES, TOO.

MMM HMM. I THINK IF I CAN WIRE YOUR TINY PHONES INTO MY DIAMOND-TIPPED DARTS...

THEN IF WE STICK THEM IN THEIR HELMETS WE COULD OVERRIDE THE NANO-TECHNOLOGY'S PRO-GRAMMING!

PLUG AND PLAY!

BOOP BOOP

THE CALCULATIONS ARE COMPLETE!

OH, I HOPE THEIR BASE IS SOMEWHERE SURPRISING! MAYBE UNDERNEATH THE STATUE OF *HACHIKO!*

PERHAPS A HIDDEN ROOM IN *ASAKUSA TEMPLE?*

OR AN UNDERGROUND, UPSIDE-DOWN VERSION OF *TOKYO TOWER?*

AW... WHAT?

AN EXIT RAMP TO NOWHERE?

BUT THE CONFIGURATIONS WERE PRECISE!

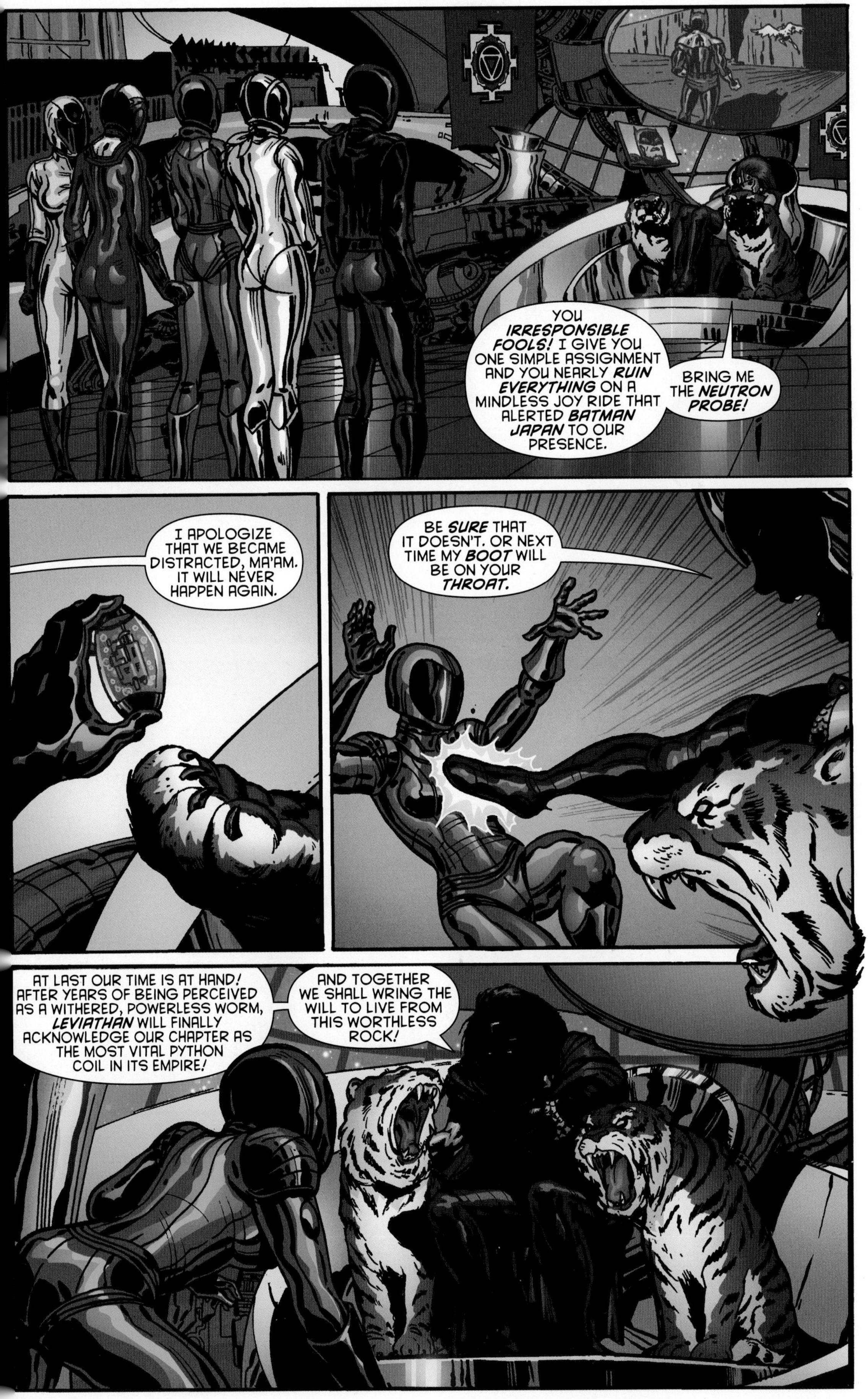
YOU IRRESPONSIBLE FOOLS! I GIVE YOU ONE SIMPLE ASSIGNMENT AND YOU NEARLY RUIN EVERYTHING ON A MINDLESS JOY RIDE THAT ALERTED BATMAN JAPAN TO OUR PRESENCE.
BRING ME THE NEUTRON PROBE!
I APOLOGIZE THAT WE BECAME DISTRACTED, MA'AM. IT WILL NEVER HAPPEN AGAIN.
BE SURE THAT IT DOESN'T. OR NEXT TIME MY BOOT WILL BE ON YOUR THROAT.
AT LAST OUR TIME IS AT HAND! AFTER YEARS OF BEING PERCEIVED AS A WITHERED, POWERLESS WORM, LEVIATHAN WILL FINALLY ACKNOWLEDGE OUR CHAPTER AS THE MOST VITAL PYTHON COIL IN ITS EMPIRE!
AND TOGETHER WE SHALL WRING THE WILL TO LIVE FROM THIS WORTHLESS ROCK!

HOLD ON, I'VE BEEN CYCLING THROUGH MY GOGGLES' DIFFERENT SPECTRUM SETTINGS, AND I'M GETTING SOMETHING WEIRD...

...IF I GAVE YOU A DISTINCT FREQUENCY, COULD YOU MATCH IT AND AMPLIFY IT?

PERFECT PITCH. MY PARENTS USED TO MAKE ME TUNE THEIR FRIENDS' PIANOS.

WOW.

SUMMIIIMASSEN

BOOM

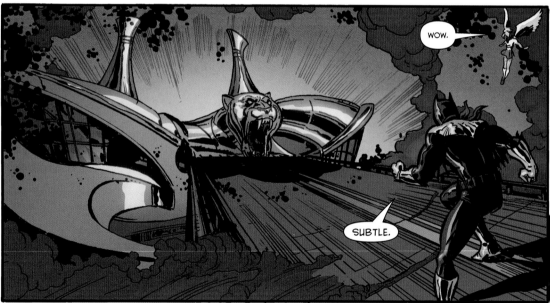

WOW.

SUBTLE.

ALERT! THE CAMOUFLAGE CLOAK HAS BEEN DISRUPTED! ALERT!

YOU *FOOLS!* GET OUT THERE AND KILL THEM OR I'LL FEED YOUR SKINS TO MY *TIGERS!*

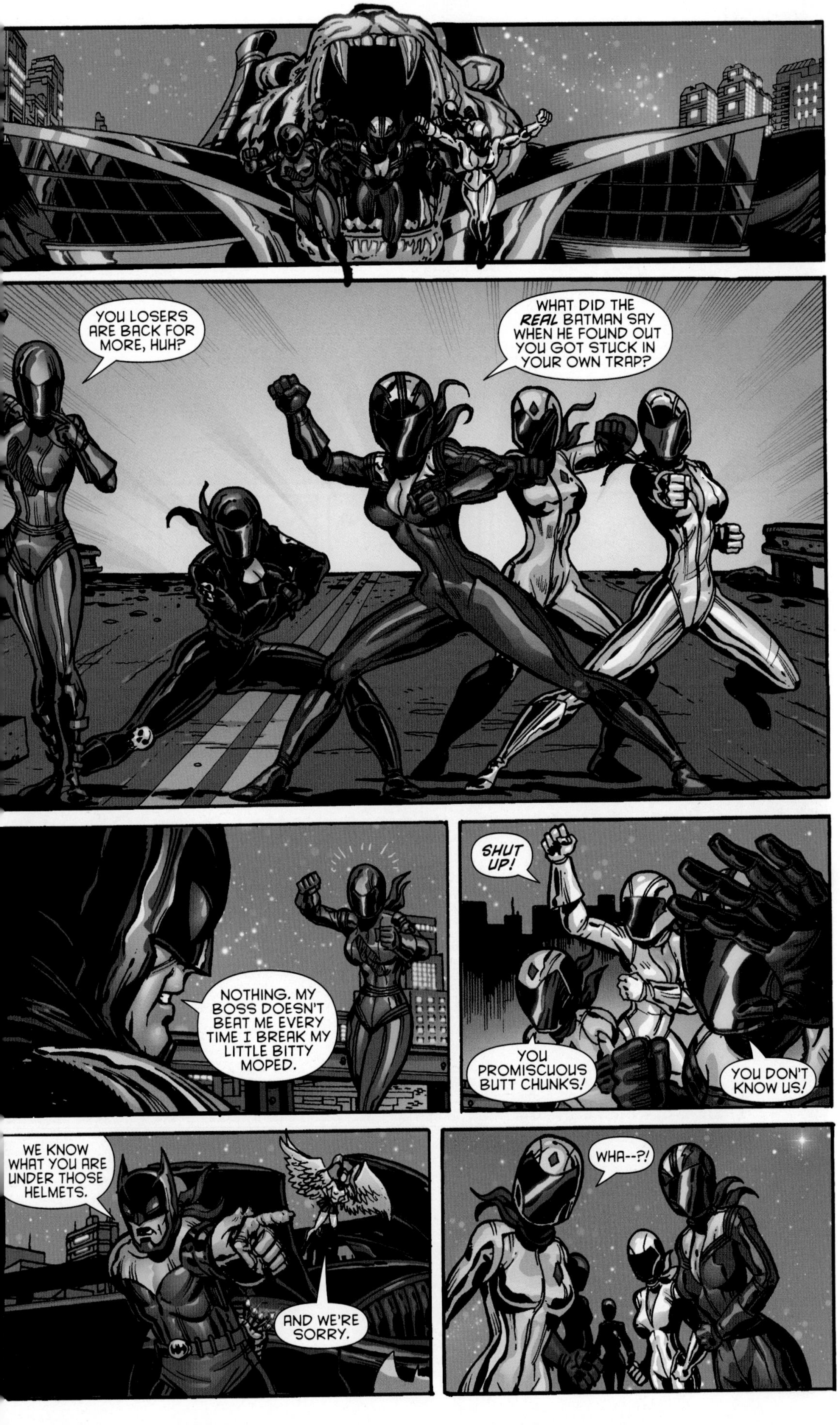
YOU LOSERS ARE BACK FOR MORE, HUH?
WHAT DID THE REAL BATMAN SAY WHEN HE FOUND OUT YOU GOT STUCK IN YOUR OWN TRAP?
NOTHING. MY BOSS DOESN'T BEAT ME EVERY TIME I BREAK MY LITTLE BITTY MOPED.
SHUT UP!
YOU PROMISCUOUS BUTT CHUNKS!
YOU DON'T KNOW US!
WE KNOW WHAT YOU ARE UNDER THOSE HELMETS.
AND WE'RE SORRY.
WHA--?!

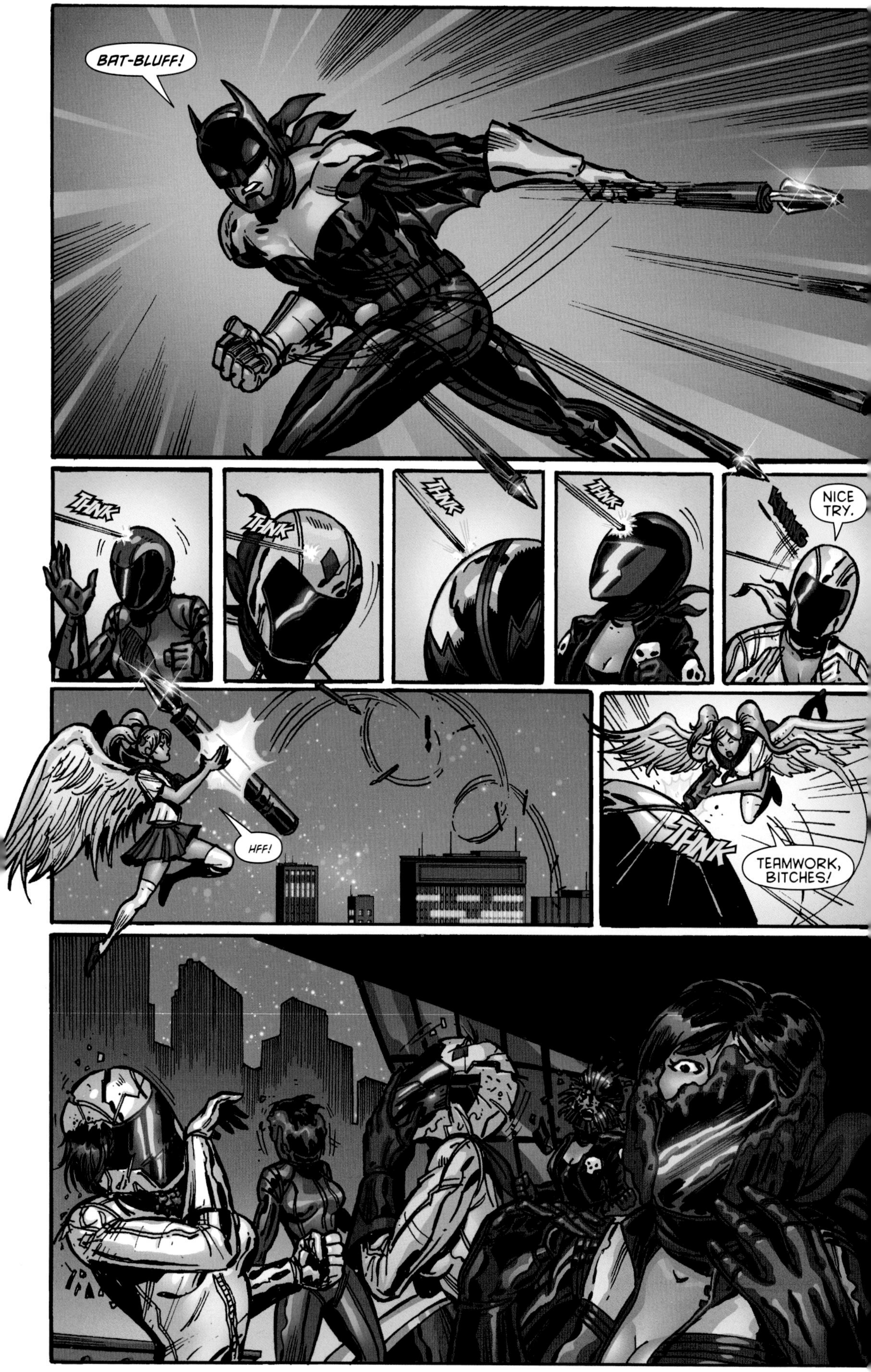
BAT-BLUFF!
THNK
THNK
THNK
THNK
NICE TRY.
HFF!
THNK
TEAMWORK, BITCHES!

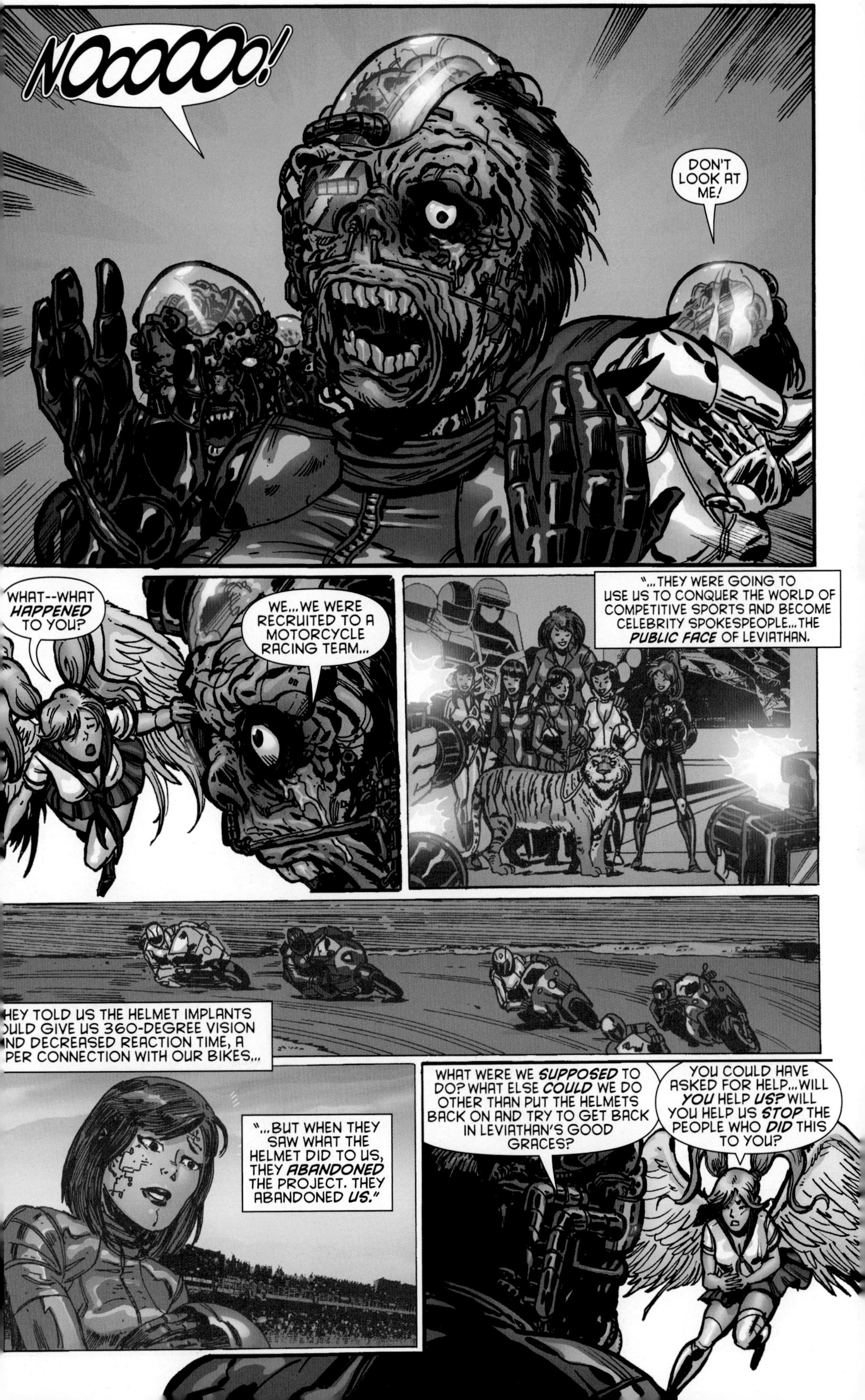
NOOOOOO!
DON'T LOOK AT ME!
WHAT--WHAT HAPPENED TO YOU?
WE...WE WERE RECRUITED TO A MOTORCYCLE RACING TEAM...
"...THEY WERE GOING TO USE US TO CONQUER THE WORLD OF COMPETITIVE SPORTS AND BECOME CELEBRITY SPOKESPEOPLE...THE PUBLIC FACE OF LEVIATHAN.
HEY TOLD US THE HELMET IMPLANTS OULD GIVE US 360-DEGREE VISION ND DECREASED REACTION TIME, A PER CONNECTION WITH OUR BIKES...
"...BUT WHEN THEY SAW WHAT THE HELMET DID TO US, THEY ABANDONED THE PROJECT. THEY ABANDONED US."
WHAT WERE WE SUPPOSED TO DO? WHAT ELSE COULD WE DO OTHER THAN PUT THE HELMETS BACK ON AND TRY TO GET BACK IN LEVIATHAN'S GOOD GRACES?
YOU COULD HAVE ASKED FOR HELP...WILL YOU HELP US? WILL YOU HELP US STOP THE PEOPLE WHO DID THIS TO YOU?

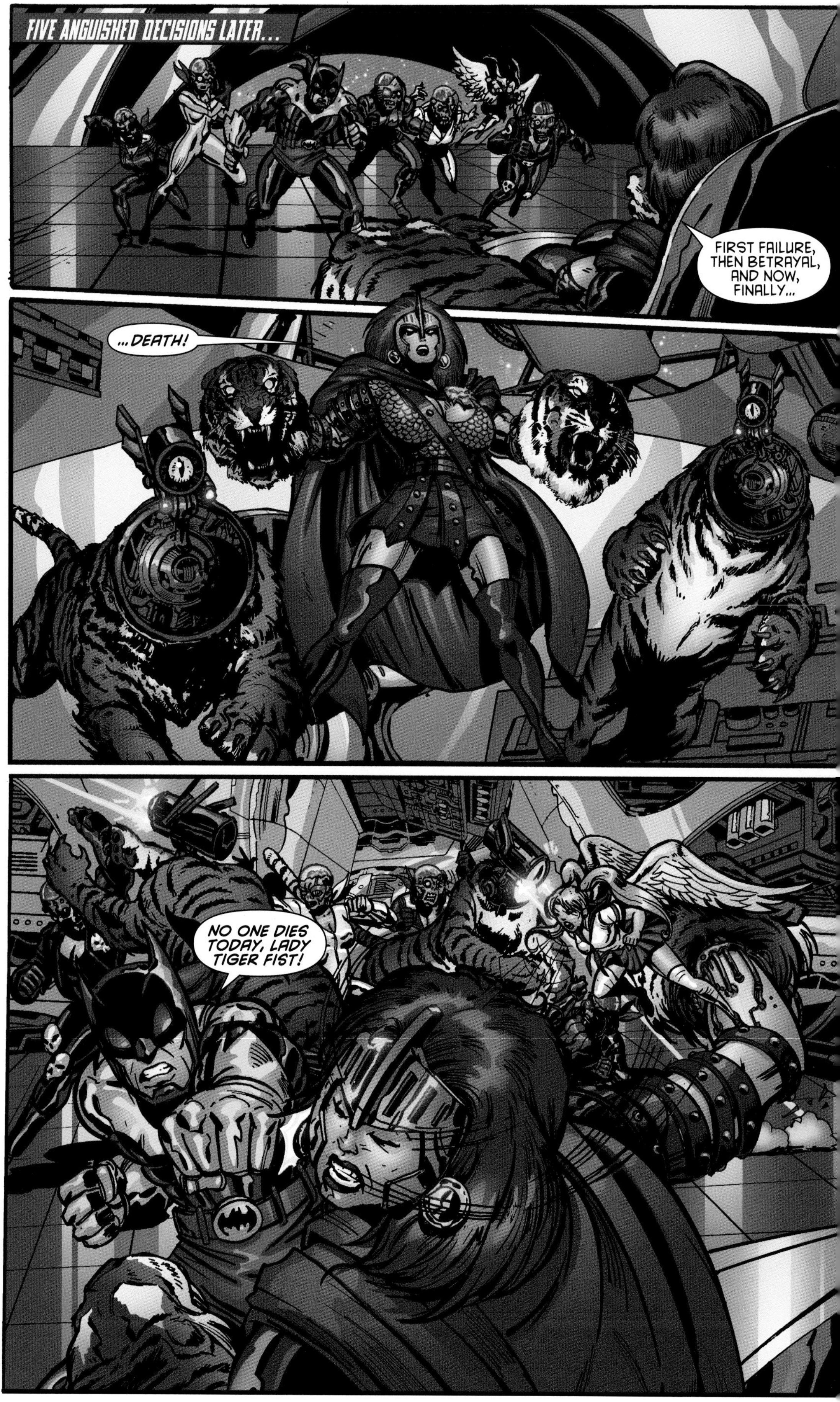
FIVE ANGUISHED DECISIONS LATER...
FIRST FAILURE, THEN BETRAYAL, AND NOW, FINALLY...
...DEATH!
NO ONE DIES TODAY, LADY TIGER FIST!

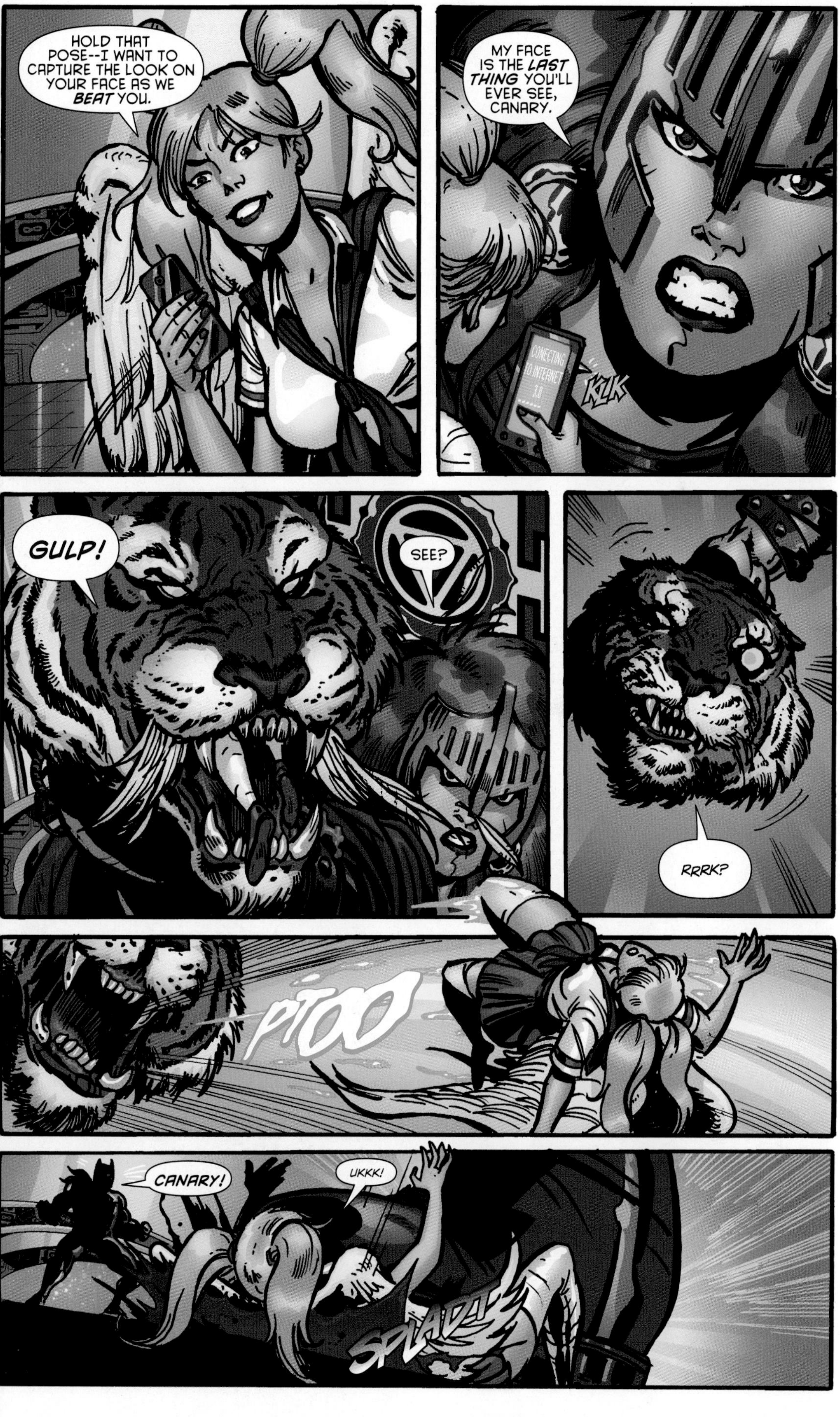
HOLD THAT POSE--I WANT TO CAPTURE THE LOOK ON YOUR FACE AS WE BEAT YOU.
MY FACE IS THE LAST THING YOU'LL EVER SEE, CANARY.
CONECTING TO INTERNET 3.0
KLIK
GULP!
SEE?
RRRK?
PTOO
CANARY!
UKKK!
SPLADT

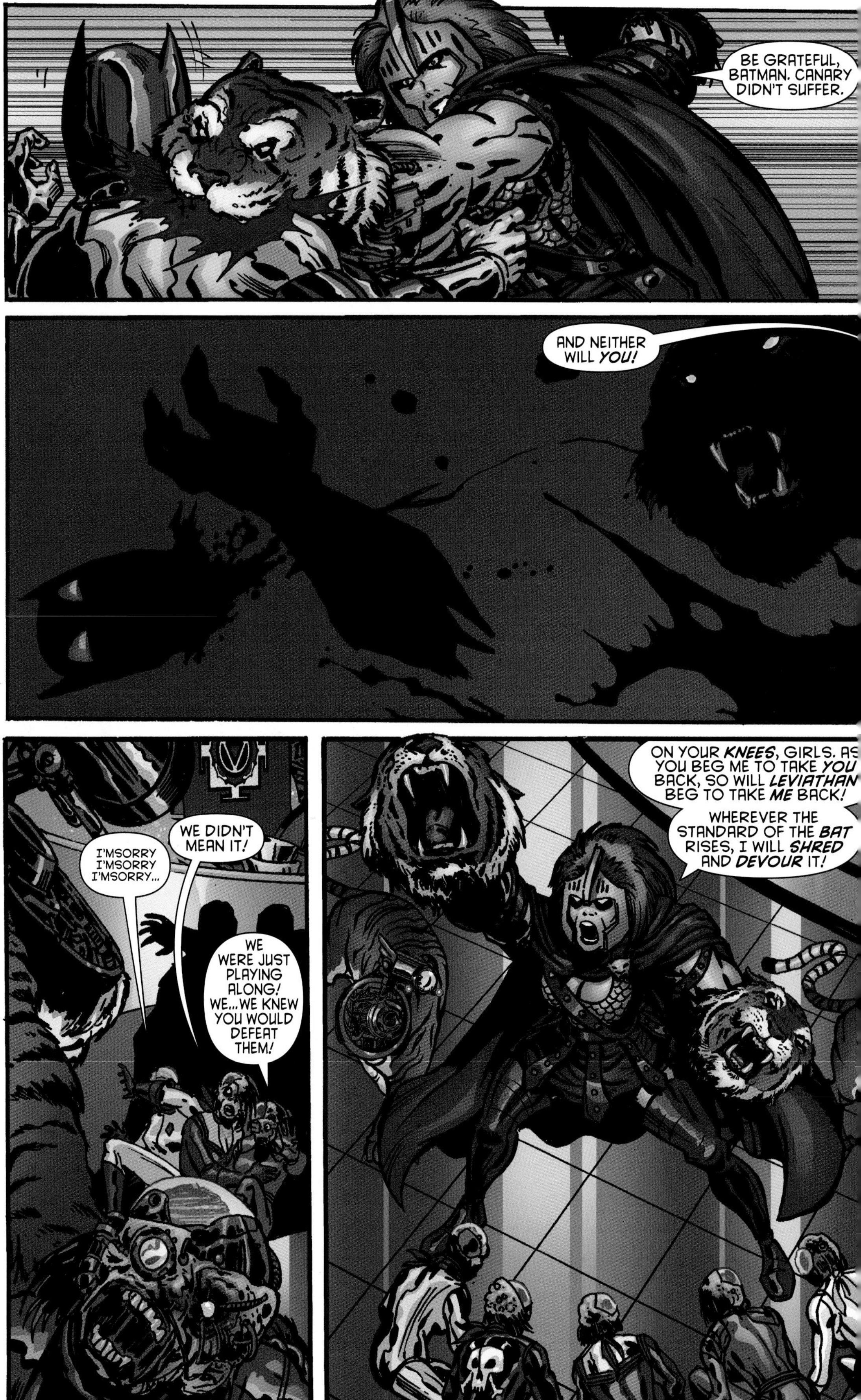
BE GRATEFUL, BATMAN. CANARY DIDN'T SUFFER.
AND NEITHER WILL *YOU!*
I'MSORRY I'MSORRY I'MSORRY...
WE DIDN'T MEAN IT!
WE WERE JUST PLAYING ALONG! WE...WE KNEW YOU WOULD DEFEAT THEM!
ON YOUR *KNEES*, GIRLS. AS YOU BEG ME TO TAKE *YOU* BACK, SO WILL *LEVIATHAN* BEG TO TAKE *ME* BACK!
WHEREVER THE STANDARD OF THE *BAT* RISES, I WILL *SHRED* AND *DEVOUR* IT!

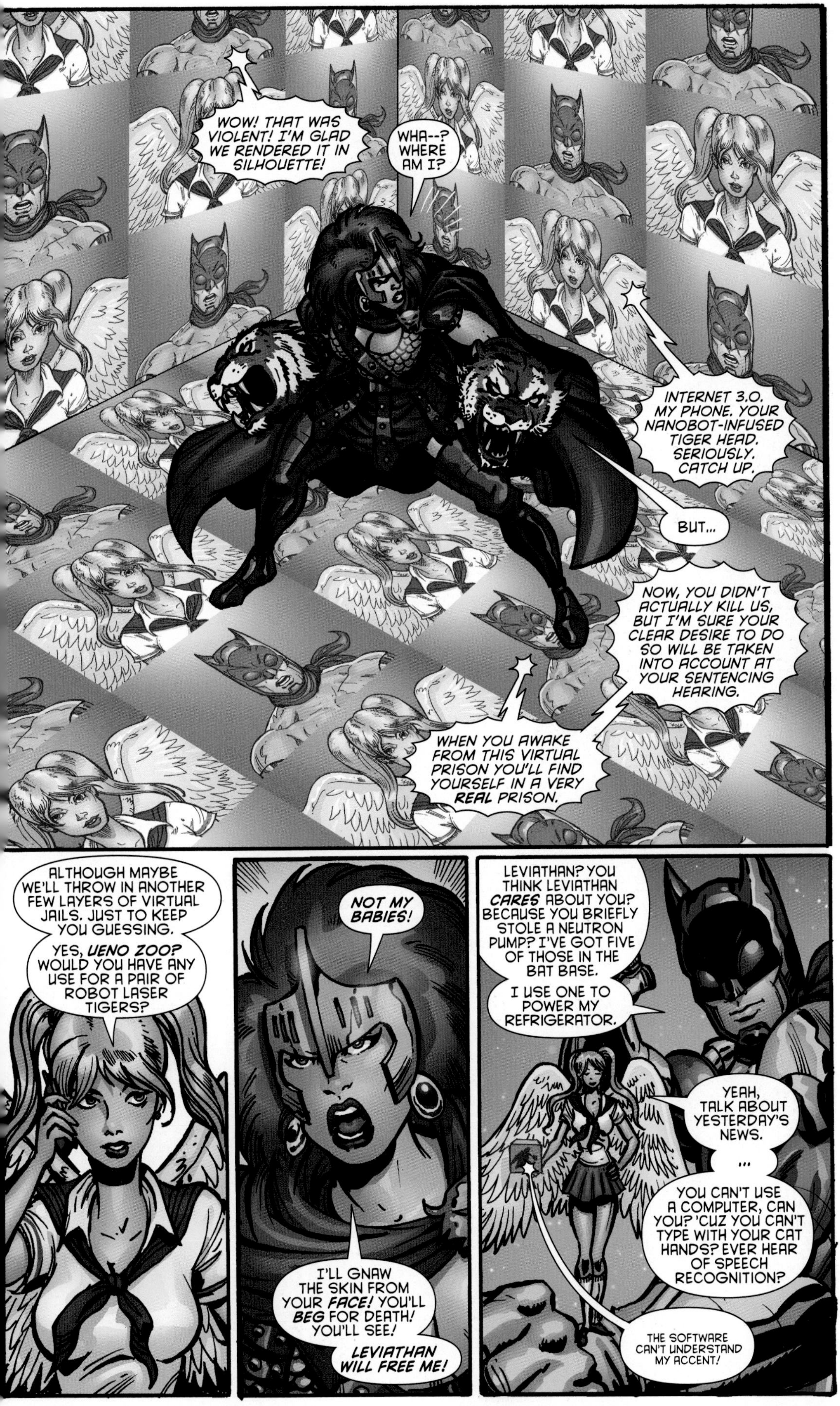
WOW! THAT WAS VIOLENT! I'M GLAD WE RENDERED IT IN SILHOUETTE!
WHA--? WHERE AM I?
INTERNET 3.O. MY PHONE. YOUR NANOBOT-INFUSED TIGER HEAD. SERIOUSLY. CATCH UP.
BUT...
NOW, YOU DIDN'T ACTUALLY KILL US, BUT I'M SURE YOUR CLEAR DESIRE TO DO SO WILL BE TAKEN INTO ACCOUNT AT YOUR SENTENCING HEARING.
WHEN YOU AWAKE FROM THIS VIRTUAL PRISON YOU'LL FIND YOURSELF IN A VERY REAL PRISON.
ALTHOUGH MAYBE WE'LL THROW IN ANOTHER FEW LAYERS OF VIRTUAL JAILS. JUST TO KEEP YOU GUESSING.
YES, UENO ZOO? WOULD YOU HAVE ANY USE FOR A PAIR OF ROBOT LASER TIGERS?
NOT MY BABIES!
I'LL GNAW THE SKIN FROM YOUR FACE! YOU'LL BEG FOR DEATH! YOU'LL SEE!
LEVIATHAN WILL FREE ME!
LEVIATHAN? YOU THINK LEVIATHAN CARES ABOUT YOU? BECAUSE YOU BRIEFLY STOLE A NEUTRON PUMP? I'VE GOT FIVE OF THOSE IN THE BAT BASE.
I USE ONE TO POWER MY REFRIGERATOR.
YEAH, TALK ABOUT YESTERDAY'S NEWS.
...
YOU CAN'T USE A COMPUTER, CAN YOU? 'CUZ YOU CAN'T TYPE WITH YOUR CAT HANDS? EVER HEAR OF SPEECH RECOGNITION?
THE SOFTWARE CAN'T UNDERSTAND MY ACCENT!

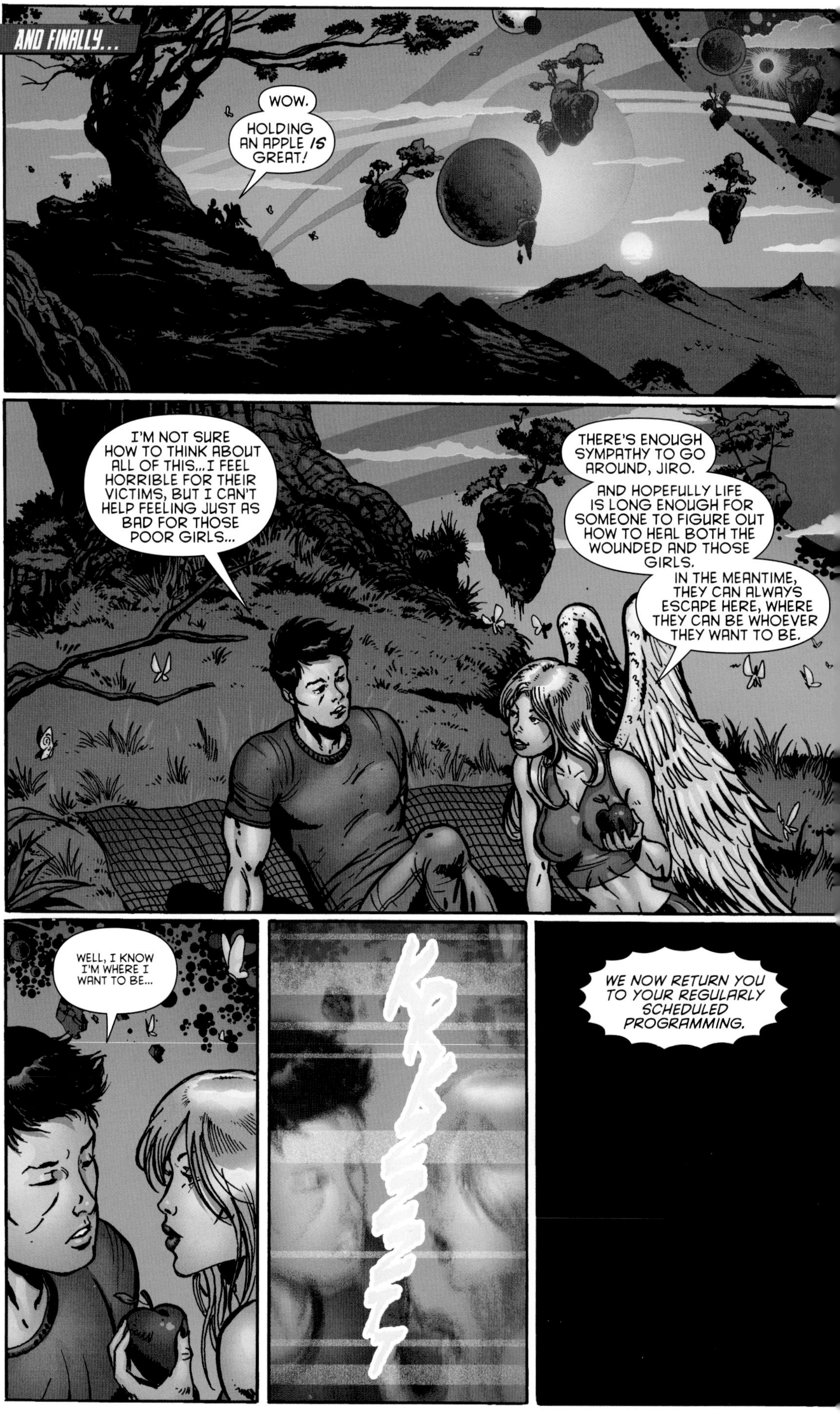

AND FINALLY...
WOW. HOLDING AN APPLE *IS* GREAT!
I'M NOT SURE HOW TO THINK ABOUT ALL OF THIS...I FEEL HORRIBLE FOR THEIR VICTIMS, BUT I CAN'T HELP FEELING JUST AS BAD FOR THOSE POOR GIRLS...
THERE'S ENOUGH SYMPATHY TO GO AROUND, JIRO.
AND HOPEFULLY LIFE IS LONG ENOUGH FOR SOMEONE TO FIGURE OUT HOW TO HEAL BOTH THE WOUNDED AND THOSE GIRLS.
IN THE MEANTIME, THEY CAN ALWAYS ESCAPE HERE, WHERE THEY CAN BE WHOEVER THEY WANT TO BE.
WELL, I KNOW I'M WHERE I WANT TO BE...
WE NOW RETURN YOU TO YOUR REGULARLY SCHEDULED PROGRAMMING.

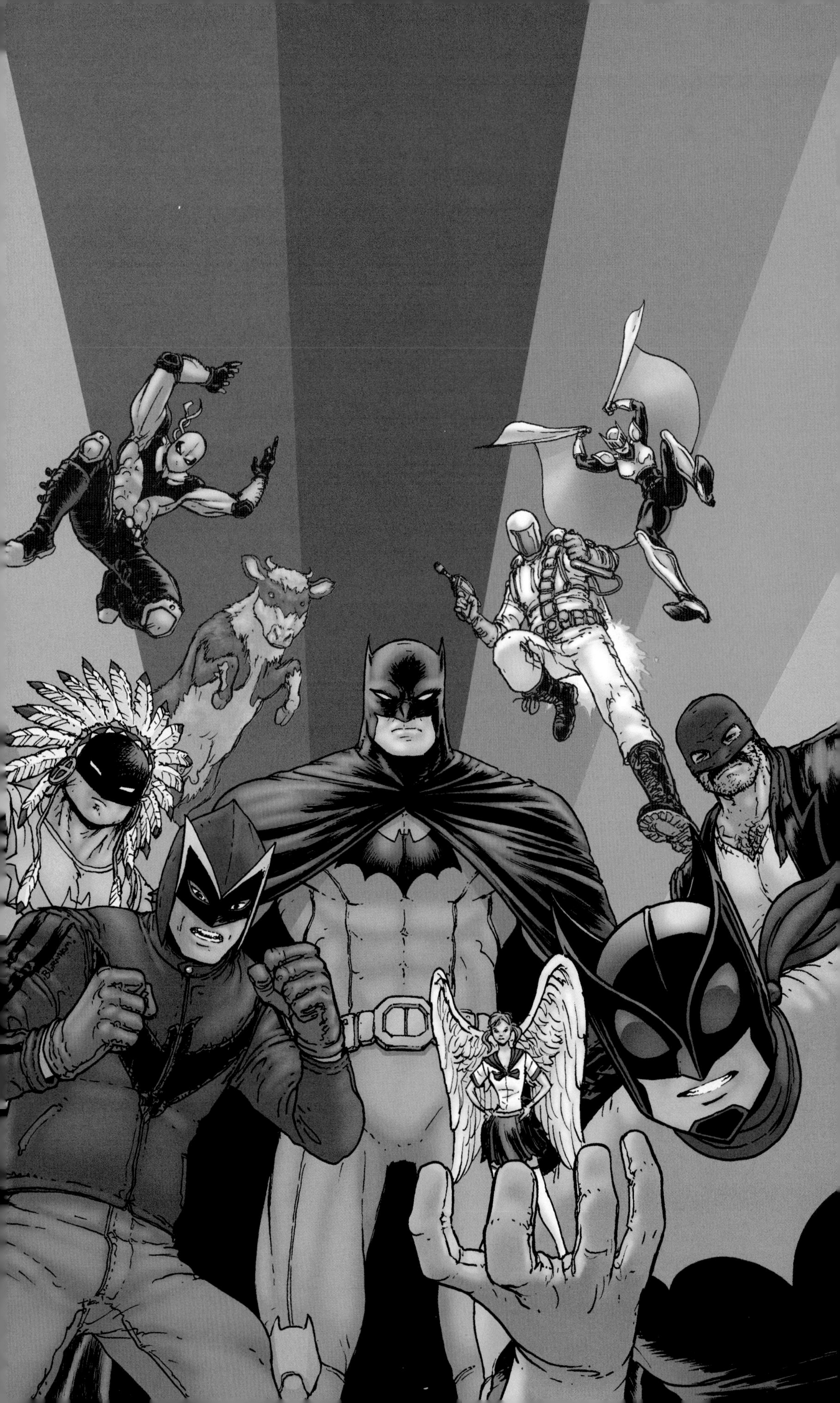

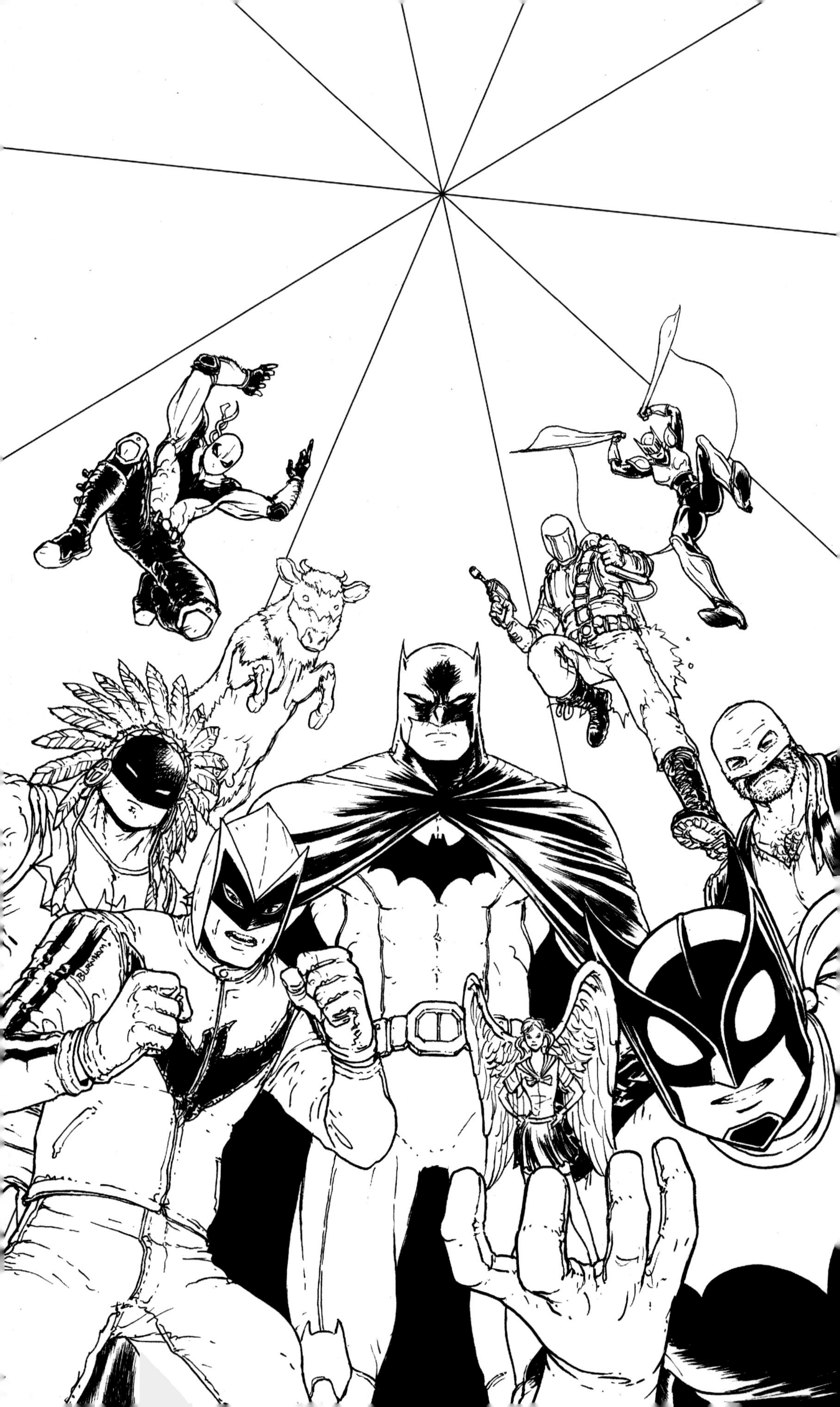

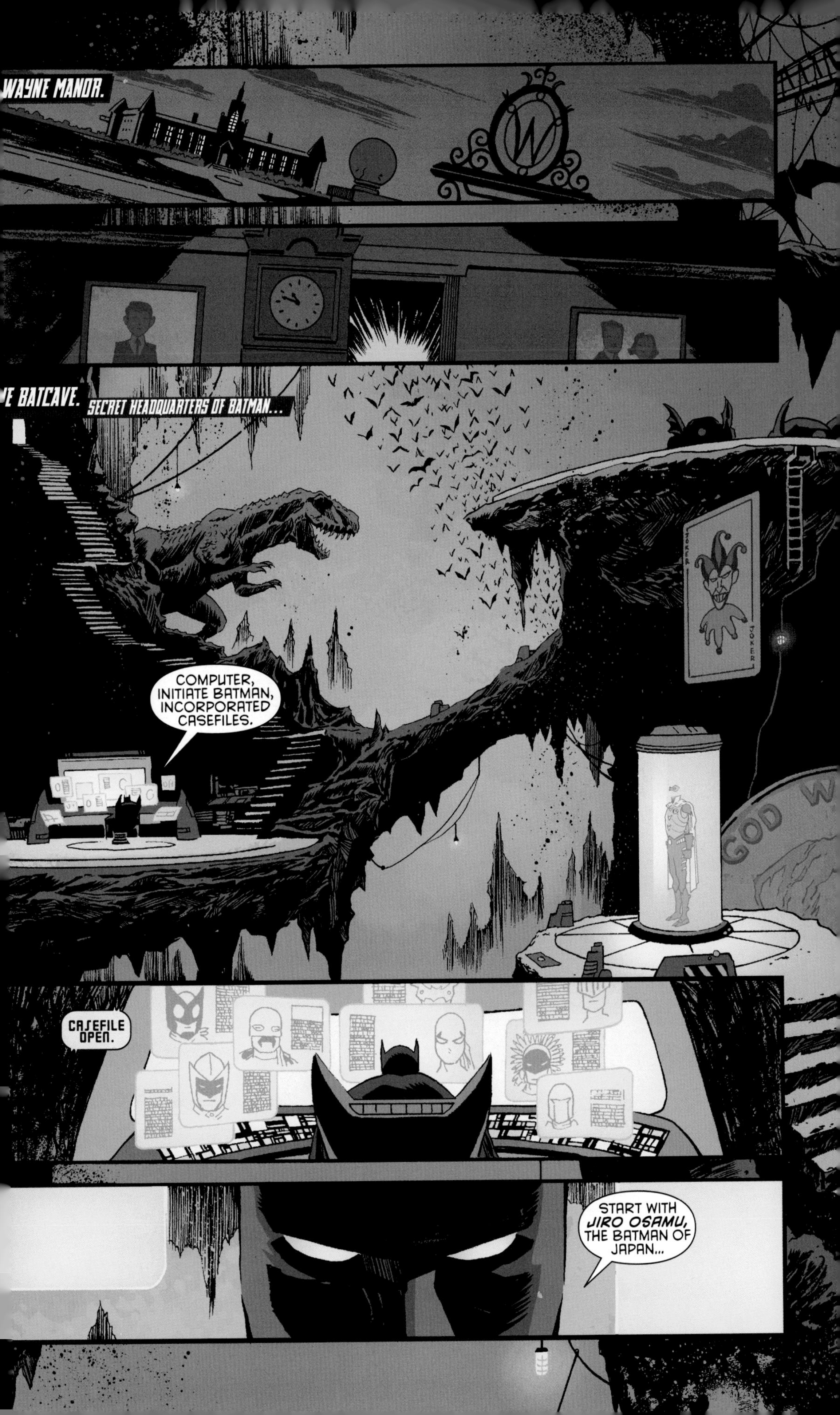
WAYNE MANOR.
E BATCAVE.
SECRET HEADQUARTERS OF BATMAN...
JOKER
JOKER
GOD W
COMPUTER, INITIATE BATMAN, INCORPORATED CASEFILES.
CASEFILE OPEN.
START WITH JIRO OSAMU, THE BATMAN OF JAPAN...

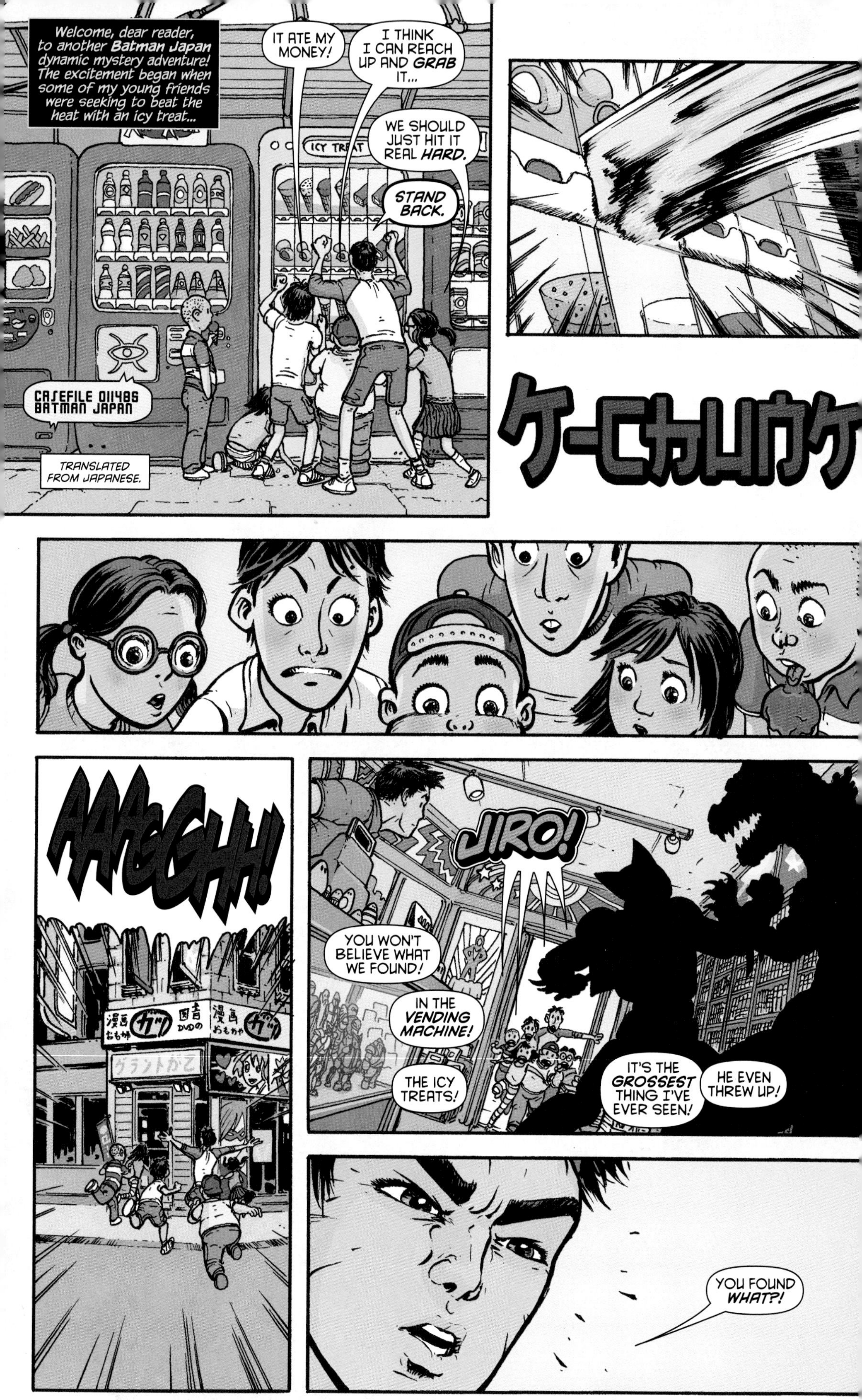

Welcome, dear reader, to another *Batman Japan* dynamic mystery adventure! The excitement began when some of my young friends were seeking to beat the heat with an icy treat...
IT ATE MY MONEY!
I THINK I CAN REACH UP AND *GRAB* IT...
WE SHOULD JUST HIT IT REAL *HARD*.
STAND BACK.
ICY TREAT
CASEFILE 01148S BATMAN JAPAN
TRANSLATED FROM JAPANESE.
K-CHUNK
AAAGGHH!
JIRO!
YOU WON'T BELIEVE WHAT WE FOUND!
IN THE *VENDING MACHINE!*
THE ICY TREATS!
IT'S THE *GROSSEST* THING I'VE EVER SEEN!
HE EVEN THREW UP!
YOU FOUND *WHAT?!*

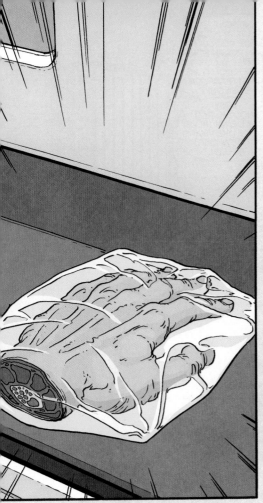

HUH.

CHILDREN, THANK YOU FOR BRINGING THIS TO MY ATTENTION. I WILL CONTACT THE APPROPRIATE AUTHORITIES.

RUN ALONG HOME NOW. COME BY THE SHOP TOMORROW AND YOU CAN EACH HAVE YOUR PICK OF *ANYTHING* YOU WANT.

THANKS, JIRO!

CANARY? IT'S JIRO.

ARE YOU FREE FOR AN *ADVENTURE* THIS EVENING?

BECAUSE THERE'S A VENDING MACHINE OUTSIDE MY STORE STOCKED WITH AT LEAST *TWO DOZEN HUMAN HEARTS, LUNGS, AND EYEBALLS.*

BLACK MARKET ORGAN TRADE?

HOW'S THIS FOR A COINCIDENCE? OUR *SHINY HAPPY AQUAZON* JUST FISHED A CORPSE OUT OF THE WATER, SECONDS BEFORE IT WAS GOING TO BE EATEN BY SHARKS.

SKIN AND ORGANS *SURGICALLY REMOVED.*

I SMELL A TEAM-UP!

WELL, I SMELL A ROTTING CORPSE. I'LL MEET YOU IN THE CITY.

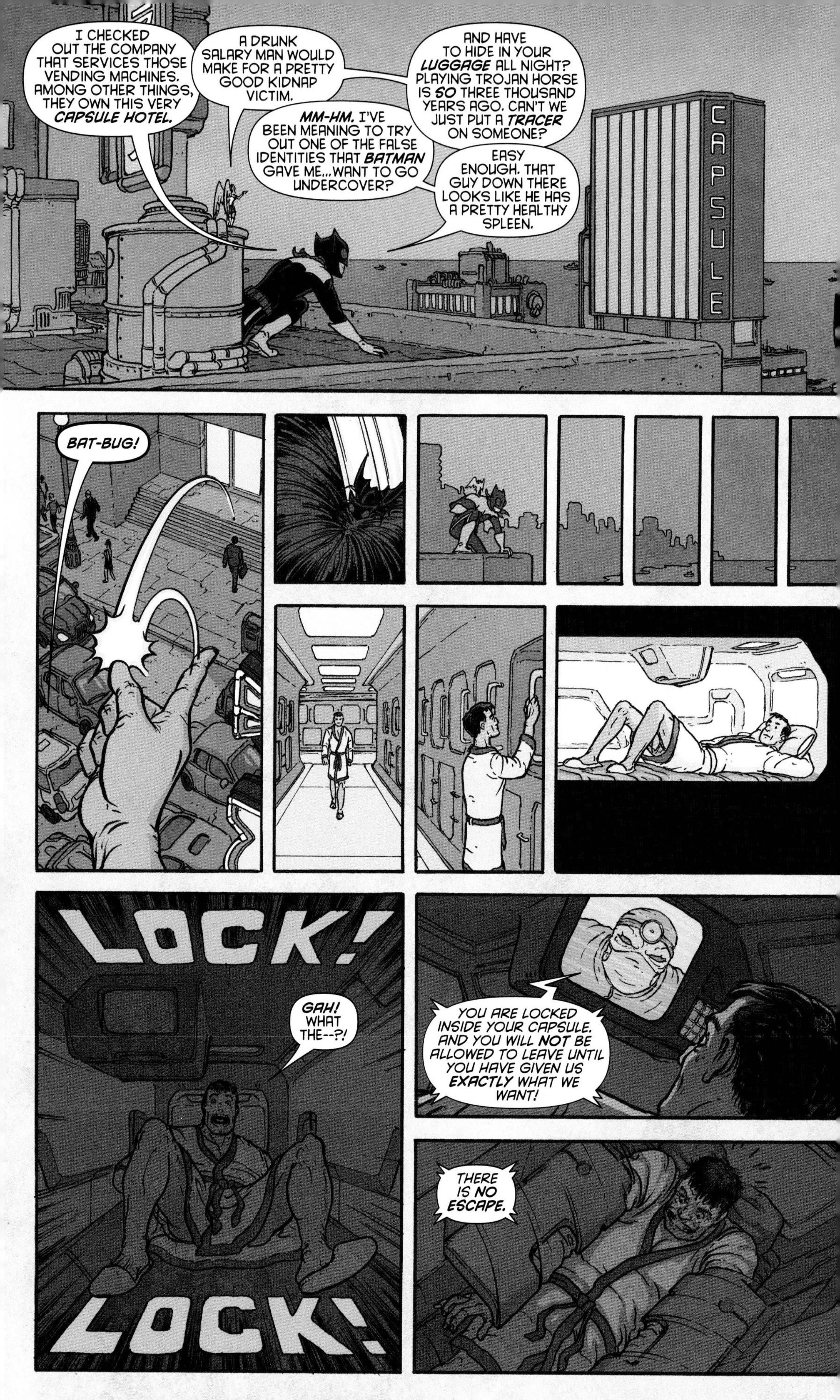
I CHECKED OUT THE COMPANY THAT SERVICES THOSE VENDING MACHINES. AMONG OTHER THINGS, THEY OWN THIS VERY CAPSULE HOTEL.
A DRUNK SALARY MAN WOULD MAKE FOR A PRETTY GOOD KIDNAP VICTIM.
MM-HM. I'VE BEEN MEANING TO TRY OUT ONE OF THE FALSE IDENTITIES THAT BATMAN GAVE ME...WANT TO GO UNDERCOVER?
AND HAVE TO HIDE IN YOUR LUGGAGE ALL NIGHT? PLAYING TROJAN HORSE IS SO THREE THOUSAND YEARS AGO. CAN'T WE JUST PUT A TRACER ON SOMEONE?
EASY ENOUGH. THAT GUY DOWN THERE LOOKS LIKE HE HAS A PRETTY HEALTHY SPLEEN.
CAPSULE
BAT-BUG!
LOCK!
GAH! WHAT THE--?!
LOCK!
YOU ARE LOCKED INSIDE YOUR CAPSULE. AND YOU WILL NOT BE ALLOWED TO LEAVE UNTIL YOU HAVE GIVEN US EXACTLY WHAT WE WANT!
THERE IS NO ESCAPE.

LET'S BEGIN WITH YOUR FULL NAME.

YOU'LL *NEVER* LET ME LIVE! IF I EVER GOT OUT, I'D LEAD THE COPS RIGHT HERE!

AH, A SMART ONE! A SHAME WE CAN'T SELL YOUR BRAIN, TOO...

IF YOU ANSWER OUR QUESTIONS QUICKLY AND ACCURATELY, YOU'LL BE *DEAD* BEFORE YOUR LIFE HAS A CHANCE TO FLASH BEFORE YOUR EYES.

MAKE US DRAG IT OUT OF YOU...AND WE'LL DRAG IT OUT LONG ENOUGH FOR YOU TO REGRET EVERY DECISION YOU EVER MADE. ONE. BY. ONE.

SNIP. BY. SNIP.

EEEEEEEEEEEEEEEEEE

EEEEEEE

WHAT *IS* THAT SOUND...?

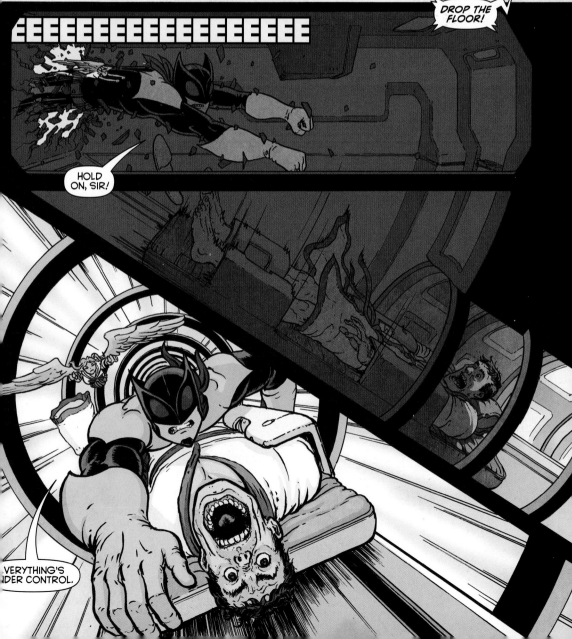

DROP THE FLOOR!

EEEEEEEEEEEEEEEEEEEEE

HOLD ON, SIR!

VERYTHING'S NDER CONTROL.

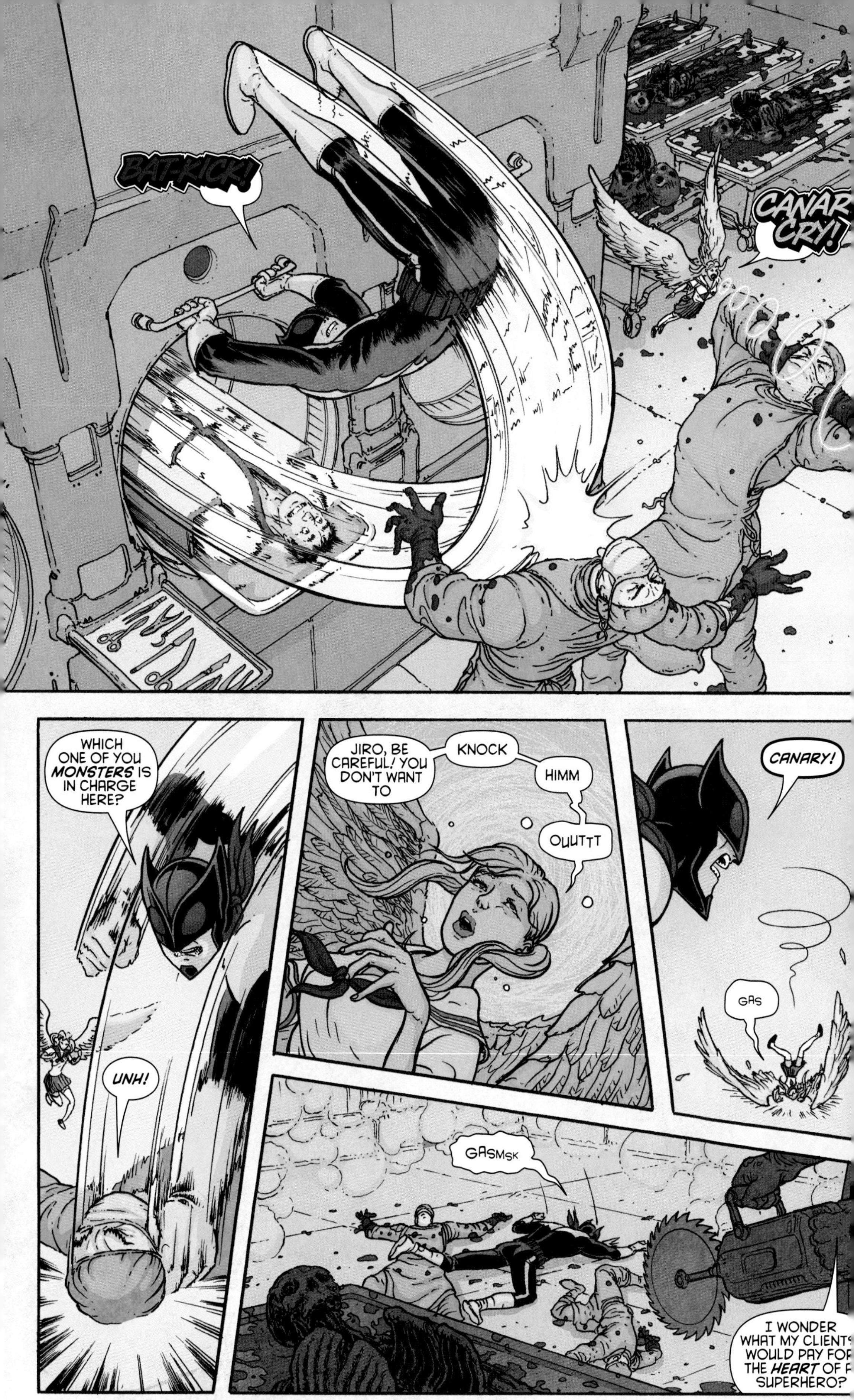
BAT-KICK!
CANARY CRY!
WHICH ONE OF YOU MONSTERS IS IN CHARGE HERE?
UNH!
JIRO, BE CAREFUL! YOU DON'T WANT TO
KNOCK
HIMM
OUUTTT
CANARY!
GAS
GASMSK
I WONDER WHAT MY CLIENTS WOULD PAY FOR THE HEART OF A SUPERHERO?

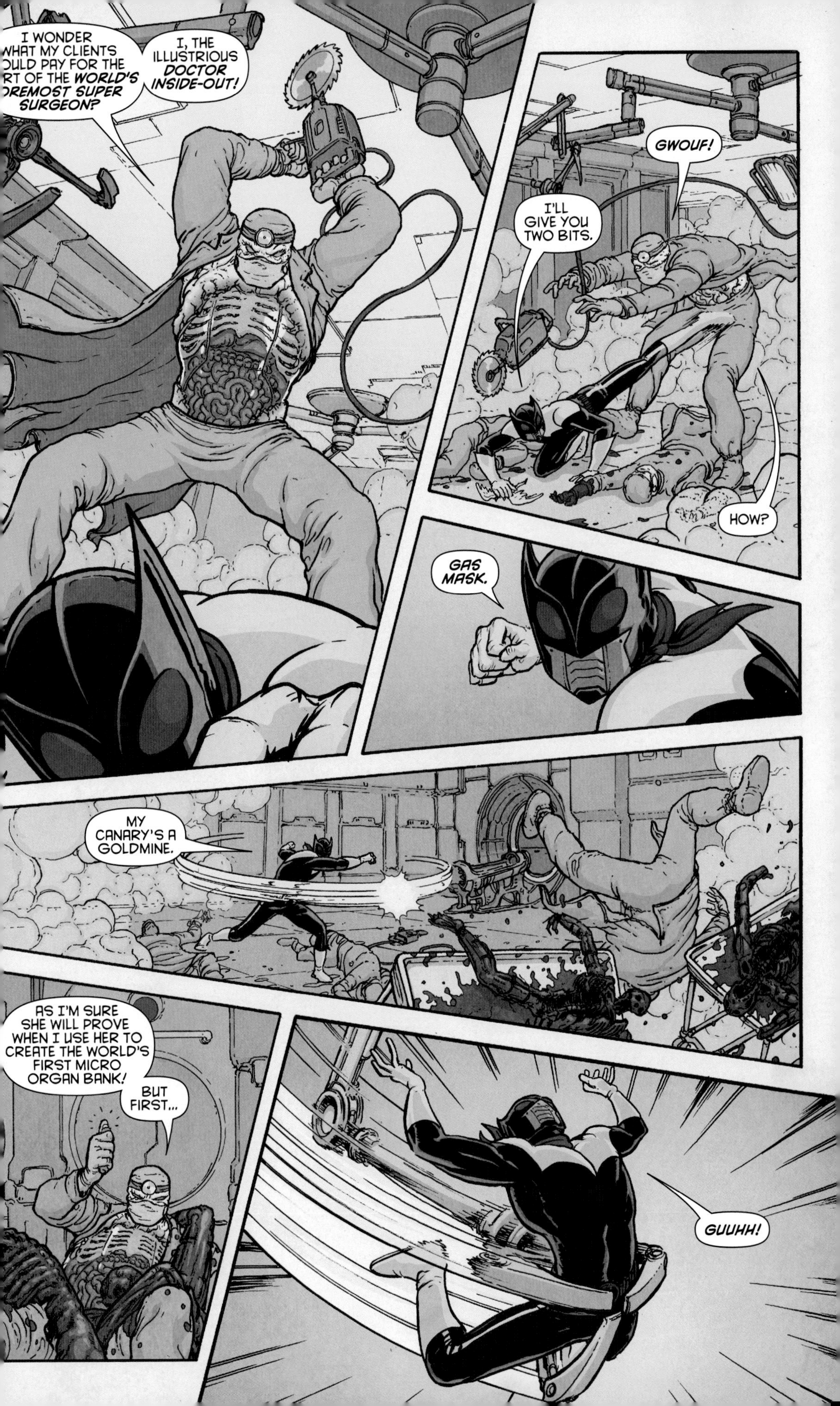
I WONDER WHAT MY CLIENTS WOULD PAY FOR THE ART OF THE *WORLD'S* FOREMOST SUPER SURGEON?
I, THE ILLUSTRIOUS *DOCTOR INSIDE-OUT!*
GWOUF!
I'LL GIVE YOU TWO BITS.
HOW?
GAS MASK.
MY CANARY'S A GOLDMINE.
AS I'M SURE SHE WILL PROVE WHEN I USE HER TO CREATE THE WORLD'S FIRST MICRO ORGAN BANK!
BUT FIRST...
GUUHH!

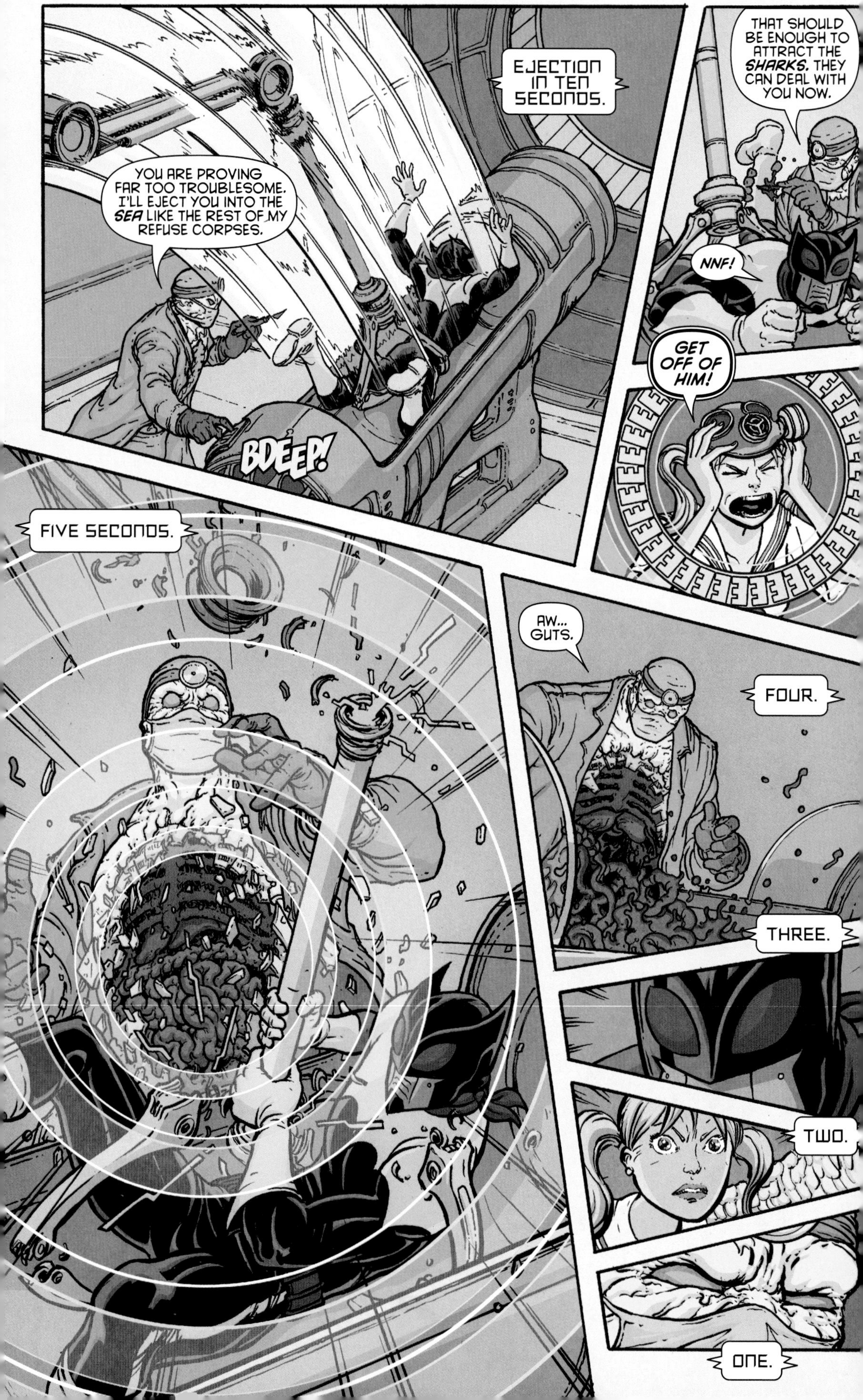
EJECTION IN TEN SECONDS.
YOU ARE PROVING FAR TOO TROUBLESOME. I'LL EJECT YOU INTO THE SEA LIKE THE REST OF MY REFUSE CORPSES.
BDEEP!
THAT SHOULD BE ENOUGH TO ATTRACT THE SHARKS. THEY CAN DEAL WITH YOU NOW.
NNF!
GET OFF OF HIM!
FIVE SECONDS.
AW... GUTS.
FOUR.
THREE.
TWO.
ONE.

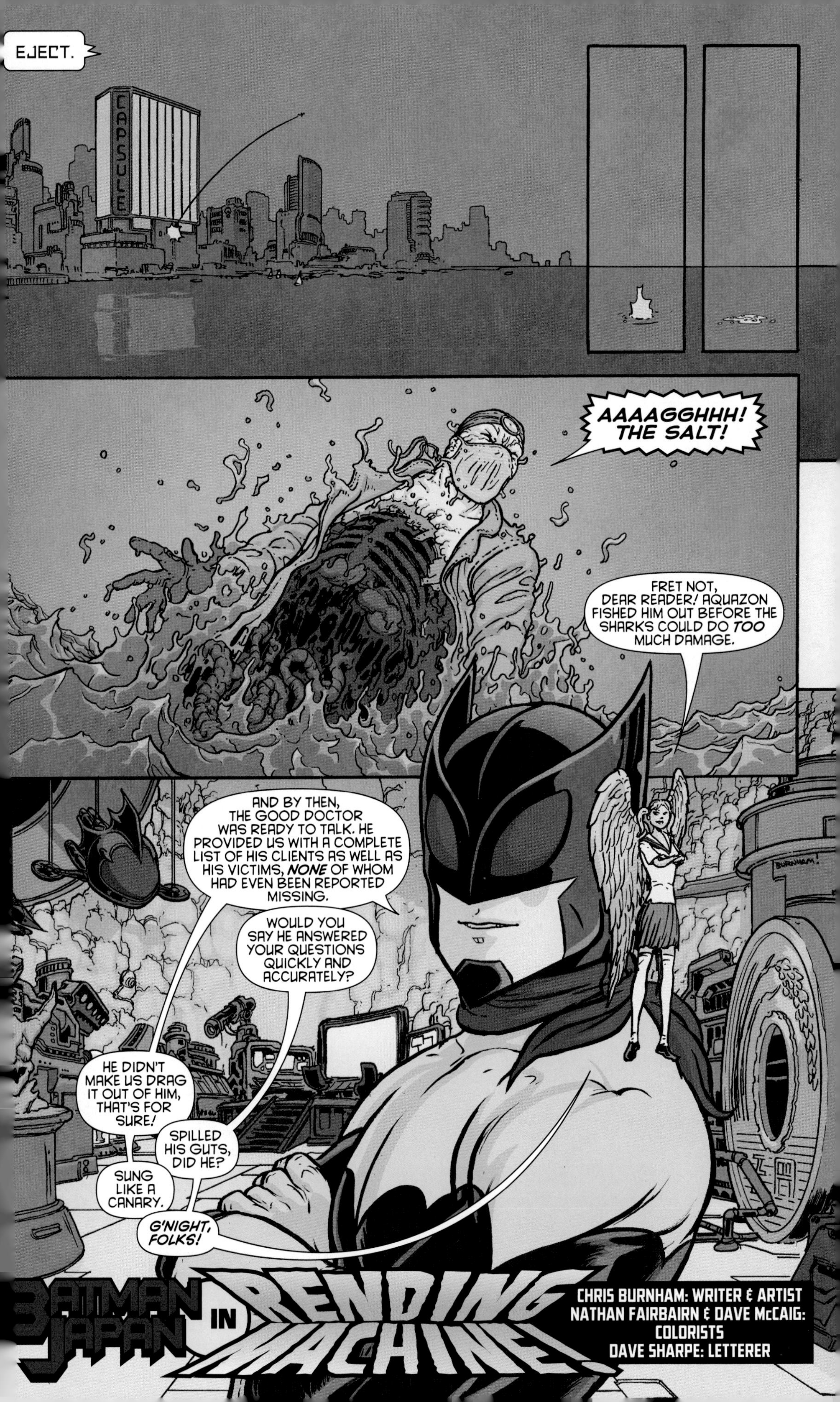

EJECT.
CAPSULE
AAAAGGHHH! THE SALT!
FRET NOT, DEAR READER! AQUAZON FISHED HIM OUT BEFORE THE SHARKS COULD DO *TOO* MUCH DAMAGE.
AND BY THEN, THE GOOD DOCTOR WAS READY TO TALK. HE PROVIDED US WITH A COMPLETE LIST OF HIS CLIENTS AS WELL AS HIS VICTIMS, *NONE* OF WHOM HAD EVEN BEEN REPORTED MISSING.
WOULD YOU SAY HE ANSWERED YOUR QUESTIONS QUICKLY AND ACCURATELY?
HE DIDN'T MAKE US DRAG IT OUT OF HIM, THAT'S FOR SURE!
SPILLED HIS GUTS, DID HE?
SUNG LIKE A CANARY.
G'NIGHT, FOLKS!
BURNHAM!
BATMAN JAPAN IN RENDING MACHINE!
CHRIS BURNHAM: WRITER & ARTIST
NATHAN FAIRBAIRN & DAVE McCAIG: COLORISTS
DAVE SHARPE: LETTERER

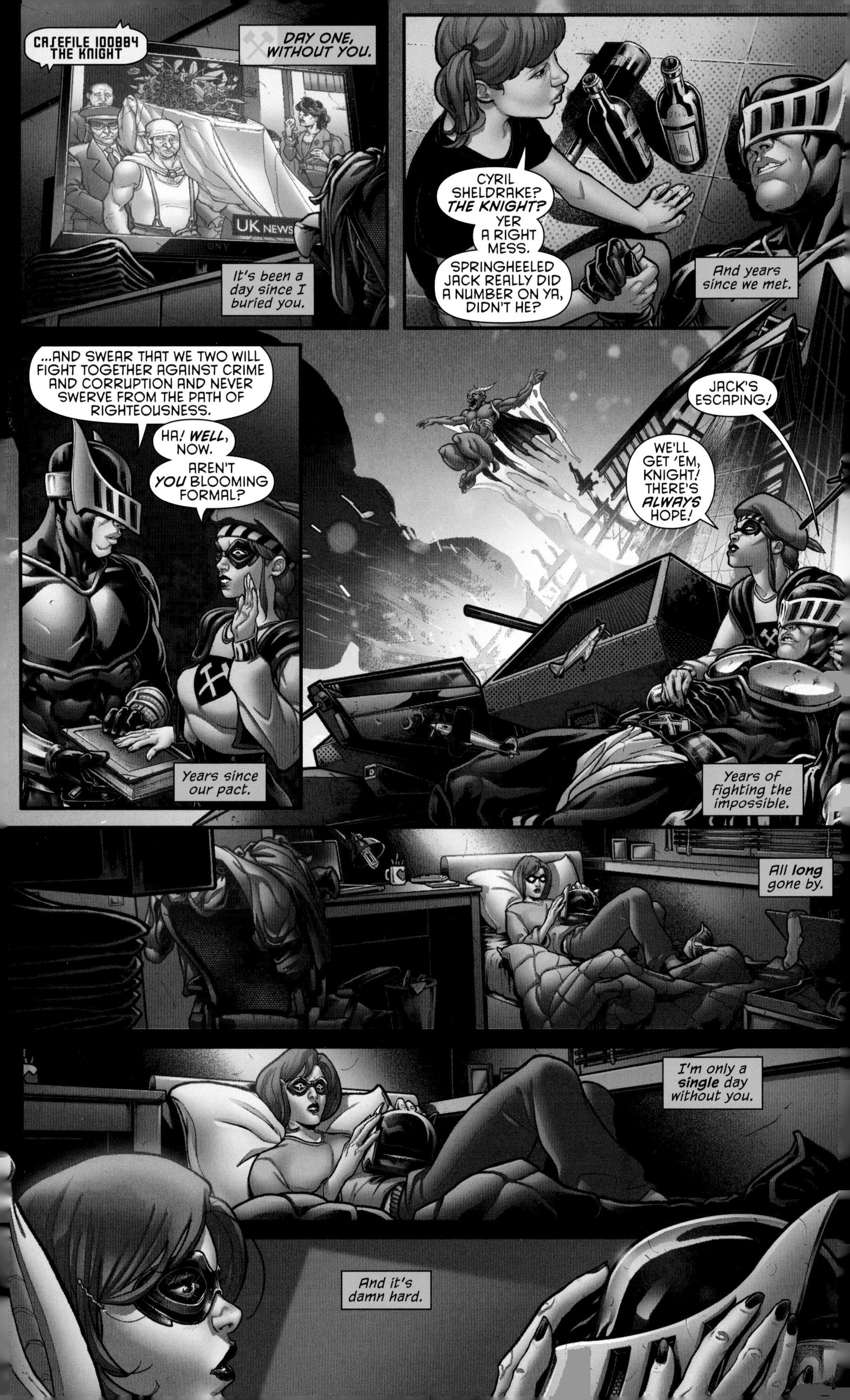
CASEFILE 100884 THE KNIGHT
DAY ONE, WITHOUT YOU.
UK NEWS
It's been a day since I buried you.
CYRIL SHELDRAKE? THE KNIGHT? YER A RIGHT MESS. SPRINGHEELED JACK REALLY DID A NUMBER ON YA, DIDN'T HE?
And years since we met.
...AND SWEAR THAT WE TWO WILL FIGHT TOGETHER AGAINST CRIME AND CORRUPTION AND NEVER SWERVE FROM THE PATH OF RIGHTEOUSNESS.
HA! WELL, NOW. AREN'T YOU BLOOMING FORMAL?
Years since our pact.
JACK'S ESCAPING!
WE'LL GET 'EM, KNIGHT! THERE'S ALWAYS HOPE!
Years of fighting the impossible.
All long gone by.
I'm only a single day without you.
And it's damn hard.

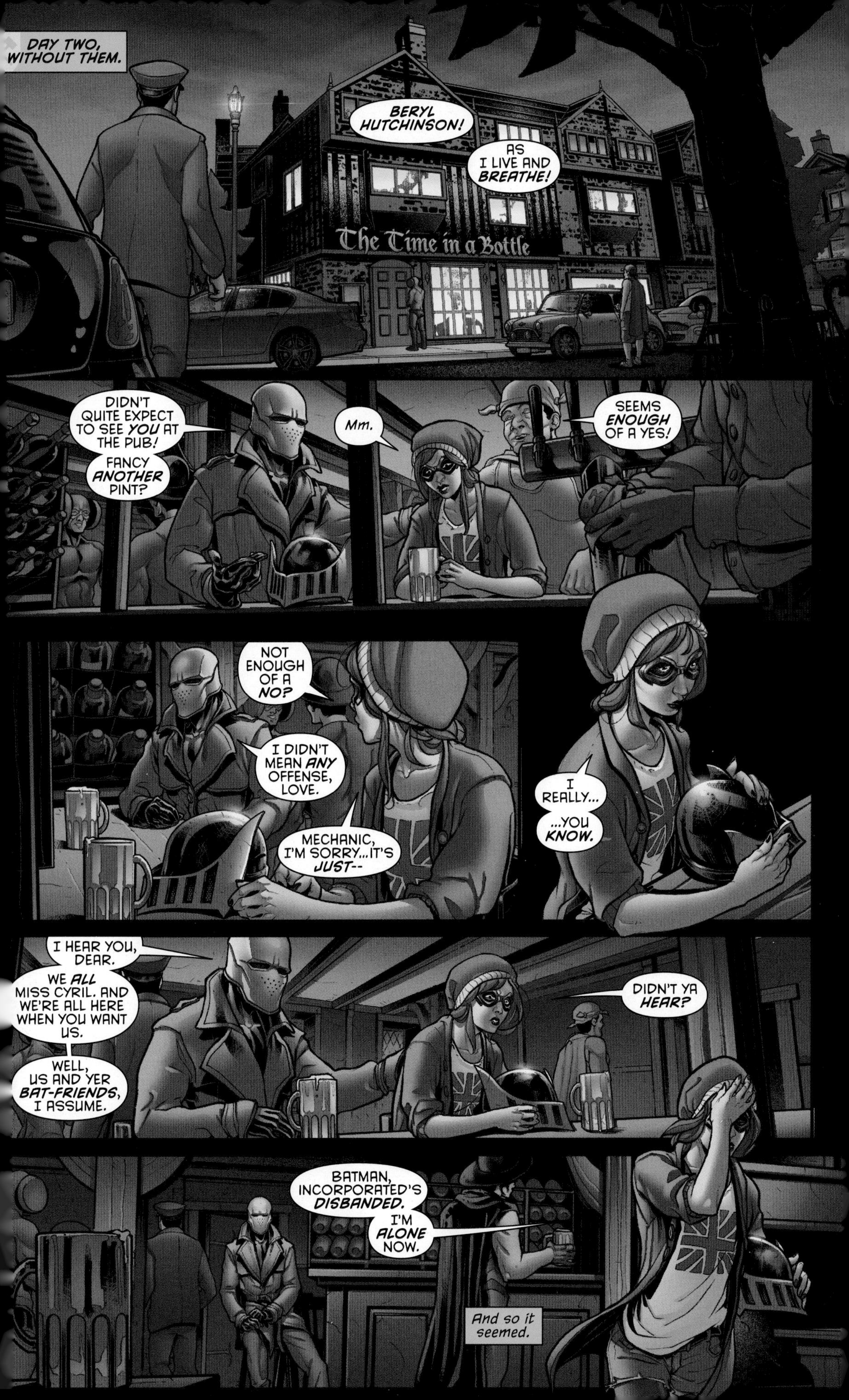

DAY TWO, WITHOUT THEM.
BERYL HUTCHINSON!
AS I LIVE AND BREATHE!
The Time in a Bottle
DIDN'T QUITE EXPECT TO SEE YOU AT THE PUB!
FANCY ANOTHER PINT?
Mm.
SEEMS ENOUGH OF A YES!
NOT ENOUGH OF A NO?
I DIDN'T MEAN ANY OFFENSE, LOVE.
MECHANIC, I'M SORRY...IT'S JUST--
I REALLY...
...YOU KNOW.
I HEAR YOU, DEAR.
WE ALL MISS CYRIL. AND WE'RE ALL HERE WHEN YOU WANT US.
WELL, US AND YER BAT-FRIENDS, I ASSUME.
DIDN'T YA HEAR?
BATMAN, INCORPORATED'S DISBANDED.
I'M ALONE NOW.
And so it seemed.

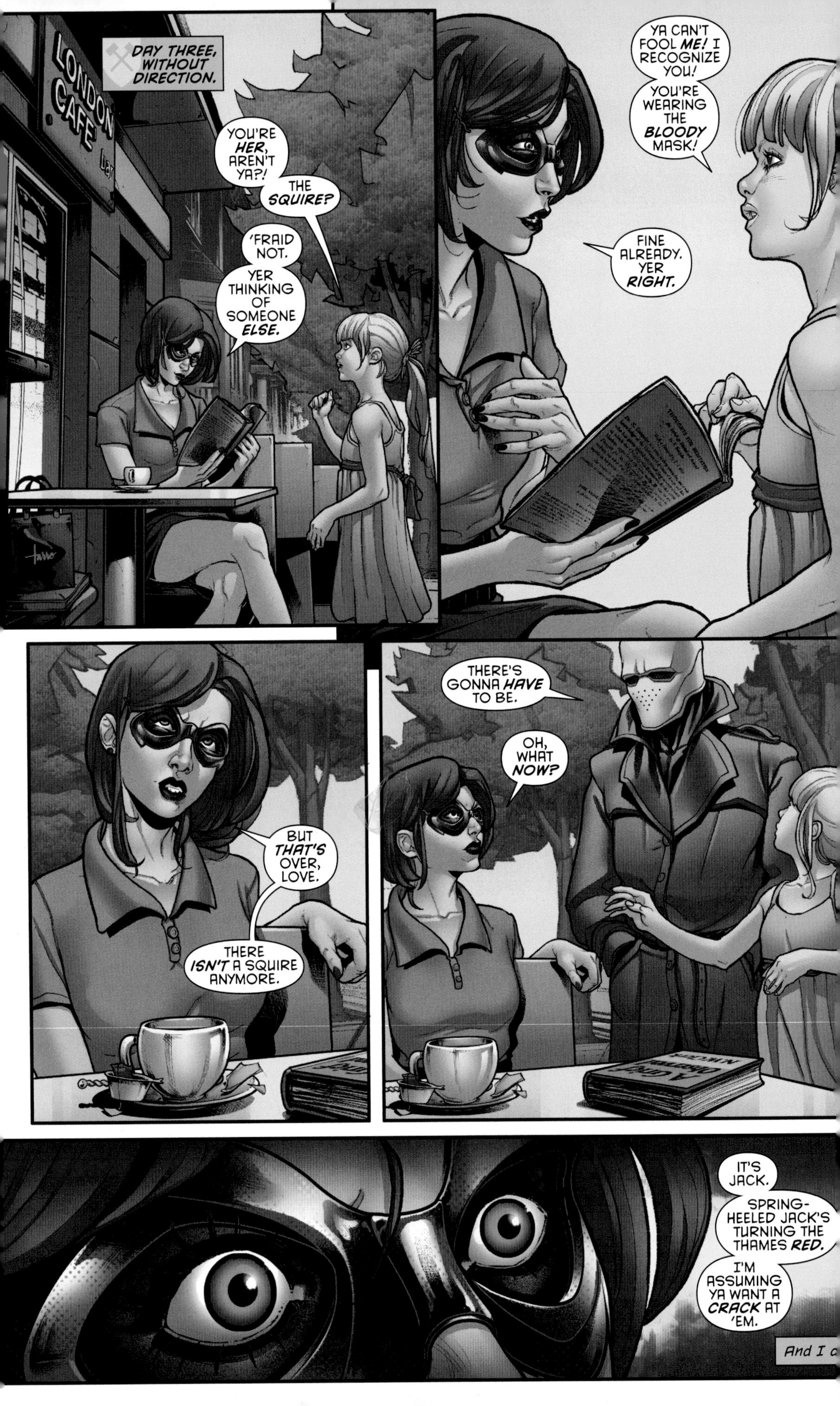

DAY THREE, WITHOUT DIRECTION.
LONDON CAFE
YOU'RE HER, AREN'T YA?!
THE SQUIRE?
'FRAID NOT.
YER THINKING OF SOMEONE ELSE.
YA CAN'T FOOL ME! I RECOGNIZE YOU!
YOU'RE WEARING THE BLOODY MASK!
FINE ALREADY. YER RIGHT.
BUT THAT'S OVER, LOVE.
THERE ISN'T A SQUIRE ANYMORE.
THERE'S GONNA HAVE TO BE.
OH, WHAT NOW?
IT'S JACK.
SPRING-HEELED JACK'S TURNING THE THAMES RED.
I'M ASSUMING YA WANT A CRACK AT 'EM.
And I c

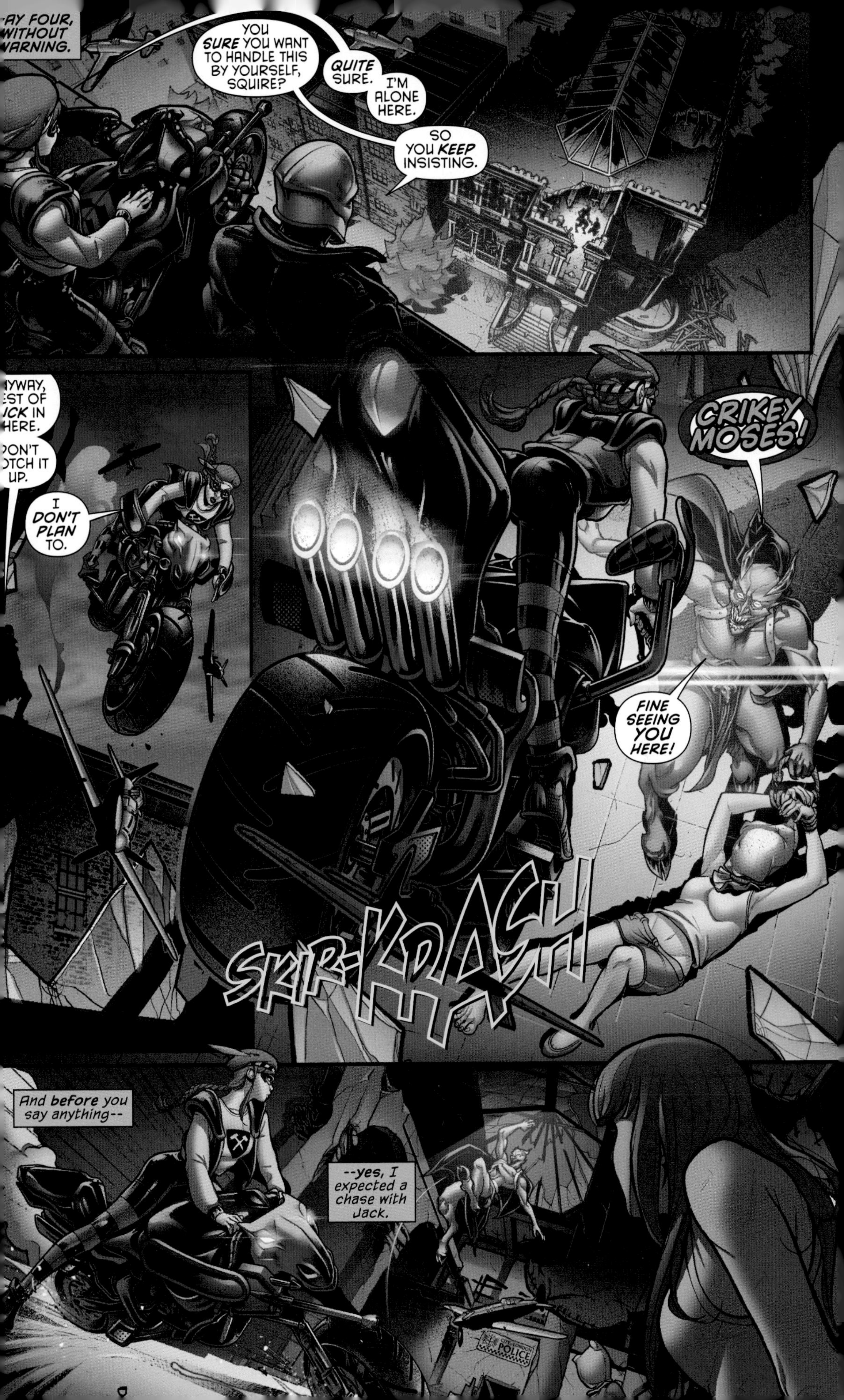

-AY FOUR, WITHOUT WARNING.
YOU SURE YOU WANT TO HANDLE THIS BY YOURSELF, SQUIRE?
QUITE SURE.
I'M ALONE HERE.
SO YOU KEEP INSISTING.
NYWAY, EST OF ICK IN HERE.
DON'T OTCH IT UP.
I DON'T PLAN TO.
CRIKEY MOSES!
FINE SEEING YOU HERE!
SKIR-KRASH
And before you say anything--
--yes, I expected a chase with Jack.
POLICE

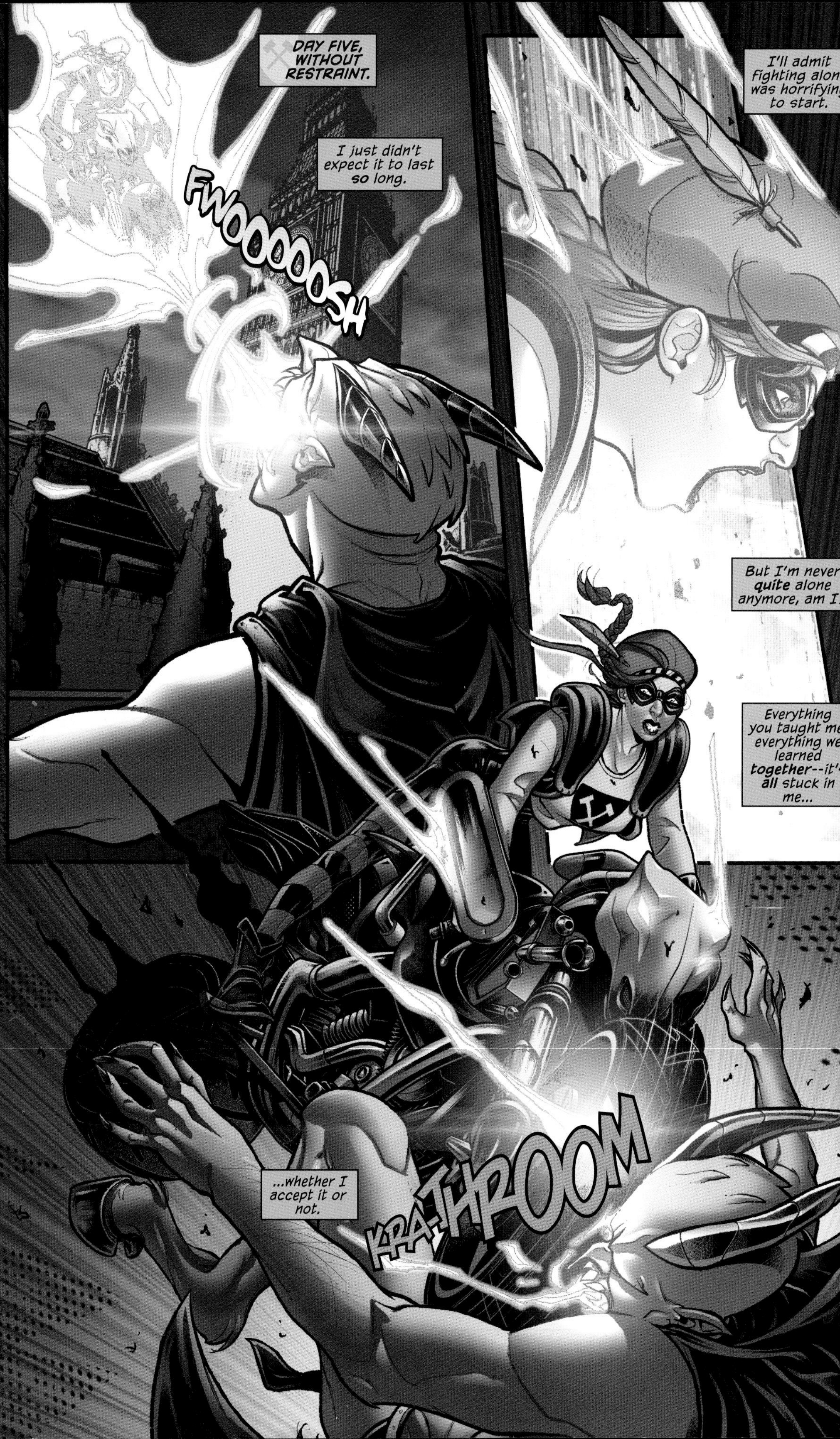
DAY FIVE, WITHOUT RESTRAINT.
I just didn't expect it to last so long.
FWOOOOOOSH
I'll admit fighting alone was horrifying to start.
But I'm never quite alone anymore, am I...
Everything you taught me, everything we learned together--it's all stuck in me...
...whether I accept it or not.
KRA-THROOM

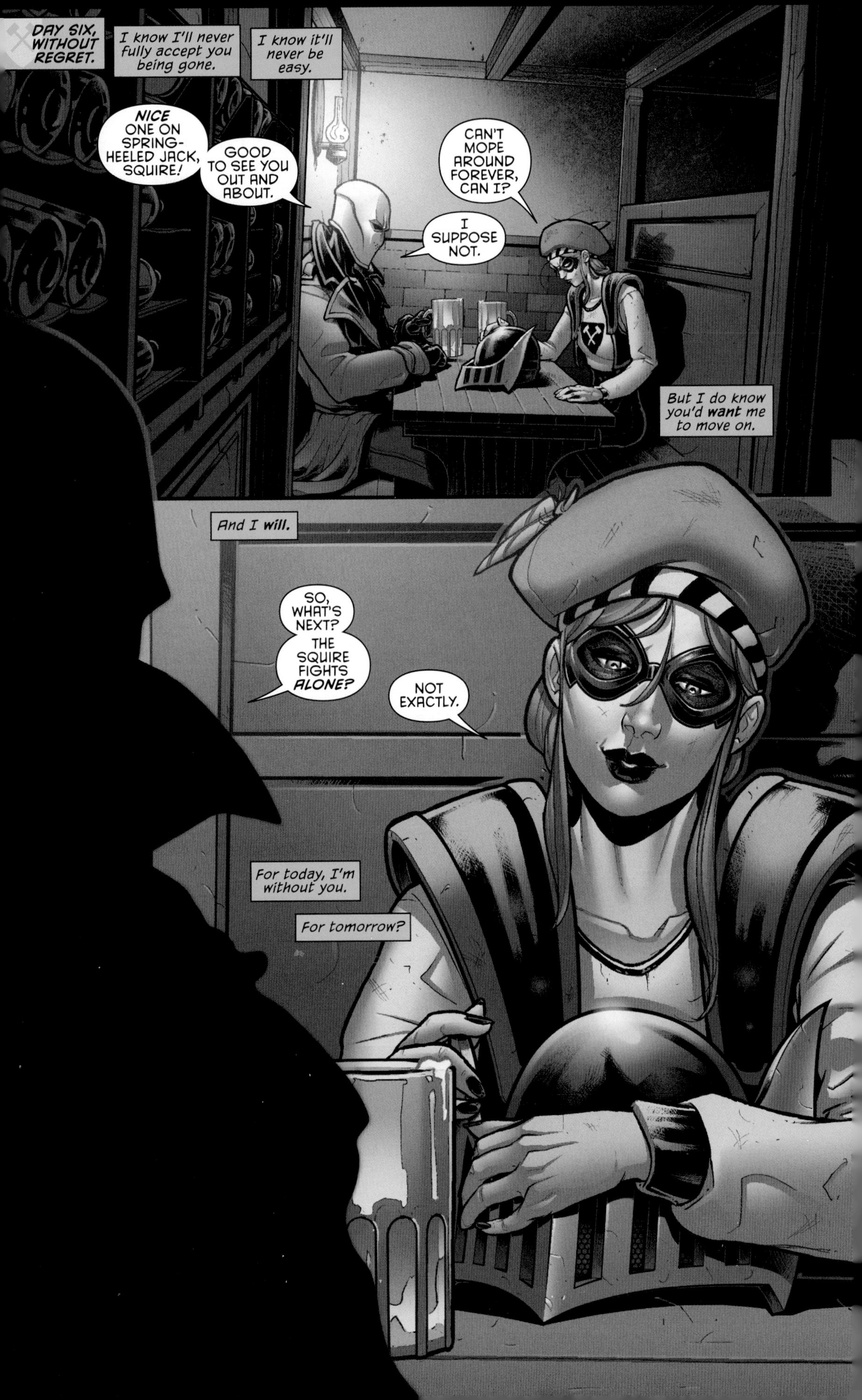

DAY SIX, WITHOUT REGRET.
I know I'll never fully accept you being gone.
I know it'll never be easy.
NICE ONE ON SPRING-HEELED JACK, SQUIRE!
GOOD TO SEE YOU OUT AND ABOUT.
CAN'T MOPE AROUND FOREVER, CAN I?
I SUPPOSE NOT.
But I do know you'd want me to move on.
And I will.
SO, WHAT'S NEXT?
THE SQUIRE FIGHTS ALONE?
NOT EXACTLY.
For today, I'm without you.
For tomorrow?

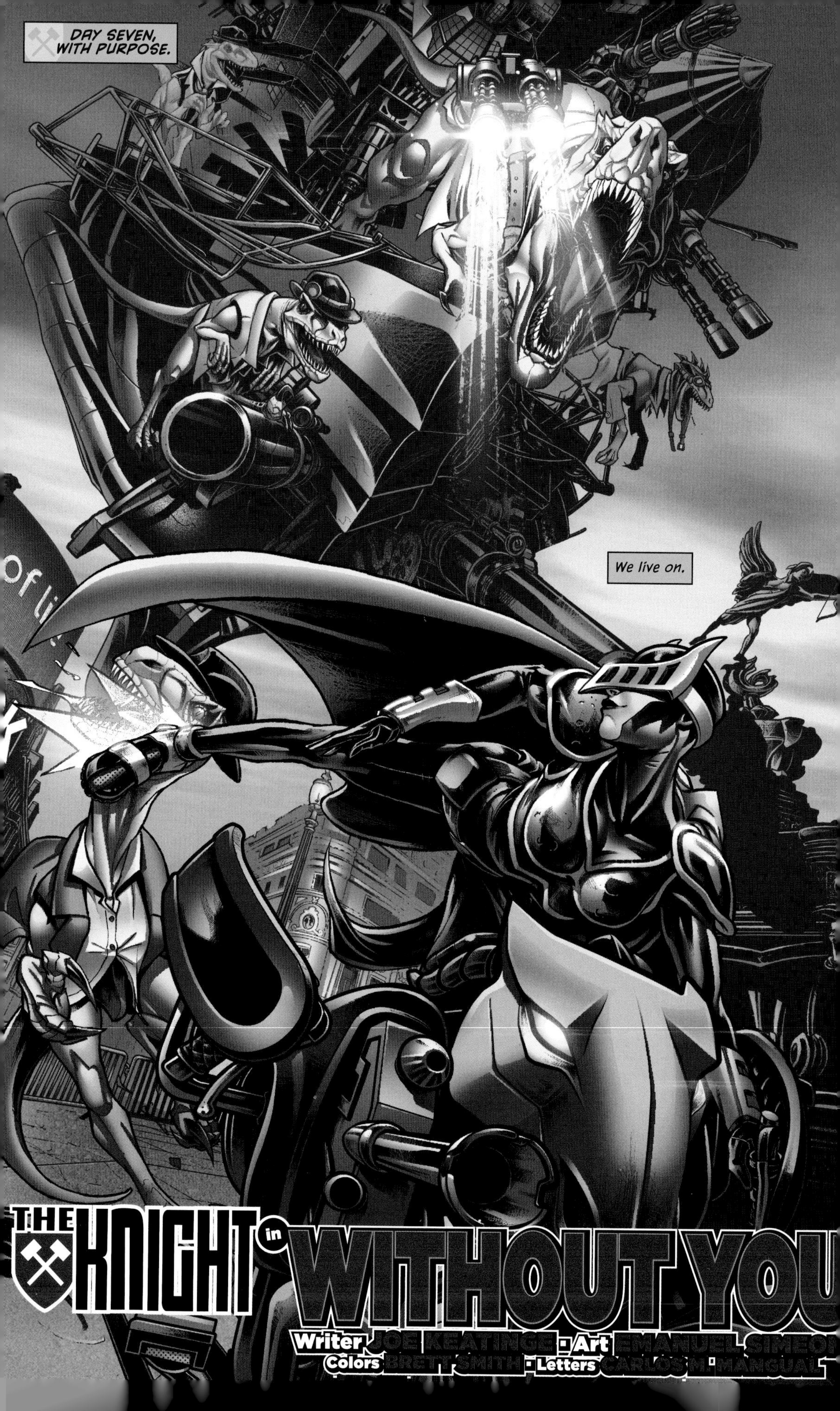
DAY SEVEN, WITH PURPOSE.
We live on.
THE KNIGHT in
WITHOUT YOU
Writer JOE KEATINGE · Art EMANUEL SIMEONI
Colors BRETT SMITH · Letters CARLOS M. MANGUAL

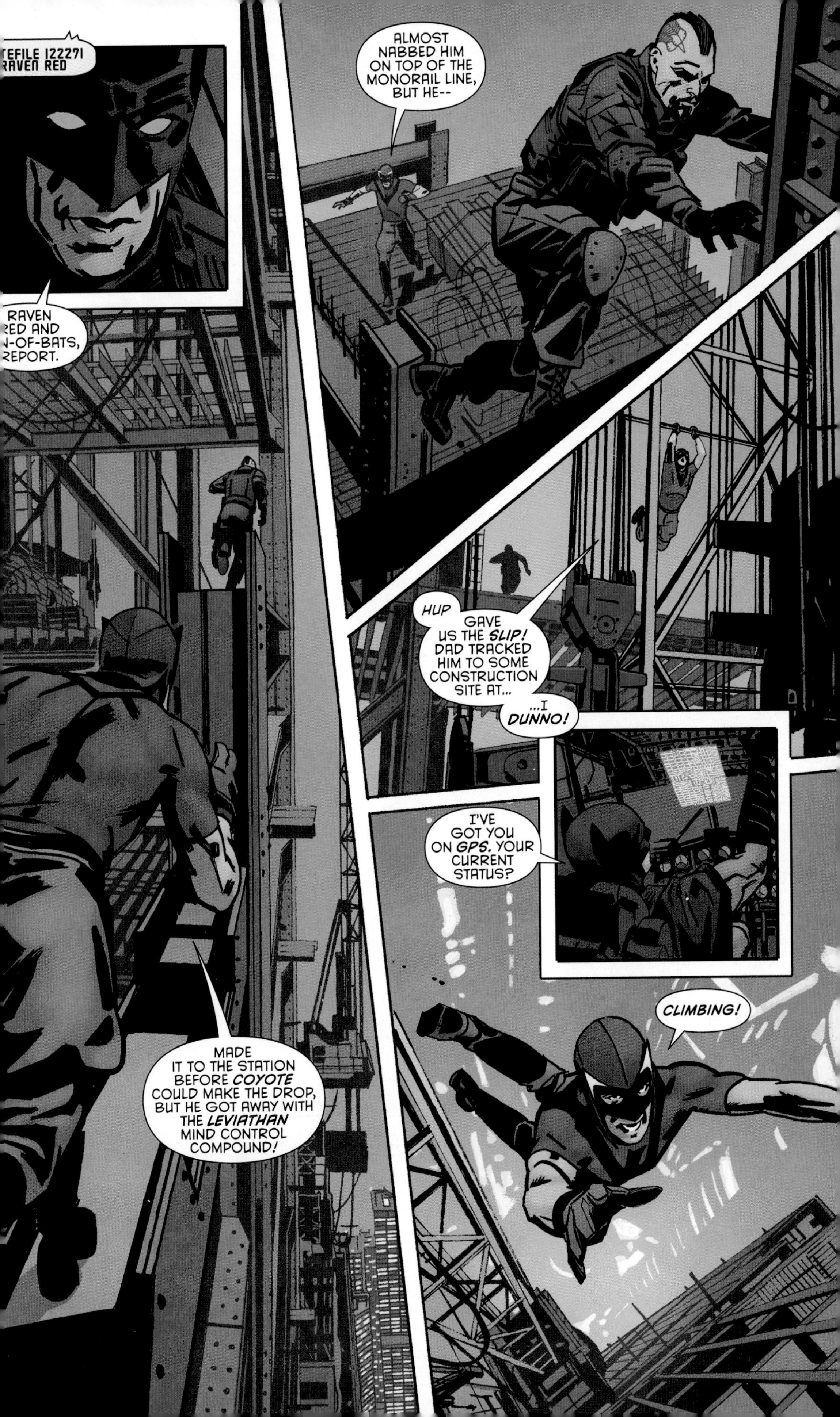

TEFILE 122271
RAVEN RED
RAVEN
RED AND
N-OF-BATS,
REPORT.
MADE IT TO THE STATION BEFORE COYOTE COULD MAKE THE DROP, BUT HE GOT AWAY WITH THE LEVIATHAN MIND CONTROL COMPOUND!
ALMOST NABBED HIM ON TOP OF THE MONORAIL LINE, BUT HE--
HUP
GAVE US THE SLIP! DAD TRACKED HIM TO SOME CONSTRUCTION SITE AT...
...I DUNNO!
I'VE GOT YOU ON GPS. YOUR CURRENT STATUS?
CLIMBING!

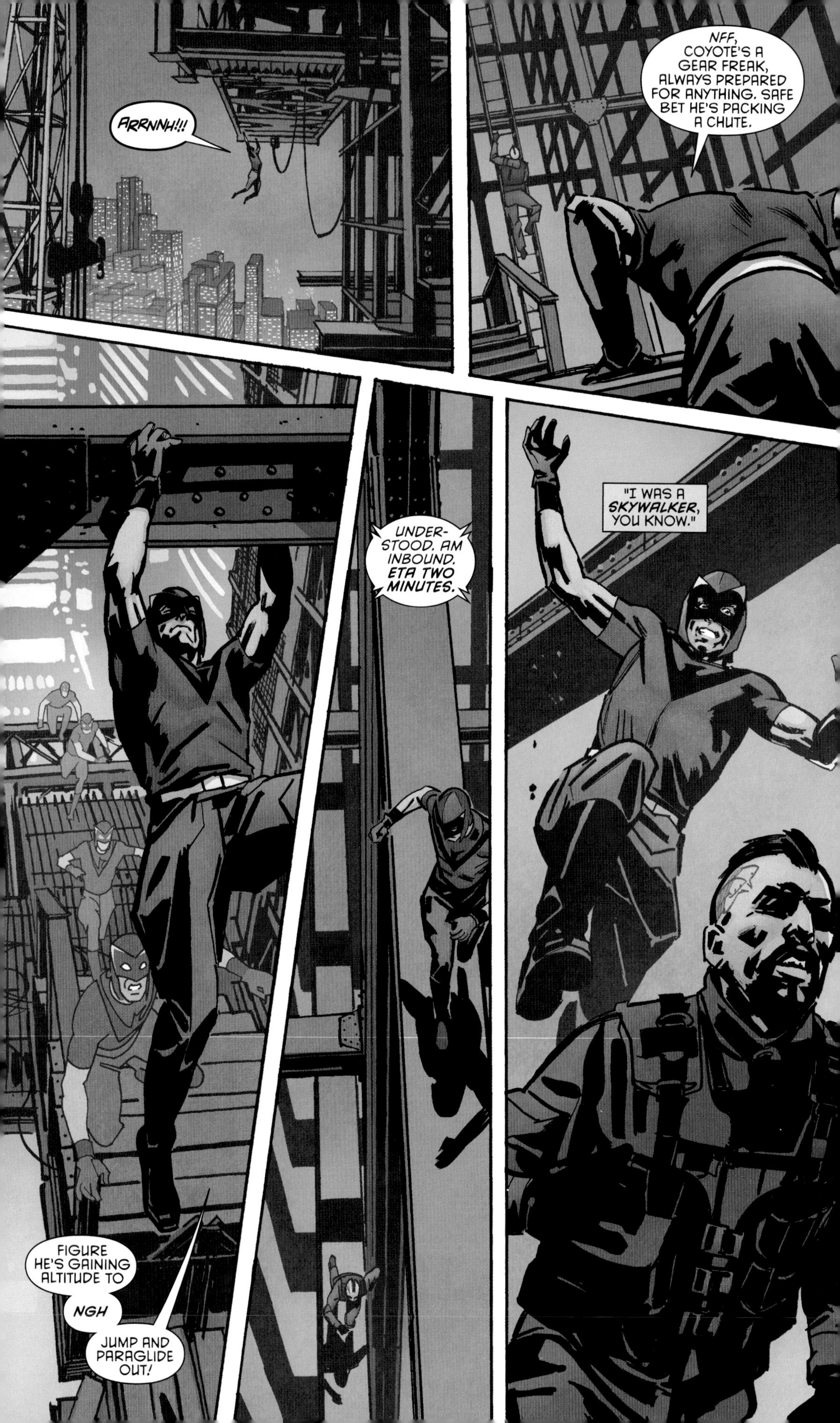

ARRNNH!!!
NFF, COYOTE'S A GEAR FREAK, ALWAYS PREPARED FOR ANYTHING. SAFE BET HE'S PACKING A CHUTE.
FIGURE HE'S GAINING ALTITUDE TO
NGH
JUMP AND PARAGLIDE OUT!
UNDER-STOOD. AM INBOUND. ETA TWO MINUTES.
"I WAS A SKYWALKER, YOU KNOW."

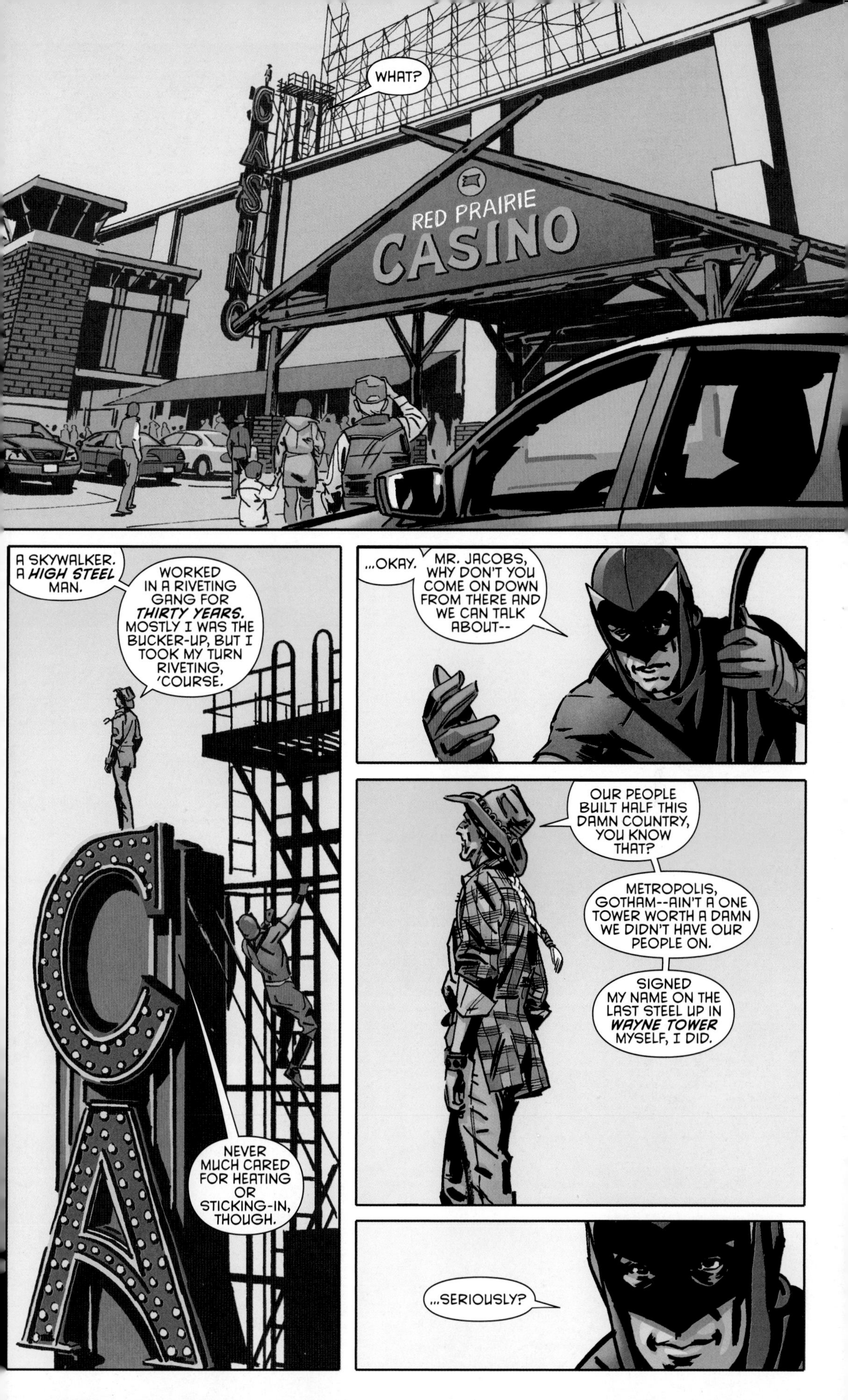
WHAT?
RED PRAIRIE CASINO
CASINO
A SKYWALKER. A HIGH STEEL MAN.
WORKED IN A RIVETING GANG FOR THIRTY YEARS. MOSTLY I WAS THE BUCKER-UP, BUT I TOOK MY TURN RIVETING, 'COURSE.
NEVER MUCH CARED FOR HEATING OR STICKING-IN, THOUGH.
...OKAY.
MR. JACOBS, WHY DON'T YOU COME ON DOWN FROM THERE AND WE CAN TALK ABOUT--
OUR PEOPLE BUILT HALF THIS DAMN COUNTRY, YOU KNOW THAT?
METROPOLIS, GOTHAM--AIN'T A ONE TOWER WORTH A DAMN WE DIDN'T HAVE OUR PEOPLE ON.
SIGNED MY NAME ON THE LAST STEEL UP IN WAYNE TOWER MYSELF, I DID.
...SERIOUSLY?

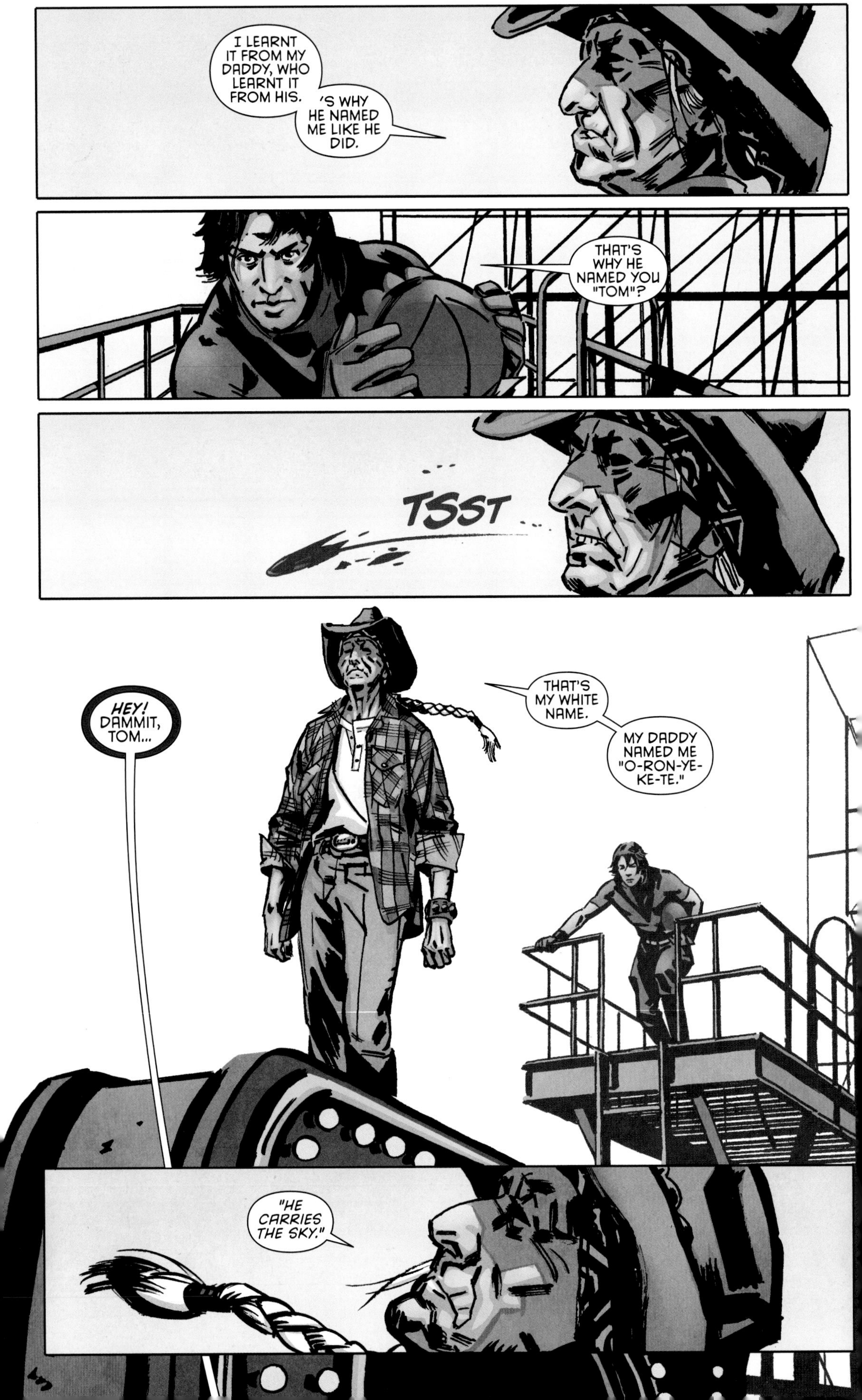
I LEARNT IT FROM MY DADDY, WHO LEARNT IT FROM HIS.
'S WHY HE NAMED ME LIKE HE DID.
THAT'S WHY HE NAMED YOU "TOM"?
TSST
THAT'S MY WHITE NAME.
MY DADDY NAMED ME "O-RON-YE-KE-TE."
HEY! DAMMIT, TOM...
"HE CARRIES THE SKY."

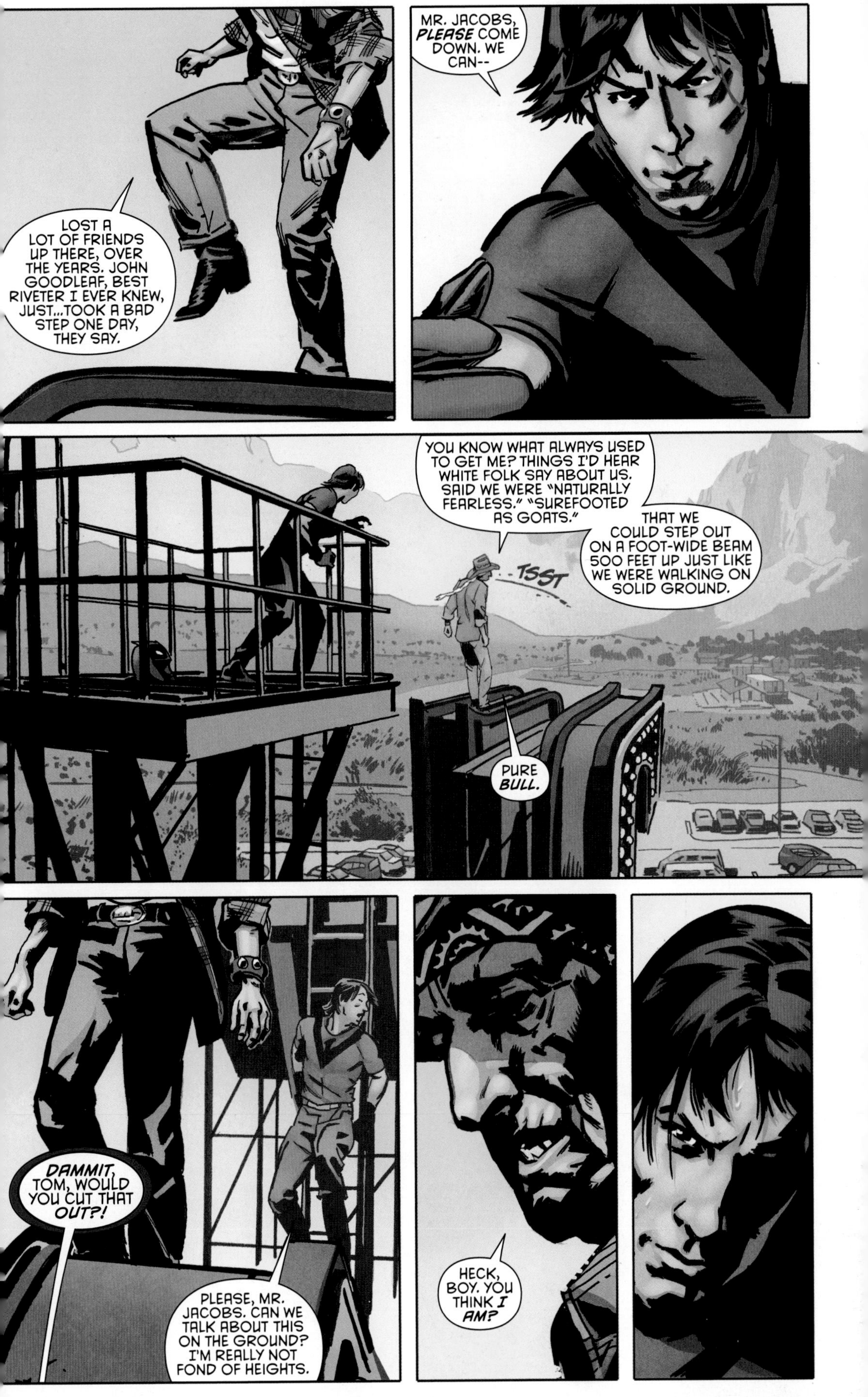

LOST A LOT OF FRIENDS UP THERE, OVER THE YEARS. JOHN GOODLEAF, BEST RIVETER I EVER KNEW, JUST...TOOK A BAD STEP ONE DAY, THEY SAY.
MR. JACOBS, PLEASE COME DOWN. WE CAN--
YOU KNOW WHAT ALWAYS USED TO GET ME? THINGS I'D HEAR WHITE FOLK SAY ABOUT US. SAID WE WERE "NATURALLY FEARLESS." "SUREFOOTED AS GOATS."
THAT WE COULD STEP OUT ON A FOOT-WIDE BEAM 500 FEET UP JUST LIKE WE WERE WALKING ON SOLID GROUND.
TSST
PURE BULL.
DAMMIT, TOM, WOULD YOU CUT THAT OUT?!
PLEASE, MR. JACOBS. CAN WE TALK ABOUT THIS ON THE GROUND? I'M REALLY NOT FOND OF HEIGHTS.
HECK, BOY. YOU THINK I AM?

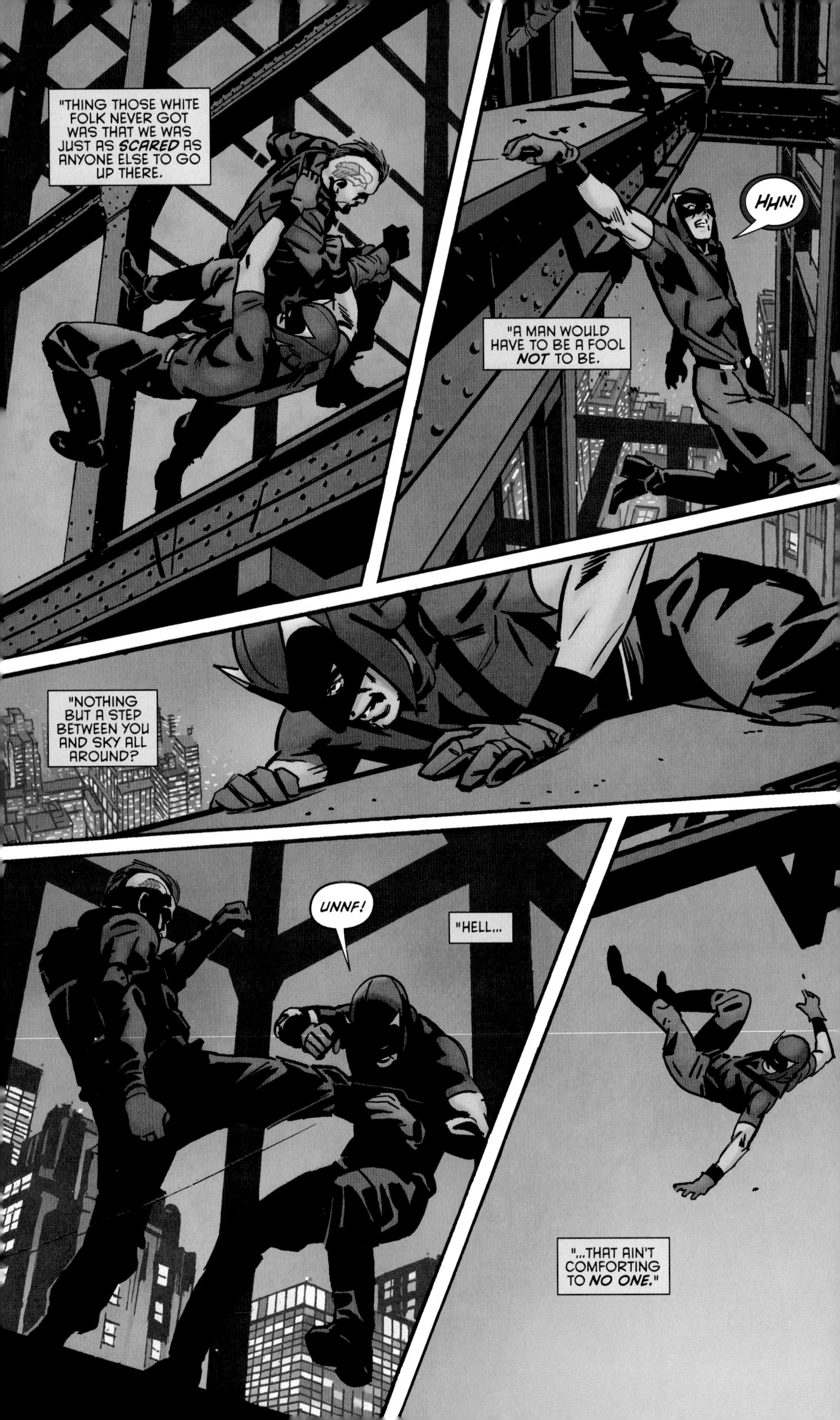
"THING THOSE WHITE FOLK NEVER GOT WAS THAT WE WAS JUST AS *SCARED* AS ANYONE ELSE TO GO UP THERE.
HHN!
"A MAN WOULD HAVE TO BE A FOOL *NOT* TO BE.
"NOTHING BUT A STEP BETWEEN YOU AND SKY ALL AROUND?
UNNF!
"HELL...
"...THAT AIN'T COMFORTING TO *NO ONE.*"

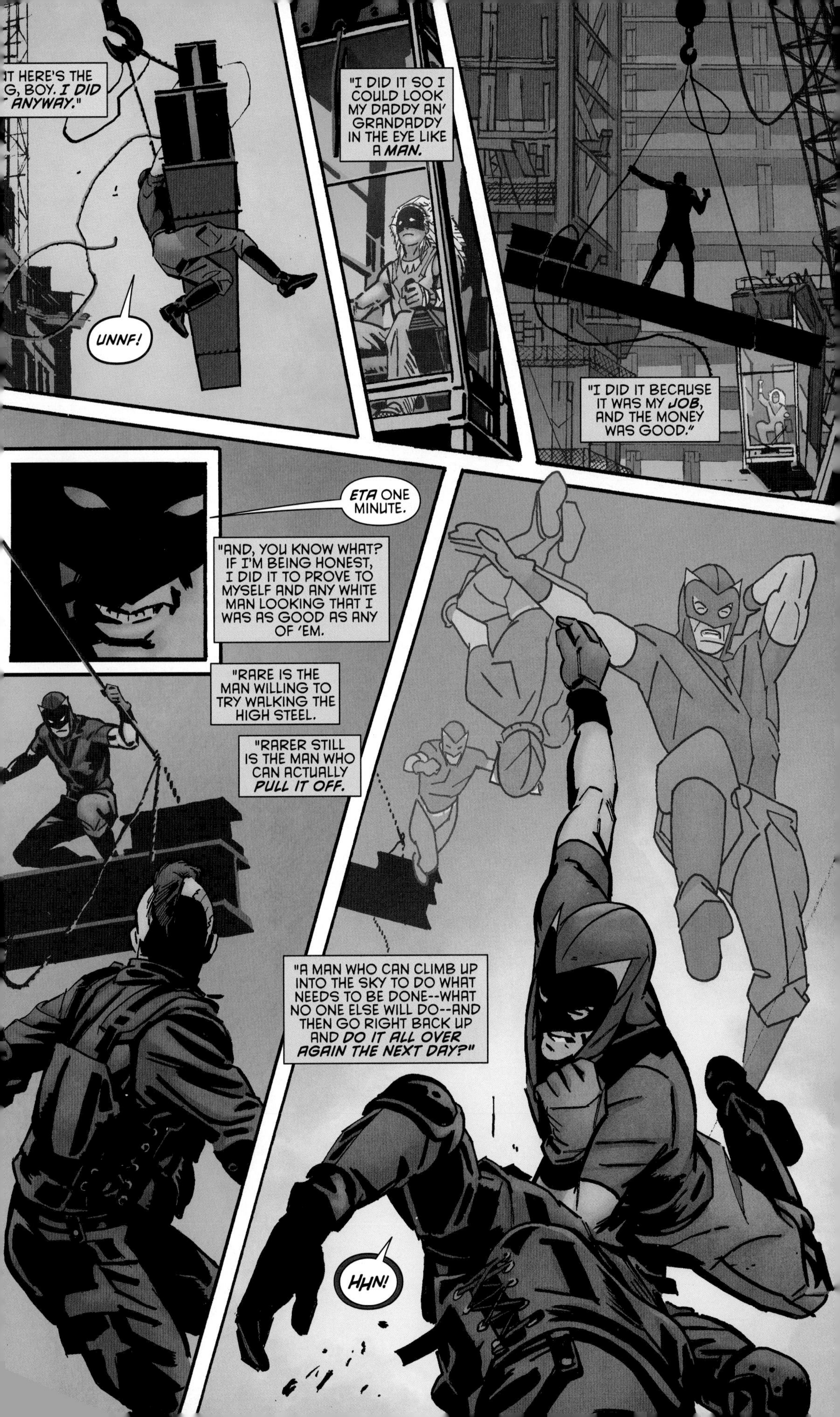

IT HERE'S THE G, BOY. I DID ANYWAY."
UNNF!
"I DID IT SO I COULD LOOK MY DADDY AN' GRANDADDY IN THE EYE LIKE A MAN.
"I DID IT BECAUSE IT WAS MY JOB, AND THE MONEY WAS GOOD."
ETA ONE MINUTE.
"AND, YOU KNOW WHAT? IF I'M BEING HONEST, I DID IT TO PROVE TO MYSELF AND ANY WHITE MAN LOOKING THAT I WAS AS GOOD AS ANY OF 'EM.
"RARE IS THE MAN WILLING TO TRY WALKING THE HIGH STEEL.
"RARER STILL IS THE MAN WHO CAN ACTUALLY PULL IT OFF.
"A MAN WHO CAN CLIMB UP INTO THE SKY TO DO WHAT NEEDS TO BE DONE--WHAT NO ONE ELSE WILL DO--AND THEN GO RIGHT BACK UP AND DO IT ALL OVER AGAIN THE NEXT DAY?"
HHN!

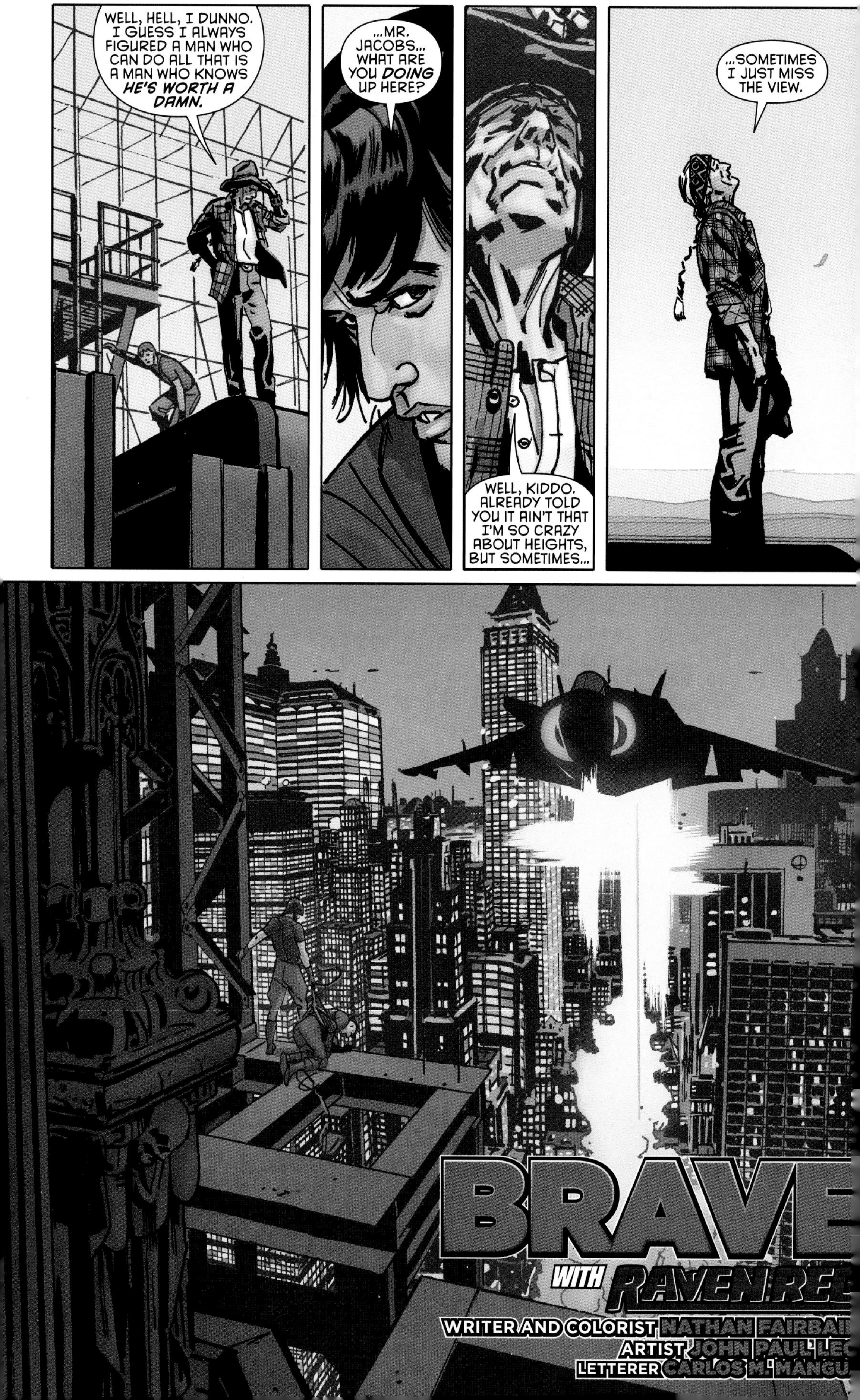
WELL, HELL, I DUNNO. I GUESS I ALWAYS FIGURED A MAN WHO CAN DO ALL THAT IS A MAN WHO KNOWS *HE'S WORTH A DAMN.*
...MR. JACOBS... WHAT ARE YOU *DOING* UP HERE?
WELL, KIDDO. ALREADY TOLD YOU IT AIN'T THAT I'M SO CRAZY ABOUT HEIGHTS, BUT SOMETIMES...
...SOMETIMES I JUST MISS THE VIEW.
BRAVE
WITH
WRITER AND COLORIST NATHAN FAIRBAI
ARTIST JOHN PAUL LEO
LETTERER CARLOS M. MANGU

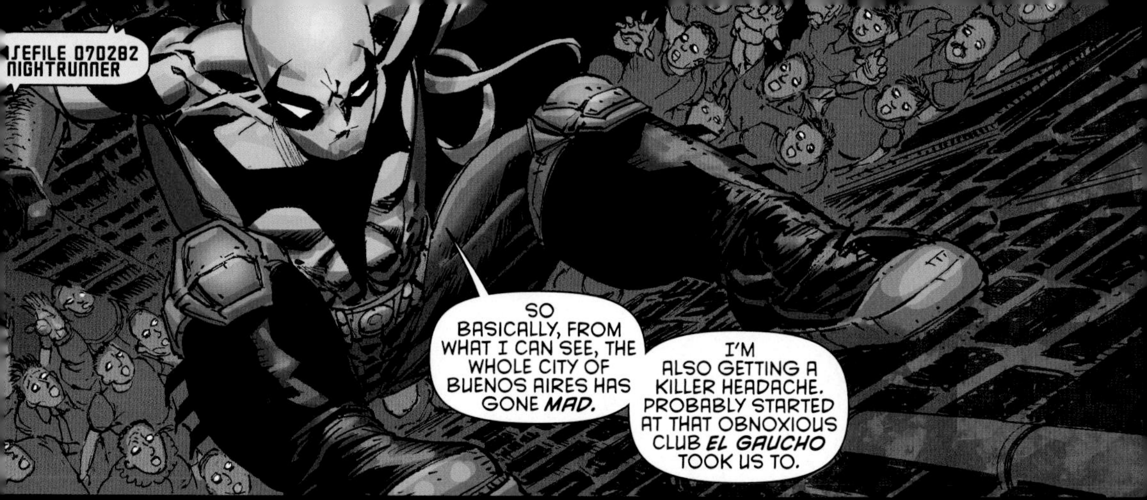
SEFILE 070282 NIGHTRUNNER
SO BASICALLY, FROM WHAT I CAN SEE, THE WHOLE CITY OF BUENOS AIRES HAS GONE *MAD.*
I'M ALSO GETTING A KILLER HEADACHE. PROBABLY STARTED AT THAT OBNOXIOUS CLUB *EL GAUCHO* TOOK US TO.

NIGHTRUNNER, DARK RANGER AND EL GAUCHO IN

HE DANGER OF LA MUERTE EN VIDA!

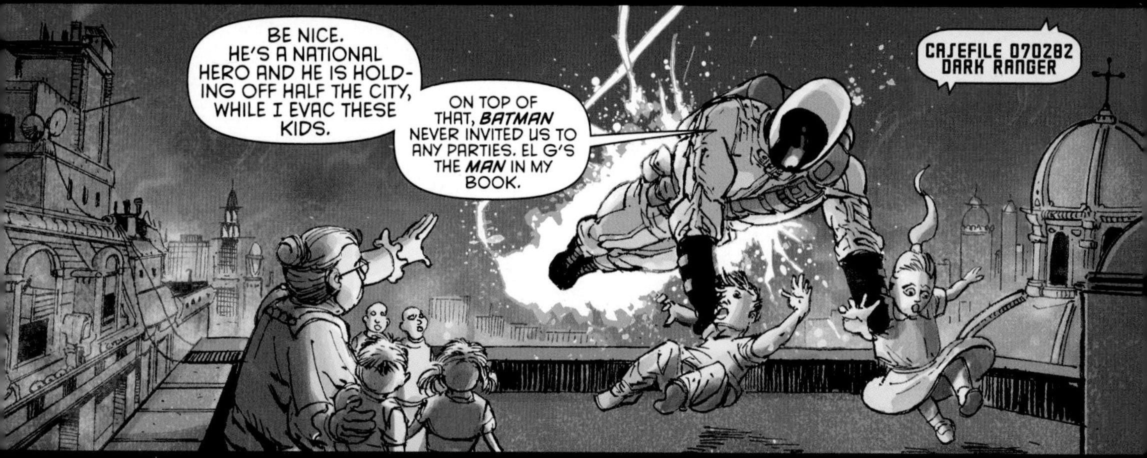
BE NICE. HE'S A NATIONAL HERO AND HE IS HOLDING OFF HALF THE CITY, WHILE I EVAC THESE KIDS.
ON TOP OF THAT, *BATMAN* NEVER INVITED US TO ANY PARTIES. EL G'S THE *MAN* IN MY BOOK.
CASEFILE 070282 DARK RANGER

WRITER - MIKE RAICHT ART - JOHN STANISCI
COLORS - ART LYON LETTERS - TAYLOR ESPOSITO

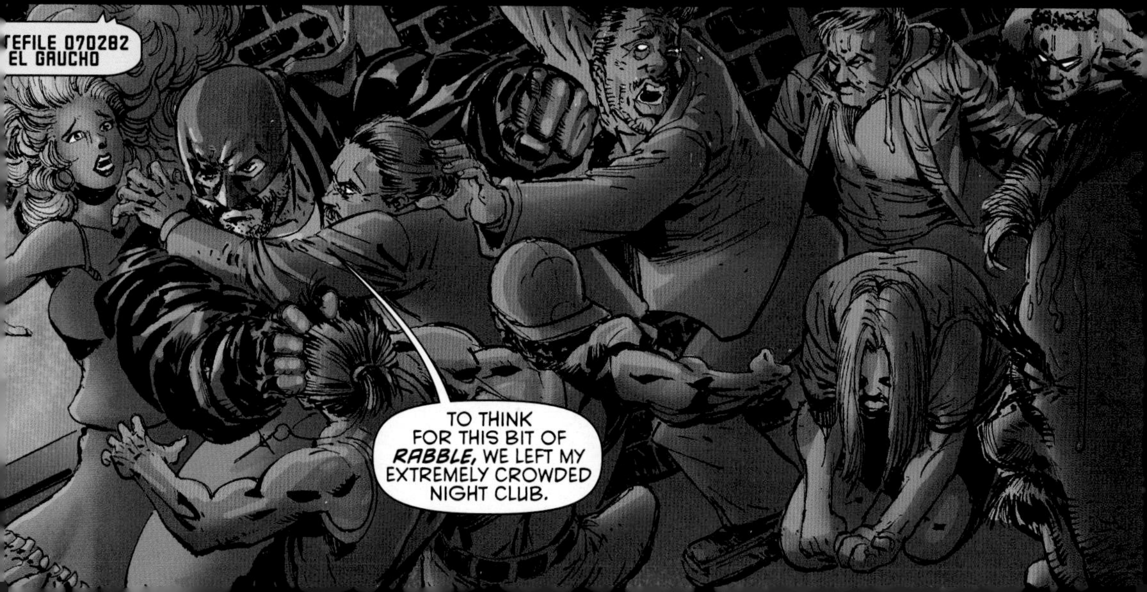
SEFILE 070282 EL GAUCHO
TO THINK FOR THIS BIT OF *RABBLE,* WE LEFT MY EXTREMELY CROWDED NIGHT CLUB.

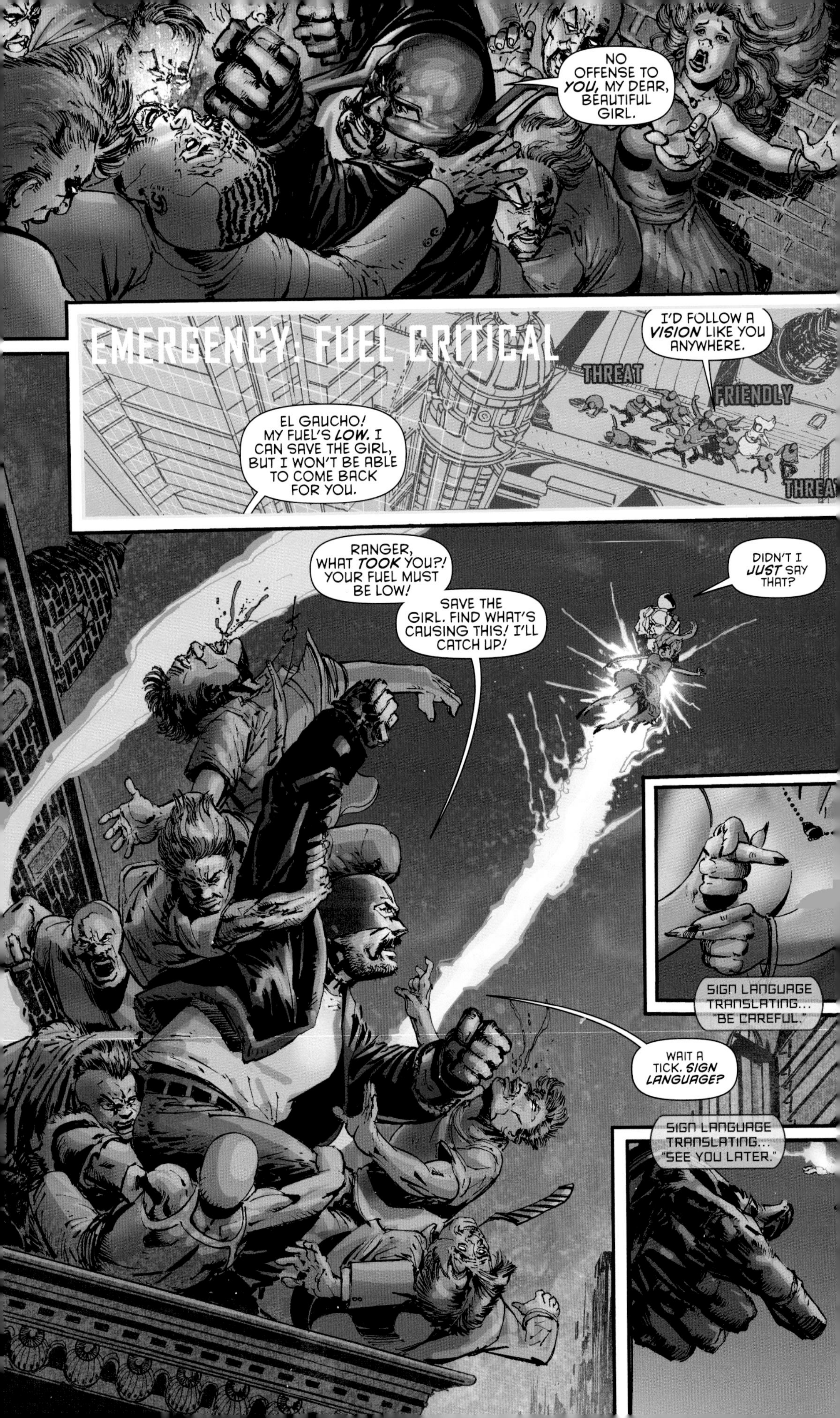

NO OFFENSE TO YOU, MY DEAR, BEAUTIFUL GIRL.
EMERGENCY: FUEL CRITICAL
I'D FOLLOW A VISION LIKE YOU ANYWHERE.
THREAT
FRIENDLY
THREAT
EL GAUCHO! MY FUEL'S LOW. I CAN SAVE THE GIRL, BUT I WON'T BE ABLE TO COME BACK FOR YOU.
RANGER, WHAT TOOK YOU?! YOUR FUEL MUST BE LOW!
SAVE THE GIRL. FIND WHAT'S CAUSING THIS! I'LL CATCH UP!
DIDN'T I JUST SAY THAT?
SIGN LANGUAGE TRANSLATING... "BE CAREFUL."
WAIT A TICK. SIGN LANGUAGE?
SIGN LANGUAGE TRANSLATING... "SEE YOU LATER."

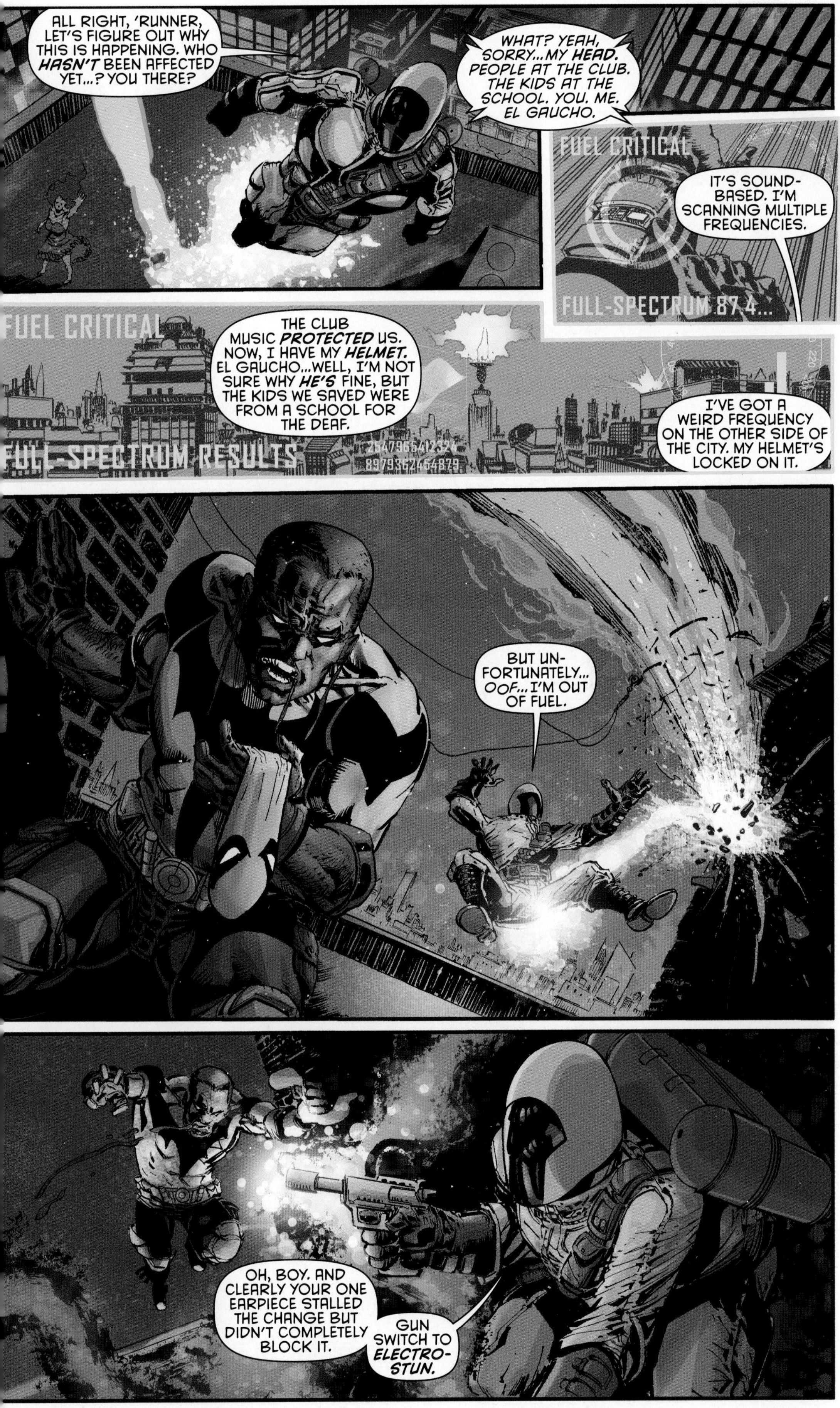
ALL RIGHT, 'RUNNER, LET'S FIGURE OUT WHY THIS IS HAPPENING. WHO HASN'T BEEN AFFECTED YET...? YOU THERE?
WHAT? YEAH, SORRY...MY HEAD. PEOPLE AT THE CLUB. THE KIDS AT THE SCHOOL. YOU. ME. EL GAUCHO.
FUEL CRITICAL
IT'S SOUND-BASED. I'M SCANNING MULTIPLE FREQUENCIES.
FULL-SPECTRUM 87.4...
FUEL CRITICAL
THE CLUB MUSIC PROTECTED US. NOW, I HAVE MY HELMET. EL GAUCHO...WELL, I'M NOT SURE WHY HE'S FINE, BUT THE KIDS WE SAVED WERE FROM A SCHOOL FOR THE DEAF.
FULL-SPECTRUM RESULTS
I'VE GOT A WEIRD FREQUENCY ON THE OTHER SIDE OF THE CITY. MY HELMET'S LOCKED ON IT.
BUT UN-FORTUNATELY... OOF...I'M OUT OF FUEL.
OH, BOY. AND CLEARLY YOUR ONE EARPIECE STALLED THE CHANGE BUT DIDN'T COMPLETELY BLOCK IT.
GUN SWITCH TO ELECTRO-STUN.

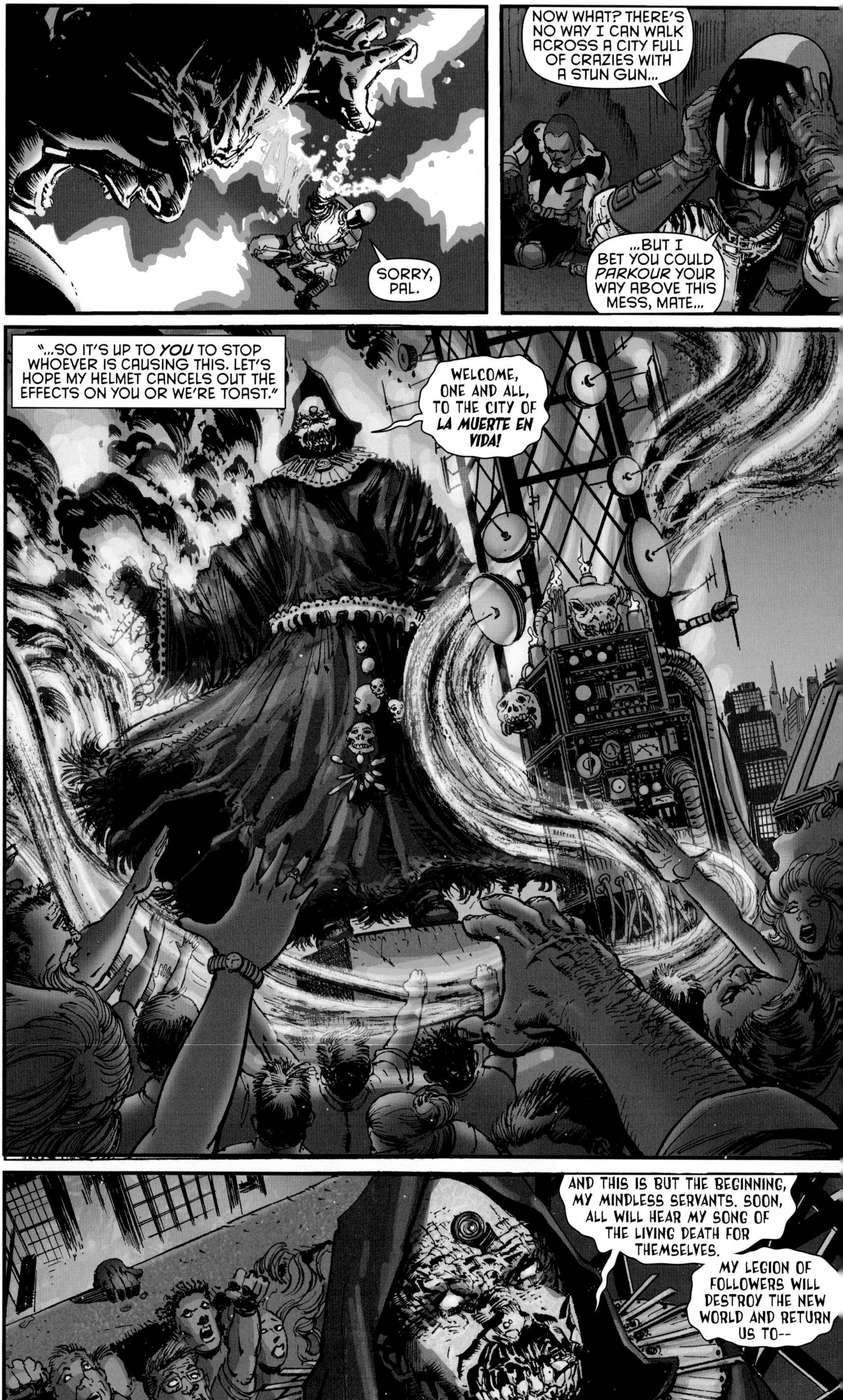
SORRY, PAL.
NOW WHAT? THERE'S NO WAY I CAN WALK ACROSS A CITY FULL OF CRAZIES WITH A STUN GUN...
...BUT I BET YOU COULD *PARKOUR* YOUR WAY ABOVE THIS MESS, MATE...
"...SO IT'S UP TO *YOU* TO STOP WHOEVER IS CAUSING THIS. LET'S HOPE MY HELMET CANCELS OUT THE EFFECTS ON YOU OR WE'RE TOAST."
WELCOME, ONE AND ALL, TO THE CITY OF *LA MUERTE EN VIDA!*
AND THIS IS BUT THE BEGINNING, MY MINDLESS SERVANTS. SOON, ALL WILL HEAR MY SONG OF THE LIVING DEATH FOR THEMSELVES.
MY LEGION OF FOLLOWERS WILL DESTROY THE NEW WORLD AND RETURN US TO--

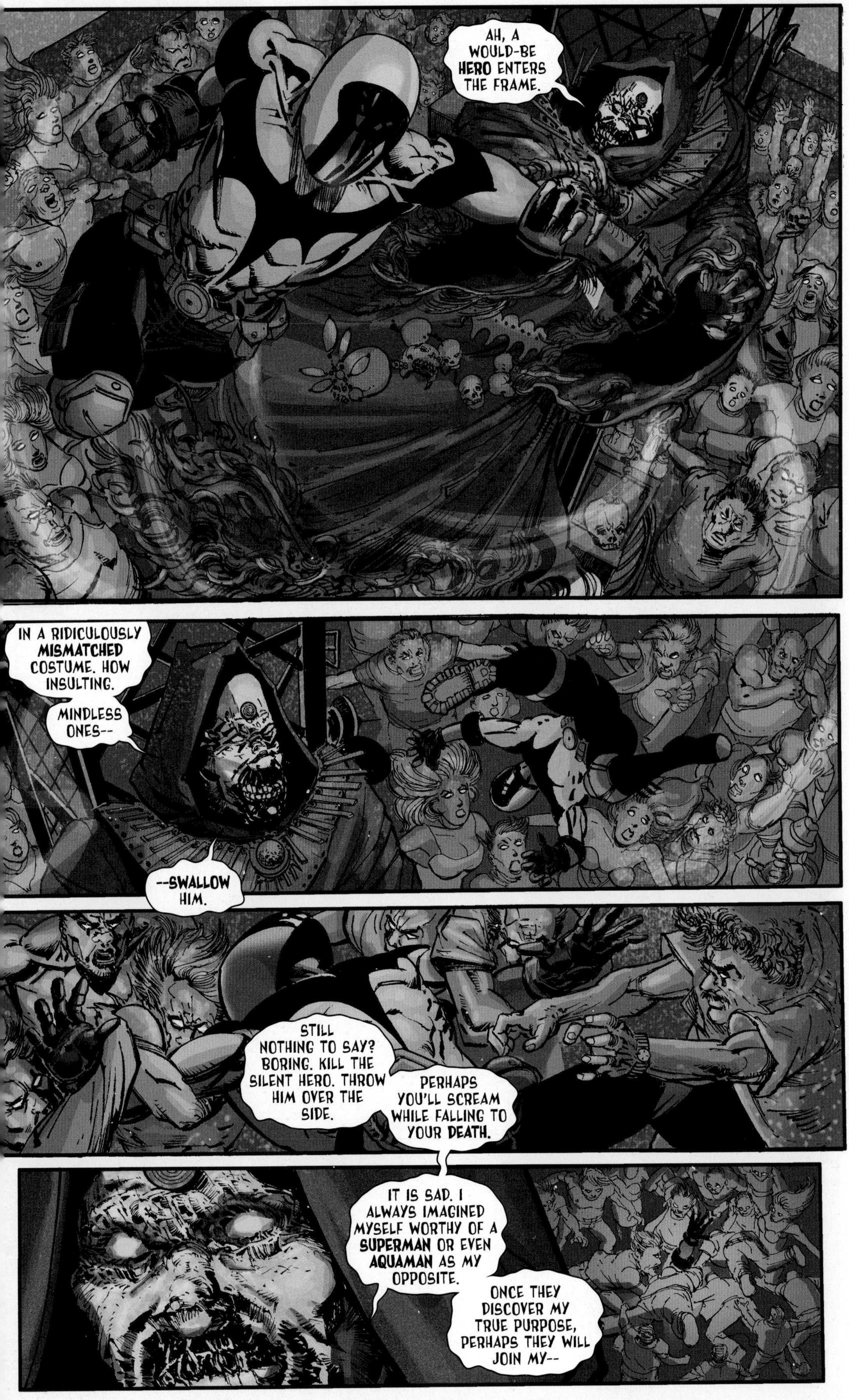
AH, A WOULD-BE **HERO** ENTERS THE FRAME.
IN A RIDICULOUSLY **MISMATCHED** COSTUME. HOW INSULTING.
MINDLESS ONES--
--**SWALLOW** HIM.
STILL NOTHING TO SAY? BORING. KILL THE SILENT HERO. THROW HIM OVER THE SIDE.
PERHAPS YOU'LL SCREAM WHILE FALLING TO YOUR **DEATH.**
IT IS SAD. I ALWAYS IMAGINED MYSELF WORTHY OF A **SUPERMAN** OR EVEN **AQUAMAN** AS MY OPPOSITE.
ONCE THEY DISCOVER MY TRUE PURPOSE, PERHAPS THEY WILL JOIN MY--

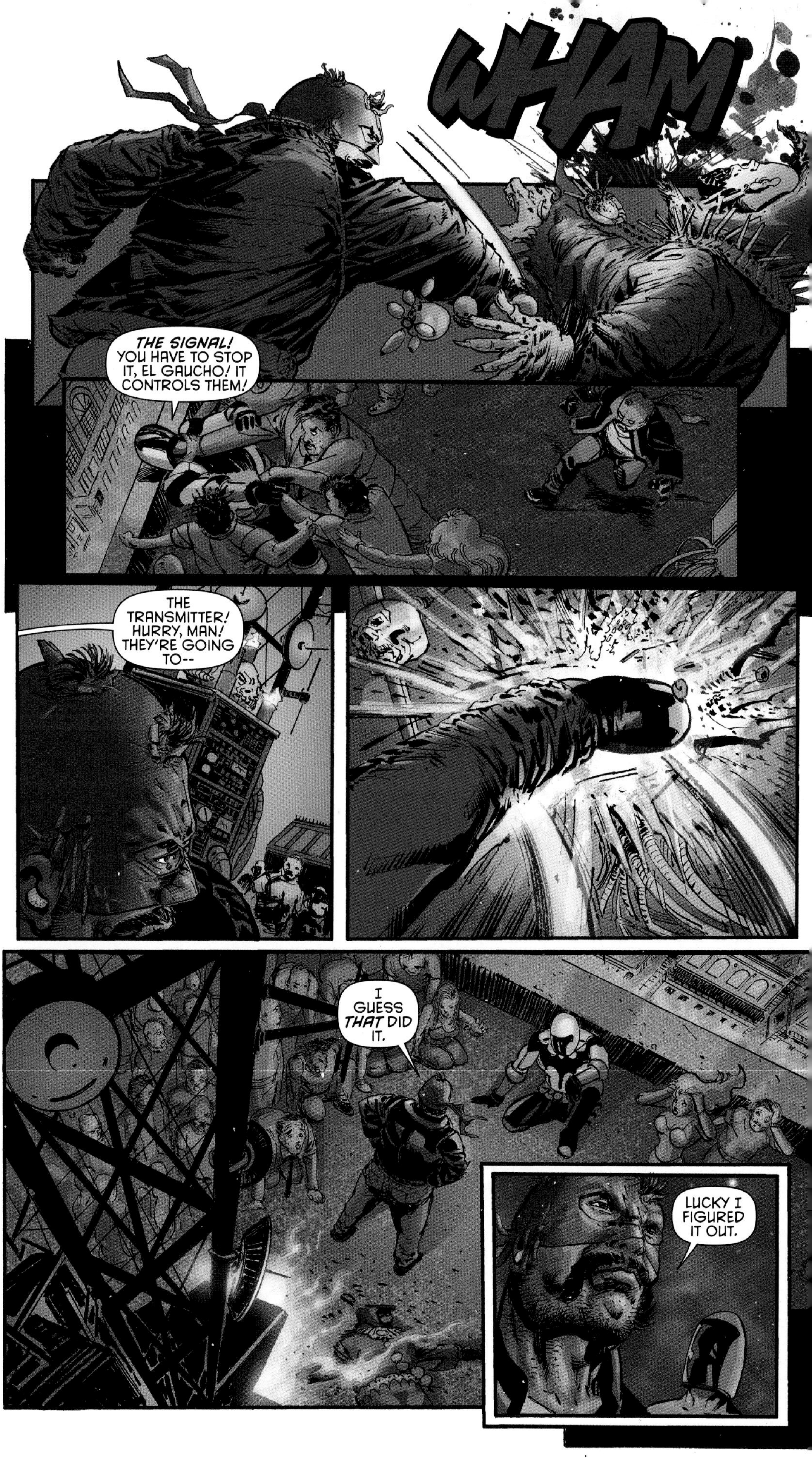
WHAM
THE SIGNAL! YOU HAVE TO STOP IT, EL GAUCHO! IT CONTROLS THEM!
THE TRANSMITTER! HURRY, MAN! THEY'RE GOING TO--
I GUESS THAT DID IT.
LUCKY I FIGURED IT OUT.

NIGHT-RUNNER! IT *WORKED.* YOU DID IT.

NOT QUITE. I COULDN'T SEE A THING IN YOUR *HELMET.* ALMOST GOT ME KILLED. EL GAUCHO SAVED THE DAY.

BUT THE SIGNAL? IT *TURNED* ME AFTER A FEW SECONDS. HOW DID HE--

AH, MY YOUNG FRIENDS, I HAVE TRAINED MY *EARS* TO BE SUPER SENSITIVE. IT CAN BE AN ADVANTAGE *AND* A CURSE.

I LOVE TO DANCE WITH THE SEÑORITAS AT THE CLUB, BUT SOMETIMES THE MUSIC IS JUST TOO LOUD.

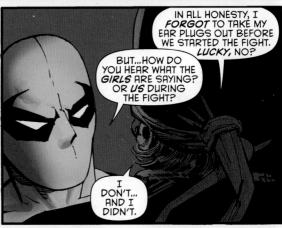

IN ALL HONESTY, I *FORGOT* TO TAKE MY EAR PLUGS OUT BEFORE WE STARTED THE FIGHT. *LUCKY,* NO?

BUT...HOW DO YOU HEAR WHAT THE *GIRLS* ARE SAYING? OR *US* DURING THE FIGHT?

I DON'T... AND I DIDN'T.

MY GOODNESS, LOOK AT THE TIME. AND US, BARELY TIRED.

I HAVE A PRIVATE JET AND FRIENDS ALL OVER THE WORLD. WHAT SAY WE CLEAN OURSELVES UP AND FIND A GOOD TIME?

COME. I WON'T LET YOU SAY NO.

YOU'RE RIGHT. HE *IS* WAY COOLER THAN BATMAN.

TOLD YOU. BUT DO YOU THINK HE'LL LET ME REFUEL MY *JETPACK?* YOU KNOW, JUST IN CASE...

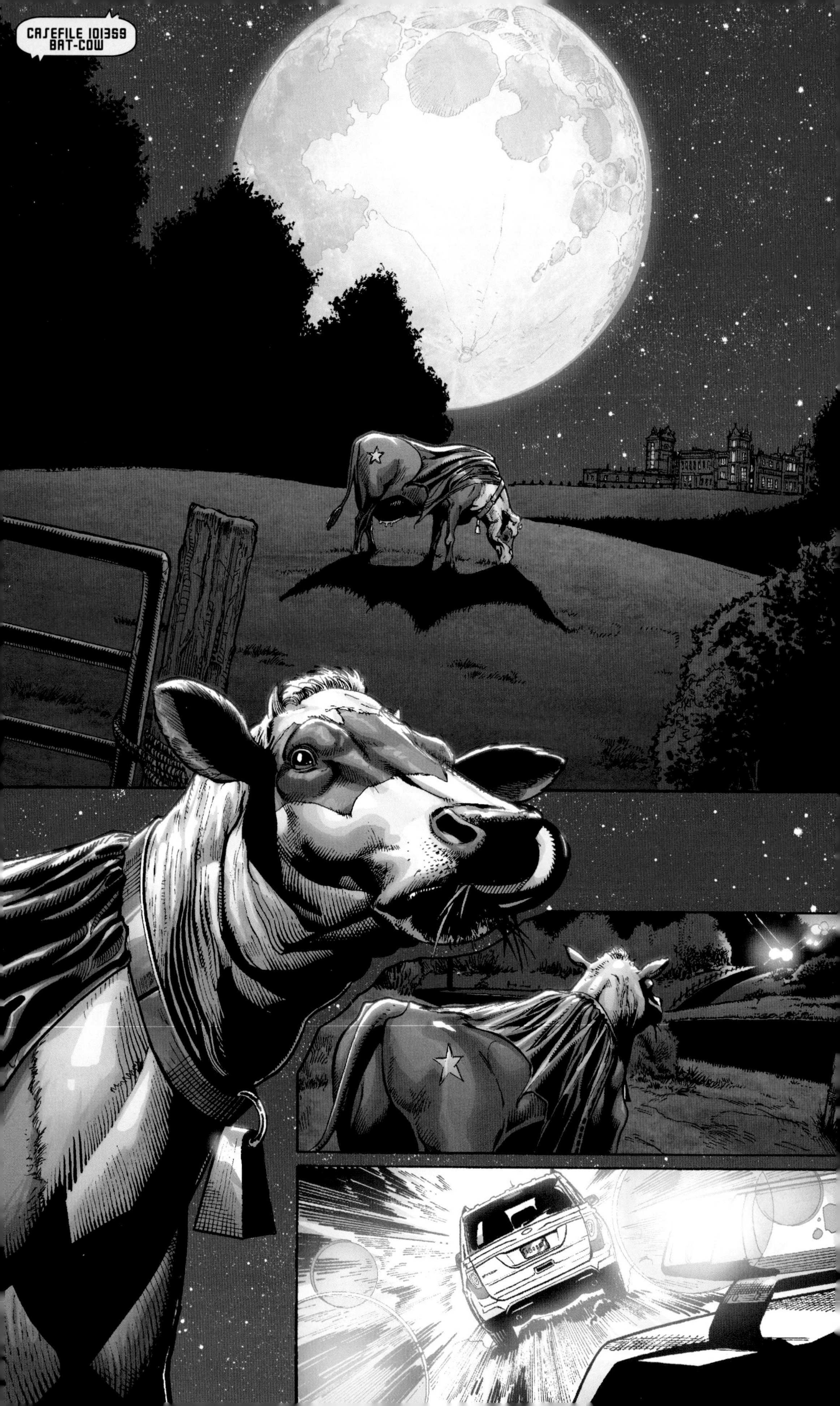
CASEFILE 101359
BAT-COW

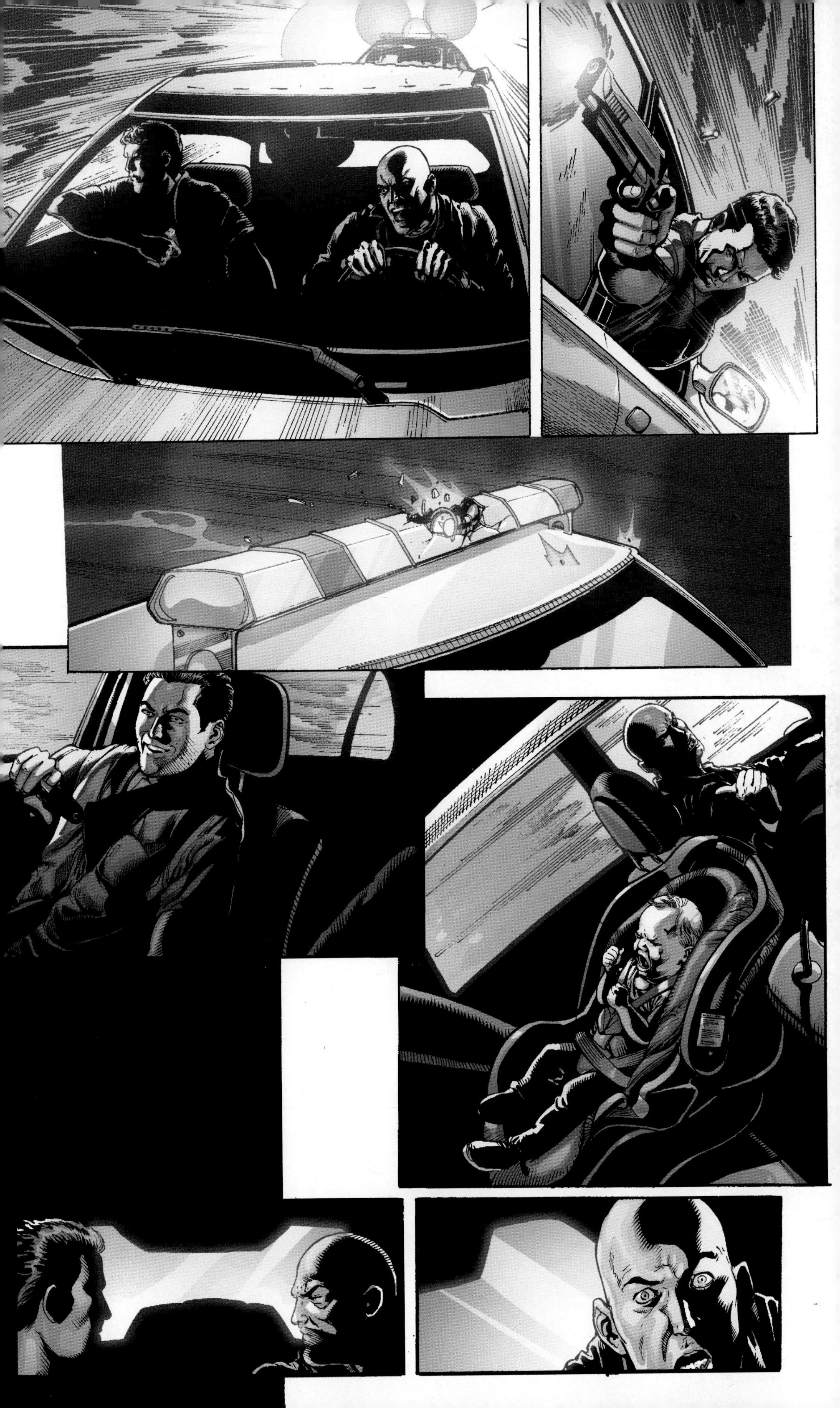

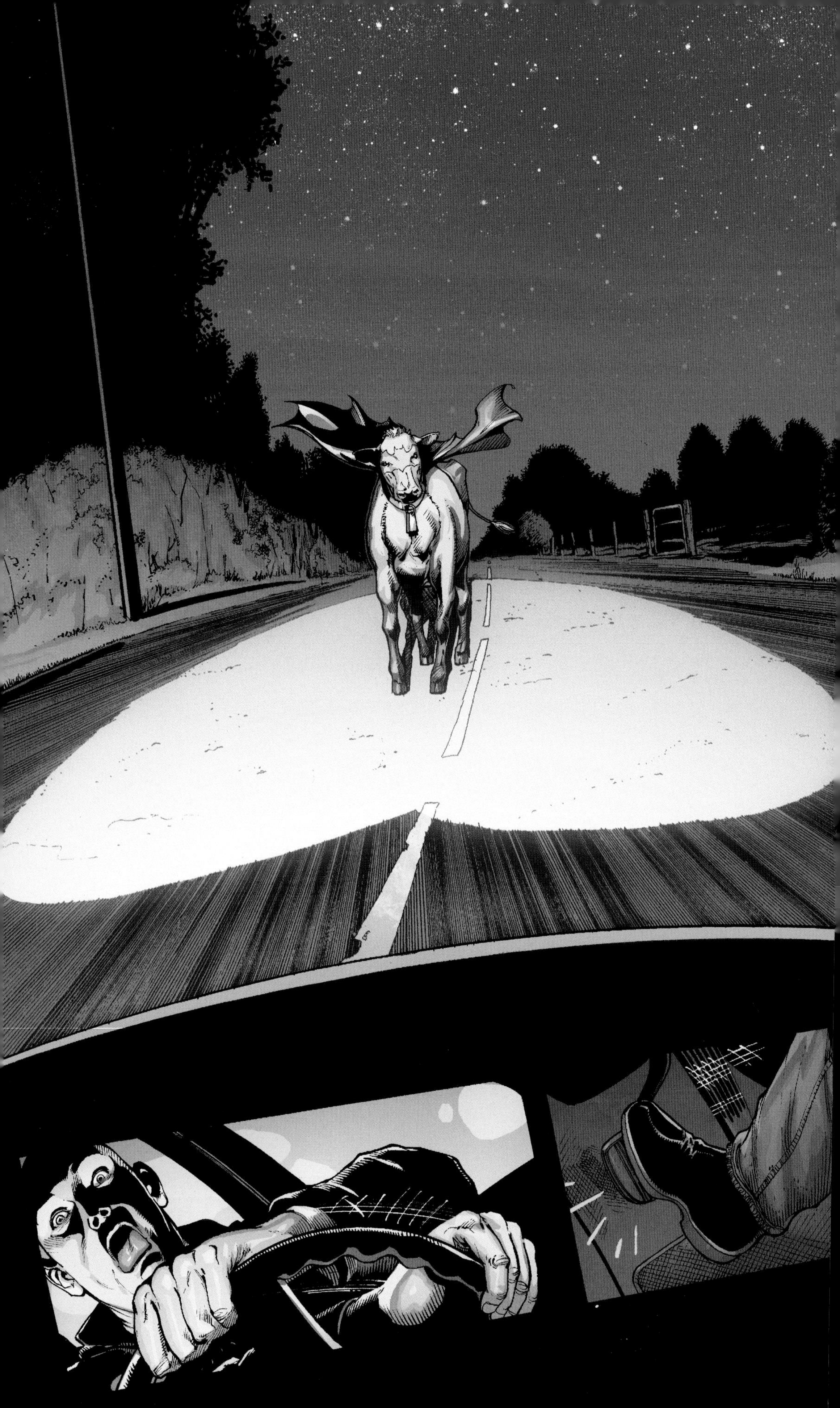

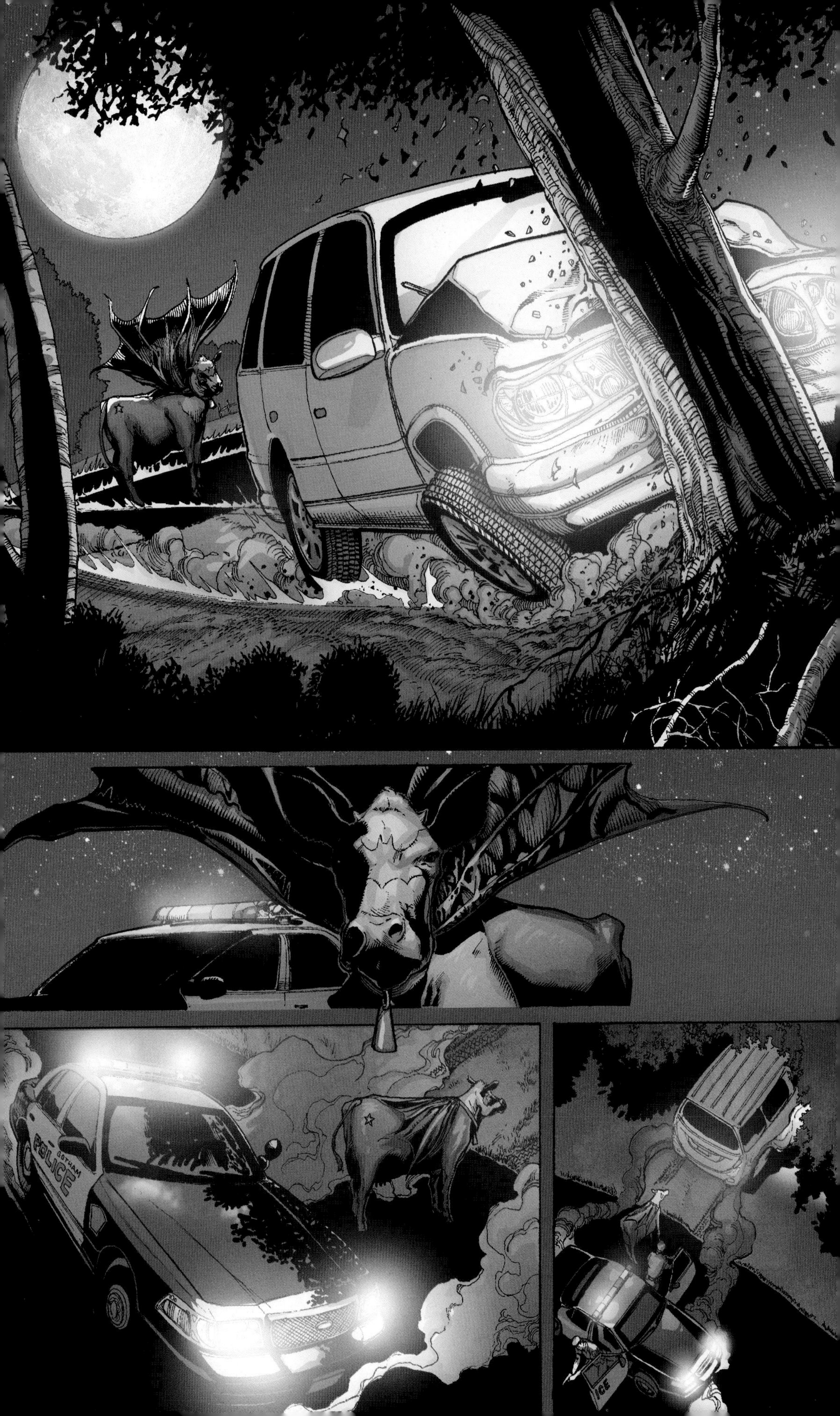
GOTHAM
POLICE

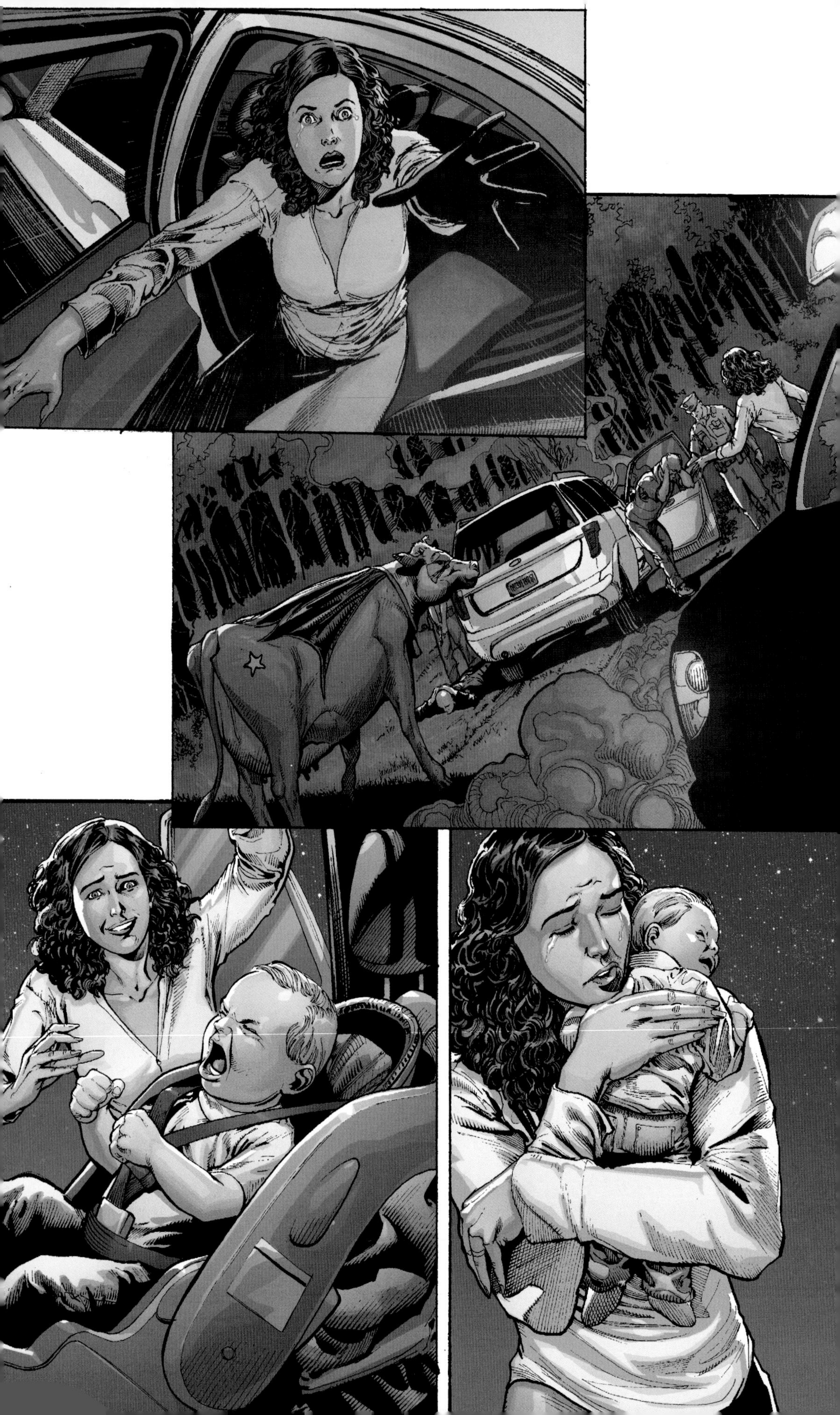

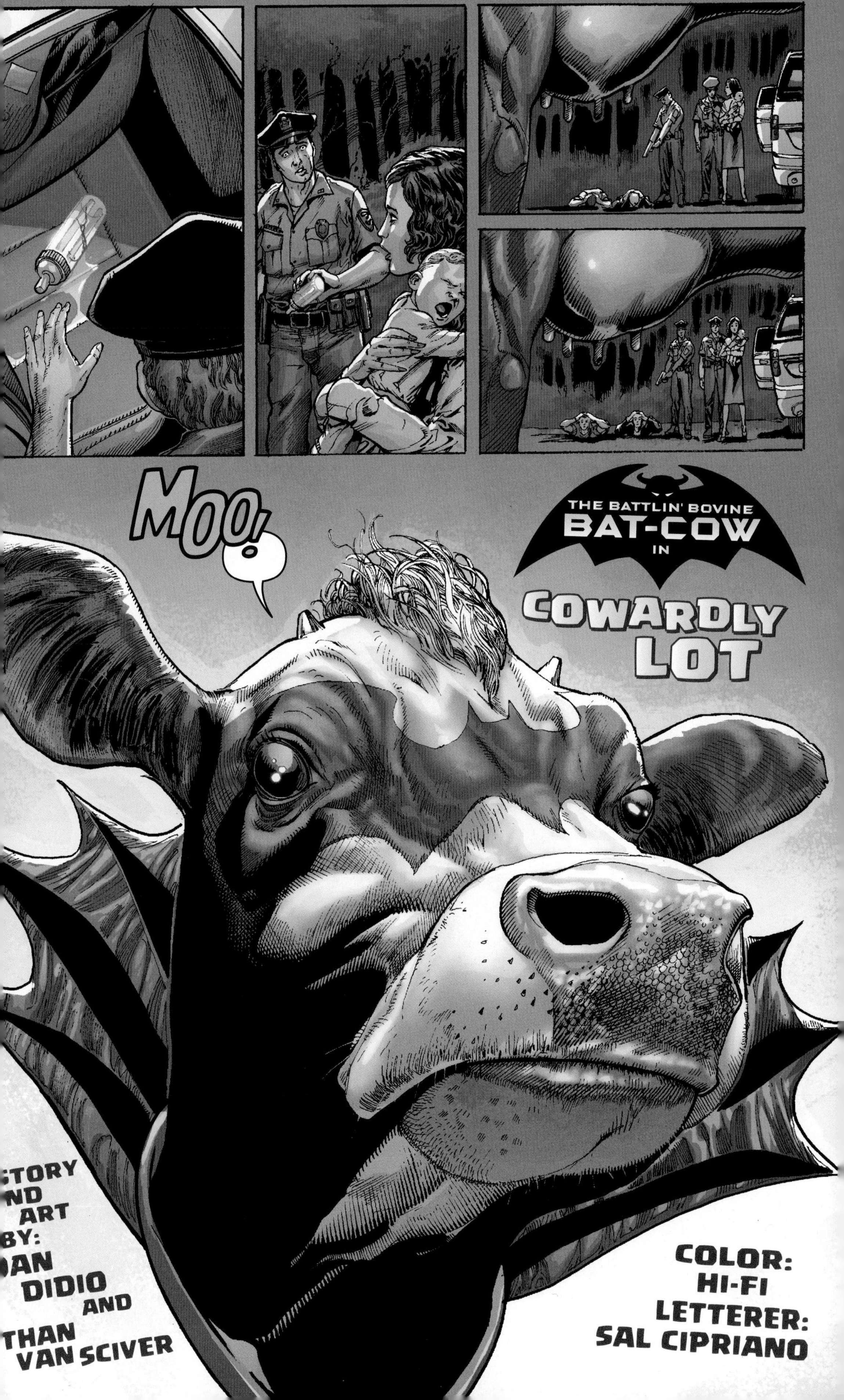
MOO!
THE BATTLIN' BOVINE
BAT-COW
IN
COWARDLY LOT
STORY
ND
ART
BY:
DAN
DIDIO
AND
THAN
VAN SCIVER
COLOR:
HI-FI
LETTERER:
SAL CIPRIANO

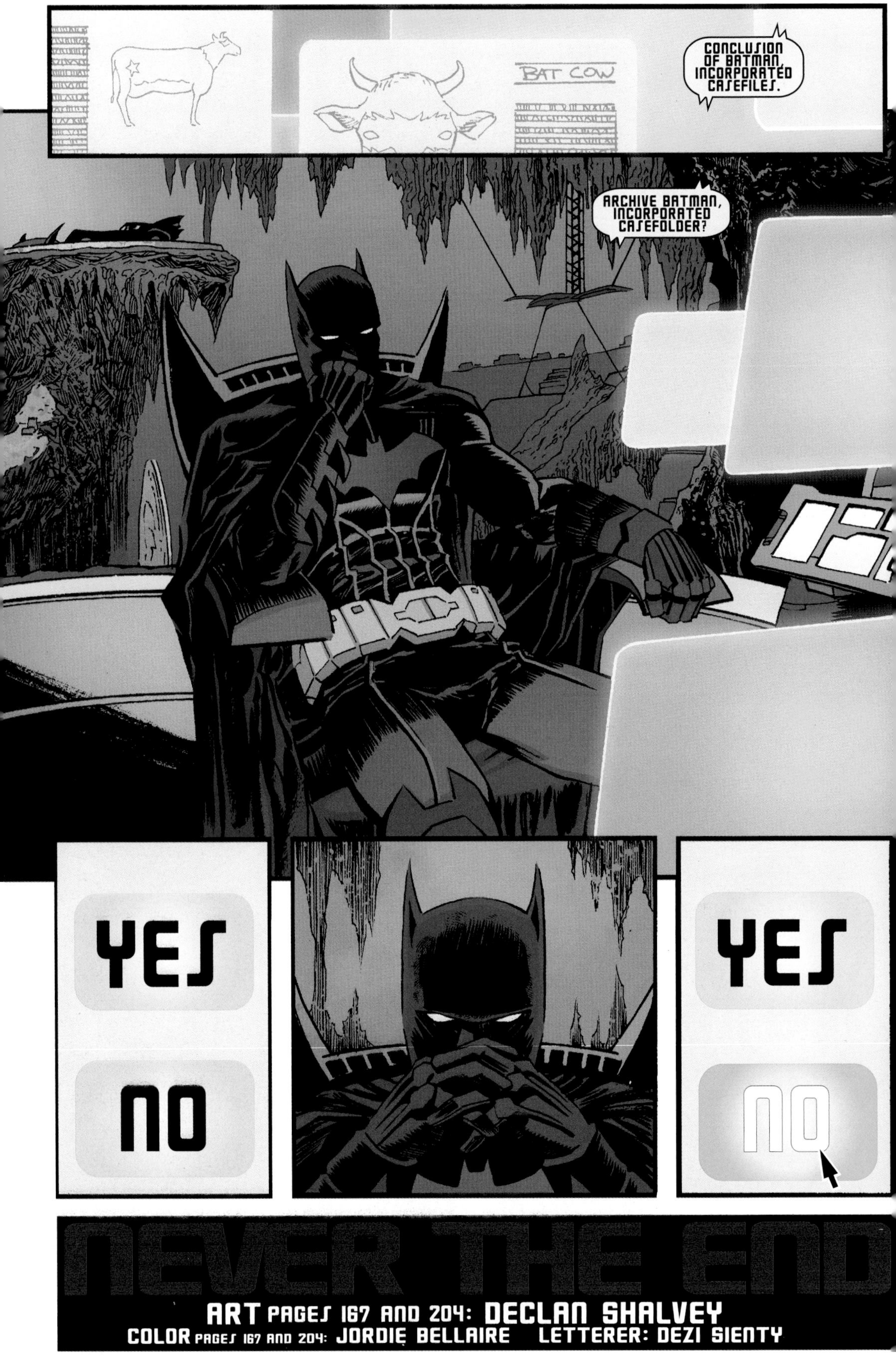
BAT COW
CONCLUSION OF BATMAN, INCORPORATED CASEFILES.
ARCHIVE BATMAN, INCORPORATED CASEFOLDER?
YES
NO
YES
NO

NEVER THE END

ART PAGES 167 AND 204: DECLAN SHALVEY
COLOR PAGES 167 AND 204: JORDIE BELLAIRE LETTERER: DEZI SIENTY

COVER: BURNHAM & FAIRBAIRN

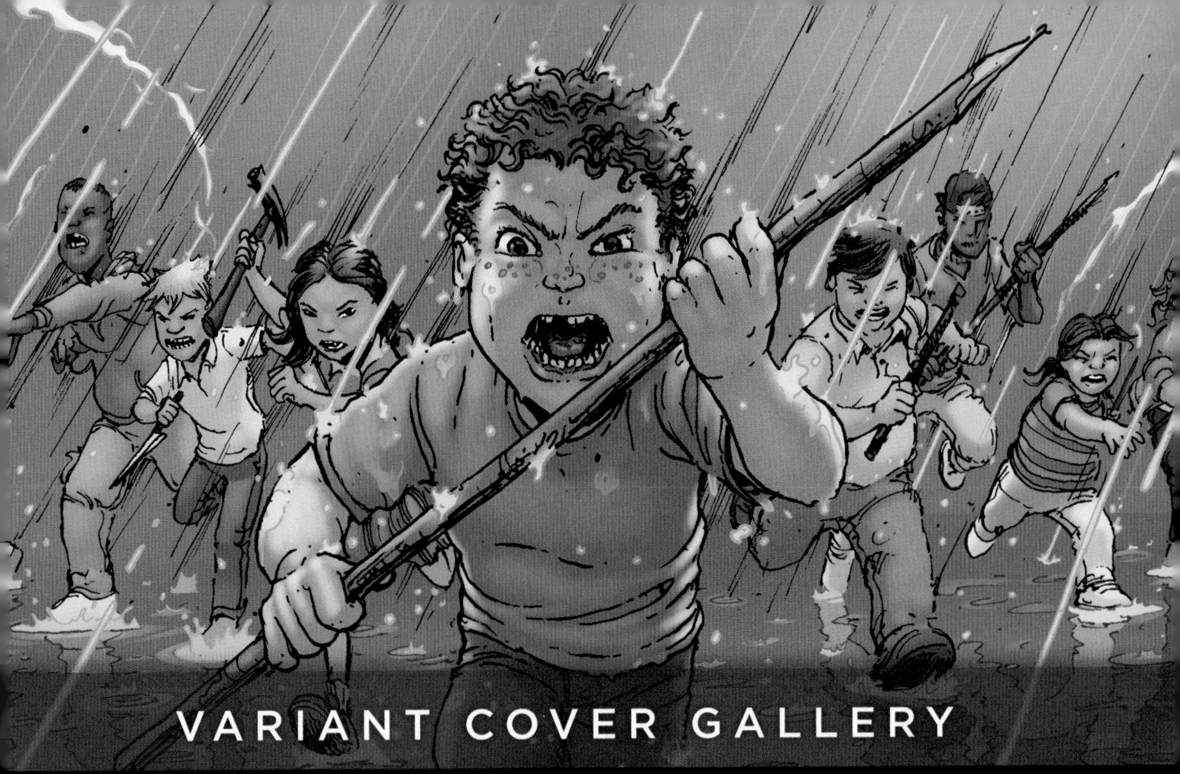

VARIANT COVER GALLERY

BATMAN INCORPORATED #7
BY TONY DANIEL & TOMEU MOREY

BATMAN INCORPORATED #8
BY CHRIS BURNHAM & NATHAN FAIRBAIRN

BATMAN INCORPORATED #9
BY CHRIS BURNHAM & NATHAN FAIRBAIRN

BATMAN INCORPORATED #10
BY JASON MASTERS & NATHAN FAIRBAIRN

BATMAN INCORPORATED #12
BY GUILLEM MARCH

BATMAN INCORPORATED #13
BY GRANT MORRISON & NATHAN FAIRBAIRN

BATMAN INCORPORATED #11
BY RICKEN

BATMAN INCORPORATED SPECIAL #1
BY ETHAN VAN SCIVER & HI-FI

BATMAN INCORPORATED #10 FULL COVER
BY CHRIS BURNHAM & NATHAN FAIRBAIRN

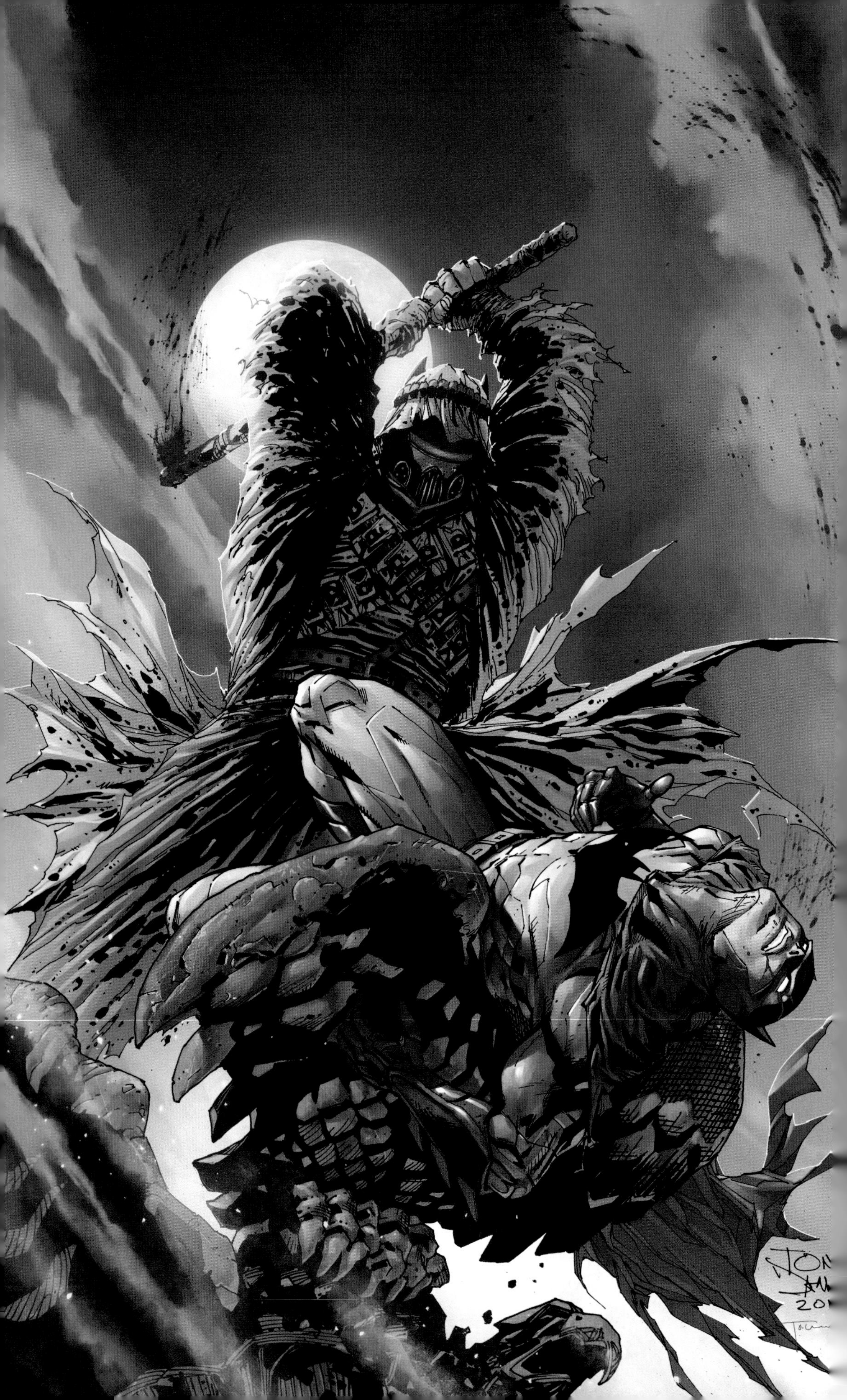

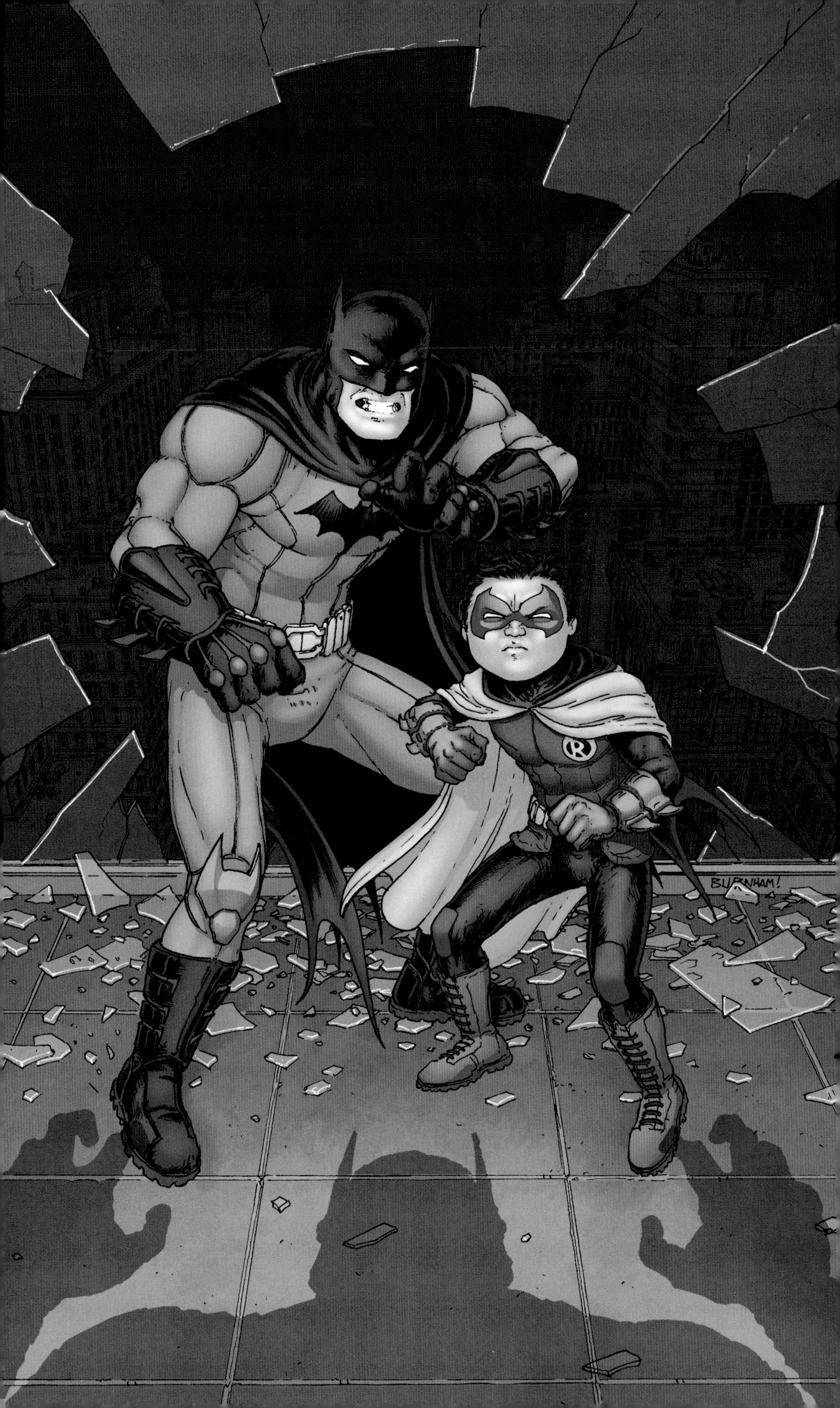
BURNHAM!

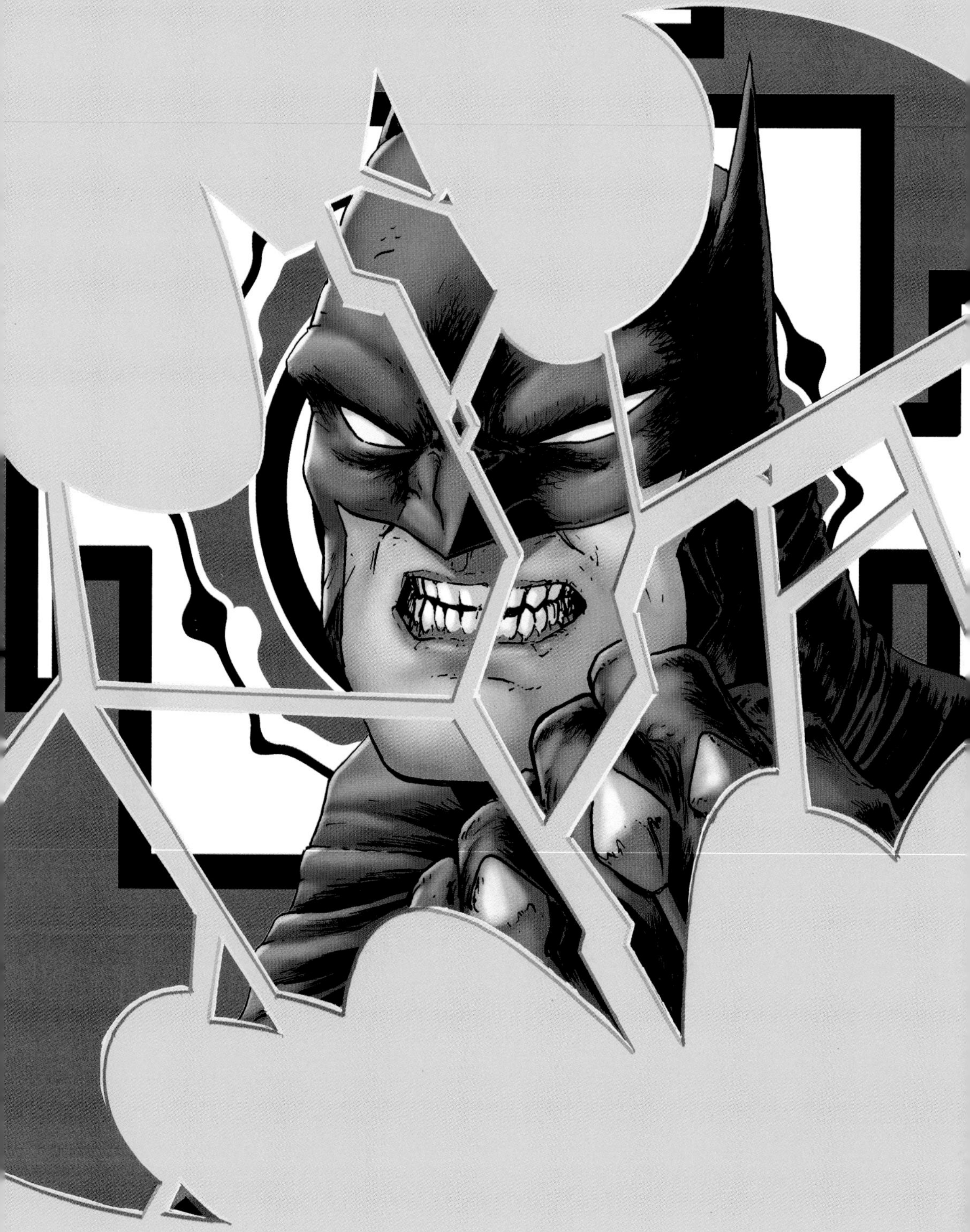

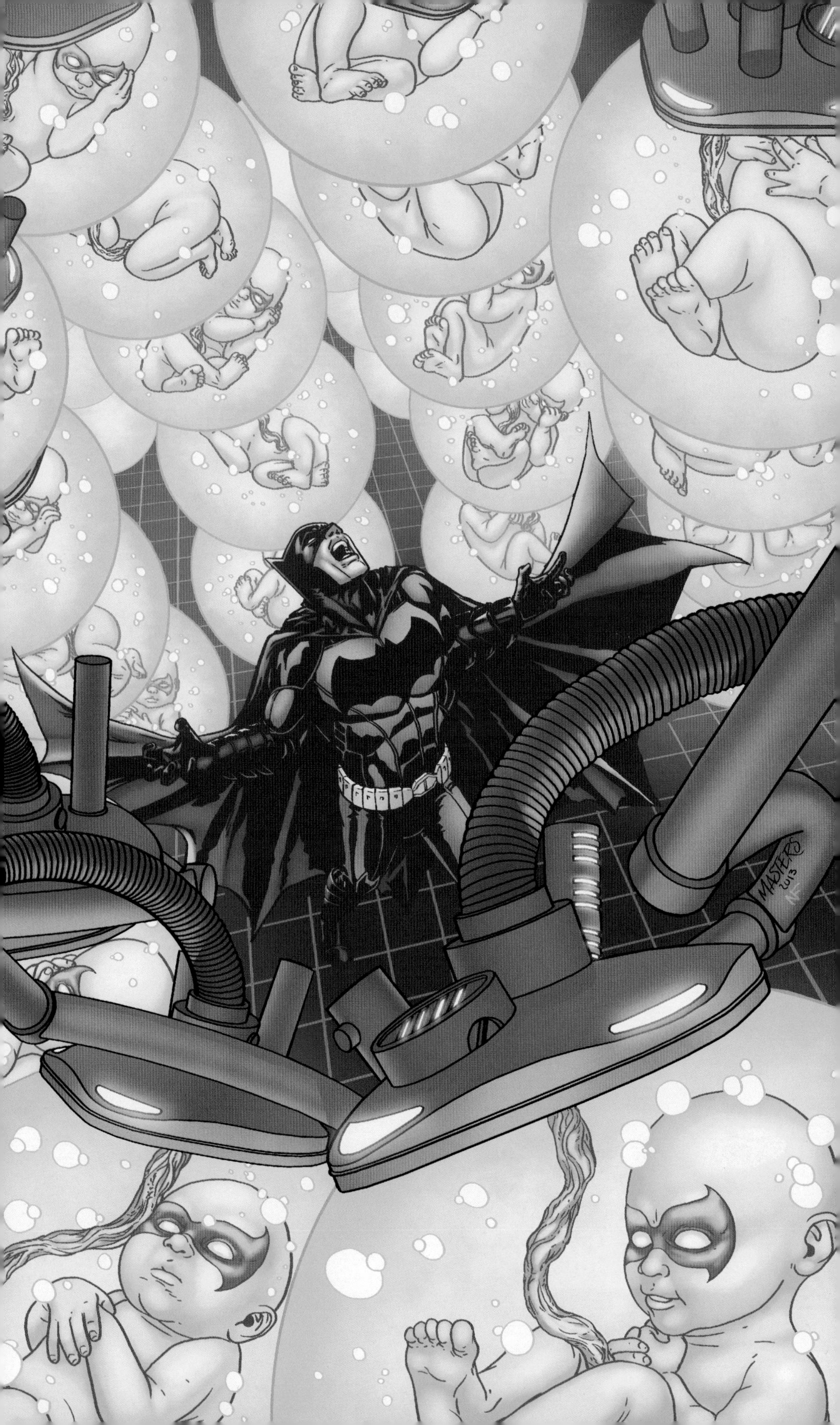
MASTERS
2013
NF

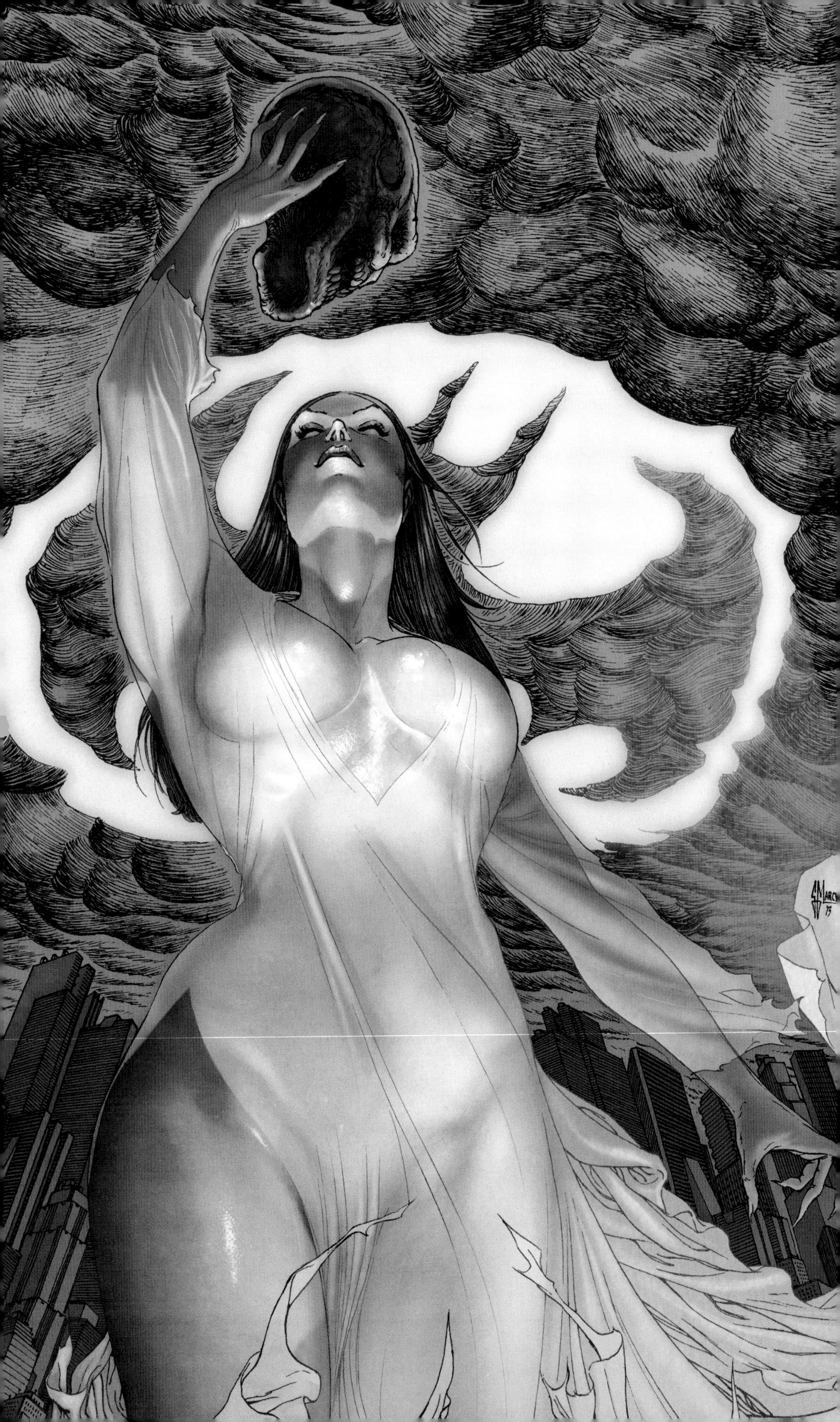

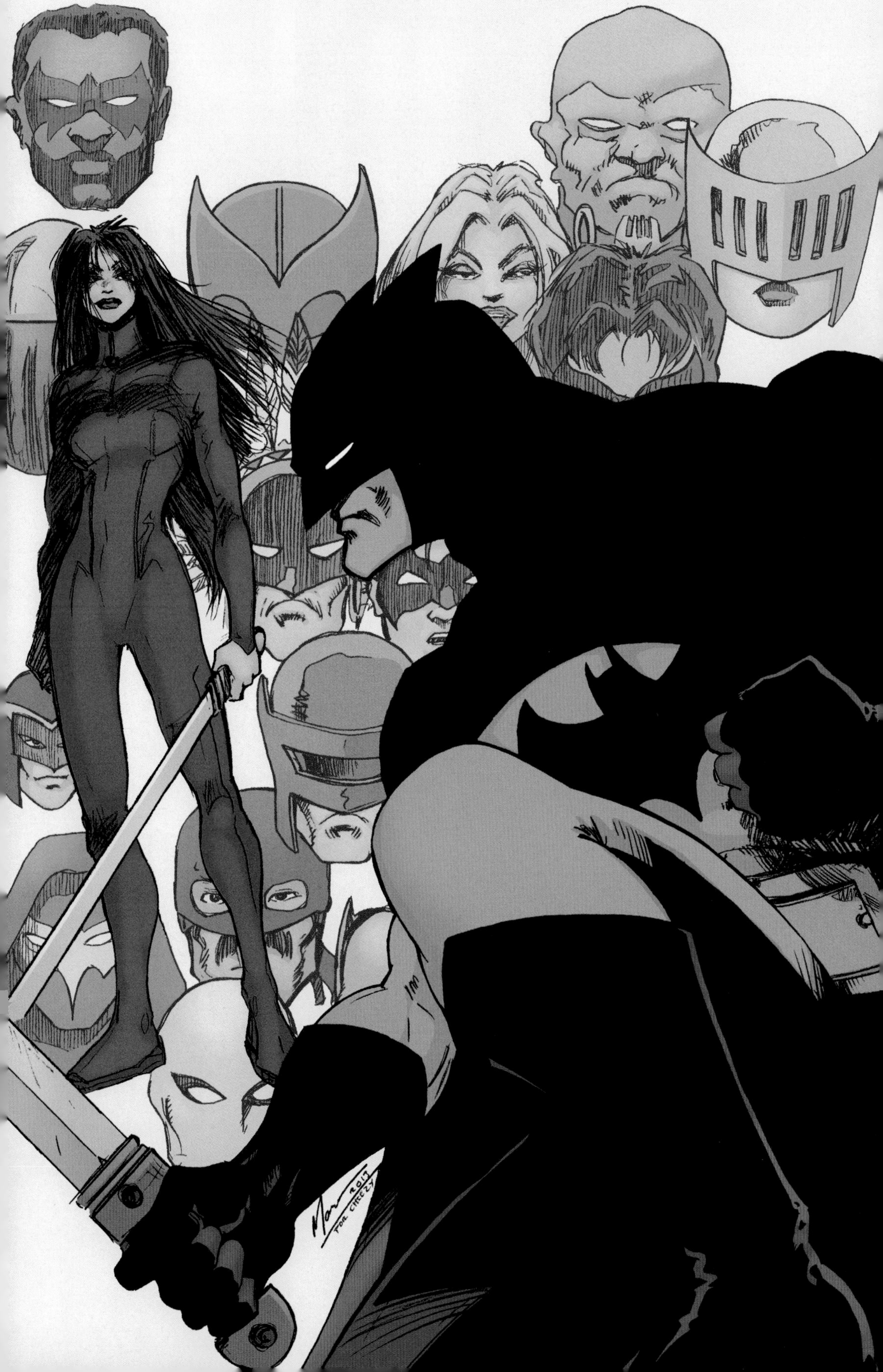

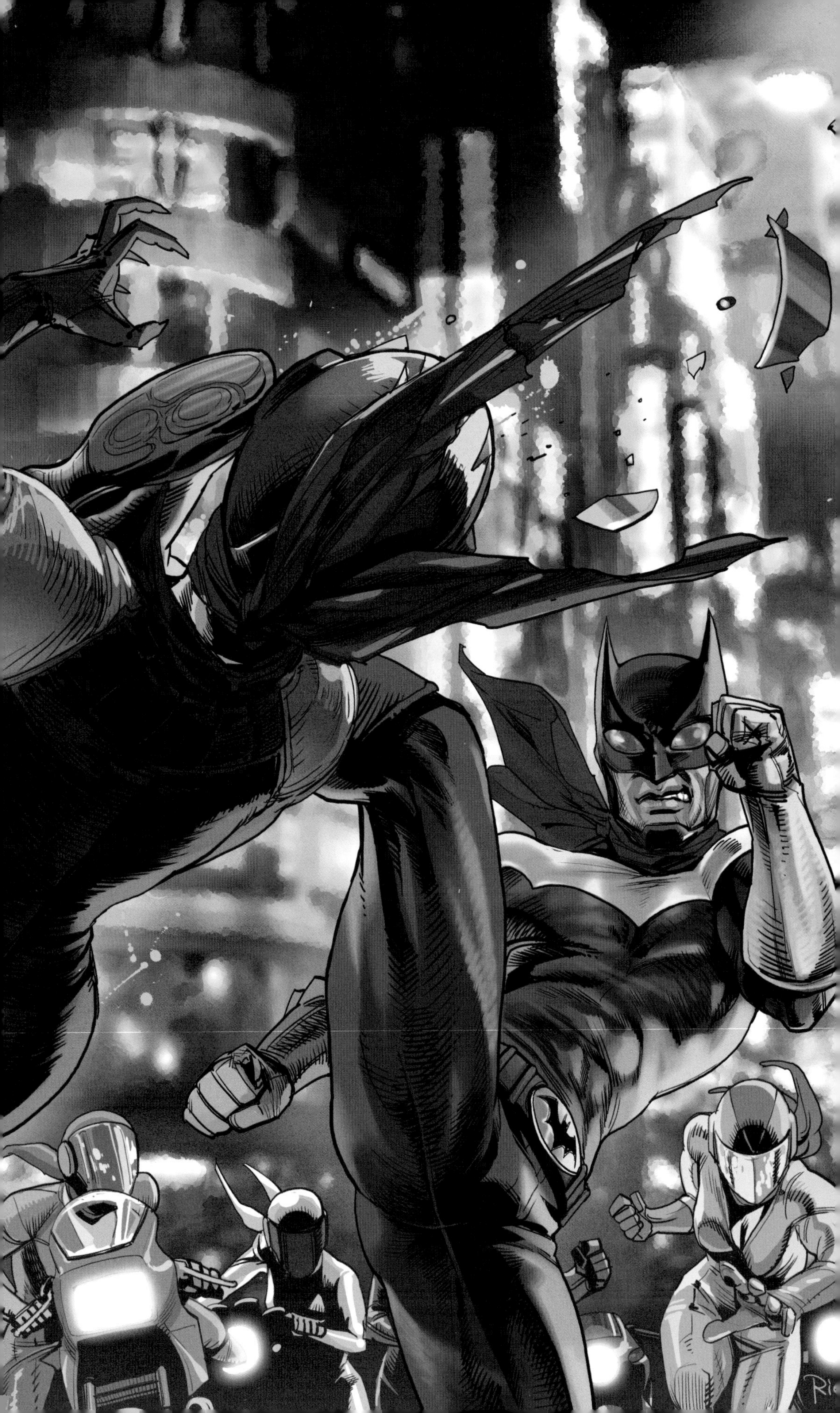

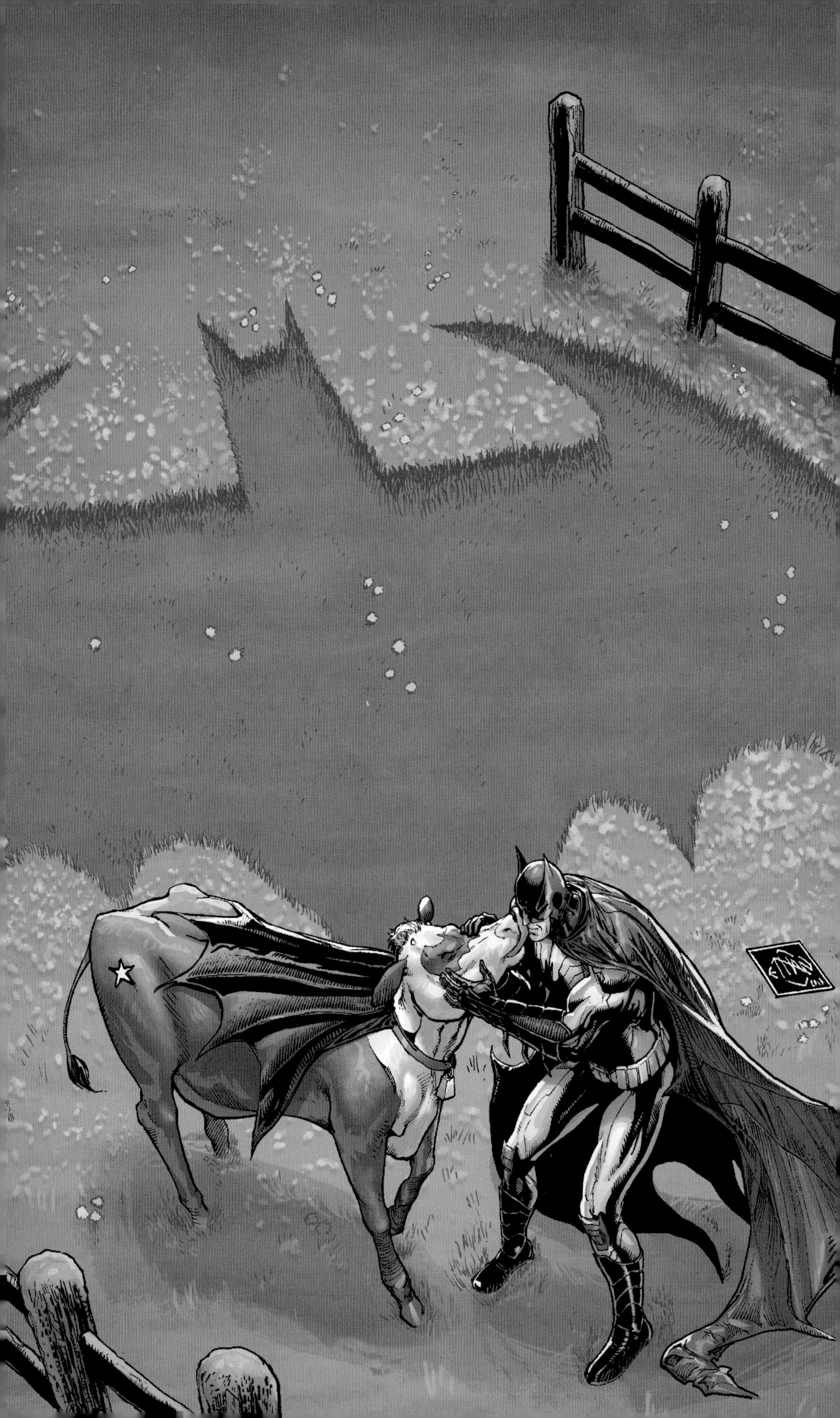

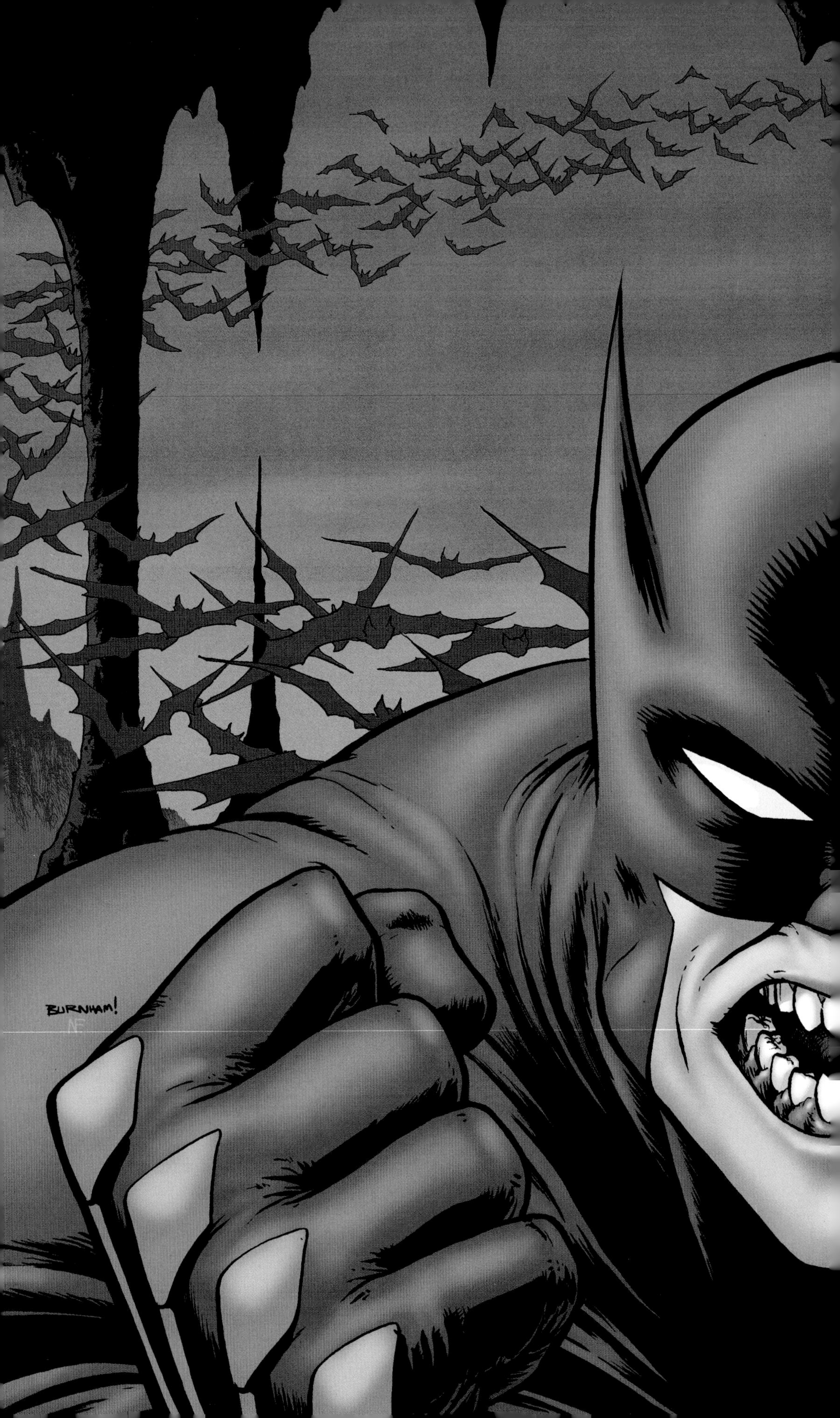
BURNHAM!

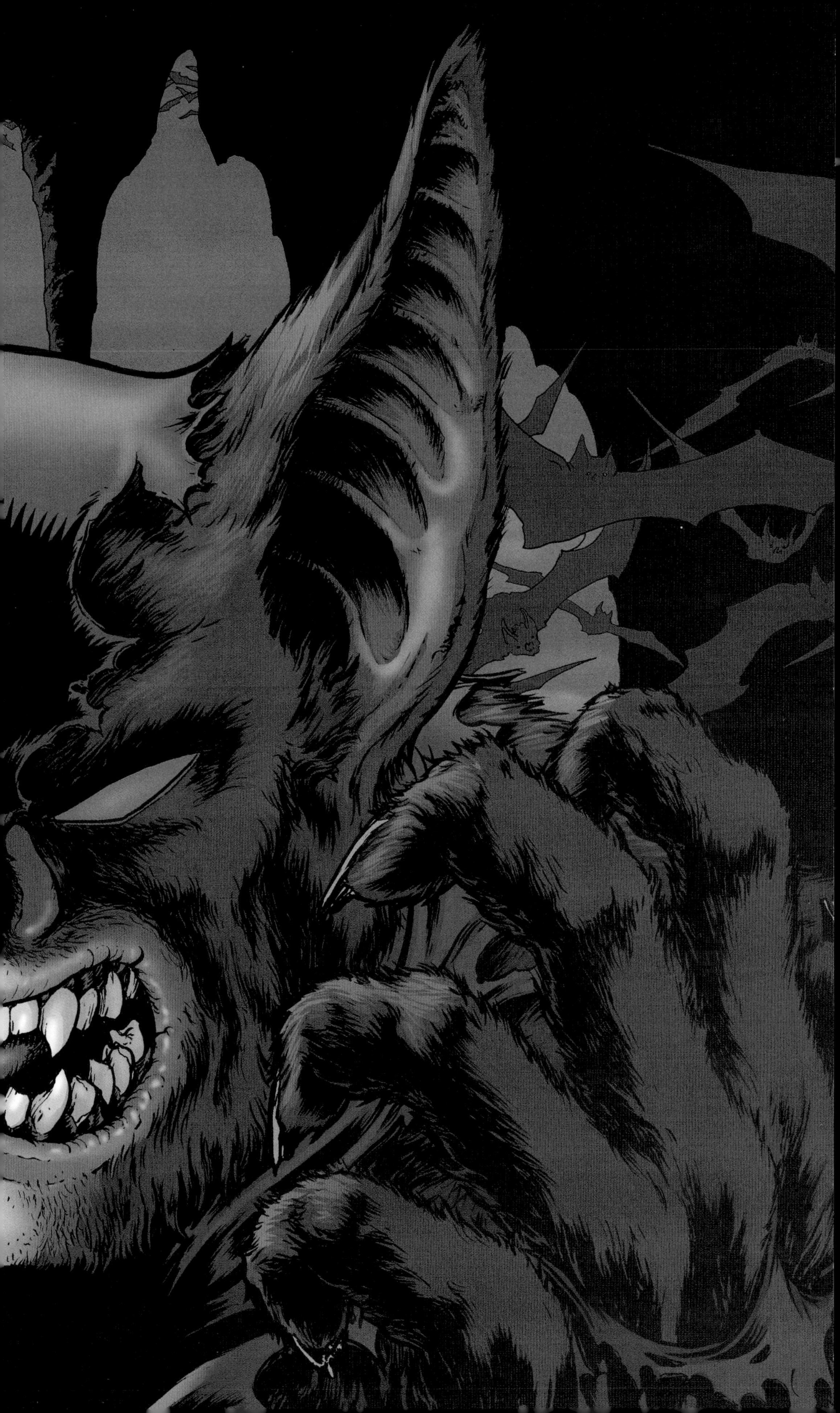

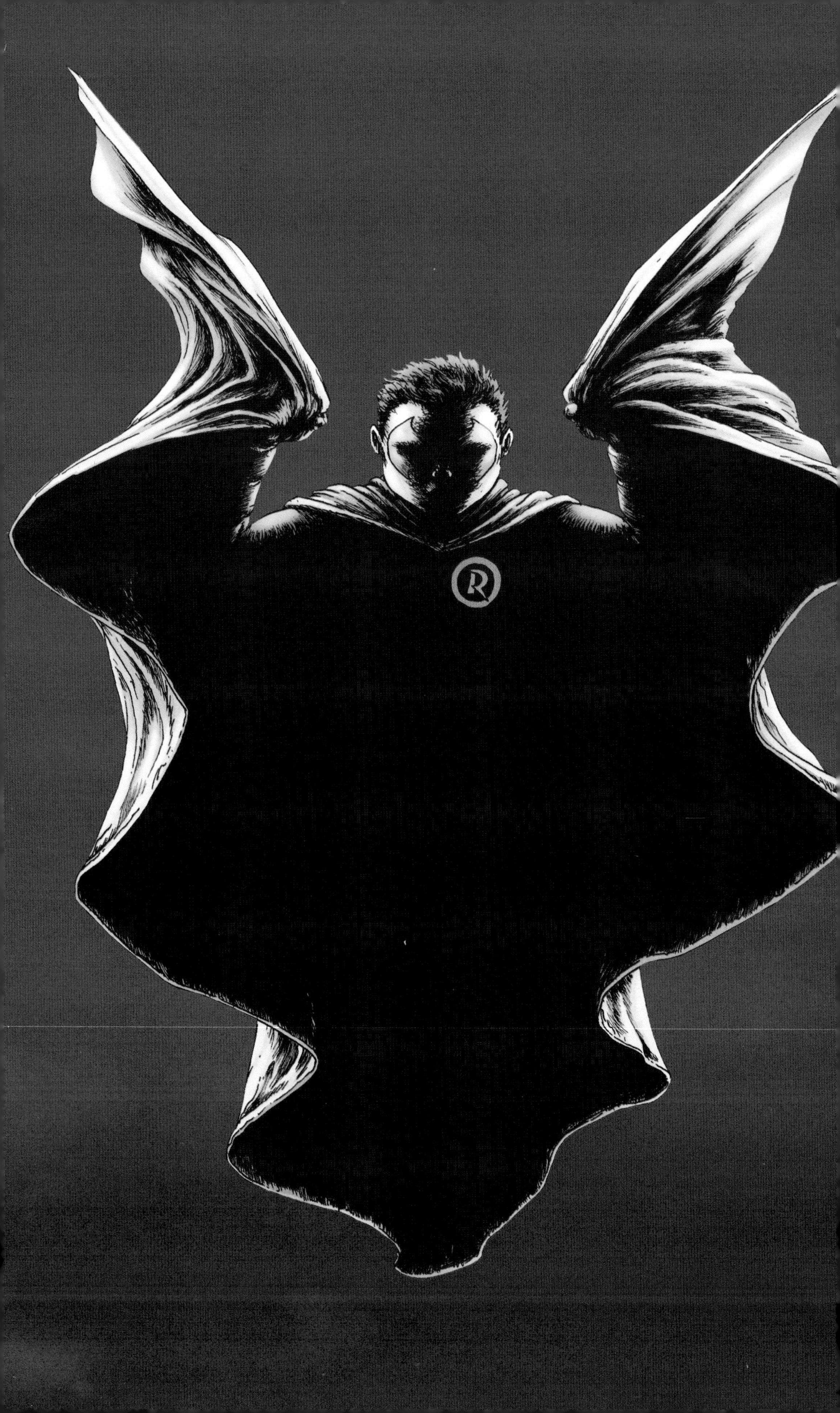

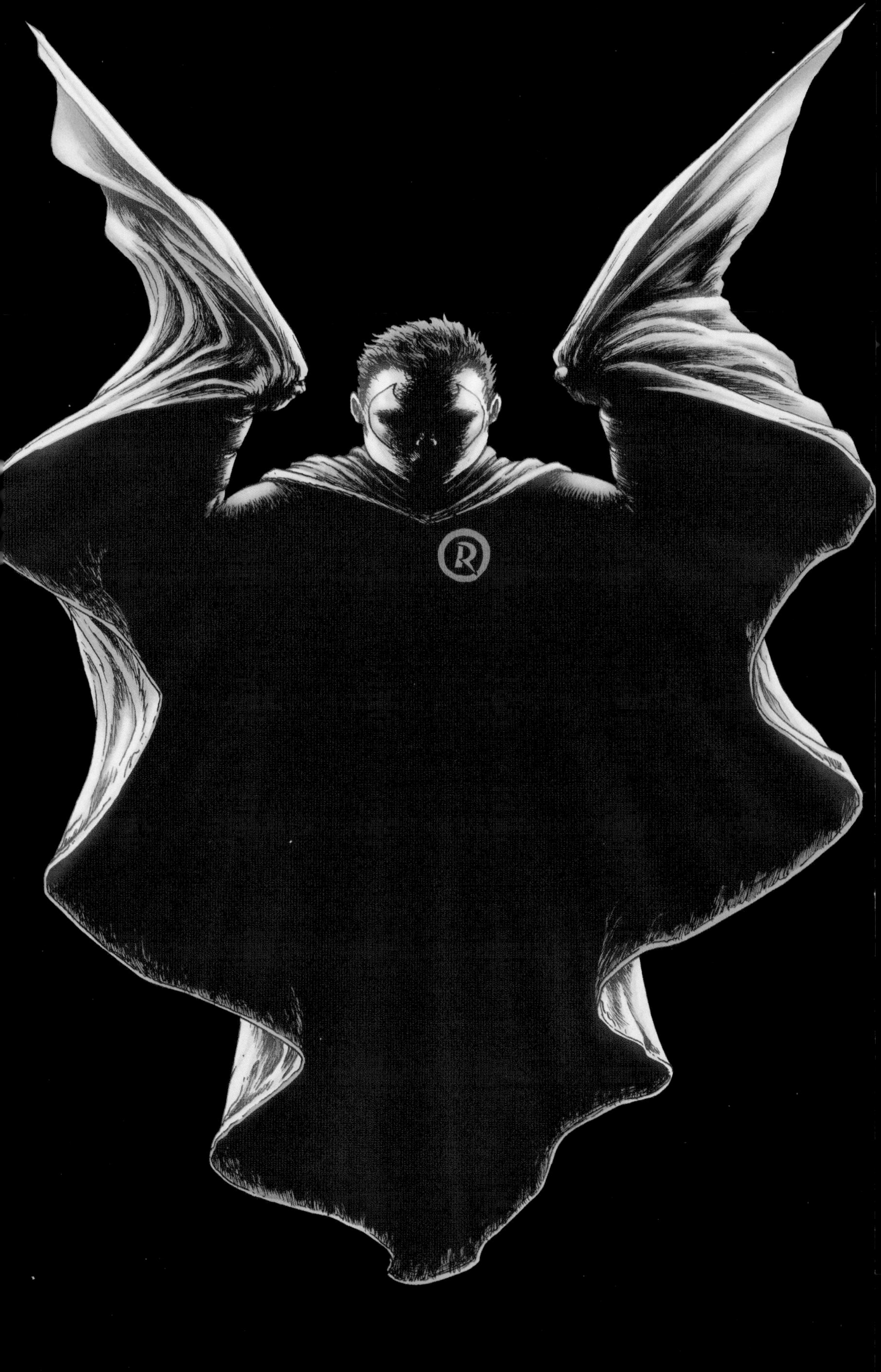

LITTLE DID I SUSPECT

when I accepted the BATMAN writing assignment back in 2006 that I'd wind up spending the next seven years writing the longest continued comic story I've ever attempted. I thought I'd said most of what I had to say about the character with Arkham Asylum, Gothic, and Batman's appearances in JLA. Clearly, I was wrong.

The original pitch was for 15 issues winding up with BATMAN R.I.P. but something happened along the way and, as I was researching his rich history, I became fascinated by the idea that every Batman story was in some way true and biographical — from the savage, young, pulp-flavored "weird figure of the dark" of his early years, through the smiling, paternal figure of the 1940s and the proto-psychedelic crusader of the '50s, the superhero detective of the '60s, the hairy-chested globetrotting adventurer of the '70s, to the brutally physical vigilante of the '80s and snarling, paranoid soldier of the '90s.

By taking his entire publishing history as the story of his life, I was able to approach Batman from a different angle, and the multifaceted character that was revealed became the subject of my story.

What would such a man be like, realistically? This was a man who had saved countless lives, faced innumerable perils, and even prevented the destruction of the world itself. This was a master of martial arts, meditation, deduction, yoga and big business. This was a man who had tamed and mastered his demons and turned personal tragedy into a relentless humanitarian crusade.

Taking that man seriously meant I had to throw out a few of the accepted ideas about Batman as a semi-unhinged, essentially humorless loner struggling with rage and guilt. The totality of his history and accomplishments made that portrayal seem limited and unconvincing, so instead, my Batman was a true superhero at the height of his powers and the peak of his abilities, surrounded by a network of friends and associates, all of whom had been inspired by his lead.

I chose to build my story around the basic trauma, the murder of his parents, that lies at the heart of Batman's genesis. It seemed to me there would be a part of Bruce Wayne that resented his parents for leaving him and especially resented his father for not being Batman that night, so the principal villains were an archetypal bad father figure in the form of Dr. Hurt and a dark mother in the form of Talia, our villain for the concluding chapters of the story.

This master theme of damaged and ruined families was nowhere more in evidence than in the creation of Damian, the first "Son of Batman" to be acknowledged in the canon. In many ways this has been Damian's story as much as it has been the story of Bruce Wayne, and it's a story that had its end planned a long time ago — for what son could ever hope to replace a father like Batman, who never dies?

And so, via Batman, Batman and Robin, Return of Bruce Wayne and Batman Incorporated. this epic tale has finally reached its finale.

Thanks to all the artists who helped realize the story — Andy Kubert, JH Williams, John Van Fleet, Tony Daniel, Ryan Benjamin, Lee Garbett, Frank Quitely, Philip Tan, Cameron Stewart, Andy Clarke, Frazer Irving, Scott Kolins, Chris Sprouse, Ryan Sook, Yanick Paquette, Georges Jeanty, David Finch, Scott Clark and of course, Chris Burnham.

Thanks to the inkers, colorists and letterers and to my indefatigable editors.

Thanks to the readers who joined in the fun and contributed to the thought-provoking debates and analyses online.

The conclusion is finally here, with only one issue to go. One issue which takes Batman to dark places he has never had to visit before. One issue and I'm done, while Batman himself continues into as yet unimagined future adventures. He'll still be here long after I'm dead and forgotten; long after all of us have come and gone, there will be Batman. It's been a joy and a privilege to spend so much time in the company of pop culture's greatest character but it's going to feel weird waking up and not having Bruce Wayne's calm, commanding, ever-so-slightly cynical voice in my head.

BATMAN FOREVER...

GRANT

GRANT MORRISON'S WACKY BATMAN ADVENTURE

Follow along with the Dark Knight, Robin, and the members of the Batman Family as writer Grant Morrison steers the course of their destiny throughout his seminal run with the Caped Crusader!

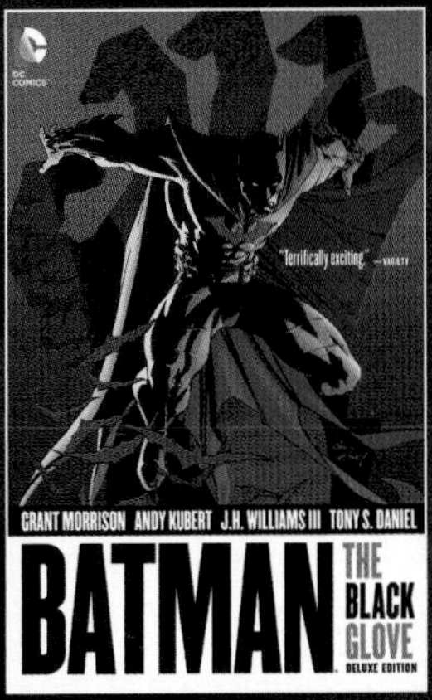
GRANT MORRISON ANDY KUBERT J.H. WILLIAMS III TONY S. DANIEL
BATMAN
THE BLACK GLOVE
DELUXE EDITION

BATMAN: THE BLACK GLOVE

- **Starting with a BANG! –** The Joker gets shot in the face, leading to major changes to the character later on!
- **Introducing Damian Wayne:** the Son of the Bat!
- **Future Shock!** Damian Wayne takes on the mantle of the Bat in a dark and dystopian future Gotham!
- **League of Batmen:** Precursor to what will become Batman Incorporated!

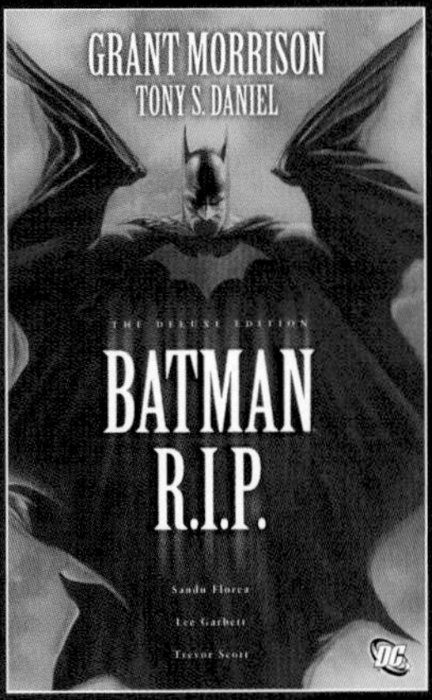
GRANT MORRISON
TONY S. DANIEL
THE DELUXE EDITION
BATMAN
R.I.P.
Sandu Florea
Lee Garbett
Trevor Scott

BATMAN: RIP

- **Meet the Members of the Black Glove!**
- **Who or what is the Batman of Zurr-en-Arrh?!!**
- **Ring the Bell –** the Dark Knight reflects on this iconic moment from the celebrated **BATMAN: YEAR ONE**

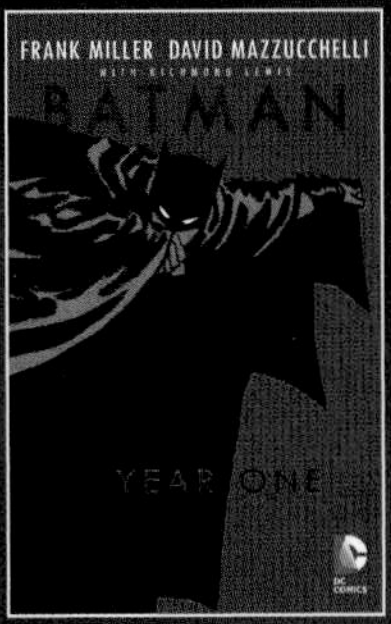
FRANK MILLER DAVID MAZZUCCHELLI
BATMAN
YEAR ONE

- **Batman Captured –** Batman imprisoned by Darkseid, tying into the events of **FINAL CRISIS**

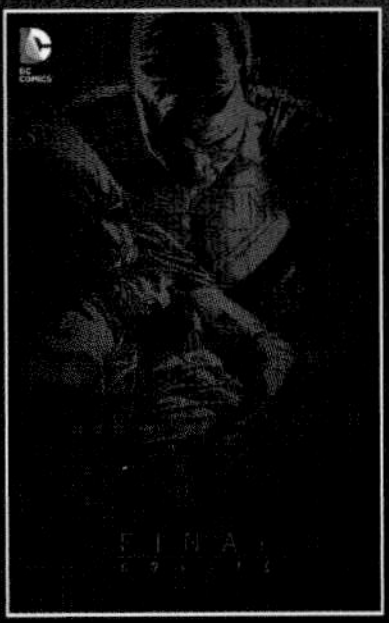

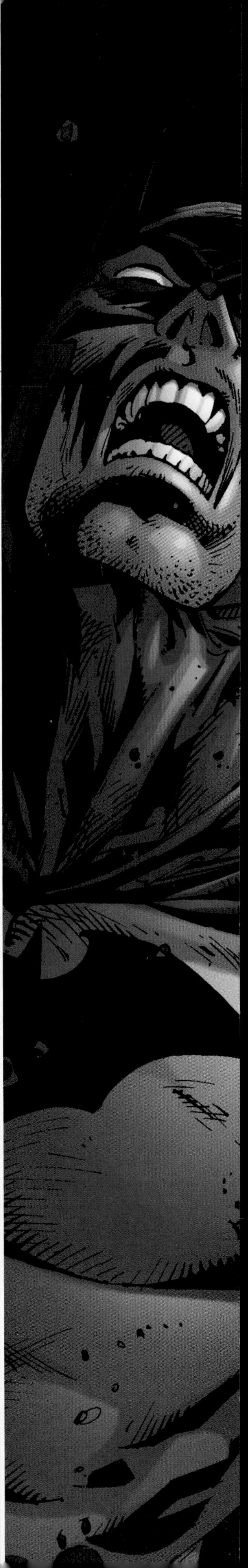

BATMAN AND ROBIN

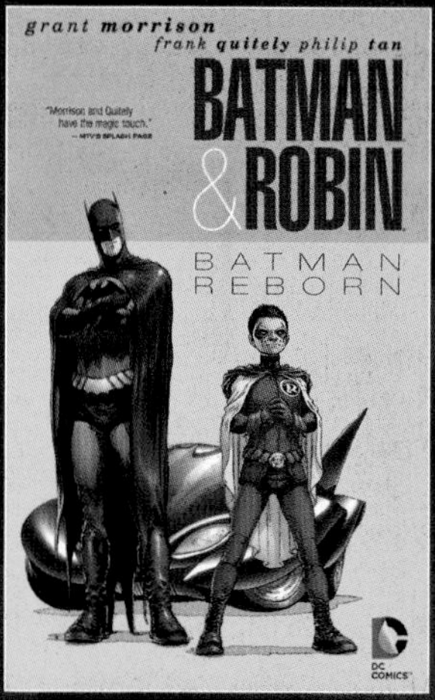
grant morrison
frank quitely philip tan
BATMAN & ROBIN
BATMAN REBORN
DC COMICS

- **Introducing the NEW Dynamic Duo!**
- **Return of the Red Hood! –** Who is under the mask?
- **The Dark Knight Returns? –** Has Batman come back from the dead?

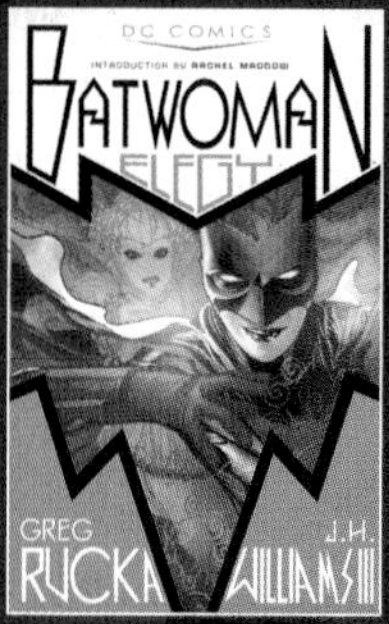
DC COMICS
BATWOMAN
ELEGY
GREG RUCKA
J.H. WILLIAMS III

- **Batman and Batwoman! –** Batwoman's early adventures can be seen in **ELEGY**!

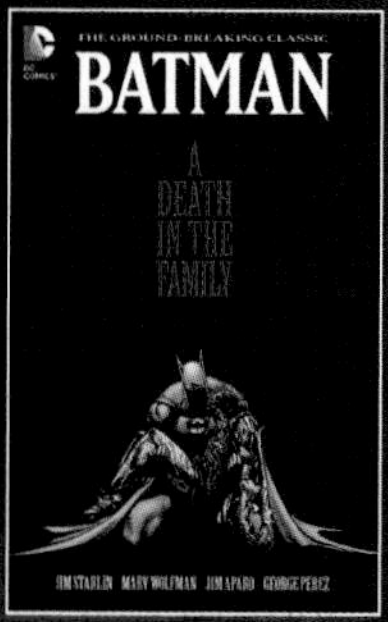
THE GROUND-BREAKING CLASSIC
BATMAN
A DEATH IN THE FAMILY

- **Joker and his Crowbars –** the Joker infamously killed another Robin with a crowbar in **A DEATH IN THE FAMILY**

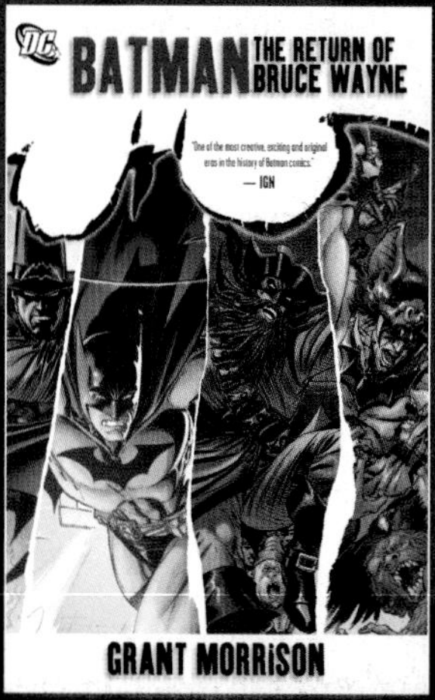
BATMAN THE RETURN OF BRUCE WAYNE
"One of the most creative, exciting and original eras in the history of Batman comics." — IGN
GRANT MORRISON

- Batman's Back! – Find out how in

BATMAN: THE RETURN OF BRUCE WAYNE

- Welcome to Batman Incorporated!

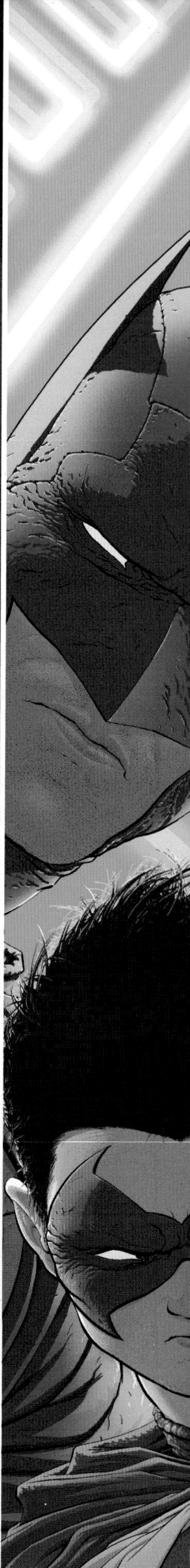

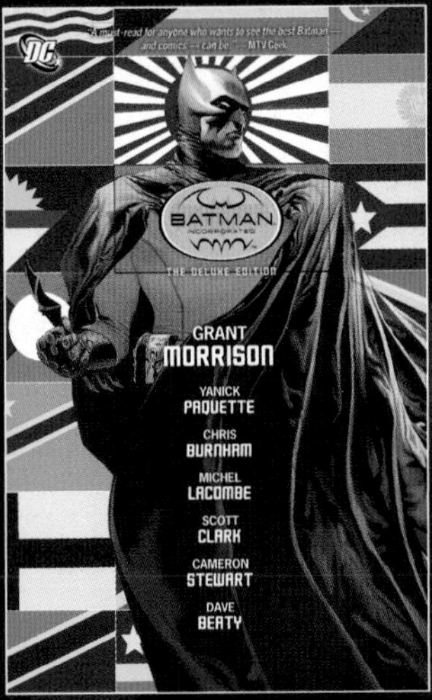
BATMAN
INCORPORATED
THE DELUXE EDITION
GRANT
MORRISON
YANICK
PAQUETTE
CHRIS
BURNHAM
MICHEL
LACOMBE
SCOTT
CLARK
CAMERON
STEWART
DAVE
BEATY

BATMAN INCORPORATED

- **Batman Inc recruits its first member:** the Batman of Japan!
- **Batwing Flies onto the Scene**
- **The Batmen of the World**
- **Leviathan Revealed –** the real threat shows its face!

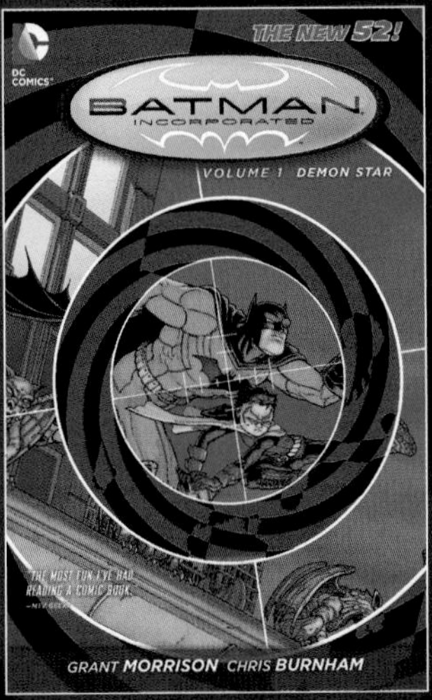
DC COMICS
THE NEW 52!
BATMAN
INCORPORATED
VOLUME 1 DEMON STAR
GRANT MORRISON CHRIS BURNHAM

BATMAN INCORPORATED VOL. 2

- **Batman & Son as the Dynamic Duo**
- **The Bat-Cow!**
- **The Origin of Talia al Ghul!**
- **Back to the Future! –** the truth behind Batman Inc finally revealed!
- **Damian Wayne and Dick Grayson:** Gotham's Greatest Reunited!
- **Death in the Family –** The Heroic Sacrifice of the Boy Wonder!

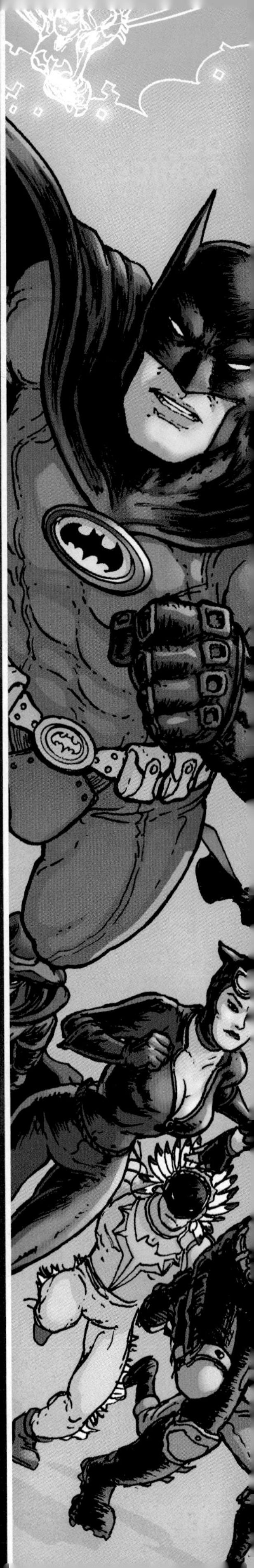

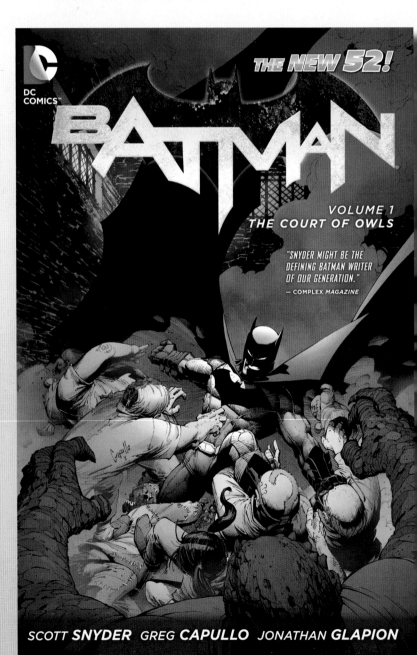

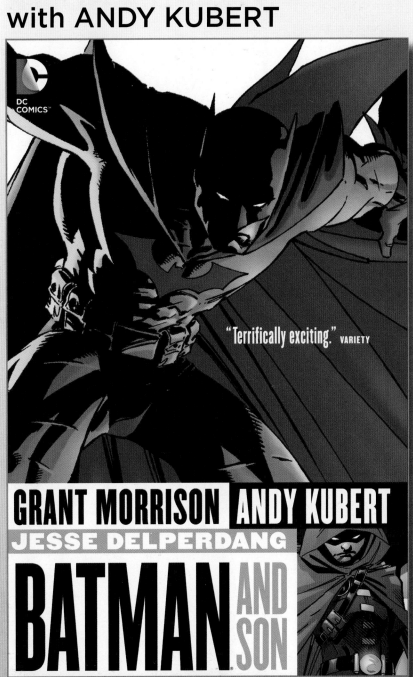

*"Stellar. A solid yarn that roots itse
in Grayson's past, with gorgeou
artwork by artist Eddy Barrows.
—IG*

START AT THE BEGINNING

NIGHTWING VOLUME 1
TRAPS AND TRAPEZES

**CATWOMAN
VOLUME 1: THE GAME**

**BIRDS OF PREY
VOLUME 1: LOOKING
FOR TROUBLE**

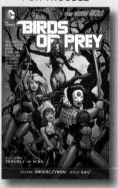

**ALL-STAR WESTERN
VOLUME 1:
GUNS AND GOTHAM**

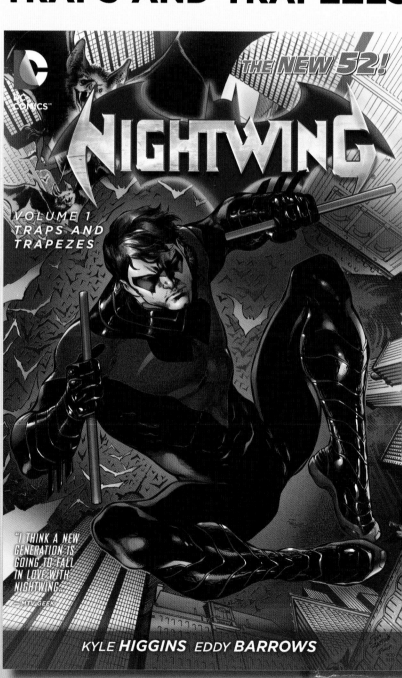